TAMING DEMOCRACY

TAMING
DEMOCRACY

"The People," the Founders, and the Troubled Ending

of the American Revolution

❧ TERRY BOUTON ❧

OXFORD
UNIVERSITY PRESS

OXFORD
UNIVERSITY PRESS

Oxford University Press, Inc., publishes works that further
Oxford University's objective of excellence
in research, scholarship, and education.

Oxford   New York
Auckland   Cape Town   Dar es Salaam   Hong Kong   Karachi
Kuala Lumpur   Madrid   Melbourne   Mexico City   Nairobi
New Delhi   Shanghai   Taipei   Toronto

With offices in
Argentina   Austria   Brazil   Chile   Czech Republic   France   Greece
Guatemala   Hungary   Italy   Japan   Poland   Portugal   Singapore
South Korea   Switzerland   Thailand   Turkey   Ukraine   Vietnam

Copyright © 2007 by Oxford University Press, Inc.

Published by Oxford University Press, Inc.
198 Madison Avenue, New York, NY 10016

www.oup.com

First issued as an Oxford University Press paperback, 2009

Oxford is a registered trademark of Oxford University Press

Library of Congress Cataloging-in-Publication Data
Bouton, Terry.
Taming democracy : the people, the founders,
and the troubled ending of the American Revolution / Terry Bouton.
p.   cm.
Includes bibliographical references and index.
ISBN 978-0-19-537856-6 (pbk.)
1. Pennsylvania—Politics and government—1775–1865.
2. Democracy—Pennsylvania—History—18th century.
3. Pennsylvania—History—Revolution, 1775–1783—Social aspects.
4. Gentry—Pennsylvania—History—18th century.
5. Statesmen—United States—History—18th century.
6. Elite (Social sciences)—United States—History—18th century.
7. United States—History—Revolution, 1775–1783—Social aspects.
8. United States—History—Revolution, 1775–1783—Influence.
9. United States—Politics and government—1775–1783.
10. United States—Politics and government—1783–1809.   I. Title.
F153.B75 2007
974.8'03—dc22   2007010410

9 8 7 6 5 4 3 2 1

Printed in the United States of America
on acid-free paper

Acknowledgments

There are far too many people to thank for a book that took so long to complete. My apologies to anyone I inadvertently leave out of these "thank you" pages. Larry Goodwyn sparked my interest in social movements and provided encouragement during graduate school, for which I will always be grateful. Larry also taught me a great deal about writing, the greatest gift I received from my education. This was back when he still smoked pretty heavily and, by the time we were finished with a marathon editing session, every fiber of my clothing was inundated with whatever ghastly brand of cigarettes he smoked. When I got home, my wife would make me take off my clothes on the balcony facing the parking lot of our multiplex apartment and put them in a thick plastic bag before she would let me inside. I always thought about those smoky clothes as a tribute to Larry's dedication and patience, a model I hope I can emulate with my own students—without the cigarette smoke.

I was lucky to have taken Peter Wood's seminar on early American history, more or less on a whim. It turned out to be the best course choice in my entire academic career. Peter's enthusiasm and his engaging way of telling a story got me hooked on the colonial and revolutionary period. He also handed me a book on a 1794 uprising in Pennsylvania, which got this project started. Over the years, he has been a gracious mentor and a thoughtful editor, who has pushed me to write clearly and forcefully.

Susan Ferber at Oxford has been a remarkable (and remarkably patient) editor. I am grateful for her diligence, excellent suggestions, and willingness to let me write the book I wanted to write.

I was also fortunate to have outstanding readers who provided encouragement and smart advice. I am grateful to Al Young, Ed Countryman, and Allan Kulikoff for dissecting the manuscript and helping me to pare it down from the behemoth they first received. I have been humbled by their dedication to making it a stronger book. I also want to thank those who offered comments on incarnations of various chapters: Alan Taylor, Elliott Gorn, Laura Edwards, Marjoleine Kars, Woody Holton, Michael A. McDonnell, Jeani O'Brien, Bill Pencak, Cathy Matson, Greg Dowd, Seth Rockman, Tom Humphrey, Reeve Huston, Drew Cayton, Jack Marietta, Wythe Holt, David Thelen, David Nord, Roger H. Brown, Owen S. Ireland, Gordon S. Wood, and Thomas P. Slaughter.

I have benefited from financial and scholarly support from a variety of sources. Jim Scott and Kay Mansfield at the Program for Agrarian Studies at Yale University let me into their academic wonderland for a year. The weekly seminar and my incomparable fellow fellows offered a model for how a scholarly community can work. Funding for that year was also supplied by the inaugural Oscar Handlin fellowship from the American Council of Learned Societies. Linda Shopes and the folks at the Pennsylvania Historical and Museum Commission provided me with several months of funding and expert navigation through the files at the state archives. Jim Grossman set me up with a carrel for the better part of a year at the Newberry Library, where Al Young and the participants in the Seminar in Early American History made me feel welcome. I received a summer stipend from the National Endowment for the Humanities and summer research funding from the University of Maryland, Baltimore County, and Winthrop University. My colleagues at UMBC have been wonderfully supportive, as were my former colleagues at Winthrop University and at Miami University of Ohio (where, as an adjunct, I was treated with respect and great kindness, for which I am especially grateful to Charlotte Goldy and Drew Cayton). I received considerable help from archivists and staff at the Historical Society of Pennsylvania, the National Archives, and the Manuscript Division of the Library of Congress. I also want to thank the unsung archivists and clerks at county courthouses throughout Pennsylvania, who educated me about legal records and even let me join the coffee pool. On a personal note, I'd like to thank Bob Bouton, Dee Abbott Youngs, Eleanor Wong, John Youngs, Diana and Mike Oliver, Russ Nagy, Jim Amspacher,

Aaron Althouse, Ginger Williams, Ed Haynes, Juliana Barr, Cynthia Herrup and Judith Bennett, Suzanne Kaufman, Ann Little and Chris Moore, and the countless coffeehouse baristas who let me steal electricity for my laptop.

Finally, I want to thank my daughter, Sophie, and my best friend, colleague, and wife, Amy Froide, who, aside from making me take off smoke-infused clothes in front of neighbors at our crummy apartment in Durham, has been the best thing in my life. Since we've been together, we've moved nineteen times, lived in eight states (and the United Kingdom), had a commuting marriage for six years between a combination of seven different universities and fellowships, and, in one unforgettable semester, made weekly trips (with a screaming nine-month-old) to Rutgers, New Jersey, where we lived in a musty basement for two-day stints before heading back to Baltimore so I could teach. After everything we've been through, nothing makes me happier than watching our three-year-old kick the gaudy "spam ball" from my office down the hall to hers.

No one mentioned above is responsible for any mistakes in the book, except for Elliott Gorn, whom I personally blame for any errors of fact—along with my parents, my high school friends, prurient television programs, heavy metal music, and violent video games.

Contents

TAMING DEMOCRACY

Introduction

Every Fourth of July, Americans gather at cookouts, parades, and firework displays to commemorate the birth of American democracy. From a broad perspective, there is much to celebrate in the story of thirteen colonies breaking away from monarchy to begin their unprecedented experiment in democratizing government and society. Even if the kind of democracy the Revolution created was in many ways more limited than the one we enjoy today, it was, nonetheless, a form of government that often provided greater freedom than Americans had experienced under British rule. The new state and national governments opened political access to ordinary folk as never before. They also tended to protect a wider range of civil liberties than had the system of rights granted by colonial governments, the British Parliament, and the king.

That said, the question remains: how democratic was the Revolution? To what extent did the Revolution actually democratize government and society? How much power did "the people" really wield? How responsive were the new governments to the interests and ideals of ordinary Americans? What kind of democracy did common folk want from the Revolution? And how happy were they with the version of democracy the Revolution brought? In short, if it was a Revolution "by the people," to what extent was it also a Revolution "for the people"?

3

Of course, in large part, the answer depends on how one defines "the people." To see the Revolution as a democratic victory for the people, one has to cut most of the people out of the story. Women received few tangible benefits from the Revolution and were almost left out of the expansion of suffrage and rights. Although many slaves obtained their freedom during the Revolution (mostly by running away), and even though propertied free blacks were allowed to vote in several northern states, it would be hard to see how the new government and society represented the interests of African Americans. It's even harder to see how any of this democratization included Native Americans. Indeed, the new governments were all dedicated to wresting lands from Indians and removing them from the democratic experiment. In short, when Americans talk about the Revolution as a victory for "the people," they generally use the phrase in the same sense as the founding generation: to refer to white men.[1]

Even if we follow the example of the so-called founding fathers and limit "the people" to just white men, the question is still relevant: did the Revolution create a democracy that, as one leading historian has put it, made "the interests and prosperity of ordinary people—their pursuits of happiness—the goal of society and government"?[2]

This book argues that most ordinary white men were disappointed by the version of democracy that emerged from the Revolution—even as it brought them new political rights and powers. These people did not think the Revolution ended with governments that made their ideals and interests the primary goal. To the contrary, they were convinced that the revolutionary elite had remade government to benefit themselves and to undermine the independence of ordinary folk. Certainly, white men (or at least those who were allowed to participate in the political system) appreciated that the Revolution had made some advances for them. But most people were convinced that the steps forward had been too small—that the government and society had not democratized enough.

Moreover, much of the revolutionary generation was convinced that, during the postwar decade, the elite founding fathers had waged—and won—a counter-revolution against popular democratic ideals. During the 1780s and 1790s, ordinary folk across the new nation perceived democracy to be under assault from elite leaders determined to scale it back from the broad ideal that had been articulated in 1776. To many people, the biggest victory in this counter-revolution was the creation of the new federal Constitution—a document that modern Americans often view as one of the Revolution's crowning democratic achievements. Most revolutionary era Americans believed that democracy survived this counter-revolution. But they also thought the version that remained had been stripped of much of its meaning and was a far less potent ideal than the one that many of them had fought a war to attain.

To appreciate the popular sense of disappointment, it's crucial to view the Revolution over its full course, from the 1760s (when the colonists began their struggle against Britain) through the 1790s (when the new state and national governments were firmly in place). Most studies of the Revolution—and especially those that place the experiences of ordinary Americans at their center—tend to examine only part of the Revolution (usually the years leading up to 1776, or the war, or the postwar period). Carved up this way, it becomes difficult to see the full range of popular ideals. An episodic approach also masks the stunning about-face made by the founding elite, many of whom championed popular ideals before 1776 and then attempted to suppress them after the war. The turnaround was so radical that the elite enacted postwar policies that were nearly identical to the ones Britain had put in place during the 1760s and 1770s, which at the time the gentry had decried as "tyranny" and "oppression."[3]

I have chosen to tell this story about democracy by focusing on revolutionary Pennsylvania. First, Pennsylvania has long been the symbolic center of the Revolution's democratic achievements. It's often called the "Cradle of Liberty" and the "birthplace of American democracy." Pennsylvania is home to the Liberty Bell and the "first" American flag said to have been designed by Betsy Ross. In Pennsylvania, we find Valley Forge, the icon for the grit and determination of American soldiers who were forced to endure that awful winter. Here too was the battle of Brandywine, a conflict that the National Park Service bills as the "biggest battle of the Revolution." And, most important, Pennsylvania has Independence Hall, the building that hosted two events central to the story of democracy: the creation and signing of the Declaration of Independence in 1776 and the closed-door convention that produced the U.S. Constitution during the hot summer of 1787.

Pennsylvania is also fitting because, in 1776, it democratized more than nearly any other colony and thus gives a much clearer sense of what was gained and lost over the course of the Revolution. Pennsylvania's revolutionaries set the standard for democratic change and framed the debates over democracy that followed in the other new states, the vast majority of which refused to go as far (except Vermont, which modeled its constitution after Pennsylvania's and in some ways went even further). Pennsylvania opened access to power far more than most colonies. While other new states kept property requirements for voting, Pennsylvania renounced them, allowing about 90 percent of adult men to vote—including many free black men. Most states retained property requirements for office holding (for example, in Maryland, only the wealthiest 5–10 percent of the population was eligible to be governor or to serve in the assembly); Pennsylvania removed such requirements. Other state governments were structured with various checks on the voices of the people (the two most frequent being a divided legislature with a strong senate and a powerful governor armed with the veto). By contrast, Pennsylvania's revolutionaries attempted to remove any barrier that kept ordinary people from being heard or their demands acted upon. This is not to say that Pennsylvania was entirely democratic: like the other states, Pennsylvania's democracy had clear limits, especially in terms of racial and gender restrictions (and wartime loyalty oaths). But, in terms of voting rights and political access, the Revolution brought a version of democracy to Pennsylvania that was unequaled anywhere in the colonies.[4]

The Revolution in Pennsylvania also expanded the definition of democracy. One of the most important aspects of this expansion was to strengthen the link between a healthy democracy and an equal distribution of wealth. In the decade before 1776, most Pennsylvanians embraced the notion that only wealth equality would keep their government and society free. In part, this emphasis was a result of the economic hardship caused by British policies, which drained the colonies of money and undermined people's sense of their own independence. That hardship convinced most people—even many of the wealthiest gentlemen who remained Loyalists during the war—that Britain was undermining American liberties by concentrating wealth among the affluent. They feared that Britain was placing too much economic power in the hands of men (both English and American) who used their wealth to transform government into a vehicle to enrich themselves. Worried that Britain was promoting tyranny within Pennsylvania's borders (most people were already convinced that Britain was promoting tyranny from without), many colonists asserted that government needed to make wealth more equal in order to protect freedom. And it was not just talk: during the 1760s and 1770s, most Pennsylvanians—even the gentry—pushed for policies to promote economic equality and to limit wealth concentrations among the affluent.

When Britain rejected the calls for change, Pennsylvania's revolutionaries expanded their ideas about acceptable forms of democratic self-expression. The failure of formal political channels (petitions, pamphlets, voting, and lobbying) caused many people to adopt a more aggressive range of strategies for getting their voices heard. This broader notion of "legitimate" politics included civil disobedience, extralegal protest, and, ultimately, collective violence. In

1776, Pennsylvanians wrote those expansive political ideals into a new state constitution that gave "the people" the right to "take such measures as to them may appear necessary to promote their safety and happiness" and even to "reform, alter, or abolish government" if they thought it necessary.[5]

By 1776, this democratic ideal became the mainstream understanding of the Revolution in Pennsylvania. It was not "radicals" or marginal outsiders who believed that government needed to extend political access, protect freedom by promoting wealth equality among white men, and arm citizens with a wide range of political weapons to defend their rights. Those beliefs were shared by ordinary people in both the city and the countryside and by large segments of the gentry. Not everyone agreed on how much the political system should be opened, the degree of wealth equality needed to protect liberty, or the virtue (or morality) of using violence to bring political change. But by 1776, there was a general consensus around a broad set of democratic values that most people believed were central to the Revolution.

This consensus shattered during the war, when much of the gentry changed their minds about democracy and began an effort to scale back its meaning and practice—in effect, attempting to tame democracy. During the war, many of the state's founding fathers abandoned their commitment to wealth equality and a democratized political system. Instead, they redefined a "good government" as one that enriched the affluent and refashioned "liberty" as a word that meant the freedom to amass as much property as one desired and to use that property as one saw fit. The elite tried to force through redistributive policies they knew would be unpopular (and even offensive) to ordinary folk. And when they met resistance, the gentry worked to restructure the state and national governments to make them less responsive to the public will—just as Britain had done during the 1760s and 1770s. The elite founders also replicated many of the economic policies that Britain had enacted, with similar results: they created an economic depression that brought hardships across the state and angered ordinary folk who saw this new order as a betrayal of the Revolution's main ideals.

In response, during the 1780s, ordinary Pennsylvanians attempted to defend their ideas of political and economic equality. Facing a situation similar to that of the 1760s and 1770s, people from across the state petitioned for the same policies they had called for a decade earlier—policies that the gentry had supported at the time. Despite the democratization of government, however, ordinary folk had a hard time mobilizing for change. They ran up against a system that, for all of its democratic innovations, still kept many obstacles in the path of the people. And, as the common folk discovered, unless they found a way to organize around those obstacles, it did not matter if most Pennsylvanians shared an agenda for change. When it came to political power, without organization, "the people" remained little more than an abstraction. As a result, ordinary Pennsylvanians achieved only limited political victories during the 1780s. The revolutionary elite rejected most of their proposals, and when they did, many people protested in the same ways they had against Britain.

Those protests prompted the elite founding fathers to create what the gentry called more permanent "barriers against democracy." They rewrote constitutions and passed new laws to diminish access to power and to out-law forms of political self-expression that many ordinary folk considered to be essential to defending their liberties. In this more hostile environment, ordinary Pennsylvanians resorted to increasingly desperate measures to pro-tect their democratic ideals. In the end, the conflict was settled by two mass popular uprisings by thousands of ordinary Pennsylvanians, one in 1794 and another in 1799. Each of these showdowns ended with federal armies march-ing through Pennsylvania to uphold a far more limited democracy than the version that had existed in 1776.

In telling this story, I am attempting to write history both from the bottom up and from the top down—to understand how the actions and ideals of ordi-nary Americans shaped the Revolution, how regular folk influenced the elite founders, and, in turn, how the gentry's attempt to enact its own vision of the Revolution affected the lives of those from the "middling" and "lower sort."

To do this, I will introduce a cast of characters who usually stand offstage in the revolutionary drama. This cast includes "Black Boy" Jimmy Smith, a Bible-toting frontiersman, who organized backcountry farmers to fight against the British during the 1760s and who helped to draft the 1776 state constitu-tion for "the people" and not for the "advantage of any single man, family, or set of men." The book also introduces Thomas Hartley, a gentleman from the town of York, pushed by small farmers from the surrounding countryside to take a stand against Britain that he said he would otherwise have "dare[d] not" make. We will meet Daniel Roberdeau, a Philadelphia merchant driven from gentility by the hardships of British policies, who, as brigadier general of the Philadelphia militia, worked against those he said were "getting rich by sucking the blood" of the citizenry. We'll witness the rise of William Findley, a weav-er and farmer, who ran for political office to save democracy from what he called the forces of "united avarice" that sought to deny ordinary "citizens their right of equal protection, power, privilege, and influence." We will see how James Martin, a county justice of the peace, used the powers of his office to shield his neighbors from foreclosure. We'll watch William Petrikin, a tailor who said he "never Spent an hour in Coledge in his life," try to organize a statewide political party of "the people" against the "moneyed men"—and almost pull it off. And we'll follow Herman Husband, a farmer and preacher who fled from North Carolina to Pennsylvania in 1772, when his attempt to "regulate" an oppressive government failed, and who then, during the 1790s, joined the "labouring industrious people" in regulating a new government run by men who wanted to live "in idleness and luxury" "upon [the] labour" of others—the kind of men, Husband said, "our Lord called vipers."[6]

Bringing people like these forward compels us to take a fresh look at the elite founders who usually inhabit center stage, men like Robert Morris (the financier of the Revolution), James Wilson (one of the architects of the federal Constitution), Alexander Hamilton, and even George Washington. This new look is not about bashing the founders. Rather, it is an attempt to see them as human beings, who acted based on ideals and prejudices shared by men of their class in the late eighteenth century. Historians have long noted the founders' elitism, their disdain for democracy, and their desire to see power in the hands of "enlightened" gentlemen like themselves. But most of this founding-father-centered history has not probed the depth of that elitism. It has downplayed or ignored the connections between elite political ideals and a culture of social climbing, speculation, and self-interest, which belied the gentry's claim of disinterested leadership. Nor has it investigated how those antidemocratic sentiments played out in the economic and political lives of ordinary Americans. Instead, when men like Robert Morris said they were working toward "combining together the Interests of moneyed Men" into "one general Money Connection" so they could muster the political "authority" to "open the Purses of the People" for "powerful Individuals," these statements have been treated as relics of prerevolutionary thinking or else as a charming character flaw. Worse yet, those words—and how men like Morris wrote laws and revised governments to bring them to life—have been ignored, and we have been told that elite attempts to concentrate wealth and power fell before popular notions of equality. Such portraits distort our understanding of the Revolution as much as do all of the popular histories that make the elite founders seem more like gods than men. This book is in part an effort to reinterpret the founding elite by letting them speak for themselves and by seeing their actions in a context broad enough to reveal their attempts—and successes—at stunting the meaning and practice of democracy for ordinary white men.[7]

The story this book tells unfolds in three parts. Part I charts the rise of democratic ideals during the 1760s and 1770s. Chapter 1 begins the tale in 1763, when British policies produced a profound scarcity of money that led both elite and ordinary Pennsylvanians to think of themselves as being oppressed. Chapter 2 reveals how the common folk pushed the Revolution in a democratic direction, which culminated in independence and a new government based on the economic and political empowerment of ordinary white men.

Part II, covering the years 1776–1787, reveals the elite founders' challenge to democracy and the attempts of ordinary Pennsylvanians to defend their ideals from this counter-revolution. Chapter 3 exposes the wartime about-face made by the new gentry as it tried to replace popular democratic ideals with what I call the "gospel of moneyed men." Chapter 4 shows how these policies replicated—and even surpassed—the widespread hardship that Britain had created a decade before. Chapter 5 explores how ordinary Pennsylvanians attempted to reclaim their vision of the Revolution in the face of this new crisis. Chapter 6 details the obstacles that blocked the path of popular reform. Chapter 7 describes the extralegal forms of resistance—what I call "rings of protection"—to which ordinary people resorted when electoral politics failed them.

Part III, roughly covering the years 1787–1799, chronicles the taming of democracy as the elite founders restructured state and national governments to limit the political influence of ordinary citizens and to stifle popular resistance to the new order. Chapter 8 recalls the conflict in Pennsylvania over the federal Constitution of 1787 that created, in the words of its supporters, "a stronger barrier against democracy." Chapter 9 follows the attempts of state leaders to outlaw popular resistance and shows the increasingly desperate measures that many ordinary Pennsylvanians developed to protect their ideals. Chapter 10 provides a narrative of the dramatic showdown in 1794 between the federal government and farmers in the central and western counties, reframing this confrontation as the outcome of more than two decades of struggle over the meaning and practice of democracy. Chapter 11 explores the parallels between the 1794 uprising and the 1799 protests in Pennsylvania's eastern counties and reflects on the internal problems that brought these resistance efforts to defeat.

The conclusion places this story of thwarted popular ideals alongside other stories about how ordinary Americans—women, African Americans, and Native Americans—were denied the Revolution they wanted. It also suggests how an account of a revolution centered on white men can help to shed new light on those other American revolutions, primarily by providing a context that helps to explain why, in the decades following the Revolution, ordinary white men became such vehement defenders of patriarchy and white supremacy and why they became obsessed with excluding everyone else from democracy's promise.

Part I

THE RISE OF DEMOCRACY

(1763–1776)

1

Oppression

THE ORIGINS OF THE AMERICAN REVOLUTION

How sweet are the labors that freemen endure
That they shall enjoy all the profit, secure
No more such sweet labors Americans know
If Britons shall reap what Americans sow.

Swarms of Placemen and Pensioners soon will appear
Like locust deforming the charms of the year
Suns vainly will rise, showers vainly descend
If we are to drudge for what others shall spend.

—"A Song to the Tune of Heart of Oak," *Pennsylvania Chronicle*, July 4, 1768

Oppression. Tyranny. Slavery. These were the words American colonists used to describe their plight under British rule. In Pennsylvania, such words echoed in political speeches, newspaper editorials, church sermons, and private writings condemning Britain for driving the colonies into poverty and stripping Americans of their independence. People from all walks of life claimed that Britain was transforming a colony once "famed, even beyond the seas" for "its wealth and plenty" into a land of "poverty, distress, and absolute ruin." It was said that even land-owning yeomen were being "lost in the ocean of poverty" as "respectable farmers, lately in good credit and having sufficient possessions" were "reduced to the lowest ebb of misfortune, and perhaps rendered incapable of ever raising" their families back to prosperity. Some said that Britain was lowering Americans to a "condition little superior to that of beggary"; others said it was like slavery.[1]

This chapter tries to explain why so many Pennsylvanians—rich and poor alike—described their situation in such harrowing terms and why they came to believe that Britain was responsible for the rise of "poverty" and "servile dependence." It begins by tracing the gradual erosion of independence that made it increasingly hard for ordinary folk to own land or to pass down farms to their children. That erosion accelerated during the 1760s and 1770s, when British policies created a dire scarcity of money that drove many families to the brink of ruin. As hardship spread across the colony, from the deepest frontier settlements to the burgeoning city of Philadelphia, it convinced most Pennsylvanians to see the conflict with Britain as a struggle between the ordinary many and the elite few. Even many wealthy gentlemen who ended up siding with Britain during the war came to believe that Britain was plotting against liberty by robbing the independence of ordinary folk to benefit the affluent. Ultimately, those shared beliefs helped to convince many Pennsylvanians that they needed to break from Britain and create a new and less oppressive government.

Eroding Independence

When eighteenth-century Americans talked about independence, they invariably meant land ownership. At a time when most white settlers farmed for a living, the American dream centered on acquiring land, harvesting enough to keep the farm solvent, and passing down land to one's children. Owning land generally brought Americans a higher standard of living than their European counterparts: they tended to be healthier; fewer died in childhood; they ate better and lived longer. Running a farm of one's own brought status, autonomy, and confidence. It meant not having to bow down (both figuratively and literally) before others. Land owners were thought to have been liberated from much of the dependency that characterized Europe, where landless tenants and serfs served landlords who commanded them and took a share of their crop as rent. Perhaps modest by the standards of modern Americans, that dream—which became something of a reality for most white Americans—was substantial. Compared with the towns and hamlets from which most white Americans had emigrated, a colony like Pennsylvania earned its reputation as the "best poor man's country."[2]

Owning land also brought many Americans political rights long denied in Europe. In America, widespread land ownership meant that most white men could satisfy the property requirement needed to vote. In Pennsylvania, where the requirement was fifty acres of land (or £50 of taxable wealth), an estimated 50–75 percent of adult white men could vote. By comparison, just 15 percent of adult men in Britain were eligible. And according to the beliefs of the day, owning land meant that ordinary farmers could speak their minds and vote for whomever they pleased without fear of reprisal. In short, land ownership brought both economic and political freedom.[3]

This is not to say that American colonists lived a trouble-free existence in relative equality of property and power. Most families lived in conditions that modern observers would consider squalid: rustic one- or two-room cabins. Farmers could be quickly pushed to the margins by one bad harvest, a drought, a flood, or an infestation of the dreaded Hessian fly. Likewise, although most white men could vote, political power remained concentrated in the hands of unelected and largely unaccountable men: the king, royal officials, proprietors like the Penn family, and a host of home-grown gentlemen who thought they were cut from finer cloth than the common folk. Ordinary men hardly ever served in political offices, many of which had property requirements that excluded all but the wealthy. Meanwhile, geographically large counties with few polling places excluded many rural folk from the process. All these factors produced low election turnout in Pennsylvania, where just 25 percent of eligible voters went to the polls— hardly the sign of a healthy and vibrant democracy.[4]

As the eighteenth century unfolded, there was also a creeping sense that Pennsylvania's famed independence was eroding. The most dramatic decay occurred in Philadelphia, where wealth became badly skewed among the city's most affluent residents. By 1760, the top 10 percent of the population owned nearly half of the city's wealth, while the lowest 60 percent owned just 8 percent. About a third of the population paid no taxes at all because they owned nothing of value.[5]

Compared to the city, the counties surrounding Philadelphia were still places of relative equality—although there, too, clear signs showed independence on the wane. Every decade saw an increase in the number of landless tenants, cottagers, and farm laborers. In many of the older counties near Philadelphia, a majority of the population was landless. These people had little prospect of becoming land owners; and, when they moved, it was not generally up the social ladder. Instead, every few years, landless farmers tended to pick up their few meager possessions (at most, a cow or a few horses) and relocate to another cottage on a different farm, perhaps working out a better deal with the landlord, but staying in the same lowly position.[6]

In terms of land owning, the colony's frontier settlements offered the greatest degree of independence. But even in these newly settled regions, landlessness was on the rise, and wealth was becoming increasingly skewed. On the eve of the Revolution, backcountry tenants represented at least

15 percent of the population—along with an unknown number of cottagers and farm laborers.[7]

Thus, although in many ways Pennsylvania remained the "best poor man's country," that reputation was increasingly challenged by the reality of rising dependence. And the problem was soon to become far worse. During the 1760s and 1770s, Britain enacted a set of policies that would bring prolonged hardship to the colonies and widen inequality across Pennsylvania.

Paying for Britain's War

The troubles began with the French and Indian War, which engulfed Pennsylvania from 1754 to 1763. The war that pitted Britain and its colonies against France and its Algonquian and Huron Indian allies took a heavy toll on Pennsylvania, which stood at the center of much of the fighting. The war strained trade and colonial finances. It also resulted in several devastating losses that sent troops and settlers fleeing for their lives.[8]

Peace with France in 1763 brought new problems rather than relief, especially when Britain turned to the colonies to pay a share of the mother country's wartime expenses. For Britain, the Seven Years' War had nearly spanned the globe and had run up a national debt of at least £132 million. Much of that sum had been spent trying to win in North America: Britain had sent its navy and thousands of troops across the ocean; it had also spent considerable sums on "gifts" used to purchase the loyalty (or merely the neutrality) of Native American tribes. The war's end incurred more expenses as Indians, dissatisfied with the new British regime, rose up behind an Ottawa chief named Pontiac and attacked frontier settlements. Even after Britain put down "Pontiac's Rebellion" in 1765, it still had to shell out funds to staff back-country forts and to guard colonial ports and shipping lanes. There was little doubt that Britain would turn to its colonies for help.[9]

Taken out of context, American anger at such a seemingly reasonable request may appear unwarranted. There were, however, good reasons that British requests rankled many colonists—aside from the familiar complaints about "no taxation without representation." First, many colonists believed that they had already paid for the war. Britain had not picked up the entire tab but had left the colonies responsible for militias, supplies, and rebuilding expenses. The colonial government taxed Pennsylvanians for such costs during the war and continued to tax them for many years after the fighting ended. Thus, even before Britain demanded that the colonies begin paying, many Pennsylvanians were convinced that they had already borne their fair share.[10]

Moreover, many Pennsylvanians, especially those who lived along the colony's northern and western frontiers, thought they hadn't gotten much for the money the colony and Crown had spent on defense. Backcountry farmers complained that they had largely been left on their own to fight Frenchmen, Indians, and, later, the warriors sent by Pontiac. Frontier settlers said that they had been forced to use money from their own pockets to defend themselves—without ever being reimbursed. Many frontiersmen were also outraged that the Quaker government refused to stop the Indian trade that put guns and hatchets in the hands of enemies who burned their farms and scalped or kidnapped their families. Backcountry anger exploded in 1763 and 1764 when, in response to a wave of Indian attacks, white settlers took revenge on Indians who had nothing to do with the attacks. They torched a village belonging to pacifist Moravian Indians and slaughtered peaceful Conestoga men, women, and children. The situation threatened to escalate into civil war when hundreds of Paxton Boys marched to Philadelphia demanding the extermination of all Indians in the colony or their complete removal. This incendiary situation guaranteed that any British calls for the colony to pay for defense would be greeted with indignation by settlers who felt that their Indian-loving rulers had abandoned them in their moment of need.[11]

The real problem was not so much that Britain asked its colonies to bear some of the burden of defense but, rather, the way it tried to collect. Britain enacted a set of policies encompassing trade, finance, and taxation that created a profound scarcity of money that brought hardship across the land. In time, anger over these policies and the distress they caused would transform many Pennsylvanians into revolutionaries.

This disastrous cash scarcity began with the attempt to eliminate the paper money issued by colonial governments. In retrospect, the move seems foolhardy. After all, in a land with few gold and silver mines, paper currencies issued by the colonial governments accounted for about three-quarters of the visible money supply. In rural America—which is to say, nearly all of America—it was often the only form of money most people knew. People used government scrip to purchase farmland or to clear more acreage for planting; they used it to buy new plows, grain seed, and livestock; paper money paid debts and taxes. Paper money was not everything: most transactions happened through book credit (a farmer would purchase cloth from a country storekeeper on credit and pay off the debt, usually not with money, but with butter his wife churned, flour ground at the local mill, or whiskey he distilled). Nevertheless, paper money remained critical to economic life. Farmers needed money to buy land, repay mortgages, and pay off debts when storekeepers refused to accept payment in flour or salted pork (which usually happened when hard times hit or when the market for farm goods dried up). In this respect, John Dickinson, Pennsylvania's most famous revolutionary pamphleteer, scarcely exaggerated when he said, "We must almost entirely rely on our paper."[12]

British officials, however, viewed eliminating currency as a fitting punishment for the colonies having allowed paper money to depreciate during the French and Indian War. In large part, the depreciation was an unavoidable result of fighting a war without gold and silver. With treasuries devoid of hard money, most colonial governments had little choice but to print money to pay soldiers, farmers who supplied the army with grain, and artisans who made shoes and blankets. The wartime money was supposed to hold its value because it was backed by taxes. That is, when a colony issued £100,000 in new money, it enacted £100,000 in new taxes to be collected several years later. In theory, the money retained its value because people would need the currency in a few years to pay those taxes. The system had worked in the past, often with great success—nowhere more so than in Pennsylvania. But now, amid a long and expensive war, paper money ran into trouble. Expenses quickly mounted, and Pennsylvania's government (like every other colonial government) could not collect taxes fast enough to absorb all the money it printed. There was really no way to avoid the depreciation: the colonies could either print money or else they could retreat before Indian and French attacks. It was that simple.[13]

Three thousand miles across the Atlantic, British officials decided that the real cause of depreciation was mismanagement and believed it was their duty to strip the colonies of the right to print any new paper money. The punishment was a new law passed in 1764, called the Currency Act, which prohibited the colonies from printing any new paper money that was legal tender—or, in other words, currency that creditors would have to accept in payment of debts.[14]

In Pennsylvania as elsewhere, this ban resulted in a desperate shortage of money. At the height of the French and Indian War in 1760, over £500,000 in currency issued by the Pennsylvania legislature circulated in the colony. Little by little, that amount shrank as old paper money was taxed out of circulation without being replaced. In 1766, the amount of currency fell to £295,000. By 1770, only £205,000 remained, with the last of the money scheduled to expire in 1772.[15]

FIG. I.I. PENNSYLVANIA TEN SHILLING NOTE, 1773. Part of the 1773 issue of currency printed by the colonial government, this note reveals the irony of the Penns' solution to the colony's cash scarcity. Although the currency depicts a prosperous farm, the Penns' stipulation that people come to Philadelphia to get loans meant that few farmers were actually able to obtain this money. Reproduced from the original held by the Department of Special Collections of the University Libraries of Notre Dame.

The only thing that kept paper money from disappearing entirely was that Britain and the Penn family occasionally permitted the printing of small amounts of non–legal tender currency. This currency's use was limited, however. Before 1773, the Penn family allowed just £50,000, most of which they demanded be spent in Philadelphia to pave city streets and to build a "bettering house" for the rapidly expanding number of poor. In short, the currency was hardly a fitting substitute.[16]

As colonists explained, by eliminating paper money, Britain forced its colonies to rely on gold and silver coins, which were always in short supply because the colonies ran a perpetual trade deficit with the mother country. Like most imperial powers of the day, Britain believed that national greatness was tied to the amount of gold and silver a nation possessed. As far as colonial relations went, this meant ensuring that hard money flowed from the colonies into the mother country. British leaders attempted to ensure a one-way flow of gold and silver (both were also called *specie*) through trade laws that forced the colonies to buy more from Britain than they sold to it. Although the extent of the deficit remains subject to debate, colonists at the time were convinced that British trade laws ensured an ever-dwindling supply of gold and silver. As thousands of Pennsylvanians explained in a 1769 petition, this trade imbalance magnified the effects of the currency ban by ensuring that "the People of this Province" were always going to be specie-poor and "greatly indebted to the Mother Country." A Philadelphia merchant was more succinct: under British laws, "[a]ll the silver and gold is shipped to England."[17]

In the past, colonial merchants had tried to ease the hard-money crunch by smuggling goods to other European empires. Technically, this trade violated century-old laws called the Navigation Acts, which Britain had passed to enforce a closed system of trade. But enforcement of those laws had been sporadic, and cheating was rampant. Smugglers filled American ports; and many of them, like Boston's John Hancock, had risen to be the wealthiest and most respected members of colonial society.

After the French and Indian War, Britain began cracking down on smuggling and, by so doing, cut off the colonies' primary means of acquiring hard money. British officials dusted off the Navigation Acts and added new laws to compel colonists to trade within the empire. To enforce those restrictions, Britain opened new inspection offices and set up vice admiralty courts to prosecute suspected smugglers. Previously, merchants accused of smuggling had been tried by American juries. Now, guilt or innocence would be decided by royally appointed judges. All these "new and stricter restraints being laid on our trade," as John Dickinson called them, prohibited the colonies from "procuring [gold and silver] coins as we used to." As a result, he said, there would be no way to compensate for the loss of paper money and a trade system that "sweeps off our silver and gold in a torrent to *Great Britain*."[18]

Making matters worse, Britain soon enacted taxes payable only in gold and silver. The effort began with new taxes on goods imported from outside the empire. In 1765, Parliament added the infamous Stamp Act that taxed newspapers, marriage licenses, shipping invoices, court papers, and nearly every other official document. In 1767, the Townshend Acts put a levy on "luxury" items like tea, glass, and lead. The amounts of each tax may have been small, and some of the taxes, like the Townshend Acts, may have targeted the wealthy; nevertheless, each new tax promised to deplete the supply of gold and silver. As Dickinson put it, with every new tax, Britain leeched the "exhausted colonies" by "drawing off, as it were, the last drops of their blood."[19]

Pennsylvanians wondered how they would ever pay those taxes—especially since they were already struggling to pay their own taxes. Indeed, a 1773 colonial report revealed the city and county of Philadelphia to be "more or less deficient in their [tax] Quotas," while the other counties had "fallen so remarkably short" that "at their present Rate of assessing themselves," they would need anywhere between eight and ten years to pay. Straining to pay old wartime taxes, many Pennsylvanians chafed when Britain added new hard-money levies to their load.[20]

Ultimately, this combination of British tax, trade, and monetary policies starved the colonies of cash. "Our paper Currency is Annually sinking, and must soon be Extinct" began a 1765 letter by a Philadelphia merchant to an English associate, which repeated what had become a familiar litany of grievances:

> Duties on . . . our imports to be paid in Silver before they are landed. The Avenues of Trade to supply us with Silver all shut up. . . . A Stamp Act staring us in the Face, should it take place together with the duties abovementioned would in short time divest us of every penny of hard money on the continent.

The Philadelphia merchant hoped for harmony "between us & our mother Country," but, with what he saw as a host of mean-spirited policies, his "Faith" in the empire was beginning to falter.[21]

"A Terrible Crush"

He was not alone. Almost as soon as Britain enacted this array of policies, the colonies experienced a faith-jarring economic downturn. In Pennsylvania, hard times quickly washed over the colony, sending waves of distress flowing from rural outposts, across the eastern hinterlands, and into Philadelphia. Those waves ebbed and crested during the decade. Nevertheless, for most Pennsylvanians, the tide of hardship remained high for the majority of the years between 1764 and the outbreak of war in 1775.[22]

Indeed, the distress was so endemic that Pennsylvanians strained their vocabularies trying to describe an economic calamity that endured for nearly a decade. They said life was "precarious and unsettled," "very gloomy," "very miserable," and "much more miserable . . . than you can imagine."[23] Others focused on the cash shortage, saying money was "very scarce," "excessive scarce," "exceedingly scarce," "monstrous scarce," "scarce beyond description," or simply "extinct."[24] Between 1764 and 1773, Quaker merchant Henry Drinker described the economy as a troublesome in-law, calling it "disagreeable," "very irksome," "very inconvenient," "quite unprofitable," "infavourable," "tedious," "truly discouraging," "distressing," and "a grievous disappointment."[25] Merchant William Pollard's descriptions over time read like a doctor's journal chronicling a slowly dying patient: "soured," "sick," "wretched," "most dreadful," "off the hinges and all out of order," "bad beyond description," and "critical and alarming." Pollard also came up with perhaps the most apt phrase to describe the crisis Britain had created: "a terrible crush."[26]

This terrible crush arrived first in the countryside, where ordinary farmers were smashed beneath the collapsing chain of transatlantic credit. Farmers had borrowed from country storekeepers, who had borrowed from Philadelphia merchants, who had borrowed from London merchants and manufacturers. When money became scarce, the full weight of this chain pounded down on farmers. As an editorial in a Philadelphia newspaper explained, English creditors pressed Philadelphia merchants to settle up, which "obliged [them] to do the same with our debtors in the country." Worse yet, many farmers had gone into debt during the war when money was abundant and prices were high; now, as money became scarce, prices dropped and farmers could not sell their crops and livestock for enough to cover the debt. Having bought high and sold low, farmers were crushed when the "great scarcity of money" made it so that the "poor debtor cannot procure cash to pay off his creditor."[27]

The resulting distress pummeled farmers whether they were tenant farmers or land-owning yeomen. In fact, observers often reported that the hardest hit seemed to be land-holding farmers of the middling sort—the kinds of people who had enough standing to obtain credit in the first place. "Money is become so extremely scarce," it was said, "that reputable freeholders find it impossible to pay debts which are trifling in comparison to their estates." One Pennsylvania storekeeper reported that he was swimming in a sea of unpaid debts from "quite able people" who "cannot get money." The same was true for a Chester County storekeeper who had only extended credit to substantial land owners. "I have about £300 entrusted in the country to persons that hold 200 acres of land," he wrote in 1773. Despite giving them an eighteen-month grace period, these middling farmers still "can't discharge the sum of ten pounds." It was the same story with a storekeeper who had loaned only to "good hands" and compelled customers to sign over property as collateral. As this man put it, "The great scarcity of cash has made it impossible to collect" even from the best of customers. A shop owner in the town of Reading offered perhaps the best summary in 1766. "People are in here who owe me money, both Rich and Poor," he said. "I am disappointed by all."[28]

Inevitably, most rural storekeepers began to "drive hard upon [their] customers." Across Pennsylvania, shop owners mounted horses and made what one Chester County storekeeper called a "long and tedious tour westward in search of the necessary Evil cause of money." All they usually collected, however, was a "repeated and inexhaustible store of supplication from my customers for a further delay." It was the same story everywhere in Pennsylvania throughout the decade. In 1764, the problem was "a greater cry for money, more than ever known"; in 1766, it was people "so craving for money"; in 1774, it was "customers" who "beg so hard for a little time that I got no money." On April 17, 1775, two days before the battles of Lexington and Concord, customers still "all plead Poverty (and I believe not without reason)." Weeks after the battles, there remained a "Universal . . . Complaint of the Scarcity of money." No matter the place or time, shopkeepers repeated a familiar refrain: "Money is Scarce here and not to be got"; "Countrey peopel Cannot pay the Small Debts in this part of the World."[29]

Things got so bad that many storekeepers closed their shops to spend all of their time dunning for debts. In 1767, one shopkeeper reported he was "doing nothing but collecting old debts and that is but very slow." In 1772, one Chester County man renounced "shopkeeping" and "rented out my store" to have "a greater opportunity for calling in my outstanding debts." In Reading, an exasperated store owner even offered to turn his shop over to the Philadelphia merchant pressing him for payment. The storekeeper invited the merchant to Reading to "look over the books and put them in some way to be collected as I can't do anything with them." He even offered to haul all the unsold goods to Philadelphia so his creditor "could dispose of them" himself. Another storekeeper, who had "shut my Books" and "quit trading," repaid his creditor with advice instead of money. "I am of [the] opinion," he wrote, "that the merchants of Philadelphia Must fortify themselves with patience. They will need it before they get all their money from the country."[30]

Philadelphia merchants, however, were in no position to be patient. Needing to satisfy British traders, many of them sued country storekeepers, triggering a chain of lawsuits across rural Pennsylvania. Some merchants gave debtors advance warning in newspaper advertisements; others sued "without giving the least notice." In response, shopkeepers across the colony put accounts "in lawyers' hands." "I am resolved to spare no man," announced a Cumberland County shop owner, who informed his creditor that "I am suing daily" all who could not pay. These lawsuits prompted customers to sue their neighbors for unpaid debts. Soon, as one merchant explained, the countryside became a jungle where "Money is very scarce and law suits multiply swingingly."[31]

With little cash around, this spate of lawsuits typically produced small returns. As a Reading shopkeeper explained, cash remained so scarce that a creditor "cannot get any money now even when he sues for it." In the spring of 1765, a shopkeeper named Peter Schuck brought lawsuits against "seventy six persons which I sue at one time." Despite a legal victory in each case, Schuck received partial payment from only four of them.[32]

When court orders could not compel payment from penniless (but not necessarily poor) farmers, property foreclosures began. Although the decay and disappearance of relevant court records make it impossible to offer a comprehensive tally, the surviving evidence paints a grim portrait. In Philadelphia County, between 1769 and 1771, the court issued 2,120 orders to foreclose land, livestock, or possessions—enough to cover 20 percent of the taxable population of the city and county. Northwest of Philadelphia in Northampton County, between 1766 and 1775, the sheriff executed 1,170 orders to confiscate or auction property—enough to cover 42 percent of the taxable population. Things were little better in neighboring Berks County, where between 1769 and 1775, the sheriff acted on more than 2,000 orders, sufficient to reach 55 percent of the taxable population. During just two years, 1774 and 1775, Northumberland County registered 981 lawsuits, which generated 553 foreclosures—enough to reach 26 percent of the population. In the cash-poor settlements on the western frontier, rural hardship was probably the most severe. In Bedford County in the foothills of the Appalachian Mountains, in the first four years of the county's existence (1772–1775), judges issued enough writs to foreclose on 57 percent of the taxable population. "Such a time never was known among the people," summarized Peter Schuck. "There is never a—week but there are some vendues of the sheriffs and constables"—the blank space representing a curse Shuck did not dare to write down.[33]

Foreclosures often did not end the matter. Many auctions finished without anyone ever tendering a bid because few potential buyers had money. "Fortunate, indeed, is the man who can get satisfaction *in Money* for any part of his debt," explained John Dickinson. "[I]n many instances, after lands and goods have been repeatedly advertised in the public gazettes, and exposed to sale, not a buyer appears." Merchant William Pollard reported that property usually went through many auctions without being sold, passing "over from court to court, the sheriff declaring he can get no person to buy."[34]

If property managed to sell, the small number of bidders tended to drive down prices. "The value got by the sheriff is always very low," declared one storekeeper, "not anything will fetch near its value." Although selling prices fluctuated, sales often returned from one-half to one-sixth of a foreclosed property's usual value. Such low prices meant that many auctions did not raise enough to cover the judgment. For example, in 1773, a Chester County shop owner complained that he had sued several of his customers to recover £200 of debts, but the county sheriff could collect only £6. Pathetic returns like these led storekeepers to grumble continually about "a bad court for collecting money." In such cases, the lawsuits continued, loading new court costs on debtors already near the breaking point.[35]

In the end, many farmers broke, and when they did, their fall often brought down others. To get a sense of how far the problem extended, consider the case of elderly and disabled slaves in Chester County, whom owners simply cast aside to save money. By 1769, many slave owners in Chester County had "become insolvent" or died, leaving debts larger than their estates could cover. When they (or their estates) put their property up for auction, no one bid on slaves who were "aged and infirm" and could not perform hard labor. As a result, the owners or their heirs—unable or unwilling to "maintain" elderly or disabled slaves—simply set them "free," which ultimately meant that they were added to the county's poor rolls. Over time, the number of ex-slaves receiving public support became so great that Chester County officials petitioned the colonial assembly to change manumission laws to fine owners who freed unproductive slaves.[36]

The ruin of farmers also sent shock waves back across the chains of credit to Philadelphia and even to Britain. John Dickinson explained in 1765 that, when "the debtors are ruined" in the countryside, the distress flowed back into the city. "Thus the consumers break the shopkeepers," he noted, "they break the merchants; and the shock must be felt as far as *London*."[37]

Such was the case in the decade before independence: Philadelphia merchants experienced difficulties when farmers across the colony (and, indeed, across America) could not acquire money to repay their debts. In 1765, merchant Henry Drinker said that the "scarcity of cash" had "greatly alarmed" him because it had "injured so many persons indebted" to his firm that he was "doubtful" he could ever collect. In 1769, Drinker remained in "peril" of "large outstanding debts" from his "able though tedious customers." That same year, merchant Stephen Collins reported "a very considerable debt of upward of eleven hundred pounds that has been several years over due." After trying to collect for two years, William Pollard concluded in 1773 that it was "almost inconceivable" to get money from storekeepers in such a cash-scarce economy.[38]

Nor could these merchants sell the goods they had imported. Most merchants were burdened with warehouses filled with goods that no one had money to buy. "I have now almost all the goods by me that I had from you the two last seasons and many of the former," explained Stephen Collins to one of his European suppliers in March 1773, "& must keep them unless I should sell them for less than they cost." Meanwhile, expenses continued to mount. "The merchants and their families must live, profits or no profits," reported William Pollard, "store rents, clerks wages, etc. must be paid."[39]

In the end, the cash scarcity drove some merchants to bankruptcy and pushed others from gentility. Take, for example, the case of merchant Daniel Roberdeau, who, in 1764, blamed the scarcity of money for the "most distressing time ever known in Philadelphia." "I have no more expectations of raising the money than I have of drawing blood out of a flint," he wrote to his English creditors a year later. "I must renew my [debts] again and again and again as long as any person will take them until I am involved in ruin." In 1767, the scarcity forced Roberdeau to abandon his "genteel life," sell his lush home, and move into "a small inconvenient house . . . to prevent impending ruin." Even these concessions failed to make him debt-free, and, during the next year, he continued to fume about how the "greatest scarcity . . . of circulating cash ever known" turned "trifling" debts into onerous burdens. Several years later, those frustrations led Roberdeau to push for a break from Britain: he chaired the meeting that called for a new state constitution; he was elected to be the first brigadier general of the Pennsylvania militia; and he represented Pennsylvania at the signing of the Articles of Confederation, the first national charter.[40]

Equally perilous for merchants was the damage the cash scarcity inflicted on their reputations. For late eighteenth-century merchants, reputation was critical. A good one could convince European lenders to extend credit and could foster lenience when times were hard. A bad one could bring a merchant to his knees. Questions about one's character or creditworthiness could prevent new lines of credit from opening, close old ones, or cause a rush of lawsuits at payment delays. Given the importance of reputation, it is hard to think merchants insincere when they wrote to British creditors that their inability to repay debts caused them "real pain," made them "ashamed to write," grieved them "to the very heart," or caused the "anguish and distress of my soul" to be so "severe" that, were it "audible," it would crash like "peals of thunder." Those expressions were prompted by fears for reputations, careers, family fortunes, and social standing—all of which the cash scarcity threatened in real ways.[41]

From here, the crush spread throughout the city. When Philadelphia merchants stopped shipping to cut losses, thousands of sailors, longshoremen, and craftspeople found themselves out of work. Throughout the prewar decade, merchants spent much time "laying on their oars doing little or nothing." Reports circulated that the city was "full of sailors who cannot procure berths," "captains waiting here for an employ," and "tradesmen" who grew "clamorous for want of employment."[42]

With so many people unemployed or working only part time, poverty spread across the city. In the mid-1760s, city leaders worried that the "want of Employment" was "reducing a large number of residents to great Straits," particularly "labouring people and others in low circumstances," who were "willing to work" but could not find "sufficient Employment to support themselves and their Families." Things had gotten so bad that, by 1772, as many as one of every four heads of household in Philadelphia could have been considered poor or nearly poor by the standards of the day. By 1774, the top 10 percent controlled more than 70 percent of the wealth, and more than half of the city's residents owned no taxable property. The cash scarcity had driven up poverty rates in Philadelphia to eight times what they had been before the French and Indian War.[43]

The worst cases ended up in jail or the poorhouse. By 1767, the city jail had filled with "numbers of unhappy people" locked up for unpaid debts. The prison's scant resources left the debtors "barely sustained" with food, causing one writer to ask that the genteel women of Philadelphia have their kitchen staffs send over table "scraps" and the "offals" of animals butchered for supper. Two years later, imprisoned debtors petitioned for release, claiming that the jail did not have enough food to keep them alive. Meanwhile, the "Scarcity of Money, and Stagnation of all Business" kept the city almshouse overcrowded with "poor and indigent Persons." Observers described deplorable conditions where "most" of the prisoners were "naked, helpless, and emaciated with Poverty and Disease to such a Degree, that some have died in a few Days after their Admission."[44]

In all of these ways, the cash scarcity united Pennsylvanians in shared distress and in a deepening conviction that their independence and liberty were under siege. As one might expect, it took little time for most people to begin assigning blame.

Defining the Oppressors

When the finger pointing started in Pennsylvania, the colony compiled a long list of offenders. Since most people viewed Britain as the main source of their troubles, the list was filled with the names of those in England who had brought hardship to America. That list also included the names of many Pennsylvanians widely considered to be part of the problem. The Penn family, which governed the colony, came in for its fair share of abuse. So too did wealthy merchants, moneylenders, and "creditors" who seemed to profit from public suffering. Indeed, as the list expanded, it grew to include nearly as many home-grown "oppressors" as Britons.

Of course, nearly everyone targeted Britain as the primary culprit. Parliament, tax officials, vice admiralty judges, and, eventually, the king all ranked high on the list of oppressors. Many Pennsylvanians began to view the British Empire as an engine of avarice, bent on taking money from "poor" Americans for its "favourites." As John Dickinson put it, Britain was willfully allowing "the welfare of millions" in America to be "sacrificed to the magnificence of a few"—whom he and others identified as wealthy aristocrats, powerful English traders and manufacturers, rich sugar planters in the Caribbean, and the British East India Company with its monopoly over tea and spices. One writer even implied that Britain should change its imperial motto to "We the King's Judges, King's Attorney's, and King's Custom-House officers, having . . . grown rich from *nothing at all*, and *engrossed* everything to ourselves, would now most willingly *keep* everything to ourselves."[45]

Adding to the sense of oppression was a belief that, under the current political system, there was little that colonists could do to change things. Aside from the colonial assembly, Pennsylvanians had no formal voice in setting the policies that governed their lives—a reality that gave rise to the slogan "no taxation without representation." Unaccountable governors at home and abroad controlled tax, monetary, and trade policies. They sent agents and troops to enforce their laws. During the 1760s and 1770s, getting change through the ballot box proved to be futile, since laws passed by popularly elected legislatures could be vetoed by the Penn family, the London Board of Trade, Parliament, or the king. When Pennsylvanians and other Americans tried to get their voices heard by accosting stamp tax collectors, taunting British soldiers, and having "tea parties" to punish those who violated boycotts of British goods, Britain's reprisal was, ultimately, repressing free speech and assembly and sending more troops to enforce its laws. Britain's intransigence in the face of public suffering and its tendency to respond to colonial protests by clamping down on political self-expression convinced many Pennsylvanians that unelected officials deserved to sit atop the list of oppressors.

Not far below them on this list were wealthy men who used their economic might to distress the public. The culprits whom Pennsylvanians identified were "men of fortune," "a minority of rich men," and "men of property" who had allowed their "morals and principles" to be debased by "the influence of wealth." They were the "*better sort*" who believed they were "made, ordained, constituted, appointed, and predestined from the foundation of the world *to govern* and . . . *possess* the surface of this globe and all its inhabitants." The guilty even included "some of our gentry" who considered the lower and middling classes to be "their property, their beasts of burden, born only to be ruled by these Lords of the Creation." "All our unhappiness," said one writer, "I believe is occasioned by a few turbulent, avaricious, and ambitious men who regard the Prosperity of Pennsylvania no longer than serves their own private Interest."[46]

Some people went so far as to accuse greedy men of being sinners destined for hell. It should not be surprising that in a society where many people viewed daily life through the prism of Scripture, Pennsylvanians saw "devilish" doings afoot and a "growing evil" in the daily "sales by sheriffs," debtors "shut up in prison," and hard-working folk unable to provide their "famil[ies] with a morsel of bread." Many Pennsylvanians believed that the men who caused this hardship had rejected the teachings of Jesus and were violating the God-given "right of the industrious to the bread he earns by his labour." With hard times spreading throughout the colony, it was easy to see, as one man did, "innocent" debtors being "greatly oppressed and ruined" by creditors who were "playing the part of Satan."[47]

No doubt, such accusations of sin were fueled by the religious revivals of the Great Awakening, which swept through Pennsylvania in the decades before the Revolution. Like other colonies, Pennsylvania had its share of itinerant preachers who toured the city and countryside, warning about pride, and who called on congregants to avoid the company of anyone who worshipped material possessions above God. In fire-and-brimstone sermons, evangelical preachers urged people to live their lives as Christ had done: to put God before everything else, to shun materialism, and to uplift the poor. Eternal damnation, the preachers said, awaited those who allowed their love of wealth to blind them to their Christian duty. Whether people were inspired by such preachers—or simply acting out their own understanding of their Christian faiths—many Pennsylvanians became convinced that their oppressors were in league with the devil.[48]

The soul searching was so widespread that some gentlemen began to worry that they themselves might be "playing the part of Satan." Take the case of John Reynell, a Quaker merchant who stewed over what to do about debtors who could not pay. In 1770, Reynell openly fretted that, as a wealthy man, he might be guilty of sin by attempting to collect debts in the cash-scarce economy. "I don't want to oppress thee," he wrote to a storekeeper who owed him for unsold merchandise. "I hate oppression and think it a great sin for the rich to oppress the poor." Reynell believed that it did not matter whether his intentions were good and that he was just trying to collect what was owed. Nor did it matter that he had civil law on his side. Reynell's idea of morality meant considering the repercussions of his actions: good intentions might produce bad results; good business decisions might be bad for his soul; what was legal in a civil court might be sin in God's court. His letter reveals a man struggling to locate the line between necessity and oppression, between a hard choice and sin. In the end, Reynell decided not to risk damnation by guessing wrong. He refused to sue the man. Instead, Reynell urged the storekeeper to "be more cautious" about "going deeper into trade . . . than thou had any stock to support," and he let the matter rest.[49]

* * *

In the end, though, it all came back to the original sin committed by Britain. The sense of being sacrificed at the altar of British ambition and arrogance drew Pennsylvanians together. The deep and enduring scarcity of money, the difficulty in paying debts and taxes, the stagnation of trade, and the rise of unemployment closed many of the ideological gaps between rich and poor, farmer and merchant, city and countryside, Quaker and Presbyterian. Hardship caused Pennsylvanians from all walks of life to see themselves as an oppressed many being overrun by a wealthy and powerful few. Ultimately, those shared beliefs would unite Pennsylvanians in attempts to solve the crises by working to make wealth and power more equal.

2

The Vision of '76

POPULAR IDEOLOGY AND THE REVOLUTION

*Do not the mechanicks and farmers constitute ninety-nine out of a hundred of the people of America? If these, by their occupations, are to be excluded from having any share in the choice of their rulers, or forms of government, would it not be best to acknowledge the jurisdiction of the British Parliament, which is composed entirely of **Gentlemen***?

—"Queries," *Pennsylvania Packet*, March 18, 1776

During the 1760s and 1770s, the hardships caused by British policies led Pennsylvanians to create a broad-based movement to democratize government and society. Part of this movement focused on transferring powers from Britain to the colonial governments—what some historians have called the struggle to establish "home rule." Here, bringing democracy meant the familiar anticolonial struggle, echoing with calls for control of taxation, finance, and trade and with demands for freedom from the coercive powers of the king, Parliament, British courts, and unpopular laws upheld by redcoat guns.

The movement to bring democracy was also about transforming Pennsylvania by fostering political and economic equality among white men. Modern Americans are familiar with the Revolution's push for political equality and how the changes of 1776 opened voting rights and brought the "common man" new powers and privileges. They tend to be far less familiar with the push for economic equality—even though Pennsylvania's revolutionaries explained that it was every bit as important as political freedom. In fact, many Pennsylvanians believed that economic equality was what made political equality possible. They were convinced that "the people" would never have political liberty until citizens had the economic wherewithal to protect their rights. To them, concentrations of wealth and power led to corruption and tyrannical rulers, while widely dispersed political and economic power promoted good government.

Guided by those beliefs, Pennsylvania's revolutionary generation—rich and poor alike—turned the Revolution into an attempt to expand political rights and ensure a relatively equal distribution of wealth. The goal was breathtaking: Pennsylvanians (even many of those who ended up siding with Britain) were attempting to shatter the bonds that had allowed the affluent to dominate economic and political life for centuries. They were throwing open the political system to give common men unprecedented access to power. And they were attempting to instill a new idea of governance in which the government worked to make ordinary white men independent property owners and to diminish the power of the affluent. These twin goals of economic and political empowerment form what I call the "vision of '76," the ideal at the heart of what most Pennsylvanians thought the Revolution was about.

This consensus was created by a political awakening among the lower and middling sorts and a changed world view among much of the gentry. During the 1760s and 1770s, ordinary Pennsylvanians began calling for political and economic power more forcefully than ever before. Meanwhile, many genteel Pennsylvanians began adopting ideas of equality that they had once considered to be the "radical" notions of common folk. Make no mistake: elite Pennsylvanians still self-identified as the "better sort"; they still wanted a society built on social rank; and they continued to think that they were the most fit to govern. Nevertheless, many gentlemen underwent a seismic ideological shift that caused them to redefine liberty as reducing wealth inequality and opening the political system.[1]

This change did not happen simply because of hard times or genteel self-reflection; members of the gentry were also pushed to transform by those below them. It could be said that ordinary folk in Pennsylvania pressured the gentry to rethink their view of the world and to work toward goals they had once found frightening. Not every gentleman yielded to demands from below. Some balked at breaking with Britain, picking up arms, or turning over political power to common men. Yet, even as the process peeled away layers of gentry support, a majority of gentlemen still came to adopt the vision of '76 as their own. This remarkable transformation helped to turn Pennsylvania's Revolution into perhaps the most democratic one in the new nation.

Equality

Equality was the key word in Pennsylvania's Revolution. More than other colonies, Pennsylvania swirled with talk of equality during the 1760s and 1770s. It was equality only among white men that was being discussed, but the terms were nonetheless dramatic: people were talking about giving ordinary men unprecedented political powers and taking serious steps toward making wealth more equal. Those voices came from poor folk, the middling sort, and even some of the colony's most affluent citizens. They were farmers, artisans, merchants, and lawyers, Quakers, Anglicans, and Presbyterians. Voices spoke for equality in the Queen's English, with a Scottish brogue, with an Irish lilt, or in guttural German cadences. Some talked of achieving equality while remaining within the British Empire; others said that equality would only come by breaking away. They were all, however, committed to the goal of bringing political and economic equality to most white men.

Such ideals flowed through petitions and political writings in Pennsylvania during the 1760s and 1770s. Farmers and artisans declared that the Revolution was about "the freemen of this Country" stating that "they do not esteem it the sole end of Government to protect the rich & powerful." Ordinary folk said that government should no longer allow "the rich" to "riot in luxury" or reward "those gentlemen who value themselves so highly on their wealth & possessions." Instead, it must "put an end to their *monopolizing schemes* and destroy their present prospects of making enormous estates at our expense" by putting "their golden harvests . . . at an end." At the same time, government should promote the interests of "the mechanicks and farmers [who] constitute ninety-nine out of a hundred of the people of America." In short, the objective of the Revolution was bringing "gentlemen . . . down to our level" and ensuring that "all ranks and conditions would come in for their just share of the wealth." The goal was a government and society that protected the biblical "right of the industrious to the bread he earns by his labour."[2]

Although many genteel Pennsylvanians found such pronouncements alarming, many more seemed to share the general objective of restraining the rich and powerful and uplifting ordinary folk. Of course, the gentry often had very different ideas about what constituted a "just share of the wealth" and "*monopolizing schemes*" and how best to bring gentlemen "down to our level" (or what "our level" meant). Nevertheless, even if most gentlemen weren't willing to go as far as ordinary folk were, they still came to believe that the survival of their liberties depended on limiting concentrations of wealth and empowering ordinary white men.

In part, the gentry's new focus on equality grew out of the ideology of republicanism that saturated the Atlantic world during the late eighteenth century. Republicanism was a set of beliefs about what it took to create a healthy self-governing republic (as opposed to a monarchy). It held that republics were unlikely to succeed in societies with great disparities of wealth because the affluent would use their economic power to dominate the political system. They would control the votes of anyone who depended on them economically and "corrupt" government toward their own ends. The best protection against such corruption was thought to be a relatively equal distribution of wealth among the citizenry. Thus, the ideals of republicanism encouraged Pennsylvanians to think that the only way to protect their freedom was to limit concentrations of wealth and make ordinary white men economically independent.[3]

Pennsylvanians articulated those ideals most clearly in complaints about British oppression and in their solutions for promoting equality. Take taxes, for example. Pennsylvanians challenged British tax laws not simply because they were "taxation without representation" or because the taxes stripped the cash-scarce colonies of money; people also condemned British taxes for promoting inequality. For instance, when Britain enacted the Stamp Act, colonial legislators denounced it as "very burthensome and unequal." In particular, people worried that the Stamp Act would drive financially strapped debtors into poverty. As John Dickinson explained, the British-induced cash scarcity had "already ruined" the "multitudes" and was "melting away" the "estates" of land-owning yeomen with lawsuits. If the Stamp Act went into effect, it would tax each legal document from debt cases: every writ and judgment, every order for a sheriff to foreclose property, every continuance issued when the case was carried over to the next court session. Debtors stood to lose livestock, land, or tools for unpaid debts—and then lose more to pay the stamp taxes on all the paperwork.[4]

According to Dickinson, this insult was compounded by the belief that wealthy creditors would pay little under the Stamp Act. Given the dire shortage of money, he said that creditors could force debtors to pay the stamp tax on any legal paperwork for borrowing money, mortgaging property, or selling land to pay debts. In these cases, "the wealthy," who "undoubtedly ought to pay the most towards the public charges," would "escape" paying taxes by passing the burden onto debtors. Thus, Dickinson said, "the whole weight" of the Stamp Act would fall "on the necessitous and industrious, who most of all require relief and encouragement." Here was the essence of tyranny: a law that bore down "extremely heavy on those who are least able to bear it." No doubt, such beliefs contributed to the widespread opposition that kept the stamp taxes from being collected and that eventually convinced Britain to repeal the hated law.[5]

Similar beliefs led many Pennsylvanians to condemn a 1772 excise tax on the alcohol they distilled, arguing that it punished the victims of the cash scarcity. As currency disappeared, whiskey often substituted for money. When farmers could not get cash, they typically distilled their crops into alcohol, which was cheaper to ship to market than corn or grain. When currency disappeared, whiskey became the primary commodity that many small farmers used to pay debts and buy necessities. Consequently, when the new excise tax was enacted in 1772, people in both the city and countryside complained that it was an "oppressive" and "heavy tax upon the middling and poorer class[es] of the inhabitants." Moreover, they said that the law was unequal because loopholes in it allowed wealthy distillers to "evade the payment." These charges that the law's inequity made it "subversive of liberty and dangerous in its consequences" were precisely the accusations farmers would repeat in 1794 when the new federal government enacted a similar whiskey tax.[6]

To replace such regressive taxes, Pennsylvanians called for progressive taxation, where the wealthy paid far more than ordinary folk. The popular cry was for taxes to be "assessed equally upon all *ranks and conditions* of men." And by "equally," most people meant taxes "proportioned to the abilities of those who were to pay them," rather than taxing everyone at the same rate. Progressive taxes were considered "equal taxation" because everyone was treated the same, according to their wealth. And, to most people, the most equal tax was one on speculative tracts of land. In particular, during the 1760s and 1770s, Pennsylvanians called for new taxes on the vast tracts of unimproved land held by the ruling Penn family. Many people believed that taxing speculative lands such as these would ensure that the wealthy paid their fair share (which is to say, a greater share than anyone else) and, at the same time, encourage them to sell to small holders at reasonable rates. Guided by this goal, the revolutionary government in 1776 would create the most progressive tax code in any of the new states—featuring taxes on speculators' holdings.[7]

Concerns about equality also stood at the center of how Pennsylvanians viewed the currency ban and how they framed their response. People across the colony from all walks of life blasted the currency ban for making wealth more unequal and turning debtors into lambs for slaughter by creditors and moneylenders. In 1769, ordinary folk from Philadelphia and from seven of Pennsylvania's nine counties (the two missing ones were in the deepest back-country) inundated the assembly with sixty-two petitions blaming the ban for forcing colonists back to the "Difficult and perplexing Method of . . . barter" that had created profound "Hardships" and inequity among the colony's early settlers. They accused Britain of stealing the independence of farmers, arti-sans, and merchants through "daily" sheriffs' auctions "for the Satisfaction of Debts" and driving the ordinary "Debtor" and "his Wife and Children" into "the utmost poverty." They said that this inequity left the common folk at "the Mercy of those few Persons who stood possessed of the principal Part of the Gold and Silver in the Colony."[8]

The same concern was expressed even by many affluent men who ended up siding with Britain. The Quaker-dominated assembly, which remained loyal to the Crown in 1776, blamed the currency ban for "impending Calamities" that increased "the Numbers of our Poor" and subjected "every *American*" to "Duress and Imprisonment, at the Will and Pleasure of his Creditor." Merchant Richard Waln, a Quaker with strong British sympa-thies, said that, by banning paper money, Britain was recreating the oppres-sions of "primitive times." Quaker merchant James Pemberton (who was arrested as a Loyalist during the war) denounced the ban for causing "those of inferior circumstances" to fall into "subjugation to the power of the rich."[9]

The solutions that Pennsylvanians offered for this crisis went well beyond lifting the currency ban: their overriding objective was creating a financial system that promoted economic equality rather than one that widened the wealth gap. The idea was to find a way to get money into the hands of ordi-nary farmers and artisans and, at the same time, provide easy access to low-cost credit. Most Pennsylvanians believed that such access was essential to keeping farms and businesses solvent and assuring that ordinary folk could achieve and sustain their independence.

Access to credit was especially important in this agrarian society, where debt followed seasonal rhythms. Farmers tended to go into debt to plant the spring crop and hoped to pay their way out with the summer and fall harvest. Borrowing was crucial, whether it was credit at a country store for tools and cloth or money borrowed from a local gentleman to hire labor to clear new acreage or to replace a broken plow. It was not just farmers who needed to borrow: in this agrarian society, almost everyone was tied to the seasonal timetable. Since farmers could only pay when they sold their crops, most arti-sans, storekeepers, and merchants also needed credit to carry them until the harvest. Access to credit could raise farmers or artisans to independence. The denial of it could keep them propertyless or cast them into dependency by bankrupting their farms and businesses. In short, the realities of farm life made credit—especially easy access to low-cost credit—central to most Pennsylvanians' notions of liberty, whether they owned land, hoped to acquire some, or worried about the future independence of their children.[10]

To bring money and credit to the masses, Pennsylvanians devised an ingenious system that turned the one thing most Pennsylvanians owned—land—into credit and cash. They called for the creation of a government-run "loan office" to offer ordinary folks low-cost mortgages as long as they owned a modest amount of land or property. To get a loan, farmers and artisans would pledge their land, livestock, or tools as collateral. In exchange, they got a long-term low-interest loan of new paper money issued by the government. Borrowers got the money at a low 5 percent interest rate and could take up to sixteen years to repay the principal.[11]

Pennsylvanians were confident that this public loan system would work because the colony had operated a wildly successful loan office for the past forty years. Beginning in 1723, the colony had issued loans of paper money to ordinary Pennsylvanians throughout the colony. Most of the loans were relatively small (the average loan was about £65). Although the borrowers were usually people of the middling sort, the loans reached a wide variety of people. Most loans went to farmers who offered land as collateral—which is why people usually referred to the loan office as a "land bank." Loans were also given to millers, barbers, butchers, carpenters, blacksmiths, innkeepers, clerks, and merchants. Even widows and spinsters could get credit. So could tenant farmers, who sometimes received loans to buy the lands they worked.[12]

The system also brought benefits to those who did not get loans by providing a stable currency that spurred economic growth and prosperity. When borrowers spent the money, it circulated through the colony (even traveling outside Pennsylvania's borders). The currency held its value well, largely because it was backed by land and property. If borrowers defaulted on their mortgage payments, the government could foreclose on whatever had been offered as collateral. There were few defaults during the land bank's forty-year run, however, and the system brought benefits throughout Pennsylvania. As a 1769 petition signed by thousands of ordinary folk put it, the land bank had satisfied the "Necessities of the People, in their various Branches of Business," bringing help to "Merchant, Farmer and Mechanic" alike.[13]

The land bank had done even more than this: it had also funded big tax cuts. The colonial government collected the annual 5 percent interest, netting the colony substantial income (for example, between 1763 and 1768, Pennsylvania took in about £9,900). The government used that money to build roads, clear waterways, provide support for the poor, and bolster colonial defenses—all without charging taxpayers a penny. In many years, the colony did not enact any direct tax because land-bank "profits" covered its expenses.[14]

This is not to say that the old system had been perfect: many people believed the land bank had not loaned enough money to enough different people. Despite the bank's great utility, its reach had been limited by elite men, who had seen it as a threat to their wealth and power. Unelected British officials, powerful colonial governors, and affluent legislators had feared that the land bank was "carried by a Levelling spirit" to bring down wealthy men. In particular, gentlemen had worried that government-issued currency would depreciate and allow debtors to pay back creditors with worthless paper. Some had condemned government currency as "Vile" and "rotten paper money" designed to "Insult Creditors" and to punish "men of ability." Such fears had led legislators, governors, and officials at the British Board of Trade to veto popular calls to expand the system to reach more people.[15]

Many Pennsylvanians hoped that a new (and more democratically run) land bank would surpass the old one and bring economic independence to a wider range of people. The goal was to put control of the land bank in the hands of democratically elected colonial legislators and to remove the ability of Parliament, the Crown, or the Penn family to veto popular calls to expand the system. As colonial legislators put it in 1767, democratic control of the land bank was "absolutely necessary to their future Liberties."[16]

In making this argument, Pennsylvanians rejected the British system and its ideals. These people were saying something quite revolutionary: ordinary people, working through their elected leaders, were better at defining the "public good" and economic policy than were the king, Parliament, the Penn family, or any other gentleman who claimed to know what was best for the masses.

They were also rejecting a system of finance like the one Britain had developed, where private moneylenders and large corporations like the Bank of England held enormous power. At the time, most Pennsylvanians believed that privatizing finance—turning control of money and credit over to private banks—promoted inequality and oppression and, therefore, posed a threat to liberty every bit as dire as control by Britain. People viewed private banks (which did not yet exist in America) as dangerous institutions that undermined freedom by putting economic power in the hands of unaccountable men. Bankers, it was said, were "wealthy persons" who wanted "money" to "center with a few"—in other words, advocates of inequality and tyranny.[17]

These anticorporate beliefs were on display in the public outrage that erupted in 1766 when a group of Philadelphia merchants attempted to create America's first private bank. The merchants, who represented eight of the city's more powerful firms, requested permission from the assembly to print £25–30,000 in new bank currency, promising this "private" money would help to end the cash scarcity. Pennsylvanians from all walks of life condemned the request as a threat to liberty. They denounced the proposed bank as the "partial Schemes of private Men" and derided the merchants as "Money Makers" and "petty banker[s]" who had been "actuated by Motives of private Gain." Ordinary Pennsylvanians petitioned that allowing "private" men or "particular Companies" to control money and credit was not in "the general Welfare." The "Power and Right" of printing paper money, they asserted, "is, and ought to be lodged in the Legislature of the Province alone"—it should not be controlled by private banks, the king, Parliament, or the Penn family. Those ideals were shared even by merchants, who emerged as some of the most vocal opponents of privatization. In December 1766, more than 200 Philadelphia merchants took out an advertisement in the *Pennsylvania Gazette* saying they would not accept any of this private money. One of the merchants who had placed the ad told a friend that "the scheme" of a private bank "is opposed by all trading people. We think public credit is too delicate for private men to interfere with." It was far better, these merchants thought, to stick with a democratically run land bank.[18]

Indeed, land-bank supporters emphasized that a government-run system of finance had promoted equality—and therefore protected freedom—far better than one based on private money lending. John Dickinson explained that "no private person would lend money on such favourable terms" as the 5 percent offered at the land bank. Likewise, no private lender would give the kind of long-term credit that ordinary folk (and especially farmers) needed. According to one farmer, "Very few" moneylenders would give loans "for longer time than a year." The land bank also made credit widely available to people of different classes and occupations throughout Pennsylvania— unlike the private bank, which was designed to lend to merchants. By law, the public bank had to parcel out the loans among the counties so that a "great number" could be "accommodated" whether they lived in Philadelphia or in the deepest backcountry.[19]

Supporters also saw the land bank as an engine of equality because no one—not even the wealthiest gentleman—could get a larger loan than could the average farmer. Under the land-bank system, advocates said, "no person is permitted to borrow a large sum." Loans were usually capped at £100; at Pennsylvania's old land bank, the average loan had only been about £65. The system allowed people to borrow enough to improve their farms and businesses, but did not provide anyone with the money to dominate economic or political life. Instead, under the land bank, "[p]eople of very small fortunes [were] enabled to purchase and cultivate land" or "carry on some business, that without such assistance they would be incapable of managing." In this way, the system was "calculated for the good of the province in general, and of the necessitous borrower in particular." It allowed ordinary people to live with dignity rather than having to beg from "usurers and exactors." It gave ordinary folk the chance of "raising up their children to industry, supporting their families with credit, [and] paying their debts with honour." In sum, the land bank bred independence rather than subservience, while discouraging concentrations of wealth.[20]

Ultimately, these arguments had little effect during the 1760s and 1770s. For nearly a decade, Pennsylvanians tried in vain to convince Britain and the Penn family to allow the legislature to create a land bank. Every proposal was rejected for reasons that future Loyalist Joseph Galloway termed "really ridiculous." Finally, in 1773, Britain and the Penn family allowed a small £150,000 land bank to open. But the money was not legal tender (which meant no one had to accept it). And, in a radical departure from previous land banks, borrowers were required to come to Philadelphia to get credit rather than being able to go to loan offices in their counties as they had done in the past. As colonial legislators put it, this change alone worked "in a great Measure to exclude the People" who "stand most in need of its Aid." Since it was prohibitively expensive for most people to travel continually to Philadelphia to get a loan and to make mortgage payments, the new land bank was essentially useless to the vast majority of the population.[21]

The message that many Pennsylvanians took away from their experiences with the attempt to create a land bank—and most of the other demands they made during the 1760s and 1770s—was that neither Britain nor the Penn family shared a commitment to preserving the economic and political independence of ordinary folk. Rather than pursuing what most Pennsylvanians thought was the public good, their unelected leaders seemed to be committed to promoting the interests of the few over the many. Britain and the Penns continued to insist on controlling taxation and finance and limiting trade. And, when the public expressed dissatisfaction, these leaders increasingly turned to British judges and troops to enforce unpopular laws.

To most Pennsylvanians, these realities engendered thoughts of independence and self-rule—even among those who eventually opposed the break with Britain. John Dickinson, who urged reconciliation in 1776, exclaimed in 1765 that Britain's willingness to promote inequality and public suffering was driving the colonies toward independence. "SHE TEACHES US TO MAKE A DISCTINCTION BETWEEN HER INTERESTS AND OUR OWN," his writing shouted. "Teaches! She requires—commands—insists upon it—threatens—compels—and even distresses us into it." William Allen, the chief justice of Pennsylvania (who moved to England at the beginning of the war), wrote in 1768 that the cash scarcity was opening "wounds" that "will not heal for an Age to come." "I ardently wish," wrote pro-British merchant Richard Waln in 1768, that we "may not be reduced to the cruel alternative of slavery or to take up arms against a people we revere as a Parent state and to whom we are attached by every tie." But, as he saw things, a showdown was brewing because Pennsylvanians were "determined not to submit to" anything else that worked toward their impoverishment and "the destruction of their Liberty."[22]

Organizing Independence

The Revolution happened, not simply because most people shared experiences and a broad set of ideals; the colonists made the Revolution by organizing on behalf of those ideals. Modern Americans tend to give the credit for this mobilization to the gentry: the elite founding fathers who formed the revolutionary committees, who created the correspondence network that connected the thirteen colonies, and who came to power in the new state and national governments. Although the gentry were unquestionably central to the story, the preoccupation with the elite founders has obscured our understanding of the critical role that ordinary Americans played in the resistance movement and in the creation of the revolutionary governments. Moreover, it has limited our understanding of the relationship between the organizing done by the founding elite and the work performed by people of the middling and lower sorts.

In revolutionary Pennsylvania, there were two layers of organizing: one by ordinary folk who mobilized in their communities and another by the gentry, which linked local resistance efforts together and connected them to the larger revolutionary movement. Appreciating these two layers is critical to understanding how Pennsylvanians organized their Revolution and why it became so democratic. (Those relationships are also vital to appreciating the problems that ordinary Pennsylvanians faced in the 1780s when the elite abandoned its commitment to economic and political equality.)

During the 1760s and 1770s, Pennsylvanians built their Revolution in an uneasy alliance between gentry-led and popular organizing efforts. The two were set apart by many factors: by class (one composed of gentlemen of wealth and standing; the other made up of the common folk with some gentry support); by tactics (the gentry favored petitions, pamphlets, and lobbying; ordinary Pennsylvanians used petitions but also relied on direct-action protests); by tone (the gentry favored a tempered resistance that avoided offending Britain; ordinary people were more brash and outspoken); and by goals (the gentry hoped to achieve justice through reconciliation with the mother country; most regular folk wanted to end oppression and were more open to the idea of independence). The result was a struggle between gentry-led and popular resistance, in which the gentry attempted to restrain the protests of ordinary Pennsylvanians, who, in turn, pushed the gentlemen to take more aggressive stances against Britain. This push-and-pull relationship carried Pennsylvania, somewhat haphazardly, down the road to independence.[23]

To get a sense of the differences, consider two examples: the first being the gentry-led committees formed in Philadelphia in 1765 to protest British imperial policies; the second being the backcountry organizations that arose about the same time that went by the names Black Boys, Brave Fellows, and Loyal Volunteers.

The gentry-led committees in Philadelphia were focused on working through existing political channels to get Britain to back down. Formed in 1765, the committees were initially composed of wealthy merchants who felt that the colonial assembly was not doing enough to oppose the currency ban, trade restrictions, and the Stamp Act. They drafted petitions and wrote pamphlets explaining their grievances. The gentry committees pressured the Penn family and the Quaker-dominated legislature to abandon their "dutiful and submissive behavior" toward Britain. They pushed the colonial assembly to complain about British policies and convinced legislators to hire lobbyists (like Benjamin Franklin) to plead their case before Parliament and the London Board of Trade. When Britain enacted the Townshend Acts in 1767 and sent royal troops to enforce its laws, the gentry committees again responded with petitions, pamphlets, and lobbying efforts. They organized a boycott of British goods and encouraged the rural gentry to form committees in the countryside to make the boycott more effective. The success of the committees was often undermined by internal bickering over strategy (many gentlemen thought a boycott was going too far; merchants complained of lost profits) and long-standing personal and political rivalries. Things were so contentious that the committees were forced to disband and reform several times.[24]

By contrast, the popular organizing of the rural Black Boys represented a far stronger and more enduring stance against Britain. This group formed in the farming communities of Cumberland County, which at the time was an enormous swath of land stretching from the Susquehanna River to the colony's western border. From the start, Cumberland farmers saw the conflict with Britain as a showdown between the few and the many. As Bible-thumping Black Boy Jimmy Smith, the group's purported leader, put it, the king and provincial government seemed to have been "erected as money-making machines" for a wealthy few. They "oppressed" the people "with expensive litigation" and "injured" small farmers by sanctioning "legal robbery." They were little more than "splendid villains that make themselves grand and great on other people's labor." Smith, who had been an Indian captive and spoke Mohawk and Ottawa, even implied that the king, the Penn family, and wealthy merchants in the colony were worse than Indians.[25]

As angry as Smith and his neighbors were with the full array of British policies, they were especially upset by the attempts of Britain and the Penn family to end Pontiac's Rebellion in 1765 by appeasing the Indians with gifts. Cumberland had been hard hit by Indian raids during the French and Indian War and Pontiac's uprising. The latest episode was a horrific attack in the summer of 1764 on a schoolhouse in Cumberland that left the headmaster and ten children dead. Rural anger intensified when hostile tribes from the Ohio Valley refused to return white prisoners taken during the war, and rumors flew about new attacks. In this environment, most people living in Cumberland thought it was unconscionable to give gifts before the Indians had signed a peace treaty and returned their white captives.

Cumberland farmers were incensed when they learned, shortly thereafter, that Philadelphia merchants had resumed the gun trade to the Indians—with the apparent blessing of the supposedly pacifist Quaker government. Farmers caught wind that wagon trains bearing the king's gifts to the Indians included hidden weapons and ammunition. They accused Quaker leaders of being in cahoots with Philadelphia merchants and Indian traders in a profit-making scheme (charges that turned out to have merit). Convinced that the government was corrupt, many Cumberland farmers decided to take the law into their own hands and regulate the Indian trade by force.

As a result, hundreds of farmers mobilized into the Black Boys (the name no doubt referring to their practice of blackening their faces in disguise; evidently they went by the name Brave Fellows when they dressed as Indians). Although this group took the law into its own hands, it was not a repeat of the Indian-slaughtering Paxton Boys (who lived farther east). Instead, the Black Boys were less interested in killing Indians than in regulating a government dominated by Britain, the Quaker elite, and eastern merchants. Their goal was policing the Indian trade: they monitored the roads and waylaid packhorse trains bound for Indian territory to inspect them for weapons. Even if the contents were marked as property of the king, when the Black Boys found weapons, they confiscated them and burned everything else as punishment.

These efforts produced frequent armed conflicts between Cumberland farmers and the British soldiers tasked with upholding the laws of king and colony. For example, in March 1765, the Black Boys found weapons stashed in an eighty-one-horse train, and, despite the fact that much of the shipment was identified as the king's property, they burned it all—an estimated £20–30,000 of goods. Most county justices refused to prosecute the Black Boys, and, as a result, the commander of the British garrison stationed at Fort Loudon (in modern-day Franklin County) decided to intervene and sent a detachment of soldiers to make arrests. After they took the first prisoners, 200 Cumberland farmers armed themselves, dressed as Indians, and surrounded the garrison. The show of force convinced the British commander to exchange prisoners and stop the arrests. When the commander insisted on keeping the prisoners' guns, however, the conflict continued. On several occasions over the next several months, hundreds of farmers surrounded the fort demanding the guns; they chased off riders trying to enter or leave the garrison; they even traded volleys with British soldiers. On one occasion, they actually kidnapped the British commander.

In all of this, the Brave Fellows believed they were acting legally—thinking that justice was on their side even though they openly opposed the authority of the king and their colonial rulers. Indeed, the Brave Fellows followed legal procedure with everything they did (even if it was not the kind of legality their rulers sanctioned). For example, the Black Boys said that they were only attempting to enforce warrants issued by Cumberland justices of the peace, who had demanded that the fort's commander return the guns he had confiscated. They justified another assault on the fort as an attempt to enforce an arrest warrant for a British sergeant who had wounded one of the Brave Fellows during a shootout. When policing the Indian trade, the Brave Fellows drew up legal commissions declaring their right to monitor the trade. They even devised a passport system to allow safe travel for Indian traders whose goods had passed inspection.

Many of these farmers believed that armed conflict was also a legal and appropriate means of politics. In September 1769, a brief war broke out between farmers and British soldiers at Fort Bedford when the Brave Fellows stopped yet another packhorse train and destroyed rifles and gun powder. When the Fort Bedford commander arrested several of the Brave Fellows, Jimmy Smith and his men decided to make a surprise attack on the garrison. The British regulars were completely unprepared for such a bold (and potentially treasonous) attack. They were so shocked that the Brave Fellows took the fort, freed the arrested men, and returned home without anyone being hurt. Years later, Jimmy Smith liked to brag that the Brave Fellows had captured the first British fort in the opening battle of America's War for Independence.[26]

Although that claim is hard to sustain, there is no doubt that the Black Boys were a model of an organization far different—and, one could argue, far more revolutionary—than the more staid committees of Philadelphia gentlemen. The Black Boys were not lawless vigilantes. But they were willing to oppose (or to "regulate") the king, the ruling Penn family, and British soldiers when they believed that their leaders were acting in oppressive ways. It was a model of organization that ordinary folk would repeat throughout Pennsylvania—and America—in the years to come.

When the two types of organization collided—as they did when ordinary folk began challenging the timidity of the gentry-led committees—the popular organizations often pushed the gentry to take far more aggressive stances than they had previously been willing to consider. Ordinary folk usually did not try to take over the committees. Rather, farmers, artisans, and laborers put tremendous pressure on the gentry to change. One could say that "the people" led by example: they took provocative actions, made declarations against Britain, and then forced the gentry to follow—however reluctantly. When the gentry proved unwilling to follow, ordinary folk demanded new leadership, which usually meant different gentlemen but, in many places, also included some of the common folk.

To get a sense of how this worked, consider the way that ordinary Philadelphians forced changes in the city committees. In Philadelphia, the upswing in popular pressure began in 1770 when craftspeople became upset with the tentativeness and elitism of the merchant-led committees. Artisans complained of "Gentlemen" who thought the "Mechanics" had no right to "*speak* or *think* for themselves" and who shunned any advice that came from below. City craftspeople also condemned the "Torrent of Corruption and self Interest" of wealthy merchants who put profits ahead of patriotism by breaking the boycotts of British goods. Believing that the gentry was incapable of regulating itself, artisans formed their own committees to enforce the boycott. By July 1770, one genteel Philadelphian started to worry that "the lead[ership] of Affairs here is (I think) now got too much out of the hands of the merchants."[27]

Such fears multiplied when Philadelphia artisans came to play an even more central role as the conflict between Britain and the colonies intensified in 1774. The catalyst was the dramatic events in New England that followed the Boston Tea Party. In response to the dumping of the tea, Britain shut down Boston harbor, banned town meetings in Massachusetts, replaced many elected officials with royally appointed ones, and shielded British officials from prosecution in Massachusetts' courts. Britain extended the punishment to the other colonies by sending additional troops and passing a new Quartering Act, which empowered British officers to confiscate (with compensation to the owner) "uninhabited houses, out-houses, barns, or other buildings." In June 1774, Parliament also enacted the Quebec Act, which extended what is now Canada into Ohio Valley lands that most Americans had viewed as future farmland for their children and grandchildren. These "coercive acts" convinced many Pennsylvanians that Britain intended to dispense with republican governance and to rule as a despotic monarchy.[28]

In Philadelphia, ordinary folk responded by pressing the gentry to take a firmer stance against Britain and to democratize the committees. Craftspeople and laborers demanded that all eligible voters be given the right to select committeemen and that committee meetings be opened to the public. The elections produced a new set of committee leaders who tended to be less wealthy and of lower status than the previous committeemen. The new men still tended to be much better off than the average Pennsylvanian, and the primary leaders usually came from the wealthiest 10 percent of the population. And, like before, many were wealthy merchants and gentlemen. Now, however, the committees also included farmers, artisans, millers, distillers, and shopkeepers. Although poor men still did not sit on the committees, the changes opened political power to a class of people long kept at arm's length by the ruling elite.[29]

Popular pressure also ensured that the new leadership was far more ethnically diverse than were the old leaders, who had mostly been wealthy Quakers and gentlemen of English and Welsh descent. Quakers still took leadership positions in the new committees, but far fewer than before (and their numbers continued to decline when the Society of Friends condemned opposition to Britain in late 1774 and later promised to disown anyone active in the resistance). The Quakers were replaced by new men who tended to come from different ethnic and religious groups, especially Scots-Irish Presbyterians and German sectarians who previously had been denied leadership roles despite the fact that they formed the majority of Pennsylvania's population.[30]

Ordinary Philadelphians exerted even more influence over the direction of the revolutionary movement beginning in April 1775, when they started forming militias after the bloodshed at Lexington and Concord. By taking the lead in mobilizing the city militia, craftspeople and laborers forced the Philadelphia gentry to approve of an aggressive act that most of them had opposed. Indeed, fears of ordinary folk leading a self-directed militia convinced some of the gentry to join up to install themselves as officers. As one member of the city gentry put it, gentlemen officers were driven less by patriotism than by a conviction that "it was Improper for the Gentlemen of America to suffer the power to get into the hands of the lowest people."[31]

Similar dynamics unfolded in the countryside, where ordinary folk often pushed gentry leaders to follow them down the path to war. Consider, for example, the case of York County, located a hundred miles west of Philadelphia, where in February 1775 county farmers compelled a cautious gentry to take up arms—two month before the battles of Lexington and Concord.[32]

In York County, the revolutionary committee was led by wary gentlemen, mostly lawyers and traders from the commercial town of York, who were convinced that the resistance was getting out of hand. In February 1775, the committee had just returned from a convention of all the Pennsylvania committees, a gathering they thought had been far too radical. The York delegation had gone to the convention hoping to calm down the resistance. Instead, a majority at the convention had voted to fight the mother country if Britain attacked New England. That majority also passed a resolution to begin making gunpowder in anticipation of war.

It could have been worse for the peace-minded York committee: some delegations had wanted to organize militias throughout the colony. The men from York had managed to join with other like-minded committees to quash the motion and focus instead on organizing another boycott of British goods. The victory was of small consolation to the York committee members, who were terrified about the prospect of going home to talk about impending war and gunpowder production with their constituents.[33]

They were so afraid that they decided to doctor their report and delete or rewrite anything they considered too radical. Upon their return, they convened a countywide meeting at the courthouse in the town of York to discuss what had happened in Philadelphia and to read the convention's resolutions. Their new version of the resolutions, however, excluded the pledge of armed support against Britain. They had also replaced the resolution calling for gunpowder production with a new one saying that Pennsylvanians should "discourage the consuming" of gunpowder since the planned boycott would cause a "scarcity" of it. The York delegates even made up a fake justification: rather than mention the impending conflict with Britain, they said that conservation of gunpowder was needed because a shortage of it might harm "our Indian trade, and the hunters in this province."

Evidently, the committeemen were not worried about anyone discovering the deception. Since the committee was the primary source for information about the resistance movement, it would be hard for ordinary folk in York County to discover what had actually happened in Philadelphia. And if newspapers or pamphlets eventually brought the news, it would take time for the truth to be disseminated and confirmed. The committeemen undoubtedly hoped that, by then, the crisis would have passed.

That dream was dashed as soon as they finished reading their bogus report. The courthouse was packed with townsfolk and farmers from the surrounding countryside. At first, the committeemen must have been pleased to see that so many rural folk had trudged miles on a winter day to take an interest in their work. None of them, however, had any idea that the farmers pressed against the walls of the crowded courthouse would soon push York County into rebellion.

When the committeemen finished their agenda, a group of farmers asked to be heard. The men identified themselves as representatives appointed to inform the committee that farmers throughout York County "had formed themselves into Companies" and were now drilling as militia in anticipation of a war with Britain. Perhaps doffing their hats in their hands, the farmers said they would defer to the committee members and wanted "to know their sentiments on the subject." If the gentlemen on the committee found the militias "disagreeable," then the farmers said they would "discontinue" training.

An awkward silence followed as the committee sat stunned. These gentlemen saw themselves as the vanguard of resistance in York County. And now, quite suddenly, the committeemen found that they were several steps behind those whom they imagined they were leading. The people had formed militias! How had this happened? Why hadn't the committee been informed?

If there was an uncomfortable pause, it was no doubt precisely the response the farmers had designed their performance to generate. After all, this was no chance gathering of farmers to display their deference. Back in the summer and fall of 1774, when farmers first began mustering, they had felt no need to ask permission of their social betters. And, as was probably clear to the committee, the militia representatives were not really asking for permission now. These farmers had already decided to stand against Britain. They had come to the meeting at York to convince the committee to join their resistance. The farmers' performance, cloaked though it was in rituals of deference, sent a commanding message that even the most obtuse of the town gentry could have detected: if you want us to consider you to be our leaders, then you must lead in the direction we point. In this subtle but powerful way, ordinary farmers brought the revolutionary struggle in York County to its defining moment.

On closer inspection, however, the display was also an admission of weakness. In orchestrating this performance, farmers had shown they could organize in their neighborhoods and throughout the county, but it also revealed that they did not think they could mobilize further without assistance. The farmers knew they were relatively isolated from the larger resistance movement. They did not know the other committee leaders in Pennsylvania

FIG. 2.1. LAND AND INDEPENDENCE. This 1788 landscape of York County highlights the importance of land to the kind of rustic independence that most farmers placed at the center of their revolutionary ideals. *View from Bushongo Tavern,* reprinted from *Columbian Magazine* (July 1788). Courtesy American Antiquarian Society.

or the men in Philadelphia who had called the convention. Nor did they know resistance leaders in other colonies. Those kinds of connections were confined to the gentry. The genteel committeemen, with their far-flung family connections and business networks, sat at the hub of communications. Quite obviously, the farmers at the courthouse did not think they had the contacts and resources to fill that critical role. Consequently, ordinary farmers turned to the local gentry to provide the connections. The gentlemen might be reluctant revolutionaries, but they provided the best way for farmers in York County to link their efforts to the wider resistance. The farmers were not placing themselves in leadership positions beyond their neighborhood committees. But they were, in effect, taking a leading role by pressuring the gentry to act as they saw fit. And by forcing the committeemen to be the kind of leaders they wanted, ordinary farmers brought a new kind of democracy to York County.

This time, the push from below worked. Rather than lose face, the committee made an instant about-face. When the silence in the courtroom broke, once-timid committeemen roared with a newfound boldness that shocked some of the gentlemen in attendance. Thomas Hartley, a prosperous lawyer from York, later reported his amazement that "the whole Committee unanimously approved" of the new militias. He was more surprised when the "old and sage" committeemen (evidently hoping to appear as leaders rather than followers) gave an after-the-fact order that "we should muster throughout the country immediately." The committee insisted, however, that the militias must be conducted with "prudence, moderation, and a strict regard to good order." More important, they demanded that each militia be placed "under the direction of a man of probity and understanding"—in other words, a member of the local gentry.

The York gentlemen were also willing to back their talk with action and take up arms themselves. "We apprehended that it would be very improper in these Inhabitants of this Town," Hartley recalled, "to recommend Measures to others which they dare not practice themselves." Consequently, the meeting quickly adjourned so Hartley and the committee could dash through the town to recruit volunteers for their own militia company. The lawyer proudly reported that "Upon an Hours Notice 36 subscribed and at the 2d meeting our Company was complete—and every Person furnished with Arms" (evidently, at the gentry's expense). "We improve in Discipline daily," Hartley wrote to a Philadelphia associate a few weeks later. "God knows how it will end, but really we have a good beginning."[34]

After Lexington and Concord, this good beginning extended throughout much of the countryside. In York County by the end of 1775, an estimated 3,350 men had enlisted in military service—about 75 percent of the male population between the ages of fifteen and fifty-five. In the eastern county of Northampton, more than 2,250 men had signed up by May 1775 (about 70 percent of the adult men). In neighboring Berks County, over 3,000 men served in the militia or in the Continental Army (over 60 percent of the adult men in this heavily German county). In Cumberland County, Black Boy Jimmy Smith and the Brave Fellows rallied an estimated 3,000 Cumberland farmers to sign up to fight Britain—about 70 percent of the county's adult men. Cumberland patriots also took the unprecedented step of levying £27,000 in taxes on themselves to defray military expenses.[35]

Not every county demonstrated such enthusiasm and, in most places, the fervor cooled as the war slogged on. There was also strong resistance to both mustering and independence in the heavily Quaker counties of Bucks, Chester, and Philadelphia. Nevertheless, the overwhelming support across much of the countryside in 1775 forced reluctant revolutionaries—and, eventually, even the pacifist general assembly—to take a more defiant stand against Britain.

Government from Below: The Pennsylvania Constitution of 1776

The drive for a new government—like with the push for war and independence—was inspired by ordinary Pennsylvanians who, although they usually did not formally lead the movement, steered the gentry down a more democratic road. The resulting government allowed a greater degree of popular participation and operated with a more expansive idea of democracy than had any previous colonial government. Not everyone was happy with the results: some thought the new government was too democratic; others thought it did not provide enough of an opening; and, during the war, the new state leaders seemed to violate civil rights more than they protected them. Nevertheless, the new government enjoyed wide popular support and was to many Pennsylvanians—even to much of the gentry—the central accomplishment of the Revolution.[36]

In many ways, this dramatic opening was caused by the inability of the Quaker-dominated assembly and the Penn family to deal with the war that was raging around them. Once deeply divided by an internal power struggle, the Penns and the gentlemen in the assembly put aside their differences after Lexington and Concord to stifle the resistance. Pennsylvania's ruling elite stalled financial support of the military and refused to coordinate with other colonies. As public sentiment increased for war and independence, the colony's governors dug in their heels. Finally, in the spring of 1776, the war dethroned them. A British gunboat sailed up the Delaware River, and the sound of cannon fire, combined with news of British "atrocities" (such as hiring thousands of Hessian mercenaries, burning a town in Maine, and provoking slave uprisings in Virginia), created an uproar that the assembly was unable to handle. As John Adams famously put it, the Quaker assembly saw the approach of independence and, rather than take action, "they started back," as if by doing nothing the whole conflict would go away. Popular discontent peaked on May 10, when the Continental Congress passed a resolution essentially calling on Pennsylvanians to overthrow their government unless it joined with the other colonies. When the ruling elite responded by redoubling its push for peace, the revolutionary committees— by now larger, more extensive, and better coordinated—deposed their leaders and brought independence to the Keystone State.[37]

In the summer of 1776, those committees—dominated by the gentry— designed a new government to prevent the oppressions of the past by empowering ordinary folk and bringing the wealthy to heel. Indeed, the creation of the 1776 Pennsylvania constitution was ripe with talk of redressing the power imbalance between the ordinary many and the wealthy few. People spoke of making a government to end the rule of "great and over-grown rich Men" who used their power to "reap the Benefits" of governance for themselves. The new system would be run by those who shared the "Passions and Interests" of ordinary citizens. It would valorize "the *common people*" over "the *rich*" and put them in a better position "to take care of their own interest[s]."[38]

In fact, this kind of thinking appeared in the very text of the 1776 constitution. "Government is, or ought to be, instituted for the common benefit, protection, and security of the people," the new document proclaimed, "and not for the particular emolument or advantage of any single man, family, or set of men who are only part of the community."[39]

Many of the framers of the 1776 constitution had wanted to go further and include a clause allowing the state to ensure equality by confiscating wealth from extremely rich people. That plank (some say it was authored by Benjamin Franklin) had declared that "future legislatures of this State should have the power of lessening property when it became excessive in individuals" because concentrations of wealth were "a danger to the happiness of mankind." The measure was voted down, however. The majority of the convention may have "embraced leveling principles," as one delegate put it, but most of them were still landed gentlemen who objected to property confiscation. Instead, they believed that government should equalize wealth through less coercive means—although the constitution remained silent on what those means should be.[40]

One of the most revolutionary provisions that did make the final version allowed nearly all adult men to vote. This opening of the political system was pushed by ordinary militiamen, who complained about the prospect of fighting for a government that denied them the right to vote. If ordinary men were going to fight for the new state, then they wanted the "Rights and Privileges of a Citizen." The 1776 constitution met that demand by removing property requirements for voting. Previously, in order to vote, one had to own fifty acres of land or £50 of property. Now, all one needed was to be a twenty-one-year-old male who had paid any state or local tax (the sons of land owners did not even have to be taxpayers). The lower requirements allowed approximately 90 percent of the adult male population to qualify—a steep increase over the 50–75 percent who had qualified in the past. The biggest gains came in the older Quaker-dominated counties of Bucks, Chester, and Philadelphia, where only about 50–60 percent of the population had been able to meet the property threshold. And, importantly, the constitution made no racial distinction, making Pennsylvania one of the few new governments that gave voting rights to free African-American males (a right they would hold until 1837).[41]

This opening represented a dramatically new way of thinking about voting and citizenship. In the past, governments had focused on limiting the franchise to adult men who owned sufficient property because it was thought that only those with property could be truly "independent" citizens. Governments had disenfranchised propertyless "dependents," whom it was thought would vote as their landlords, employers, or creditors directed. It was said that preventing dependents from voting would keep wealthy men from corrupting the political system. As Pennsylvanians broke from Britain, they also abandoned this old way of thinking about voting. The new focus was to protect against corruption by giving the vote to men who held little or no property. The idea was that an expanded electorate would protect against corruption better because, with so many voters, there would be too many people to buy off. At the same time, it was thought that allowing ordinary folk to vote would give them the power they needed to get access to money, credit, and land and become independent. And with property in many hands, it would be even harder for the affluent to control political life. There were remnants of the old thinking in this new ideal: Pennsylvania's revolutionaries still considered the propertyless a possible threat. But they now believed that giving the vote to ordinary folk was the only way to keep the wealthy in check.

No doubt, similar reasoning explains why the framers of the 1776 constitution did not require representatives in the Pennsylvania assembly to hold property. Most of the other states kept high property requirements for political office. Pennsylvania allowed "all free men" the right "to be elected into office." This did not mean that poor men suddenly won political office. Indeed, the new state assembly tended to be composed of the same gentlemen who sat on the revolutionary committees. Most were wealthy or at least well-off. But the relaxed rules also allowed into office some new men, who were not wealthy: small farmers, weavers, and tailors of modest means.

The new constitution was also revolutionary in that it offered much stronger protections for civil liberties than had the colonial government. The 1776 constitution protected freedom of religion, speech, assembly, and the press. It also included a right to trial by jury, rights against self-incrimination and unreasonable search and seizure, and a right to bear arms. It even included a right to revolution. The constitution stated, "[T]he community hath an indubitable, unalienable and indefeasible right to reform, alter, or abolish government in such manner as shall be by that community judged most conducive to the public weal." The document declared that government was "instituted and supported for the security and protection of the community" so that people could "enjoy their natural rights." "Whenever these great ends of government are not obtained," it held, "the people have a right, by common consent to change it, and take such measures as to them may appear necessary to promote their safety and happiness." As we shall see, most Pennsylvanians took those rights seriously, believing that the constitution not only sanctioned protest but, in fact, required "the people" to take action when they thought political leaders were violating the public will.

The framers of the 1776 constitution hoped that they could restructure government so that people would never again feel the need to rebel. Thus, in the new system, most of the important offices in the state and county governments were elected rather than appointed. The new system equalized political power by linking representation in the assembly to a county's population, rather than allowing the older counties in the east to wield power well beyond their numbers (Quakers had filled one-third of the seats in the assembly, although they were only about 10 percent of the population).

The 1776 constitution also attempted to remove internal checks against the will of the citizenry. Modern Americans are accustomed to thinking about the height of democratic government as a divided legislature (house and senate) and a powerful executive (president) armed with the veto. Pennsylvania's revolutionaries thought otherwise. They viewed such a government as checking democracy rather than promoting it. After all, divided government was a British legacy, where the king and the upper chamber of Parliament (the House of Lords, filled with titled aristocrats who served for life) checked the democratic branch (the House of Commons). Most Pennsylvanians believed they had suffered under such a system. Consequently, they wanted a new government that would remove the barriers that had kept their voices from being heard.[42]

The solution they developed was to put most of the power in a new state assembly with an unchecked unicameral house. The idea, as Thomas Paine wrote, was "common sense." If the lower house in the legislature was the voice of the people, then any check on the house—such as a senate or a governor with a veto—was a check on the will of the people by the rich and well-born. Guided by this belief, the framers of the 1776 constitution refused to institute a senate. They also intentionally created the state executive without veto power. In fact, this new executive, called the "President of Pennsylvania" could do little more than advise the legislature and enforce laws. As observers at the time commented, this was the most democratic government in the new nation; according to Benjamin Franklin, that meant it was also "the safest and best."[43]

Additionally the framers included provisions to encourage politicians to remain faithful to their constituents. They instituted annual elections for every representative, giving people a yearly chance to hold their leaders accountable. They tried to set term limits, hoping to avoid career politicians who might develop interests apart from their communities. The framers also tried to make the operations of government as transparent as possible by keeping the doors of the assembly open to the public and by publishing a detailed record of votes and debates so people could read what their legislators had said and see how they had voted. Finally, the constitution called for the creation of public schools in each county to ensure that citizens had the education to make informed decisions.

As dramatic as this political opening was, however, it had clear limits. For example, the new government did not open the vote for everyone. Women were denied the franchise—as they were in every other new state (with the brief exception of New Jersey). Slaves were prohibited from voting. It is uncertain whether the small communities of Native Americans, mostly Christian converts, were able to vote. And despite the focus on empowering white men, the tax-paying stipulation denied the vote to many of the very poorest whites, whose poverty exempted them from taxation. Finally, from 1777 until 1786, the state disenfranchised anyone who refused to support the revolutionary government. Like most other states, Pennsylvania enacted "test oaths" that required voters to denounce the king and pledge their allegiance to the new state. Although the law was unevenly enforced, especially after the war, these oaths denied the vote to many Loyalists, Quakers, and religious pacifists.

There were also limits regarding who was eligible to serve in office. In practice, the phrase "all free men" really meant Christians. The 1776 constitution required that "before he takes his seat," each assemblyman must declare a belief in God and "acknowledge the Scriptures of the Old and New Testament to be given by Divine inspiration." This was actually more lenient than the oaths required by the colonial government. Despite the Quakers' reputation for tolerance, they had insisted that legislators acknowledge the Holy Trinity and declare, among other things, that believing in the saints was superstitious and following the pope was idolatrous. Such provisions, clearly designed to keep Catholics from holding office, were abetted by other civic penalties on Catholics, Unitarians, Jews, and Muslims—all of which were absent in the 1776 constitution.[44]

Likewise, the 1776 constitution's protections of civil rights initially applied only to patriots. During the war, the government narrowed free speech and assembly in the name of security. Bear in mind, Pennsylvania was frequently a battlefield; the government itself had to flee Philadelphia when Britain occupied the city in 1777. Nor were Loyalists harmless: they revealed troop movements, gave intelligence to British commanders, and supplied British forces. The same could be said for the many Quakers who refused to pay taxes or supply the American war effort at the same time they traded with the British. Nevertheless, if the concerns were genuine, the government often silenced or imprisoned those suspected of helping the enemy on flimsy evidence and with little real cause. At the same time, revolutionary leaders often looked the other way as patriotic vigilante groups took the law into their own hands against those they deemed to be enemies to the cause. The repression was often brutal, sometimes targeting people whose only crime was a religious belief in pacifism.[45]

There were even clear limits on what promised to be the new government's most revolutionary act: the abolition of slavery in Pennsylvania. Swept up in the ideals of the Revolution (and pressured by antislavery groups, Quakers, and slaves themselves), the new government passed a gradual abolition law in 1780. "Gradual," however, was the key word. The law did not free any slaves outright; instead, it only freed the children of current slaves when they reached the age of twenty-eight. Indeed, slavery continued in Pennsylvania long after those who passed the law had died. The fact that Pennsylvania's law became the model adopted by the revolutionary governments in most of the northern states revealed, more than anything else, the stark limits on popular notions of democracy during the American Revolution.[46]

Despite these limits—and, at times, perhaps because of them—the 1776 constitution enjoyed widespread popular support in the state. The surest sign of that support came in early 1779, when a group of state leaders attempted to call a new convention to overturn the constitution because they believed it was too democratic. In response, ordinary people across the state launched a petition drive to support the 1776 charter. Conditions were not favorable for such an effort: many people were more focused on British and Indian enemies than they were on political doings in the state; most of the Pennsylvania Line was encamped in northern New Jersey and upstate New York and, therefore, could not defend the constitution under which they were fighting. Nor did the weather cooperate: the winter of 1779 was the coldest of the war. Despite wartime chaos and frigid temperatures, in a little more than a month, over 16,500 Pennsylvanians signed petitions expressing their approval of the 1776 constitution. To put this effort in perspective, consider that eight years later, in 1787, only about 6,800 Pennsylvanians voted in favor of the federal Constitution (and only about 13,000 cast votes in the ratification elections). In sum, more than twice as many Pennsylvanians voiced support for the 1776 state constitution than for the 1787 federal Constitution.[47]

*   *   *

In the end, the clearest measure of this transformation was the support it enjoyed among the gentry. Indeed, even many elite Pennsylvanians who disliked the 1776 constitution were quick to say that they approved of the Revolution's larger objectives of empowering ordinary folk and displacing the wealthy few. Shortly after the passage of the 1776 constitution, Dr. William Shippen (a member of one of Pennsylvania's most prominent and powerful families) celebrated the downfall of those "who have heretofore been at the head of affairs" and who now were "ousted or at least brought down to a level with their fellow citizens." Likewise, an elitist writer who complained that Pennsylvania's revolutionary government consisted "*chiefly* of illiterate men who are altogether unqualified for their offices" felt compelled to declare his distaste for the thought of "wealthy men" coming back "into power." For the time being, even many of the elite Pennsylvanians who thought too much power had fallen into the hands of ordinary men reaffirmed their commitment to working for the interests of the many over the few. That commitment would soon change radically.[48]

Part II

CONFRONTING THE COUNTER-REVOLUTION

(1776–1787)

3

The Gospel of Moneyed Men

THE GENTRY'S NEW IDEALS

This wise, this necessary preservative against tyranny [the 1776 Pennsylvania Constitution] has given very great offence to some of our gentry who regard you as their property, their beasts of burden, born only to be ruled by these Lords of the Creation. . . . I have been repeatedly told by them that gentlemen would not submit to have power so much in the hands of the people. The people, they say, are not fit to be the guardians of their own rights.

—"The Examiner," *Pennsylvania Evening Post*, October 15, 1776

The Possession of Money will acquire Influence. Influence will lead to Authority, and authority will open the Purses of the People.

—Robert Morris, "Observations on the State of Affairs," January 13, 1783

Amid the chaos of war, the Revolution in Pennsylvania reached its decisive turning point. The turning point was not a military loss or victory but rather a radical rethinking by the gentry of what they wanted the Revolution to be. In a stunning reversal, many genteel Pennsylvanians abandoned the vision of '76. They did not just give up on the ideal of empowering white men: the gentry, in fact, made a complete about-face. They began condemning the Revolution's democratic achievements and started calling for important decisions to be removed from popular control. Much of the gentry also replaced its support for wealth equality with a new belief that the only way to make America great was to put most of the money and land in the hands of the wealthy. In short, during the war, much of the gentry came to embrace ideals that had far more in common with the beliefs of their former British masters than they did with the ideals of 1776.

The similarities to Britain were even starker in the ways the gentry tried to bring that ideal to life. They enacted policies nearly identical to the ones Britain had passed during the 1760s and 1770s: they tried to eliminate paper money and public land banks and then tried to enact new taxes payable only in gold and silver. Knowing their policies would be unpopular, the revolutionary elite also attempted to roll back democratic reforms to make it harder for ordinary folk to stop them—much as Britain had done during the 1760s and 1770s. They also tried to adopt a British model for finance by transferring government powers to new private corporations that were free from popular control.

This chapter is an attempt to understand how and why the Pennsylvania gentry made this radical turnaround and how it came to embrace ideals and policies it had once labeled tyranny.

Enemy Democracy

As the War for Independence raged around them, many genteel Pennsylvanians perceived the rise of a new enemy: it was not Loyalists or British regulars or Hessian soldiers; rather, the new enemy was democracy. America, they believed, was being ruined by the democratic forces unleashed in 1776. Many Pennsylvania gentlemen were especially concerned by what they saw as the extreme version of democracy that infested their home state. As one gentleman put it, Pennsylvania's revolutionary government had sent "evils afloat" by allowing "bad men [to] have too much sway" over those who were "wise and honest." Some went so far as to say that Pennsylvania was under the control of "Wicked men" who were "opposed to Heaven and its laws." They said that the democratic government would "go to the devil for popularity" and was creating an earthly "damnation" filled with "ruin, poverty, famine and distress, with idleness, vice, corruption of morals, and every species of evil."[1]

For some gentlemen, such feelings began with the passage of the 1776 state constitution. These men were upset that "a set of *plain* men" had "assembled together to make a government." Some among the "higher classes" complained that "Power had fallen into low hands" and worried about the rising "power and consequence" of people whom they called "inferior." Others feared their declining status in this new democratic society. "*This damned simplicity* of their's will make us simple freemen," fretted one gentleman, who blamed the gentry's social fall on "so many plain country folks being in the Convention" that created the 1776 constitution. One Lancaster gentleman simply said that the 1776 document had been created by and for "numsculs."[2]

What had caused the gentry suddenly to view democracy as an "evil"? The short answer is that the war and the Revolution had changed the gentry. Wartime problems had soured many gentlemen on democracy. At the same time, the social upheavals caused by independence had brought genteel status to new men, who then abandoned their faith in equality as they refashioned themselves as gentlemen of the highest social order. By the war's end, the interplay of wartime troubles and the rise of a new gentry would create a governing elite dedicated to limiting democracy.

For much of the revolutionary gentry, democracy's fall from grace came when the new state and national governments seemed unable to administer the war effort. In particular, the new governments faced severe financial problems that made it hard to supply the army or pay troops. Much of the trouble could be traced to the familiar problem of fighting a war without gold and silver—the same problem that had plagued the colonies during the French and Indian War. As it had during that conflict, the government funded the war against Britain by printing paper money. And as before, the fighting made it difficult to collect the taxes needed to manage the millions of dollars printed. As a result, paper money plummeted in value once again, plunging to near worthlessness by 1781. The currency issued by the Pennsylvania assembly performed much better, continuing to trade throughout the war. Nevertheless, most gentlemen still came to view all government-issued paper money as a black eye for the state and nation.[3]

Like British officials during the French and Indian War, the revolutionary elite tended to blame this depreciation on democratic control of money. According to one Philadelphia merchant, elected leaders had played "tricks" with currency and engaged in financial "Follies" to appease the masses by printing money any time the public asked for it. Giving voice to what quickly became the received wisdom among elite Pennsylvanians, this man attributed all of the nation's financial problems to the "Imbecility" of democratically elected politicians.[4]

Of course, this was exactly how Britain had viewed the situation when the value of paper money had plummeted during the French and Indian War. Back in 1764, Britain had claimed that American legislators could not manage money. At that time, American gentlemen had vehemently denied the charge, saying that currency had depreciated only because the war had been so long and expensive. Now, less than a decade later, many of these same men adopted the British view (a view they had once called tyrannical).

Equally ironic was how the gentry blamed democracy for problems with tax collection. During the 1760s and 1770s, the gentry had called British taxes oppressive and demanded leniency in collection. Many gentlemen had even sanctioned tax resistance. Now, however, when ordinary folk complained about the high tax burden from the Revolutionary War and local officials were lenient with those who had trouble paying, these same men viewed such resistance as a problem. Joseph Reed, the president of Pennsylvania, blamed the "Easiness" of tax collectors who refused to act with "Firmness and Vigour." "We believe," Reed said on behalf of his fellow state leaders, that county officials were "equally dangerous" because they were infected with "a vicious Spirit of popularity" and would not press the collectors to action. According to Reed and his colleagues, this kind of democracy—one where local officials responded to their constituents rather than to state orders—threatened the war effort and the republic itself.[5]

In part, the changed views of men like Reed are typical of what happens when political outsiders suddenly become insiders. The assembly looked far different from the inside than it had from the coffeehouses and taverns where the revolutionary committees had organized their bid for independence. Faced with setting up and administering a government during wartime, many of the leading revolutionaries changed their ideas about the main problems facing the state. They now viewed popular dissent and resistance as troublesome, much as British officials had been irked by protests during the 1760s and 1770s. Thus, someone like Dr. Benjamin Rush, who had been a strong advocate for democracy when he helped to draft the 1776 state constitution, left the war believing that politicians were more likely to "injure their constituents by voting agreeably to their inclinations, than *against* them."[6]

The change was also due to the rise of new leaders. During the war, many of the men who had been most active in designing the 1776 constitution either took positions in the military or else retired from politics altogether. Some left out of the frustration of running a war on a shoestring budget. Others were driven out by popular discontent over a war that seemed to be dragging on with little end in sight. Whatever the case, many of those who had helped to build the vision of '76 were replaced in office by men who were far more skeptical of popular government and the idea of equality.[7]

At the same time, the composition of the gentry transformed as the old elite was replaced by a new set of "gentlemen." The War for Independence rearranged Pennsylvania's social hierarchy. Much of the colonial ruling elite had remained loyal to the Crown, many of them eventually fleeing to

Canada, England, and British-controlled New York. Their departure left a void at the top of polite society, which others rushed to fill. Lesser gentry tried to join the highest social circles. Many outsiders claimed gentility for the first time. Small merchants, prosperous farmers, successful privateers, counting-room clerks, artisans who had won government contracts to supply the army, and new immigrants—all now purported to be "gentlemen." To old-money Virginian Arthur Lee, wartime Philadelphia reeked with the stench of the nouveaux riches and social climbers "intoxicated with a sudden change of manners and unexpected elevation."[8]

When the aspiring gentry began to adopt genteel airs, they also started distancing themselves from ordinary folk. Those who had once identified as the many now said they belonged to the few. Many members of the new gentry renounced democracy and egalitarianism. Instead, they started treating the common folk with contempt, as if they could prove that they belonged in polite society merely by reaching new heights of snobbery.

Nowhere was this kind of self-refashioning more extreme than in the officer corps of the Continental Army. Many officers had entered the service as young men from modest social backgrounds. During the war, however, they believed that they had risen dramatically in social rank. The army gave these men their first real taste of privilege, power, and status. It also exposed them to the manners of Old World gentility as they rubbed elbows with allied officers in the French army, some of whom held aristocratic titles. Many American officers convinced themselves that they were of a similar social caliber as the European socialites with whom they shared meals, fine brandy, and tours of the ballroom dance floor. (Genteel balls continued during the war: in fact, while the enlisted men froze at Valley Forge, army officers attended balls in the nearby town of York.)[9]

Those experiences transformed many officers, causing them to shun the lives they had known before the war. For example, former Continental Army captain Alexander Graydon expressed horror when, after leaving the service, he was called upon in 1780 to take a tour of duty in the Berks County militia. Graydon explained that he was so dedicated to preserving the "Distinctions and Graduations of Rank" that he had acquired in the Continental Army that his "feelings would have been wounded by being obliged to perform the Duty of a private Centinel in common with a set of men (the Peasantry of the Country) with whom from their Education and manner of Life he could not associate." No doubt men like Graydon disparaged ordinary folk and the "Principles of Equality" in an effort to distance themselves from a past life that could be labeled as "common." To prove they belonged in polite society, the rising gentry loudly condemned the masses as if to say: how could anyone possibly confuse *me* with *them*?[10]

It was not enough simply to be a snob or proclaim gentility, however; one also needed to live the gentry's expensive lifestyle. And expensive it was. Some estimates place the initial cost of a suitable gentleman's townhouse, furniture, and carriage at no less than $12,000. Those who truly wanted to appear refined needed to spend an additional $5,300 for a serviceable country seat, thereby raising the opening demands of civility to well over $17,000—a small fortune for the day. None of this included the costs of operating an estate: servants' wages, landscaping expenses, and the funds to keep the pantry stocked with tasty delicacies, imported rum, and fine wines. Nor did it include accounts at tailors' and dressmaker shops, the cost of invitations to teas and balls, or the salary of the children's tutor.[11]

The question for the new gentry (and for established gentlemen trying to rise in polite society) was: how to afford those costs? Stodgy Virginian Arthur Lee observed that the price tag seemed to pose little problem for the merchants and government contractors "who have made large fortunes during this war" and who set about bathing themselves in "Extravagance, ostentation, and dissipation." Other social climbers, however, did not have pockets deep enough to afford the trappings of the title. The costs were especially daunting for Continental Army officers who had made the great leap from obscurity to gentility. Once retired, the officers had few prospective sources of income. "They cannot return to their former employments," General Arthur St. Clair of the Pennsylvania Line explained, "their habits are much too changed." A British visitor confirmed this by noting that former Continental Army "Captains, Majors, and Colonels" shunned working with their hands and only deigned to perform the "*easy* occupations of domestic life."[12]

Although they lacked income, the new gentry still managed to purchase luxuries—a fact noted disdainfully by Europeans. As the war drew to a close, even the French court at Versailles was abuzz with the "rapid Progress of Luxury at Philadelphia." In Britain, reports circulated that the social routine in Philadelphia was so extravagant that it was probably "more expensive than in London." Neither the French nor the English looked favorably on the spending spree. Indeed, they only differed on who was to blame. The French accused the British, saying that Americans were trying to replicate the "taste they have inherited from their luxury-loving former masters, the English." The English blamed the French, saying that genteel Americans had caught the disease of luxury from "associating with their gay volatile allies" (aristocratic French officers and diplomats) "in camps & cities" during the war.[13]

Whatever the case, foreign observers became convinced that the gentry was spending money it did not have (or rather, spending money loaned by European creditors). One British merchant in America at the end of the war reported a disturbing "propensity" among gentlemen for "living on the proceeds of effects procured on credit" and using borrowed money to fund their "show, expense, and dissipation." He predicted that most of the genteel pretenders would not be able to repay their debts, which would "eventually destroy credit" and plunge them back down to "their usual level."[14]

The same worries echoed across Pennsylvania. Farmers chastised the new gentry for "living far above their abilities" and running "themselves so much in debt that they are almost all bankrupts." In 1781, Pennsylvania president Joseph Reed fretted over the gentry's "extravagant opinions of the plenty, riches, ease, and luxury" awaiting them. He said that many of the state's leading men would soon "find themselves most egregiously disappointed" when the bills for their spending sprees arrived. Occasionally, even genteel Pennsylvanians admitted that they had been "extravagant rather beyond our capacity."[15]

Such admissions, however, seldom led gentlemen to cut their purchases. As Philadelphia merchant Stephen Collins explained to his son in 1784, it was too hard to abandon luxury living. Collins confessed that genteel men were "going to the Devil very fast" because they could not afford their lifestyles. But he could not bring himself to condemn the overspending. Nor did he "begrudge" the merchant who, upon being sentenced to debtors' prison, "would not go to gaol without ordering up his coach to ride there . . . in taste." Collins told his son that, although gentlemen might try to observe "strict economy, frugality, and industry," restraint usually fell before the love of luxury. "This my son is a lesson every day to train by," he advised. "So let thee and I at least learn to take warning by it as we value ease."[16]

Others were not so calm about the growing gap between income and spending; many army officers were nearly in a state of panic. General St. Clair explained that, without sufficient income to fund their genteel lifestyles, the officers faced the "melancholy prospect" of returning to their former stations, which he said would make them "the most abject and despicable people on the face of the earth." As St. Clair saw it, without the money to maintain gentility, the officers' lives were essentially over.[17]

The growing anxieties over status were heightened by what the new gentry perceived as increasing disrespect from ordinary Pennsylvanians. Indeed, at the same time that these men were embracing gentility, many ordinary folk intensified their disdain for snobbery. The newly minted gentlemen officers of the Continental Army and militia faced some of the strongest defiance. Genteel militia officers were confronted by enlisted men who did not accept the social distinctions that they believed set them apart as "Officers and Gentlemen." Militiamen demanded the right to vote for officers, and many soldiers, like the privates in the Philadelphia militia, claimed they were "entitled to an equal consultation" on matters such as the choice of uniform (enlisted men wanted everyone to wear simple and inexpensive "Hunting Shirts" to "level all distinctions" between privates and officers). The focus on equality was so extreme that when one militia captain was asked how many men were under his command, he replied, "Not one, but I am commanded by ninety."[18]

If the hierarchy was clearer in the Continental Army, there was still friction over rank and status. Enlisted men complained about haughty officers and bristled at beatings for misconduct. In the Pennsylvania Line, such anger exploded with mutinies in January 1781 and again in 1783, and each time enlisted men cited ill treatment by superiors among their grievances.[19]

Gentlemen on the home front faced similar indignities. Members of the gentry (and nearly everyone else) who did not display enough enthusiasm for the revolutionary cause often found themselves ridiculed by superpatriots from the middling and lower classes. Crowds of ordinary Pennsylvanians punished Loyalist gentlemen and genteel Quakers, whose pacifism was usually equated with treason. Crowds also targeted merchants who seemed to be profiting from wartime scarcities and "getting rich by sucking the blood" of the citizenry. Calls went out to *"Rouse! Rouse! Rouse!"* against the "rich and powerful" for allegedly hoarding food and necessities and driving up prices. The offending gentry, whether suspected price gougers, Loyalists, or pacifists, often had their homes and businesses vandalized and faced a variety of humiliating punishments: they were beaten, had their hair cropped off, were marched through jeering crowds and thrown in jail, or were bathed in hot tar and feathers (and sometimes all of the above).[20]

In Philadelphia, class warfare nearly broke out as genteel men exchanged gunfire with crowds of the "lower sort." The most alarming incident was a 1779 showdown between the Philadelphia militia and a lawyer named James Wilson, who was suspected of wartime profiteering and aiding the British. Upon hearing a rumor that a scheduled march by the Philadelphia militia was actually a plot to arrest Wilson for treason, the lawyer assembled a group of armed gentlemen at his home. When the militia paraded by, someone inside fired a shot into the crowd. A gunfight ensued, and by the time the shooting had ended, several militiamen and a few gentlemen lay dead.

(Wilson would survive to become one of the primary architects of the new federal Constitution designed to remove power from the hands of ordinary people such as these.)[21]

Incidents such as these (along with the nation's economic troubles and the gentry's own financial problems) convinced many genteel Pennsylvanians that the Revolution was out of control and that they—the very men whose fortunes and social standing had grown as a result of the Revolution—had become its victims. In their new world view, it was not the few who oppressed the many but, instead, the many who oppressed the few. "The contest," reported one gentleman visiting Pennsylvania in 1779, "is between the respectable Citizens of Fortune & Character" and "People in lower Circumstances, & Reputation." And members of the elite were convinced that common people (men like their former selves) were winning this battle as a result of their new democratic powers.[22]

Many genteel Pennsylvanians concluded that the only solution was for the gentry to take control of the government and turn back the tide of democracy. They called for "righteous men" to come to power to save Pennsylvania from the "divine vengeance" that God would bring as punishment for democratizing society and government. Naturally, most gentlemen imagined the new prophets being just like themselves: "men of business" and "men of thriving fortunes" who possessed "education" and "estates." They were the "properly enlightened" who could reinstate "the moral fitness of things" by casting out bad men and their bad laws. Anyone who supported unfettered democracy would be deemed "a prophaner of the rites and worship of the sacred temple of liberty." By preaching "the truth," the new prophets would absolve the "great national sin" of democratic excess and restore "the divine blessing on ourselves and on our posterity."[23]

The belief that wealthy men must take control was so strong that—amazingly—many gentlemen actually hoped that the war would last longer so that they could amass the power needed to scale back democracy. "In this City," observed one Philadelphia merchant in 1782, "the prospect of Peace has given more general discontent than anything that has happened of a long time, particularly amongst the mercantile part of the Community." Elite men wanted to scale back democracy, and they believed that "a continuance of the War is Necessary" to reach that goal. "The favorable moment both to gain and establish Power, is at the close of a War," said one of the leading voices for change. "For all are then recently convinced of the necessity, and few are inclined either to dispute the Grant, or oppose the Exertion." Here was the surest mark of the gentry's transformation: their complaints about an autocratic Britain had given way to Machiavellian desires to prolong a bloody conflict so that they could grab power.[24]

Robert Morris to the Gentry's Rescue

Just as the situation looked the bleakest, a champion for the gentry's interests—a Philadelphia merchant in his late forties named Robert Morris— emerged with a plan for salvation. Although most Americans have never heard of him, Morris was one of the iconic figures of the Revolution. Today, his image adorns the inside of the rotunda of the U.S. Capitol building: he is pictured as the heir of Mercury, god of commerce, in the fresco that centers on a Christlike George Washington ascending to heaven. That giant Robert Morris on the Capitol ceiling ably captures his larger-than-life persona. If his passion led at times to overindulgence, Morris was nonetheless a man who made things happen. As a merchant, he was the king among princes, so aggressive in his dealings that he took risks that others would not dare—such as when he single-handedly tried to corner the nation's tobacco market. When Morris built his dream mansion, it was so palatial in scope that it was never completed and came to be called "Morris's Folly." When he invested in land, Morris leveraged his fortune to buy at least 6 million acres, a gamble that would leave him in debtors' prison when the speculative bubble burst in the mid-1790s. Even when he ate, Morris could not stop at the average portion. As a result, he had a moon face with sagging jowls that draped over a bulbous neck. Not even finely tailored waistcoats (or portrait artists intent on flattery) could hide his bulk. Heavy and six feet tall, he was a man whose physical attributes reflected his ambition: Morris was large.[25]

Nowhere was Morris's audacity better displayed than in his radical plan for rescuing the gentry and, as he saw it, making America into a great nation. Morris envisioned gentlemen taking control of the government, using it to enrich themselves, and then scaling back democracy so it did not threaten their interests. He did not give his plan a name, but with his belief that it would bring "Salvation," it is fitting to call Morris's program the "gospel of moneyed men."[26]

The basic premise of Morris's plan was this: America would only stand alongside the nations of Europe when government dedicated itself to putting wealth into the hands of the affluent. Morris wanted the government to channel money to the wealthy, either through direct payouts or by privatizing the most lucrative parts of the state and turning them over to new for-profit corporations owned and run by the gentry. If Morris had proposed his agenda

FIG. 3.1. COMMERCE. This Brumidi fresco, which is part of the *Apotheosis of Washington* that adorns the ceiling of the U.S. Capitol's rotunda, reveals Robert Morris's central place in the pantheon of founding fathers. Morris is symbolically deified through his connection to Mercury, the Roman god of commerce, and by his place in the apotheosis—a word that literally means "risen to the rank of a god." Architect of the Capitol.

today, it might be called "neoliberalism" or supply-side/trickle-down economics. Indeed, Morris came close to using such language himself when describing his new creed. He said that the interests of the wealthy went "hand in hand" with the public good: what was good for the rich was good for America. He declared that national greatness would come by "distributing Property into those Hands which could render it most productive"—a group of people he identified as "monied men" and "the mercantile Part of Society."[27]

According to Morris, the chief obstacle to this plan was democracy. He knew that ordinary Pennsylvanians were committed to the vision of '76 and its principles of political and economic equality and would oppose his plan for redistributing wealth to the rich. Given his past failures to persuade the public, Morris had no illusions that he could gain converts among the common folk. Morris had never embraced the ideals of Pennsylvania's Revolution; he had initially opposed the Declaration of Independence; and he was among the most vocal opponents of the 1776 state constitution. He viewed the common people, who forced the Revolution on gentlemen like himself, as "vulgar Souls whose narrow Optics can see but the little Circle of selfish Concerns." Morris considered them to be incapable of understanding the sacrifices he believed they needed to make for his plan to work. To him, "the people" were part of the problem, not the solution.[28]

Consequently, Morris hoped to use government-provided wealth to gain the political power needed to bypass democracy. His own experiences provided the model. A prosperous merchant before the conflict, Morris had used government positions to make a killing from the war. In 1775, the Continental Congress appointed him chairman of its Secret Committee of Trade, which controlled war-related spending. Morris used the position to direct nearly a million dollars' worth of business through his own mercantile firm and through businesses in which he had an interest. He used government ships to transport his private cargo free of charge to markets in the West Indies and Europe. If the ships sank or were captured, the public subsidized Morris for his private losses. In all of these ways (and critics alleged that he also embezzled another $80,000), Morris used the government to turn himself into probably the wealthiest man in America.[29]

That wealth made him into one of the most powerful men in the nation's history. In desperate financial straits in 1781, both Congress and Pennsylvania turned to him for financial assistance. Morris promised to use his private fortune to assist the state and nation in exchange for sweeping authority over finance, including the printing of money, the collection of taxes, and the funding of the war effort. Congress gave him the right to appoint or dismiss any official—not just in the Office of Finance that he headed but in any agency of government that dealt with collecting or spending government money. He had so much power that one of his strongest critics, Pennsylvania president Joseph Reed, called Morris "a pecuniary dictator," a man "whose dictates none dare oppose, and from whose decisions lay no appeal." Although Reed exaggerated, Morris was the most powerful man in America—aside, perhaps, from George Washington. Indeed, the degree of authority he possessed over the economy was probably never matched in the subsequent history of the United States.[30]

As powerful as he was, Morris knew much of his authority would only last as long as the war; to establish real power, he needed to recruit other moneyed men to his cause. His primary recruiting tool was wealth provided by the government. He believed that he could use the state to buy the political support of "powerful Individuals." Morris had little faith that his fellow gentlemen would act out of altruistic principles, patriotism, or republican virtue.

Instead, he was convinced that the affluent only truly responded to "the strong Principle of Self Love and the immediate Sense of private Interest." "We shall Only have to Appeal to the interest of Mankind which in most Cases will do more than their Patriotism," he wrote to Thomas Jefferson in 1781. Thus, his goal was using government to direct wealth toward "combining together the Interests of moneyed Men" into "one general Money Connection."[31]

Morris believed that this "Money Connection" would have the power to thwart any opposition from ordinary Americans. Once united, the gentry could create stronger and less democratic governments that would become effective vehicles for transferring wealth to the rich. Writing to Benjamin Franklin in September 1782, Morris said that the goal was "drawing by Degrees the Bands of Authority together" and "establishing the Power of Government over a People impatient of Control." He later distilled his beliefs into a simple mantra: "The Possession of Money will acquire Influence. Influence will lead to Authority, and authority will open the Purses of the People."[32]

FIG. 3.2. THE "WHITE HOUSE." The building shown here is Robert Morris's townhouse in Philadelphia, where George Washington stayed while he chaired the Constitutional Convention in 1787. Washington also made this building his home when the federal government relocated from New York City to Philadelphia in 1790. Engraving by T. H. Mumford, reprinted from John F. Watson, *Annals of Philadelphia* (Philadelphia, 1879–1881).

It is important to keep in mind that Morris was not some fringe radical: his ideas had wide support among the Pennsylvanian and national elite. Morris was the ultimate political insider. Consider his central role in subsequent political developments. In 1787, Morris would be one of the primary organizers of the convention that reframed the national government under a new U.S. Constitution. Most of the delegates who assembled in Philadelphia that summer were somehow connected to Morris: they were involved in his business deals, had prospered from his government patronage, had borrowed money from him, or were his personal friends. George Washington counted Morris as a close friend and confidant. Washington even lived as a guest in Morris's house for several months during the Constitutional Convention, which met just a block away. In 1790, when the national government moved to its temporary home in Philadelphia, now-President Washington once again lived in the Morris mansion (making it that day's version of the White House). Washington wanted Morris to be the first Treasury secretary; Morris turned him down, choosing to enter the Senate instead. Alexander Hamilton, who took the position, had learned at Morris's feet, and his financial ideas, often called "Hamiltonian," were in many ways a repackaged version of Morris's philosophy. In short, his ideals became the ones around which most of the nation's founding fathers rallied during the postwar decade.[33]

Yet, if Morris's ideas were consistent with those of much of the gentry, they were decidedly out of step with popular notions of what the Revolution was supposed to be about. The gospel of moneyed men was, in many ways, the antithesis of how most ordinary Pennsylvanians viewed the Revolution. Morris narrowed the definition of the public good from something determined by the citizenry to an ideal defined solely by moneyed men. He recast republican government as a far less democratic institution, where important decisions—especially those about finance—were decided by rich men rather than by democratically elected representatives. He scaled back the concept of independence from a word that meant widespread property ownership to a new (or, rather, an old) standard that judged the independence of the nation by how much property the affluent controlled. And he redefined freedom by rejecting the notion that a truly free society required government intervention to promote an equal distribution of wealth. Instead, Morris now defined freedom as the absolute right to use one's property without interference from government, no matter the social consequences.

When the gospel of moneyed men went into effect, the consequences for ordinary Pennsylvanians (and Americans) were tragic. Each part of the gospel widened the gap between the theories Morris preached and the results his programs delivered. As that gap grew, however, Morris refused to change course. Like with most things he did, Morris clung to the belief that he was right, no matter how much reality showed otherwise. Like the true disciple of any religion, Morris and his followers lamented the signs of distress but always believed that the promised land lay just around the corner.

The Perils of Privatization

The troubles with the gospel of moneyed men began in the same place where Britain's problems with the colonies had started: paper money. To a large degree, Morris's plans mimicked what Britain had done at the end of the French and Indian War: he wanted to eliminate all government-issued paper money. "It may be considered as an incontrovertible Proposition," he wrote to Congress in July 1782, "that all paper Money ought to be absorbed by Taxation or otherwise and destroyed before we can Expect our public Credit to be fully reestablished." It was an eerie echo of speeches in Parliament on behalf of the Currency Act that had banned paper money in 1764.[34]

This time around, however, Morris believed that he could avoid a cash scarcity by replacing government paper money with a new kind of currency printed by private banks. His ideas about currency were part of a larger plan to privatize finance by removing powers once held exclusively by government and turning them over to private corporations. Morris saw privatization as a cure for wartime inflation. He believed that if the government's power to print money was lodged in private companies, the moneyed men running those companies would never print too much money. He believed that the bank's directors would respond to the will of the stockholders, who, because they were creditors, would never depreciate money and would not allow debtors to repay them with worthless currency.

In many ways, Morris intended finance under private banks to be less democratic than it had been under British rule. While Britain had allowed politicians elected in Pennsylvania to maintain some influence over monetary decisions, the Morris plan purged government from the process. In his idealized system, no public forum existed for the American people to influence decisions about the nation's central monetary questions. The bankers would never have to respond to popular calls to print more paper money, no matter how fervently the public clamored for cash (or how desperately the economy

FIG. 3.3. ROBERT MORRIS BY CHARLES WILLSON PEALE, FROM LIFE, C. 1782. Behind Morris's chair and through the velvet curtain, stands his creation, the Bank of North America, the first private bank in the United States. (Independence National Historical Park.)

needed an infusion of money to avoid an economic depression). If the bankers believed that more money would cause inflation, they would simply say no. To Morris, removing finance from democratic control like this was the "change in our Monied Systems" that was an "*absolute Necessity*" to "work Salvation."[35]

Morris believed that the primary agent of "Salvation" would be the bank he created in Philadelphia in 1781—the first private bank chartered in the United States. His ambitions were reflected in the name Morris gave to the institution: the Bank of North America—as if the continent needed no other bank. Morris promised that his bank would be "a principal Pillar of American Credit," fulfilling much of the credit and currency needs of Pennsylvania and the nation. He said that the money in the bank's vaults would come only from private individuals, who would be the primary stockholders. The only role for government, as far as Morris saw it, was to charter private banks—which meant giving them the protections of limited liability. A corporate charter (which could only be given by the government) would shield stockholders from being sued if the bank ran into financial troubles. With a charter, stockholders only stood to lose the money they had invested in bank stock. Without one, the stockholders could lose their homes and personal property if the bank failed.[36]

Although Morris imagined that there would eventually be many private banks in America, he was averse to competition that would cut into his bank's profitability. Thus, Morris wanted to kill the public land bank, which would eat into his bank's profits with its fixed, low-interest loans. He also opposed chartering too many private banks. Thus, while Morris thought it was good that New York chartered a bank (which was too far away to compete with his Philadelphia bank), he was dead set against Pennsylvania chartering any banks that would compete with his. Indeed, during the 1780s, Morris and his fellow bankers would use all of their political clout to oppose the creation of several rival banks.[37]

Morris insisted on limiting rivals, in part, because a lack of competition fostered one of his larger goals: funneling wealth to moneyed men. He wanted his bank to reap steep profits as the region's primary moneylender. As Morris told potential investors, "Few will find the Other parts of their Fortunes to Yield them so large or so certain An income as the Stock they have in the Bank." Those predictions would prove to be accurate. In 1783, the bank paid a dividend of 14.5 percent and paid 13.5 percent in 1784—hefty returns, especially given that so few other investments at the time were even turning a profit.[38]

Morris also believed that privatization would reward wealthy creditors with its tight control of money. He believed that the bankers would tie the amount of currency in circulation to the amount of gold and silver in the vaults and, therefore, the money would never lose its value—making it more likely for creditors to profit on the money they loaned. Morris knew that moneyed men also stood to profit from the shock of privatization, as government currencies disappeared. As money became scarce, its value would increase, making it more expensive for debtors to repay with currency and ensuring that creditors received a magnificent return on what they had loaned. The price shock would even allow the rich to prosper as borrowers. Since wealthy gentlemen in America tended to borrow from European merchants or financiers, a tight money supply would benefit these men when they converted the bank's money to British pounds, Spanish dollars, or French livres when they went to repay their overseas debts (provided, of course, that the gentry's own debtors could scrape together the money to repay them).

And it was here—when it came to the role that debtors played in the equation—that Morris's plan fell apart. His privatization plan assumed that ordinary Americans had the money to repay their debts. It was a strange assumption to make considering that the other parts of the plan entailed removing money from circulation, taking away the primary source of credit for ordinary folk (the land-bank system), and stacking the financial deck in favor of creditors. This glaring oversight turned privatization into a disaster for most

Pennsylvanians. Morris's policies replicated the cash scarcity that Britain had caused and made a bad wartime situation far worse. It caused an abrupt drop in the money supply, as cash disappeared and credit dried up. As early as 1782, ordinary folk across Pennsylvania complained, once again, about a profound scarcity of money—and they would continue to complain for at least a decade.

The biggest problem with privatization was that Morris's bank currency proved to be a poor substitute for government-issued paper money. Since the new bank only printed money in close correlation to the amount of gold and silver in its vaults, it needed to have an enormous supply of specie. Morris's protégé Alexander Hamilton reasoned that, in order to support the massive infusion of currency the economy required, the Bank of North America needed about $4 million in its vaults. Hamilton said that making a go of it with anything less "would be fatal." To put this figure in perspective, Hamilton estimated that the entire nation held just $6 million in specie or "one fifth of the circulating medium before the war." This meant that the Bank of North America would have to amass two-thirds of the entire hard-money supply in the nation.[39]

If $4 million was the bottom line, the bank failed miserably. When the Bank of North America opened for business in 1781, it had only $400,000 in capital. Moreover, most of this money came from the government rather than private investors. Moneyed men had purchased just $146,000 in bank stock, meaning that Morris had to borrow $256,000 from Congress to "privatize" the financial system. The startup capital was woefully inadequate and Morris knew it. "The Capital proposed falls far Short of your Idea and indeed far Short of what it ought to be," he confessed to Hamilton. Morris understood that, with such a small base, the bank could not print enough money to compensate for the loss of government paper. "Four hundred thousand Dollrs. are not sufficient for [the purposes of government] nor those of private Commerce," he reported to Congress, "because no considerable Circulation of Paper can be founded on so narrow a Basis." Despite this admission, Morris insisted that the experiment in privatization continue.[40]

Morris tried to compensate for his underfunded bank by issuing paper money of his own creation—so-called Morris notes—but they proved to be inadequate as well. Morris printed a relatively small number of notes, which tended to circulate only among merchants and government contractors. The other problem was that the smallest denomination of the Morris notes was $20, far too large for the average American to acquire. Hamilton warned Morris of this shortcoming by explaining that Morris notes "do not enter far into ordinary circulation."[41]

Morris's response to Hamilton revealed the depth of his contempt for the American public. "If my Notes circulate only among mercantile People, I do not regret it," he stated, "but rather wish that the Circulation may for the present be confined to them and to the wealthier Members of other Professions." He was convinced that people of the lower and middling sorts would not preserve his money's worth. "Had a considerable Quantity been thrown into the Hands of that Class of the People whose Ideas on the Subject of Money are more the Offspring of Habit than of Reason," he predicted, "it must have depreciated." In particular, Morris was suspicious of the country's farming majority. "For you must know that whatever fine plausible Speeches may be made on this Subject," he wrote to Hamilton, "the Farmers" were "not very violently devoted to" paper money. It was a peculiar statement, given that farmers—by Morris's own admission—had long been the biggest supporters of paper money. Odd too was Morris's unwillingness to change his plans even when he admitted privately that bank paper and his own notes were "as is said, and as I really believe, deficient."[42]

Indeed, Morris refused to bend even when his policies began to undermine the war effort. Faced with the choice of printing more money or letting the army go unpaid and undersupplied, Morris kept the printing presses silent. When he could not muster enough money to procure horses for the army, Morris declared that he would prefer that the army "never moved than that they should distress or destroy the little Public Credit which I have established." His orders to the deputy quartermaster general for the southern army were more explicit: "It is better that any Part of the public Service remain unperformed than that you should pay these Notes away at the smallest degree of depreciation or by giving one farthing more for Articles or service than the same could be procured for with hard Money in hand." Things were so bad that a British spy wrote encouragingly of Morris's policies: "Money is exceedingly scarce, so much so that they cannot comply with their Contracts, the consequence of which is that most of the Contractors for the Army have declined for the want of Cash, which they were to have been furnished with from the Bank." As this spy realized, Morris's whole supply effort rested upon hard money, and there was not enough gold and silver in America to equip the army. Thankfully for Morris—and the nation—all of this happened after the victory over General Charles Cornwallis had essentially sealed the American victory, and Morris's intransigence did not imperil the war effort as it surely would have earlier in the conflict.[43]

The problems of the currency scarcity were exacerbated by the credit crunch that privatization caused. Although Morris frequently said that the Bank of North America would loan money to ordinary folk and replace the land bank, it did not. Indeed, it could not: the bank's own bylaws prohibited it from accepting land as collateral for loans. Instead, the bank loaned almost exclusively to merchants and other affluent men. For example, in its first year of operation, from 1782 to 1783, the Bank of North America made 1,806 loans to people living in Pennsylvania. Of those, 99 percent went to Philadelphians. People in the rest of the state received just 21 loans. Those identified as farmers—the primary beneficiaries of the old land-bank system—received just 2 bank loans. In short, privatization had eliminated a public credit system that extended loans to Pennsylvanians across lines of geography, occupation, and (relatively speaking) wealth. By contrast, the private bank loaned money almost exclusively to affluent Philadelphia merchants.[44]

The result of this credit crunch was soaring interest rates. Unable to borrow from the bank, ordinary Pennsylvanians (and members of the gentry outside the privileged banking circle) were forced to turn to private money-lenders, who began charging usurious rates. The jump was astounding. Before privatization, the land-bank system had kept interest at 5–6 percent *per year*. With privatization, interest shot up to between 5 and 12 percent *per month*. Needless to say, these punishing rates meant real trouble for ordinary farmers and artisans who needed credit to run their farms and businesses.[45]

Taxes in Gold and Silver

The situation worsened when the state legislature—at Morris's insistence—began enacting new taxes in 1782 payable in gold and silver. If Pennsylvania and the nation were no longer going to fund the war using paper money, then they had little choice but to tax the public in gold and silver. The plan was certainly optimistic, especially given Alexander Hamilton's estimates that the supply of hard money was about one-fifth of what it had been before the war. It would also prove to be unrealistic.

To most Pennsylvanians, the new taxes were yet another replay of British transgressions. Consequently, they began to complain just as they had in the 1760s and 1770s when Britain had followed its currency ban with hard-money taxes. One petition signed by people in half of the counties in Pennsylvania (mostly in the east) said that the new taxes were "much more than can be raised on the Inhabitants, without great distress in the general, and the utter ruin of many individuals." A York County writer explained that the math did not add up. His county had little money and yet faced huge tax quotas of approximately $89,000 in gold and silver for 1782 and another $47,600 for 1783. "By calculation it appears, that the quota of taxes for the county of York, will require two waggon load of silver," he estimated. "It will puzzle the inhabitants to scrape so much together."[46]

Farmers in the state's western counties were so upset by the new specie taxes that, rather than petition, they held meetings in 1782 to consider seceding from Pennsylvania and forming a new state. Westerners complained that the new "Tax was very large and only to be paid in Gold and silver, [which] the people were not able to do." They also believed that the tax undermined their efforts to defend the frontier. Congress had provided limited troops to defend the backcountry, meaning that locals had shouldered much of the financial and military burden of defending the western front. With a new Indian assault imminent, westerners had asked for military support. Instead, they got a heavy tax bill to fund "the general war"—a term westerners mocked because it never seemed to include Indian fighting on the frontier. Under these circumstances, western farmers viewed the new specie taxes as an insult. As one local official put it, his neighbors were incensed that "they are not assisted with either men or money to defend themselves [against] the Savages, and yet are obliged to pay a Tax in Specie which they have not."[47]

Initially, the widespread protests shocked state leaders—just as Stamp Act protests and the rise of the Brave Fellows had shocked British officials and the Penn family. They were so surprised that, for a little while at least, doubts began to creep in among the faithful. In private moments, even Robert Morris admitted that his program had big problems. He was "Sensible of this Truth" that "hard Money is scarce" and that it would be "as difficult to pay your [tax] Quota without Money as it was of old to *make Bricks without Straw*." He lamented the "truly alarming . . . Scene of private Distress" about him. Morris worried that people were being crushed by an even "greater Weight as the Collection of Taxes creates a general Demand for Money." His fears deepened when he considered that people could not raise money because "those who have Articles of Produce on Hand cannot possibly vend them" due to the cash scarcity and closed markets. Projecting into the future, Morris foresaw continued distress. "Few Persons even here are acquainted with the Extent of this Calamity which is now only in its Commencement," he said in May 1782. "If not speedily checked," he predicted, the cash scarcity would "produce the most fatal Consequences."[48]

In this moment of candor, Morris was even willing to make some concessions to alleviate the worst of the suffering. For example, he responded to the harrowing situation in western Pennsylvania by allowing inhabitants to pay their specie taxes in flour rather than gold and silver. The concession failed to work. Westerners had already sold "that little which they did raise" to feed the soldiers stationed at Fort Pitt—for which they had received IOUs that they could not use "to purchase necessarys for their Familys" or even pay their taxes. Without even "a sufficient quantity of grain" to feed their children, westerners wanted Morris to take government IOUs as payment. When he refused, farmers became deeply skeptical about his motives. Most westerners were convinced that this was merely another of Morris's schemes to enrich himself by trying to acquire "the Flour at his own price" and then send it to New Orleans where he would "sell it to the best advantage & put the proffits in his own pockett." Such fears were not farfetched: Morris and other high-ranking public officials had employed similar practices elsewhere for personal gain. Regardless, the episode did little to improve Morris's negative view of ordinary citizens (or their negative impression of him).[49]

If anything, this encounter relieved Morris's conscience and convinced him that the money scarcity was not as serious as people made it out to be. When farmers rejected his offer, Morris began to believe that they were lying about the crisis. At best, he thought the scarcity was a great "Delusion." "The Idea that Taxes cannot be raised because of the Want of Specie is very general, indeed it is almost universal, and yet nothing can be more ill founded," he sermonized:

> The Complaint made by the People of a Want of Money to pay their taxes it is nothing new to me, nor indeed to any body. . . . The Complaint is I believe quite as old as Taxation and will last as long. That Times are hard, that Money is scarce, that Taxes are heavy, and the like are Constant themes of Declamation in all Countries.

Morris even said that the scarcity must not be real because so many people were complaining about it. "The very Generality of the Complaint shows it to be ill founded," he concluded.[50]

Morris began to argue that the government needed to force the public out of its delusion by compelling tax collection. "If the People be put in the Necessity of procuring Specie they will procure it," said Morris. "They can, if they will." It was an extraordinary leap of faith: cause the public to need money, and money will appear. To spread this faith, Morris told a former navy chaplain that he and the nation's religious leaders "must preach Taxation into practice."[51]

Pennsylvania legislators, many of whom shared Morris's beliefs, took things one step further: they actually hired a minister to travel the state to preach tax collection. In 1783, the legislature gave the job to the Reverend James Finley, a Presbyterian minister and a graduate of Princeton College. Finley's task was to stop the secession movement in the western counties and get the backcountry to pay the specie taxes. Finley trekked over the Appalachian Mountains and met with the "ill designing men" and with "Ministers & other Gentlemen" whom he hoped could stop the resistance. On his first Sunday, he took to the pulpit and preached a "Sermon against having any hand in such Schemes."[52]

Despite the reverend's best fire and brimstone, however, his new flock remained unmoved. "Some approved of my conduct," Finley reported, but most people "alleged I was too officious." Moreover, as Finley witnessed the westerners' daily struggles, he began to question the righteousness of his cause. His congregation asked him how they were supposed to pay a tax in specie when there was no money in the countryside. After an uncomfortable pause, Finley confessed that he "could not answer." It was an epiphany that transformed the good reverend.

Soon after, Finley abandoned his mission; instead, he became an advocate for "a people always & justly pleading their want of such cash." He wrote to state leaders, telling them that the specie taxes were totally unrealistic and that their policies were causing great hardship. Finley pleaded for state leaders to "adopt some easy measure" for taxpayers "until money shall circulate more extensively." Most legislators paid little heed to Finley's story of spiritual awakening. They embraced a different faith and were not swayed by his sermon. No doubt, the whole experience merely convinced them that they needed to be more careful about whom they hired to preach compliance to the "deluded" public.[53]

Speculating in the War Debt

For those who saw the currency ban and new specie taxes as oppressive, the greatest insult was yet to come with Morris's handling of the Revolutionary War debt. Morris considered the war debt to be the primary engine of wealth redistribution to enrich moneyed men. He explained the plan to Congress in 1782: encourage gentlemen to speculate in nearly worthless government IOUs that were "in a manner dead"; then, once the wealthy had acquired the IOUs "at a considerable Discount," the government would bring these dead slips of paper "back to existence" by paying off the IOUs at top dollar. Moneyed men would spend little and reap huge rewards—paid for by new taxes on the American people. Morris told Congress that this massive redistribution of wealth would provide the affluent with "those Funds which are necessary to the full Exercise of their Skill and Industry." As Morris saw it, taking money from ordinary taxpayers to fund a huge windfall for war debt speculators was exactly the kind of thing that needed to be done to make America great.[54]

The debt Morris wanted to use to generate this windfall was about $27 million in IOUs, which Congress had issued during the war. It was a hodge-podge of paper. About $11 million of the debt was, essentially, war bonds, that is, interest-bearing certificates that Congress had sold to wealthy investors or used to pay military contractors when they would no longer accept Continental currency. About $5 million of it was back pay and a pension set-tlement for officers in the Continental Army, given out in lump sums rang-ing from $1,600 for lieutenants to $10,000 for generals. Another $6 million was back pay for between 20,000 and 30,000 soldiers, who usually received between $200 and $300 apiece. (Morris had opposed any kind of pension for enlisted men, saying, "I cannot conceive that when Soldiers are well fed and clad they will have much Need of Money and, therefore, considering what Kind of Men usually fill up the Ranks of an Army too much would be rather pernicious than useful.") The final $5–6 million was generally composed of IOUs to suppliers of the army: an invoice receipt given to a merchant for bar-rels of sugar; the scrawled note of a quartermaster who had purchased boots from a cobbler; scraps signed by an army officer who had impressed livestock and wagons from a village.[55]

Nearly all of this paper came into the hands of moneyed gentlemen. Sometimes, gentlemen acquired debt certificates by purchasing them direct-ly from the government or, more likely, when Congress essentially turned the war bonds into currency to pay contractors. Most of the concentration hap-pened because ordinary Americans sold their IOUs. There was good reason to sell. Virtually every other slip of paper the government had issued during the war had depreciated, and, fearing that the same thing would happen to the IOUs, most people sold them for whatever they could get. Morris would not allow them to be accepted for taxes. And most people could not afford to wait years for the government to repay them. The demands of running a farm or a shoemaker's shop or, in the case of soldiers, simply the costs of traveling home drove most people to sell.

Those who hung on to their IOUs quickly learned that neither Congress nor the state government was going to pay them back anytime soon. Even trying to collect the yearly 6 percent interest on the IOUs proved futile. Collecting entailed a costly journey to Philadelphia and a long wait for an appointment with finance officers—only to be told there was no money to be had. In August 1783, state officials reported that many IOU holders, "after coming from the remote parts of the state, and having a liquidation of their certificates refused," had left their offices "with murmurs and discontents." Many of these people no doubt sold their IOUs before they left town and brought home tales of frustration that convinced most of their neighbors to sell too.[56]

In the end, probably more than 90 percent of farmers, artisans, and soldiers sold their certificates—most of them shortly after receiving the IOUs. It was estimated at the time that "the certificates passed from the original holders in the proportion of probably nineteen-twentieths." The rates for soldiers' certificates were thought to be even higher. "I think we may safely calculate," one observer said in 1785, "that there are 20 (perhaps indeed 50) soldiers certificates in the hands of speculators for one that remains with the original owners." If these estimates are accurate, over 95 percent of ordinary Pennsylvanians sold their IOUs.[57]

Moreover, as Robert Morris hoped, the certificates quickly concentrated among affluent men, who had the financial resources to sit on the certificates and the political clout to pressure the government to pay them. In Pennsylvania, as elsewhere, the concentration was astounding. By 1790, over 96 percent of Pennsylvania's $4.8 million share of the war debt was held by just 434 people. Even this remarkable figure is skewed. The top 28 investors (nearly all of whom were Philadelphia merchants, lawyers, and brokers) owned over 40 percent of the entire Pennsylvania war debt.[58]

As one might expect, there was considerable overlap between those who bought the war debt certificates and the wealthy men involved in the Bank of North America. The stockholders and clients of the Bank of North America held certificates representing 67 percent of the war debt. The top thirty-five men from the banking circle, each with over $20,000 in certificates, held about 44 percent of the total.[59]

The wealthy acquired the vast majority of these certificates for pennies on the dollar. The IOUs were worth far less than the amounts printed on their faces, even at the moment they were issued. The selling prices usually ranged between one-sixth and one-fortieth of the face value, depending on the type of IOU. Soldiers' certificates were said to have sold at "one tenth, and many not more than one thirtieth" of their face value, meaning that a certificate with "$100" printed on its face could have sold for about $3.50. Other kinds of certificates tended to sell at rates where a $100 certificate could be had for $10–17 and perhaps for as little as $2.50.[60]

Even the gentlemen who had purchased war bonds directly from the government usually obtained them at a fraction of their face value. Wealthy investors usually bought war bonds using greatly depreciated paper money, allowing them to pay about one-fifth of the bond's face value. Likewise, merchants who accepted bonds as payment insisted on receiving, as Robert Morris put it, "Sums vastly beyond the Value of the Services and Articles obtained." The only group of gentlemen who had not acquired certificates at a small fraction of their face value was the army officers, who received them as part of their pension settlement. Yet, there was speculation here too: many army officers also purchased war debt certificates from the enlisted men under their command in order to bolster their holdings. (Despite this, officers actually held relatively few certificates: the 101 officers who could be identified in war debt records held $160,000 in certificates, or merely 4.5 percent of the Pennsylvania war debt.)[61]

Although the certificates had never been worth anything approaching the amounts printed on their faces, the men who amassed the IOUs demanded payment at full face value. If they had paid $10 to a soldier for a certificate that said "$100" on its face, they wanted the government to pay them the $100. They also wanted the government to pay them 6 percent per year in interest until the full principal was paid off—along with any back interest that the previous holder had been unable to collect. Needless to say, the proposed returns were stunning. The interest payments alone would often repay the cost of the initial investment in a few years. And with a return on the principal of probably ten to thirty times—or more—war debt speculators stood to make fortunes if they could get the government to pay off the IOUs at face value.

Speculators stood to make even more if they could get the government to pay them in gold and silver rather than paper money. Speculators (along with army officers) insisted that they not be paid in paper money. Instead, they demanded that the government tax the public in gold and silver and step up enforcement of tax collection to make sure ordinary people paid, whether they had hard money or not.

Of course, those taxes would be laid on the very same farmers, artisans, and soldiers who had sold the IOUs for pennies on the dollar. Thus, ordinary people received little for their wartime sacrifices. They had served as soldiers or given crops and livestock to provision the army or shod horses for the cavalry—all for IOUs that had never been worth very much from the moment those slips of paper touched their hands. They could not even use the IOUs to pay the taxes the state enacted to pay the interest on the IOUs. Instead, they had to pay taxes in gold and silver, in large part so that affluent men could receive an extraordinary windfall. And they were supposed to view all of this as serving the "public good."

*   *   *

In the end, the gospel of moneyed men bore a striking resemblance to British oppression during the 1760s and 1770s. The policies were similar, as were the justifications for limiting democracy and the easy dismissal of criticism by the public. Like British officials and the Penn family, Morris and others believed that power over money and credit needed to be removed from democratic control because they said that popularly elected governments could not manage finances. Like Britain, they killed the land-bank system without offering a good alternative for getting money and credit into the hands of ordinary folk. When ordinary people complained about a scarcity of money, the revolutionary elite called the charges unfounded and said the public was lazy, greedy, and ill informed—just as Britain had. And like Britain, the revolutionary elite enacted new taxes payable in gold and silver to fund the war and government expenses.

The immediate results were also the same: just as British policies caused a dire scarcity of money and a prolonged economic depression, so too would the Morris plan.

4

The Sheriff's Wagon

THE CRISIS OF THE 1780S

I need not observe that for want of money the interests of our country are every day receiving lasting wounds. Wherever we turn we see the marks of public poverty and distress.

—Timothy Pickering, Philadelphia County, March 24, 1781

Never have we seen a crisis that wore so gloomy an aspect as the present, for want of cash; which puts it entirely out of our power to discharge our public debts and other demands, such as land-office fees, surveyors fees, and . . . lawyers fees, which are worst of all.

—"A Farmer," *Pittsburgh Gazette*, December 9, 1786

When it comes to symbols for the spirit of 1776, Pennsylvania has almost a monopoly. After all, it is home to the Liberty Bell, Valley Forge, and Independence Hall. It was the location of the First Continental Congress and the birthplace of the Declaration of Independence. These symbols speak of the triumph of liberty and democracy and have been celebrated, with good reason, by Americans ever since.

There is, however, another symbol of the Revolution that complicates the ending to the traditional story. And although this symbol has disappeared from cultural memory, in the years after the War for Independence, it was to many Pennsylvanians the most potent icon of the Revolution's outcome. The image was this: the heavily loaded wagon of a county sheriff bearing the foreclosed property of debt-ridden citizens. The power of this icon came from its ubiquity. During the postwar decade, the sheriff's wagon could be seen nearly everywhere. With its load of foreclosed property, it struggled up the narrow gullied roads of the backcountry, groaned along the wide smooth lanes of the Delaware Valley, and rattled down the bumpy cobble-stone streets of Philadelphia, the richest city in the new nation. As was to be expected in a largely agricultural society, the wagon made most of its stops at the homes of small farmers. Yet its flat wooden bed was just as likely to hold the confiscated tools of a blacksmith, the grindstone of a miller, or the inventory of a small merchant. Indeed, one striking comparative fact is this: there were more Pennsylvanians who had property foreclosed by county sheriffs during the postwar decades than there were Pennsylvania soldiers who fought for the Continental Army.

This chapter probes the depths of the postwar depression by following the travels of the sheriff's wagon from the courthouse steps, through the homes of financially strapped debtors, and to the auction block where property was sold to cover unpaid debts or taxes. It provides an intimate portrait of how the new cash scarcity reawakened the specter of mass economic dependency that many Pennsylvanians had initiated a revolution to escape.

Ending at the Beginning

To many of those who lived through the War for Independence, it was some-times hard to tell what the Revolution had changed. Certainly, on many lev-els, most Pennsylvanians felt freer: government was more open; most adult white men could vote; and citizens were protected by a strong bill of rights in the state constitution. But in terms of the economic well-being that gave independence its meaning, life in postwar Pennsylvania resembled the dark days of the 1760s and 1770s. The similarities were obvious to Pennsylvanians of all classes and regions, as cries of a scarcity of money stretched from the western backcountry to the metropolis of Philadelphia.

Popular complaints about the new scarcity could be heard across the coun-tryside. In 1784, ordinary folk from across Pennsylvania petitioned against the "Sad and awful effects" they had "personally Experienced" due to the "General Scarcity of hard money." Petitioners said they had watched the "Public Trade and Private transactions of Human Life . . . nearly reduced to a total Stagnation." And they warned that, if government did not print new paper currency to com-pensate for the shortage, there was "just reason to Dread" that "Still more fatal Calamities" would follow "at a Period not far Distant."[1]

As one might expect, things were worst in the western counties. "The sit-uation of this Country at present is very alarming for the want of Money," explained a frontier merchant in Pittsburgh in 1787. "Very few in this Town can procure Money to go to market, and as to pay or recover a Debt it is out of the question." In neighboring Washington County, citizens assembled that year at a "patriot convention" to express their alarm over the "daily draining [of] our circulating medium." "Our lands must be patented, that cannot be done without cash," they wrote in a petition, "our proportion of the national debt must be paid, and that cannot be done without cash; our private mutual contracts must be discharged, and this, in many respects, cannot be done without cash." "The discharge of our taxes and debts," they noted, were "demands that cannot be put off without apparent ruin."[2]

Next door in Westmoreland County, weaver-turned-politician William Findley reported in 1786 that ruin was fast approaching for those who could not pay the mortgages on their land. His constituents were diligently trying "to pay the state its due" so that they would "be able to call the lands their own." But with so little cash around, they could not make their payments. In desperation, some farmers had sold "the last cow and sheep to procure a little money (for nothing but cows and sheep will find money there)." "I myself have been urged to take the last cow—to take anything they had in order to secure their lands," Findley confessed. "They raise the last shilling they are able—and plead as if for life that we may add a few dollars to the scanty sum." Despite such efforts, most people could not acquire enough money. The results were grim: "Our real estates are subject to be sold for debts; and are actually daily selling in this manner."[3]

The situation was little better in the central and eastern counties. "There is nothing here but a General outcry of the Scarcity of Cash," reported a Northumberland County official in 1788. In 1787, an observer in nearby Cumberland County had declared that "money is almost invisible," leaving citizens without the necessary funds to reimburse county storekeepers for what this man estimated to be $65,000 worth of goods. "Collecting cash here is almost out of the question at this time," reported a storekeeper in the town of Lancaster. In 1784, Lancaster tax officials said that they could not collect because "the circulation of cash in the county was not one fifth part sufficient for the medium of trade." Revenue officers in Northampton County noted the same "distress of the people" caused by the "scarcity of money." Even in Chester County, home to some of the richest farmland in the state, tax collectors "all say there is no Money."[4]

Money was also scarce in Philadelphia, where each passing year seemed to make the dearth more severe. "The scarcity of money is now the cry & rings through the city almost as much as the bells do in the case of fire," observed merchant Stephen Collins in December 1782. In July 1783, Collins reported that it was "impossible to command any money without murdering" his customers to get it. In January 1784, Collins informed an acquaintance that the blaze had spread, making things "worse and worse & money is so scarce that I can assure you my good friend it makes me almost sick." In 1785, he told his creditors, "The shopkeepers in Town & Country are breaking fast, so that I think [it] best to be on ones guard." Two years later, in September 1787, he wrote (from an office blocks away from the Constitutional Convention) that "times have grown so bad, money so scarce [that] amazing quantities of real estate of every kind [are] selling at both public and private sale." In sum, this was a statewide—indeed, a nationwide crisis—that left most people struggling to remain solvent.[5]

By nearly every measure, the postwar scarcity was even more severe than the one that had generated the Revolution. There was certainly less currency in circulation. On the eve of independence, when colonial Pennsylvanians had complained of a profound "scarcity of money," there had been approximately $5.30 per person in government paper in circulation. By comparison, in 1786 there was only about $1.90. At the end of 1790, the amount of currency stood at a mere 30 cents per person. During the prewar decade, Pennsylvanians had struggled to pay their financial obligations with a handful of paper bills. During the postwar decade, they had only pocket change.[6]

Indeed, the postwar crisis was probably comparable to the nation's most cataclysmic stretch of hard times, the Great Depression of the 1930s. Even a cursory comparison of the decline in national production during the periods tells a chilling story. From 1929 to 1933, national output plummeted by 48 percent. Although estimates from the revolutionary years offer only rough approximations, the drop in production before 1790 may have been as much as 46 percent of prewar output. And, while the Great Depression spanned a decade, some figures indicate that the revolutionary economy did not reach the level of output it had achieved in 1774 until sometime after 1805—an almost thirty-year economic trough.[7]

In terms of property foreclosures, the downturn in the revolutionary economy may have surpassed the Great Depression of the 1930s. When thousands of Pennsylvanians could not pay their debts, mortgages, and taxes, they found themselves facing lawsuits from creditors and the government. In communities held together by networks of book credit, the financial downfall of even one community member often triggered ripples of catastrophe that flowed through court docket books. If a father could not pay his debts, the court foreclosed a promissory note from his son. When the son was unable to pay cash, the court prosecuted the neighbor who owed the son for butter and flour. If that neighbor lacked cash, the chain continued until every possible debt had been called in. The webs of economic interdependence led court officials to family members, friends, neighbors, and business associates. So complicated were the tangles of debt that cases sometimes found satisfaction only after proceeding through a line of six different people. In such instances, it was entirely likely that defendants in debt suits lost property or land to men they did not even know.[8]

The collapse of credit networks throughout Pennsylvania unleashed an epidemic of property foreclosures. The surviving evidence suggests that foreclosures spread across Pennsylvania, becoming more rampant the greater the distance from Philadelphia. In the eastern county of Berks, a decade of debt litigation between 1782 and 1792 produced 3,400 writs of foreclosure for a taxable population that averaged about 5,000 families—or enough to foreclose 68 percent of taxpayers. In neighboring Lancaster County, the court issued 3,900 writs of foreclosure between 1784 and 1789, enough to cover 66 percent of the county's taxable population of 5,900. In Northumberland County on the northern frontier, between 1785 and 1790, the sheriff delivered more writs of foreclosure (2,180) than there were taxpayers (2,140).[9]

Things were even worse in the frontier counties on the western side of the Appalachian Mountains. For example, in Westmoreland County, over the decade spanning 1782 to 1792, judges issued a remarkable 6,100 separate orders to foreclose goods and land. These orders brought the sheriff into the homes of at least 1,200 different families to seize property or to hold a land auction. Since Westmoreland County averaged only about 2,800 taxpayers during this period, the sheriff foreclosed no less than 43 percent of the families in this jurisdiction.[10]

Such numbers take on added weight when one considers that creditors often tried to avoid lawsuits. Many creditors were worried that lawsuit costs would leave debtors too poor to repay. Consequently, some of them urged agents to "adopt every other expedient before they proceed to that extremity" of suing, which would be "attended with a good deal of expense and delay." Rather than rack up court costs, Philadelphia merchant William Sitgreaves wrote threatening letters: in the three-year period between January 1791 and January 1794, he sent at least 195 letters to indebted storekeepers promising to sue if they did not pay accounts long overdue. Other creditors preferred "coaxing" money out of debtors rather than suing because, like merchant Stephen Collins, they were "afraid to sue . . . for fear that [their debtors] would go to gaol," and the debt would be "lost" because they would be unable to earn income while in prison.[11]

At first glance, the debts in question appear to have been rather trivial. In Westmoreland County, where the most complete set of foreclosure records has survived, the bulk of court activity was initiated to recover outstanding debts or taxes of around $67. Much of the litigation was over more modest sums. In several cases, people were foreclosed because they could not repay debts of $3.[12]

When such figures are put in perspective, it becomes apparent that these seemingly small amounts of money often represented much of a family's yearly income. In what is a rough estimate, yearly income in Pennsylvania was $25–30 per person (a figure that takes the postwar depression into consideration). With an average of five to six people per family, most households probably earned between $125 and $180 each year. If these estimates are correct, the typical debt case involved as much as half of a family's yearly income.[13]

Court costs compounded the problem. Debtors or taxpayers who lost their cases generally had to pay the costs. And, as in the modern legal system, the amount was often steep. Nearly every time a court official raised a pen or stood up from his chair, a fee or tax was added to the bill of costs. There were filing fees, bench fees, and appearance fees, along with taxes for warrants, subpoenas, and depositions. Whenever a lawyer completed some basic procedure like bringing an action, filing a declaration, or obtaining a judgment, a court clerk added another set of taxes in the ledger. Of course, the attorney taxes were separate from the actual fees that lawyers billed to their clients. If the case went to trial, the defendant was responsible for no fewer than ten additional fees. Every time the county sheriff became involved, there was yet another litany of costs. For each summons the sheriff delivered, every indictment he served, and every recalcitrant debtor he apprehended, a new fee was invoked. Furthermore, defendants were required to compensate the sheriff for the mileage he traveled to dispatch any kind of legal paper. Perhaps the most exasperating charges were reserved for citizens whose possessions were foreclosed. After the sheriff loaded the goods into his wagon and sold them at auction, he left behind a bill covering the fees for inventorying and auctioning the property as well as for the distance he had to travel.[14]

Unfortunately for most debtors, drawn-out lawsuits kept this cycle of taxes repeating, thereby escalating court costs. Due to the scarcity of money, debtors typically returned to court several times before they could pay everything. In well over half the cases that led to foreclosure in Westmoreland County, debtors made at least five separate trips through the court system before the legal action ended. As a result, most cases remained on the dockets for a number of years, some for over a decade. While the duration of lawsuits allowed debtors some breathing room, the drawn-out cases amassed heavy court fees.

In the end, accumulated court costs were often a daunting burden. To modern observers, the court costs in revolutionary America probably seem modest. For example, in Westmoreland County, the price of litigation, while it could run as high as $60 for a single case, usually hovered around $13.[15] But under economic circumstances where debts of less than $30 routinely led to foreclosure, a court cost of $13, by itself, was often prohibitive. Farmers in Cumberland County complained that the costs of paying the sheriff to travel "Ten or Twelve Miles" to reach their farms often generated fees that were "more than the debt." "At a time when national poverty has overwhelmed our country," began a similar petition from Westmoreland County farmers, "We have seen poverty itself shamefully oppressed and the fruits of honest industry totally swallowed up . . . to satisfy the rapacious demand of a Bill of Costs." They concluded that "the costs of the law" had become "one of the greatest curses that have ever visited our country." These petitioners knew of what they spoke: in Westmoreland County between 1782 and 1792, one out of every four foreclosures was produced merely by unpaid court costs.[16]

Making the Rounds

As the court churned out writ after writ foreclosing property, the sheriff sat quietly in his chair arranging the names of debtors by township and mapping out his route. He would handle some business himself and parcel the rest out to the constables of each township. After organizing his affairs, the sheriff set out on his travels. It was the identical routine month after month.

At each stop, his work was the same. With ledger in hand, he made his way around the property to take an inventory of its worth. He wandered the fields where crops grew and noted the quality of the future harvest. Taking a small spade from his sack, he dug into the earth to determine the richness of the topsoil. On the way back from the fields, he stopped by the pasture where sheep and cows grazed and jotted reminders about the health and age of each beast. His next stop was the barn, where he made similar notes about the horses. He checked their teeth, eyes, and hooves and noted which animals appeared capable of hard labor. He looked around the barn for carts, wagons, bridles, and saddles and assessed their condition. He did the same for axes, plows, and any other tools he could find. He finished here by inspecting the grain bins and climbing the wooden ladder to see what was stored in the hayloft.[17]

If this was the home of an artisan, he headed over to the work shed. If the man was a cobbler, the sheriff searched for awls and binding equipment, counted the inventory of leather, and studied the finished shoes and boots. If he was a blacksmith, the sheriff examined the large hammer and contemplated the help he would need to retrieve the heavy anvil. If the man was a distiller, he determined the capacity of the stills, inspected the fixtures and lines, and counted the kegs and casks in storage.[18]

Then the sheriff entered the house. Inside, he tested chairs and tables to make sure they were sturdy. Opening cupboards, he clanged pots and pans and jotted notes about their make. If the plates and mugs were pewter, he included them on the inventory; wooden plates and utensils would not sell. If there was a spinning wheel, he gave its pedal a few pumps to ensure that it could perform its duty. If the debtor was a slave owner, this was as suitable a time as any to record the name, age, sex, and racial mix of each slave, noting also the marketable skills they possessed.[19]

Finally, the sheriff located the bedroom or, in most houses (which were one-room cabins), he simply walked across the floor to the sleeping area. Here, he opened drawers and inspected clothes, hoping to find something that might draw a bid. Turning to the bed, he kicked the frame and bounced the mattress. He recorded the color and pattern of any blankets he could find. Then he folded back the bed covers and ran his fingers through the linens (if there were any) and made notes about their quality. Then he closed the ledger.[20]

The sheriff would return to his wagon to summarize the situation. If the creditor had made a specific request to confiscate grain, furniture, or tools, the sheriff calculated the combination of goods it would take to fulfill the debt. Then, he gathered the items and loaded them onto the wagon. If the creditor wanted grain, he went to the storage bins and scooped the appropriate amount into large sacks. If it was before harvest time, the sheriff made the farmer sign a note ceding the "grain in the ground" to the creditor. When the order called for livestock, the sheriff coaxed cows from the fields or led horses from the barn. Being careful not to tangle the lines, he tied each animal to an iron cleat on the backboard. Then, he boarded the wagon and began the long slow trip to the creditor's home to deliver the foreclosed property.

More likely though, in this cash-starved economy, creditors desired money over possessions, and, as a result, they generally ordered the sheriff to auction property to cover the debt. Most creditors had their own bills to pay, usually to overseas lenders. "I want money . . . very much to pay my debts with in Europe," wrote Stephen Collins to a country lawyer in 1787. "Old houses & lands will not do to make remittances in," he said. "Besides if I was to take his land," Collins reasoned, "I could never sell it for cash for much more than 10 [shillings] in the pound"—about half of what it was typically worth. It was this last consideration that drove most creditors to opt for sheriffs' auctions instead of confiscation. As Collins understood, if he cleared the debt by taking land, he would probably only get half his money. If Collins had the sheriff auction the debtor's property, he would eventually be able to collect the whole debt no matter how low the selling price. Given these realities, most creditors understandably opted for an auction.[21]

The sheriff would be kept busy preparing for the auction. State law required him to advertise foreclosed property at common places throughout the county. He had to transcribe the inventory to parchment and nail the notices to trees near churches and meetinghouses. If there was a local or regional newspaper, the sheriff took out advertisements listing the name of the debtor, the property foreclosed, and the time and place of the auction (the debtor was charged for the costs of the ad).[22]

On the specified day, usually a few weeks later, the sheriff returned to the debtor's home to hold the auction. Since most homes were not considered "public places," the sheriff usually transported the possessions to a site that was more accessible. There he sat with his cargo, awaiting bidders and their wagons.[23]

Despite all of the preparation, however, auctions were often unsuccessful. Many people refused to bid because they were hesitant to participate in bankrupting neighbors. Others did not have the money in this cash-scarce economy. Fending off foreclosure themselves, many people had no need for another cow or a chest of drawers.[24]

Even when bidders arrived with cash, the auction rarely produced enough money to free debtors from their obligations. With so few people willing or able to bid, sale prices remained low, often less than half of the property's estimated worth. "I have seen some of the collectors and they all say there is no money," reported the treasurer of Chester County in southeastern Pennsylvania. "I attended a Sheriff's vendue last week where horses and stock etc. sold for [a] quarter of their value. I bought a feather bed and furniture for one pound and six pence." In other counties, property sold for as little as one-eighth to one-tenth of its estimated value.[25]

Sometimes, unscrupulous bidders did what they could to drive prices even lower. The most extreme example was probably in 1786, when a landlord in

Cumberland County had the local constable auction the cow and horse of a tenant farmer named William McKinney, who had fallen £10 behind on his rent. McKinney had "begged" his landlord to "take hogs or grain in the ground and property of value or notes equal to cash, and spare my milch cow and my plow horse for the sake of my family." But the landlord had refused, leaving McKinney in "the utmost distress." Resigned to the sale of his property, McKinney hoped at least to keep court costs to a minimum. "On the day of the sale the constable came for the property, I desired he would sell them on the premises as it was a public place," McKinney remembered, "but he refused to do it and drove them a mile further and sold them there, for which he charged me four shillings." Having lost even this small concession, things looked bleak.[26]

Then, at the auction site, a miracle seemed to happen. When the constable began the bidding, McKinney's landlord arrived and halted the auction. McKinney recalled that his landlord "made a proposal before the public that he would buy all for me and return the goods [to me] which stopped the intended buyers from bidding." It seemed that McKinney's landlord—the man whose lawsuit had brought matters to this disastrous end—had changed his mind and come to save the day for his tenant. Compelled by this emotional scene, the other potential buyers agreed to tender no bids so that the landlord could purchase McKinney's property at a bare minimum.

Not long after the crowd had dispersed, the miracle vanished. Despite the landlord's public promises, he kept the cow and other possessions for himself. He had rigged the auction to keep others from bidding so he could obtain his tenant's belongings for virtually nothing. The landlord also refused to erase the £10 debt. The case continued, and on "the orders of the landlord, the constable came eight or ten days after and sold a horse" of McKinney's.

Although most auctions were free from such shenanigans, goods still typically did not sell for enough to cover the debt. For example, in Westmoreland County, the sale of goods did not procure enough money to satisfy the debtor's obligations in over 92 percent of cases. This meant that virtually everyone who had his or her livestock, tools, and furniture sold at auction was still unable to get out of debt and could expect more auctions and new court costs.[27]

For most debtors, such sales meant that it was now even harder to pay their way out of debt because the sheriff invariably sold the things they needed to make a living. This truth shook Thomas Cheyney, a judge of appeals in Chester County, who reported to state tax officials in 1785 that "the

Complaints of the People" being foreclosed for unpaid taxes were "truly distressing." Due to the "Scarcity of money," farm prices had fallen so low that his neighbors could not "Toss out their grain to discharge" their debts and taxes. In futile attempts to pay, local farmers were "driving off their stock and selling them at Little more than half of their Value." But with the low sale prices, even if they sold "all their goods & tools for carrying on their Trades and business for the Support of their Little Children," it would still not be enough to "pay the Demand." To Cheyney, stripping people of the means to pay was more "discouraging to Industry" than "anything that has ever befell the People in this Part of the Country." Without tools, plows, and livestock, how would farmers feed their families, let alone pay overdue taxes?[28]

The process of divesting debtors of the means to pay found its most extreme example in the confiscation of land. When there were no more cows, horses, and tools to foreclose, creditors and tax officials went after land. Some creditors, guessing that their debtors did not have enough goods to pay, went after the land first, fearing they might lose out to rival creditors. Others hoped to wrest land from debtors quickly to preserve its value. One Philadelphia creditor insisted on foreclosing his debtors' lands in Cumberland County because he worried that the current owners, "despairing of ever being able to discharge the large demands against them, are letting the estate go to ruin and are impoverishing the land by getting all they can out of it." In last-ditch efforts to work their way out of trouble, many farmers ignored good farming practices and used every inch of cleared space to produce an immediate harvest of cash crops instead of rotating crops. Others cut down as many trees as they could, hoping to pay their debts from the sale of timber. For creditors who suspected that their debtors were devaluing property in these ways, the pressures to foreclose land must have been intense.[29] As a result, land frequently appeared on lists of foreclosed property. For example, in Westmoreland County, from 1782 to 1792, the sheriff confiscated real estate or held a land auction at least 425 different times, a figure that represented nearly 20 percent of his caseload and about 10 percent of the families in the county.[30]

Even as he sold land to cover debts and taxes, the sheriff knew that, most likely, the matter was still far from over. Like with auctioned goods, land sold by the sheriff brought only a fraction of what it was typically worth. "We brought a suit against one of our neighbors for upwards of £70," explained two country storekeepers in 1789. "The sheriff levied a tract of land for which the man three years ago paid £100. And this tract of land when put up to sale actually brought no more than £10.10." The storekeepers hoped this example would give their Philadelphia creditor "a tolerable idea of our poverty in money matters." Such low selling prices ensured that most land sales did not earn enough to repay the debt. Indeed, in a decade of auctions in Westmoreland County, 67 percent of land sales failed to cover the debt. Thus, the entire process of foreclosure—even after it had stripped debtors of their livestock, tools, and land—often did little to relieve citizens of their financial burdens.[31]

The sheriff knew from experience that these people would probably join the growing ranks of propertyless debtors. It was a sobering social truth in this litany of debt peonage that fully 20 percent of the households the sheriff visited contained nothing of value for him to foreclose. These people possessed no spinning wheel, wagon, furniture, or linens to auction. In a decade of foreclosures in Westmoreland County, the sheriff walked away with an empty inventory ledger approximately 1,200 times.[32]

As a result, many impoverished debtors found themselves thrown in the county jail. In Westmoreland County, a decade of sheriff foreclosures forced citizens to prison on 357 different occasions. These actions brought into jail at least 270 different people, or about 10 percent of the taxable population. Many debtors made two or three separate tours of the county penal system. Some stayed in jail for a week, others for months, and a few remained imprisoned for over a year.[33]

Bail was available, if the creditor and judge were willing—and if the debtor could find someone willing to support a bond. There were, however, considerable disincentives to put up bail for a debtor. By bailing a debtor out of jail, neighbors and family members pledged their own property that the debt would be paid in a timely fashion. Thus, providing bail often served only to draw friends or relatives into the cycle of debt, foreclosure, and possibly prison.

Many of those who saw little hope of ever paying their debts followed a desperate and timeless option: they gathered their families and remaining belongings, and they fled. While it is impossible to know the precise number of debtors who ran away to other states or to the unmapped backcountry, it is perhaps enough to observe that more than a few cases in the Westmoreland County dockets ended with entries like "Gone to Kentucky" or "Indian Country."

Most debtors, however, stayed until their cases were settled, and then, when they had little property left, they packed up their families and moved. Here is the figure that probably best summarizes the human toll of the postwar scarcity: in Westmoreland County, the majority of debtors foreclosed during the 1780s had left by the end of the decade. Of the 980 citizens whose property was foreclosed between 1782 and 1789, 540 could not be found on the 1790 census rolls anywhere in Pennsylvania west of the Appalachian Mountains. Thus, for more than half of foreclosed families, the arrival of the county sheriff signaled the end of a homestead and the beginning of an arduous journey to carve a new farm out of the land somewhere else.[34]

The Distribution of Pain and Wealth

When the sheriff had placed the last debtor on his docket in jail, the horses pulling his wagon could take a rest. In the moments before the wagon starts its travels again, it is important to pause and consider more closely the people who found themselves foreclosed. A few points deserve emphasis. First, the cash scarcity brought hardship to a wide range of people across the state, not just poor backcountry farmers. Second, although the crisis hurt some gentlemen, most of the pain was borne by those of the middling and lower sorts. And, finally, property redistribution performed by the sheriff ended up greatly widening the gap between the rich and everyone else.

The victims of Morris's policies were not simply the poor. Indeed, the entire problem of foreclosure largely bypassed the poor because they could not get loans or credit in the first place—and certainly not the $60 that represented the typical debt of foreclosed citizens in counties like Westmoreland. Those foreclosed were the kinds of people whom creditors felt confident entrusting with a relatively large sum of money: middling farmers, most of whom probably owned their land.

Although land-owning yeomen represented the largest casualties of sheriffs' auctions, the pain also reached above them. In the countryside, the scarcity afflicted many gentlemen. For example, in Cumberland County, Matthias Hollypeter, who owned an estate estimated at $8,000, faced foreclosure because he could not muster enough cash to pay $19 in taxes. Likewise, in Philadelphia, the scarcity thinned the ranks of merchants, eliminating many smaller firms and taking down several prominent trading houses. Between 1784 and 1790, no fewer than sixty-eight mercantile firms petitioned for bankruptcy. During the year ending June 1785, Philadelphia merchants went out of business at the rate of over one firm per month.[35]

Even lawyers felt the pinch. Certainly, there was considerable debt-related business to be had by even the most incompetent lawyer. But clients who could not afford to pay small debts usually could not afford lawyers' fees. As a Cumberland County lawyer declared in 1784, "I confess I have been very inattentive about this suit and without any excuse, except my clients not having given me a fee." "The last court at Carlisle was a *beggarly one*," he reported. "If the next court is not better, I shall pray that beggary may attend the whole county without the exception of *an individual*."[36]

While most people felt the pain, poorer folk were usually hit the hardest. In the city, the postwar decade was among the toughest on record for artisans and laborers of the lower sort. In the countryside, where a good year often meant just getting by, the cash scarcity made the margin of error desperately thin. Factor in bad weather or a failed crop and that margin could evaporate. For example, in 1789, cash-poor farmers in Westmoreland County faced an abnormally cold spring that ruined the early harvest. With the "almost total failing of the corn crops" that summer, farmers faced a severe food shortage that one inhabitant said was "very near" to being "a famine." By August, with no money to buy food, "great numbers" of farmers "were borrowing meal in dishfuls and few to lend." To feed their families, "many were bailing grain before it was fully ripe." Any hopes that a late-season crop would remedy the crisis were dashed by an "early frost in the fall." That winter "produced a great death of cattle," as farmers could not afford to keep their livestock fed. The spring of 1790 brought empty grain reserves, creating what one resident called "the greatest appearance of scarcity of bread in the western country that I have ever observed." "Many families were already in great distress," he said in May, "and the prospects of putting in Spring crops are very unpromising, the horses being too poor to work through want of feed." The situation was desperate, he concluded, "several poor people have lost all."[37]

In the end, the unequal distribution of pain translated into a widening gap between the wealthy and nearly everyone else. Although some individuals of the middling and lower sorts may have prospered, the lowest 90 percent of the population lost ground. By 1800, most citizens now possessed far less of the state's wealth—land, money, livestock, tools, furniture, pots and pans—than in the past. In Philadelphia in 1780, the lowest 90 percent of the population held over 56 percent of the wealth. By 1789, they held only 33 percent. By 1795, Philadelphia's lowest 90 percent owned only about 18 percent of the total assessed wealth—a staggering downward shift in only fifteen years.[38]

It was the same story in the countryside. In Chester County, just outside the city, in 1775, the lowest 60 percent of the population held about 26 percent of the wealth. By 1799, it had fallen to just 16 percent. Even in the western counties an increasingly small percentage of the population owned land, and land owners watched the size of their holdings shrink. A typical citizen in western Pennsylvania owned a 100-acre farm in the 1780s. By the mid-1790s, that farm was just a 50-acre homestead. In Fayette County in the western corner of the state, the typical settler was actually landless by 1796. Throughout the countryside, the number of tenant farmers soared. "There are now three times the number of tenants to be found in all the old countries of the state, [than] there was before the war," estimated one Pennsylvanian. "This dependant class of people are created only by the impossibility of borrowing money upon interest," he observed, "which formerly was the principal source of the freeholds;—and of course, of the free and independent spirit of our country." Whatever the effects on freedom and independence, it was clear that Pennsylvania had undergone a dramatic economic shift. Whether the setting was urban or rural, most people now earned less and owned less than they had on the eve of the Revolution.[39]

At the same time, a much smaller number of men with favorable connections to money and credit made impressive gains. Well-financed retailers and merchants commanded larger market shares and drove their competitors out of business. Commercial farmers with government contracts and ties to eastern merchants expanded production by buying their neighbors' farmland. Many of those who prospered established considerable investment portfolios of bank notes and stock, government securities, and bonds from various capital projects. Almost everyone who turned a profit acquired speculative holdings in city and town lots or in backcountry lands. As wealth accumulated, fine new townhouses and country estates appeared in the urban and rural landscapes. Along the roads leading to these houses, there traveled an emerging corps of portrait painters vying to capture the families of prosperous men on canvas.

Increasingly, those who prospered situated themselves at the hub of economic activity. They shaped the flow of commerce and credit, and, in a very real sense, they determined who shared the benefits of credit and money and who did not. Even in the backcountry, where mythology holds that things were more egalitarian, relatively few men controlled access to land and credit. Increasingly, they also controlled the grain trade, the most important source of farm income. The cash scarcity accelerated the trade's concentration. Farmers desperate for money sold the rights to much of their wheat and corn long before harvest, usually at prices well below the going rate. As increasing numbers of farmers mortgaged their crops, well-to-do farmers came to own much of the local harvest. As one grain merchant put it in 1788, "wheat . . . is very scarce. Nobody has it but your wealthy farmers." The trade became controlled by men such as John Wilkins of Pittsburgh, who in 1791 used the backing of some moneyed friends to purchase 800 barrels of flour at bargain rates from western Pennsylvania farmers. Wilkins profited by keeping the grain off the market and waiting until the scarcity produced "a greater price." Then, he sold the flour downstream or back to the very farmers who had sold it to him in the first place. Undone by the cash scarcity and bad weather, western farmers had little choice but to pay whatever men like Wilkins demanded. In 1790, one resident observed that farmers who had sold grain at a rate of four shillings per bushel were buying it back for ten shillings. Undoubtedly, many farmers mortgaged next year's crop to cover the costs, increasing their indebtedness and the control that local moneyed men exerted over trade.[40]

These kinds of profits encouraged some elite Pennsylvanians to see the cash scarcity as a blessing. According to one York County gentleman, writing in 1791, the cash shortage had been divinely inspired. Pennsylvania was experiencing "what we call hard times or the scarcity of money." But he assured his readers that this was all part of God's plan to teach people the value of money by forcing them to go without it. Economic deprivation would compel the public to work harder and observe greater "industry and economy." "The scarcity of money is the only thing that will save this people," he declared. The York gentleman concluded that, rather than complaining about the inadequate circulating medium, everyone should "let this circumstance excite in us gratitude to a kind of Providence for connecting future prosperity with present scarcity." It was a remarkable argument: the mass foreclosures and personal suffering imposed by the artificial scarcity of money was a gift from God.[41]

Whether divinely inspired or not, the scarcity enhanced the power of those who could command cash and credit. Moneyed men in Pennsylvania were not omnipotent; their control was not absolute. As a class, they seemed to scratch and claw at one another more often than they acted in concert. At times, they appeared mystified by the currents in the economy, and many of them faltered by guessing wrong. And, as we shall see, many prominent men made wild speculations that brought them to ruin. Nevertheless, those at the top of society were ascendant during the postwar decade, and their rise often came at the expense of those below them.

*　　*　　*

These then were the central facts of the revolutionary economy. Most citizens in Pennsylvania were mired in debt. Unable to acquire money or credit, they prayed that their families would be spared the worst of the depression. At the same time, they watched some men make fortunes, acquire enormous tracts of land, and live in refined opulence. That a cause-and-effect relationship underlay the losses and gains was an interpretive leap that few citizens failed to make.

Moreover, this was not just a Pennsylvania crisis: when leaders in other states enacted their own versions of the Morris plan (at Morris's prompting), they set off a nationwide crisis. Thus, in the postwar decade, the sheriff's wagon was in motion from South Carolina to the northern reaches of Maine.[42]

As hard as they tried, most Pennsylvanians could not reconcile the sight of the heavily loaded sheriff's wagon with their vision of the Revolution. The piles of writs, the intrusive inventorying, the confiscation of property, and the demoralizing auctions fit few people's definition of liberty. And so, when ordinary Pennsylvanians saw their vision of the Revolution slipping out of reach, many of them decided to fight back.

5

Equal Power

"THE PEOPLE" ATTEMPT TO RECLAIM
THE REVOLUTION

No observation is better supported, than this that, a country cannot long preserve its liberty, where a great inequality of property takes place. Is it not therefore the most dangerous policy in this infant republic, to combine the wealthy in order to make them powerful?

—Petition of yeomen from across Pennsylvania

A democratical government like ours admits no superiority.

—John Smilie, Fayette County, 1786

During the 1780s, ordinary Pennsylvanians launched an attack on the gospel of moneyed men and the hard times it created. These people demanded that state leaders save democracy by ending the policies that concentrated wealth among moneyed men. They called for new policies to make wealth more equal. And they demanded a return of a vigorous democracy. Those calls—which came in the form of petitions, newspaper editorials, and speeches by profarmer politicians—revealed that most ordinary Pennsylvanians had not only kept their faith in the vision of '76 but, in fact, had deepened and extended their ideas about equalizing wealth and power. They also showed that the people's ideas of democracy had expanded well beyond the right to vote to embrace a belief that ordinary folk had the right to make public policy on taxation, credit and debt, monetary issues, land policy, and a host of other matters. Needless to say, these popular ideals posed a direct threat to the Morris plan and to the moneyed men who depended on it.

Preserving Equal Power

Several things about the popular challenge to the Morris plan need to be kept in mind. First, by the 1780s, the ideas about political and economic equality expressed by ordinary Pennsylvanians represented mainstream thinking about the Revolution that could be traced at least as far back as the 1760s and 1770s. The proposals for making wealth and power more equal were not the ideas of radical fringe groups. Instead, they represented the thinking of the majority of the population. Second, ordinary folk were not simply out to soak the rich. Instead, their commitment was to protecting equality and developing solutions that tried to balance everyone's interests— even those of speculators, bankers, and creditors who had attempted to gouge the public. Indeed, given the profound hardships the Morris plan had created, the restraint of popular proposals appears striking.[1]

The basic ideals were perhaps best stated by a backcountry politician named William Findley, who was in many ways himself an embodiment of the Revolution's achievements: he was an ordinary man who rose from obscurity to take a seat in government and challenge the wealthy gentlemen who were accustomed to ruling. Findley certainly looked ordinary. He was in his forties during the 1780s and had a long weathered face, small sad eyes, and thick bushy eyebrows. His shoulder-length brown hair was graying, unruly, and thinning slightly on top, receding enough to reveal a brow creased with furrows. Findley's average looks mirrored his humble origins. Born in the north of Ireland in the early 1740s, he was trained as a weaver. He had emigrated to Pennsylvania in his mid-twenties, arriving at the end of the French and Indian War, and eventually he bought some land, which he farmed as he worked his trade. When war with Britain broke out, Findley joined the Cumberland County militia. He entered as a private, but showed a gift for leadership and quickly rose through the ranks, making captain by the war's end. That leadership catapulted Findley into the Pennsylvania General Assembly in 1784 as a representative from the new western county of Westmoreland. Findley saw himself as a champion of "the people" and an advocate of small farmers in particular (he often wrote under the pseudonym "A Farmer"). His efforts made him the most popular politician in the western counties and eventually launched him into Congress.[2]

According to Findley, the Revolution's biggest accomplishment was giving "citizens their right of equal protection, power, privilege, and influence." By this, he meant a government that provided ordinary folk with the same rights and access to power as the wealthy. Thus, equal protection meant that government needed to pay as much attention to looking out for the rights of

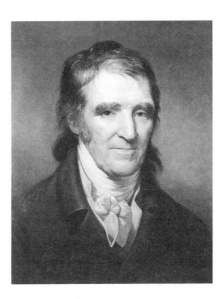

FIG. 5.1. WILLIAM FINDLEY BY REMBRANDT PEALE, FROM LIFE, 1805.
The Ulster-born Findley rose from obscurity as a farmer and weaver to
become the most popular politician from the western counties. He began his
political career, which spanned four decades, as an outsider who championed
democracy and "the people." During the 1790s, he tempered his democratic
ideals and became part of the political establishment he had once railed
against. (Independence National Historical Park.)

ordinary folk as it did for the wealthy. Equal power meant preventing the
affluent from oppressing ordinary folk. Equal privilege meant distributing
rewards to commoner and gentleman alike. And equal influence meant preventing rich men from using their wealth to sway the government or, in
Findley's words, ensuring that "No man has a greater claim of special privilege for his £100,000 than I have for my £5."[3]

To Findley, protecting all of these different kinds of equality meant that
the government must preserve a basic equality of wealth. The biggest threat
to democracy, Findley said, was the growing gap between the rich and everyone else. "Enormous wealth, possessed by individuals," he declared, "has
always had its influence and danger in free states." The only way to thwart
that danger was for government to promote wealth equality. As Findley put
it, "Wealth in many hands operates as many checks."[4]

This is not to say that Findley—and, by extension, most ordinary
Pennsylvanians—was in favor of creating an absolute equality of property
where everyone had exactly the same amount of wealth. No doubt, some
people supported the idea of confiscating land and property from wealthy

gentlemen and redistributing them to ordinary citizens along the lines of what Europeans called "agrarian law." If any such plans existed, however, little evidence of them has survived.

Instead, the majority opinion was that some differences in property were inevitable, natural, and even preferable. This position was made clear by petitioners from across the state, who identified themselves as land-owning "yeomen" farmers and who protested the accumulation of property in the hands of "a few wealthy and powerful citizens." Although these farmers argued for "an equality of rights" and some kind of "equal division of property," they stated that there would always be some level of "inequality" in society. "We know that a difference will always take place in society," they said, "according to the physical and acquired abilities of its members." Some farmers were better at growing crops; some cobblers made better shoes; some lawyers were better at arguing before a jury; some merchants more adept at sniffing out profitable deals. They believed that this kind of "inequality," born of talent and ability, "so far from being a source of evil, is the true basis of public prosperity." Society needed good farmers and artisans and merchants, and the petitioners believed that people should be rewarded for their skills and abilities.[5]

That said, these farmers also believed that there was a line where inequality crossed into the danger zone. And although they were not specific about where the line was, the farmers were clear that government had no business magnifying natural inequalities and pushing society toward that line. The core lesson of history and of the Revolution was that "a country cannot long preserve its liberty, where a great inequality of property takes place." The "social compact," they said, established "a perfect equality among citizens." Too great a concentration of wealth threatened that equality and undermined liberty. Consequently, any government policy that worked "to combine the wealthy in order to make them powerful" was "the most dangerous policy in this infant republic." Instead, the government should work to ensure some basic equality of property so that ordinary folk had the means to check the wealthy and preserve liberty.[6]

According to these farmers, equality of wealth was more than a check— it was a way to ensure that equality remained an American value. Equality promoted social harmony by pushing people "of the same society to mutually assist each other according to their abilities." An equal distribution of wealth promoted social equality by causing citizens to be scornful of those who adopted elitist pretensions. It shaped how Americans framed their ambitions and how they defined success. It caused people to value wealth "not as an end" in itself but, as Findley put it, as something that allowed them "to procure the necessaries and a competence of the comforts of life" and attain a basic level of "happiness and independence." Findley explained the formula: "An equal circulation of . . . wealth tends to promote equal interests—equal manners—and equal designs." As long as government worked to ensure wealth equality, people like Findley believed that it would promote a culture that would keep democracy safe.[7]

Ordinary folk often contrasted this democratic culture of equality with one that promoted selfishness and oppression. Findley argued that making wealth accumulation the highest social value was not only bad for America but also bad for "the human soul" because it "dries and shrivels up" compassion and leaves only the desire to amass more wealth and power. "It was the saying of a wise writer," Findley recalled, that "when riches increase," men "increased in their appetite for riches, and in their endeavors to procure them." "Enriching" oneself at the expense of others was un-American and immoral, he said. It was "a means of obtaining wealth" that "all the generous feeling[s] of the human soul forbid."[8]

Many ordinary Pennsylvanians put a Christian spin on those same beliefs, announcing that a moral gulf separated them as good Christians from state elites, whom they considered to be depraved secularists. To these people, Christianity was about creating a government and a society based on the teachings of Jesus which, to them, meant shunning oppression, fostering equality, and working to uplift the poor. Many Pennsylvanians believed that "Robert [Morris] and all [his] monied friends, bankers and brokers" were attempting to install an un-Christian government that mocked Jesus' message. According to many Christians, members of the state elite were creatures of the Enlightenment who thought Christianity was at best an "inconvenience" and at worst a "radical evil" "professed by a great many of the vulgar in this country." It was said that the elite worshipped the "religion of nature" where the only commandments were to "fill your coffers" and create "distinctions amongst mankind." Some people even said the gentry were incapable of being Christians. Following Jesus would require gentlemen to abandon "every genteel amusement" and stop "grasping at honours and distinctions" (sacrifices it was thought the gentry would never make). When gentlemen used religion in appeals to "the people," it was viewed as cynical attempts to "awe the minds of the vulgar, and keep them in subjugation."[9]

Seen in this way, the opposition to the Morris plan was not just about ending the cash scarcity or protecting democracy; in a larger sense, many ordinary Pennsylvanians believed that they were checking the selfishness that corroded society and, instead, promoting the empathy and compassion needed to create a humane, just, and Christian republic. Of course, in many ways, the ideas of compassion held by ordinary Pennsylvanians were narrow (especially when it came to matters of race). Nonetheless, for the day, this represented a very real attempt to create a moral society free from oppression (even as that "moral" society embodied the biases and prejudices of the day).

During the 1780s, ordinary Pennsylvanians attempted to advance those values in the arenas of money, credit, banking, corporations, the war debt, taxation, and land policy.

Money and Credit for "the good and Benefit of the whole community"

The defense of equal power began by repeating a battle that ordinary Pennsylvanians thought they had already won: the creation of widespread access to money and low-cost credit. Indeed, the struggles over finance in the 1780s closely resembled the ones waged against Britain during the 1760s and 1770s. In this new struggle, however, ordinary Pennsylvanians confronted not just a ban on paper money, but an alternative system of finance centered in a powerful private bank—the kind of institution Pennsylvanians of all ranks and classes had united to oppose in 1769. As a result, ordinary Pennsylvanians framed the battle as one between a private system governed by and for the wealthy and a public one that spread the tools of economic independence far more equally among the population.

Most Pennsylvanians saw Morris's experiment in privatization—along with the rest of his program—as a disaster. People complained that the Morris plan led only to the "distress or ruin [of] many valuable citizens" and allowed "men of wealth" to buy "the farms of the poor, and to sweep away" years of hard labor "for a trifling price." Morris's policies drove away "Great numbers" of farmers who had fought against Britain and "assisted in procuring independence." They allowed bankers and "a few wealthy men" to become "sole lords of the soil" and replace land-owning yeomen with "tenants, who will be dependent upon their landlords and vote as they direct." Many people were convinced that "the boasted equality of Pennsylvania" was about to be replaced by "servile dependence" that "must eventually subvert the fundamental principles of a free government." Others said that Morris's policies were "weakening the state, and destroying that equality of property on which the safety of the republic rests."[10]

Many ordinary Pennsylvanians saw the Bank of North America at the root of the problem, saying it offered nothing to regular folk—especially compared to the old public land-bank system. In 1785, thousands of people from across Pennsylvania signed petitions saying that it was "impossible" for them to get loans at the Bank of North America. They also noted that the bank only loaned money to merchants for forty-five days and that most people in this rural society needed loans for a much longer period (remember that the colonial loan office had loaned money for up to sixteen years). They noted that even land-owning farmers who "could furnish the best security are distressed" because they could not "find men willing to lend" or were forced to turn to "gripping usurers, who extort enormous premiums, far beyond what the profits of trade can support." The end result, according to the petitioners, was a situation where those with a "debt to pay" were dragged through court in a process that "too often ends in bankruptcy."[11]

Most people also believed that the bank was illegal under the 1776 Pennsylvania constitution. Popular petitions during 1785 and 1786 declared the bank to be "founded on principles incompatible with the nature of our government, and fraught with evils of the most alarming kind." Petitioners said that the government had unlawfully given "a few private citizens" rights which they believed could only be entrusted to a democratically elected legislature. William Findley explained, "The government of Pennsylvania being a democracy, the bank is inconsistent with the bill of rights thereof, which says, that government is not instituted for the emolument of any man, family, or set of men." The legislature had "no right, no constitutional power" to grant the bank corporate status and thereby hand out "special privilege" to "favourites." It was illegal to "incorporate bodies for the sole purpose of gain" or hand out "privilege, profit, influence, or power" to "congregated wealth." The Revolution, he said, was about equality and uplifting ordinary folk, not about advancing the "principles of united avarice."[12]

More than this, people worried that the bank would eventually destroy democracy. Thousands of Pennsylvanians complained in their petitions that bankers (many of whom, like Morris, were also politicians) had begun "to acquire influence in our public councils, and an ascendancy in the government, subversive of the dearest rights of the people." They were worried that "a small number" of "monied men" and "perhaps a single stockholder" could eventually use the bank's growing economic might to begin "actually governing" the state as a shadow government. Others spoke of how it was "highly dangerous" and "Contrary to [the] spirit of a republican government" to have an "institution" that was "placed out of the reach of the legislature," noting that not even "the former government" had been willing to create a private "influence" so "powerful and alarming."[13]

It was not that these people thought bankers were somehow innately sinister; instead, they worried about what Findley called the "nature of the institution." As a profit-driven company, the bank operated under "natural principles" of doing whatever it took to make money. Findley said it was the "indispensable duty of the directors" to turn as much profit as possible for their shareholders and that meant trying to "engross all the wealth, power, and influence of the state" they could. The problem, as Findley framed it, was that, in a democracy, no one had the power to check the bank. "We are too unequal in wealth to render a perfect democracy suitable to our circumstances," he declared, "yet we are so equal in wealth, power, etc. that we have no counterpoise sufficient to check or control an institution of such vast influence and magnitude." "Like a snowball perpetually rolled," he declared, the bank "must continually increase its dimensions and influence." In the end, Findley predicted, "Democracy must fall before it."[14]

The belief that profit-driven corporations pose a grave threat to democracy led many people to declare that they all should be made illegal. Echoing the phrases in popular petitions, some state legislators said for-profit corporations were "totally destructive of that equality which ought to prevail in a republic." "The accumulation of enormous wealth in the hands of" a company with corporate status, they declared, "will necessarily produce a degree of influence and power which cannot be entrusted in the hands of any set of men whatsoever without endangering the public safety." Others spoke of the "dangerous tendencies" of for-profit corporations or talked about corporate power as "an engine of destruction" that enabled "a few men to take advantage of their wealth." Even one of the state's leading writers on economics argued that any institution chartered for "its own immediate profit [was] incompatible with the interest of the State." "So powerful and uncontroulable a combination of property in private hands," this economist declared, could only lead to "an undue exercise of influence" over economic and political life—just as private corporations like the Bank of England had an "injurious" hold over the British Parliament.[15]

This anticorporate belief was so strong that, during the postwar decades, few government actions prompted the kind of swift, widespread, and visceral public condemnation as did the attempts of state leaders to grant corporate status. Aside from the bank, the most notable outpouring of anticorporate sentiment was triggered by the attempts of some Philadelphia gentlemen to form a company to build canals and turnpikes. In response, farmers from across the state petitioned against giving "a few wealthy and powerful citizens" such "partial and dangerous privileges." "We observe, with great anxiety," they wrote, "wealthy incorporated companies taking possession of public and private property." Their concern was that corporate status made "a few men . . . sufficiently powerful by privileges and wealth, to purchase, or to destroy, the property and rights of their fellow citizens." "The inequality introduced by such establishments," they said in a blanket condemnation of all for-profit corporations, "must destroy the liberties of our country." Some people were so opposed to for-profit corporations that they said there should not be a single "incorporate[d] Company of Men in the Universe."[16]

Convinced that banks and other profit-driven corporations would under-mine equality and democracy, ordinary Pennsylvanians pushed instead for government to take a more active role in providing public services—like the land bank that had offered low-cost credit to the common folk. Indeed, peo-ple throughout the state had started calling for a new land bank as soon as Morris began privatizing finance in 1781. Petitioners challenged the attempt to eliminate paper money as a scheme that allowed "a few Individuals [to be] made rich by the losses of the whole Community!" Instead, they called for a new land bank that would loan money to anyone with sufficient collateral, not just those who were wealthy or had connections to a banker. This pub-lic system of credit, they said, worked for "the good and Benefit of the whole community" and was the only way to "save this State from inevitable ruin."[17]

In arguing for the return of a land bank, people dismissed claims made by men like Morris that government money was no longer credible—noting that Britain had said the exact same thing at the end of the French and Indian War. No doubt hoping to remind the elite that they had once balked at a ban on government currency, ordinary Pennsylvanians explained that, like before, the money problems were a wartime aberration. "Your petition-ers are persuaded, that with proper management, now that we are relieved from the burdens and calamities of war, public faith might be restored," went one version of a document signed by thousands of Pennsylvanians. "The State of Pennsylvania is now in a Situation entirely Different from any they have been in Since the beginning of the late National Contest." "We now stand upon entire new ground, so firm, that nothing but an unwarrantable timidity can occasion distrust." The trauma was over. Normal conditions had returned, and state-issued paper could once again resume its position as a secure medium of exchange. It was time to revive "the Ancient, Safe and Successful plan" of a land bank. As most people saw it, nothing could be more reasonable. Besides, compared to the mess of wartime paper—Pennsylvanians had dealt with seven different types of state money that all traded at different and constantly changing values, not to mention the numerous different issues of Continental currency—a new land bank with its single currency would be far easier to manage.[18]

The point, they said, was to create a new and stable financial system that spread benefits equally across society. Having suffered from the depreciation of wartime currencies, most people wanted new money that held its value. "We do not want any kind of paper imposed on the people," declared a York County farmer, "but such as will stand on its own foundation," like paper money backed by the "permanent foundation" of land. And despite the pain caused by privatization, people were clear that they were not looking for revenge on the creditors and bankers who had advocated it. As Westmoreland petitioners put it, they did not want to "injure the interest of any private individual or that of any particular Corporation, nor . . . obstruct the Extension of trade." They thought that allowing debtors to escape paying creditors with worthless money was unequal and wrong. Instead, people believed that the new system would "enable the citizens of this state to discharge their debts" honorably—but without resorting to "Sad and awful" sheriffs' auctions. In short, the goal was equity for everyone.[19]

"THE PLAN" for the War Debt

The same concern for equality shaped popular ideas for dealing with the Revolutionary War debt—solutions based on trying to balance the interests of everyone involved in the matter: taxpayers, the soldiers and farmers who had sold near-worthless IOUs, and even speculators. To be sure, a few people spoke about "throwing off the whole debt" and paying speculators nothing as punishment for their willingness to impoverish ordinary folk. Most popular plans, however, proposed "virtuous" solutions that considered everyone's needs, even those who had tried to profit at the public's expense. Speculators themselves might not have seen these efforts at balance as right or just. But, to ordinary Pennsylvanians, they were a genuine attempt to be fair and equal, despite widespread anger.[20]

Popular plans for the war debt were based on a belief that it was unjust to pay war debt speculators the full face value for IOUs they had purchased for pennies on the dollar. "Why then should we make crafty speculators, who have neither had the credit of their county, the welfare of their fellow citizens, nor even their own honor in view, the most wealthy men in the state," asked a writer from Franklin County, "on the ruins of those who have [displayed] real patriotism under the severest trials?" The central issue was one of equity: "For my part I am clearly of opinion, that no person who possesses the smallest degree of patriotism, or love for his country, ought to expect more than a reasonable compensation for the service he has rendered it." He insisted that it was "unjust and cruel" for the "trading people" who had purchased certificates at a fraction of their face value to demand "any more than they have paid for them, with a sufficient [payment of interest] for the use of their money." If the government paid war debt speculators the full face value of the certificates, "it will make a curious change in property; those to whom it should have been paid [soldiers and farmers], and who perhaps well deserved it, will be nothing richer; while those who have no claim (except that of having paid perhaps two shillings and six pence in the pound) will receive all the benefits." Indeed, this writer insisted that "if the certificates I refer to are made equal to specie," then war debt speculators will "have acquired fortunes with an unheard of degree of rapidity" funded by taxes on the very people who had sold the certificates for a pittance. In his opinion, this would be "countenancing a scene of villainy which every honest man must abhor." "Our people," agreed a York County farmer, "will never consent to pay such an enormous perpetual tax, purely to enrich a few men who have bought up the certificates for a mere song." It would have been better for soldiers, farmers, and artisans "if they had never received any public acknowledgments at all for their services" and had marched against the British or offered up their wagons and grain to the army for free.[21]

Popular ideas for bringing equality to the war debt were best summarized by a set of policies that people simply called "the Plan." Developed from public debate in Cumberland and Franklin counties, the Plan brought together popular ideas raised in petitions about the war IOUs that dated as far back as 1780. With its publication in 1786, the Plan became a rallying point, inspiring people across the state to adopt its ideas.[22]

The basic idea of the Plan was redressing what people saw as two separate and unequal systems for dealing with the war debt: one for ordinary folk and another for wealthy speculators. People argued that when most of the IOUs had been in the hands of ordinary folk, the government had treated them as worthless scraps of paper and would not even accept them for payment of taxes. This was true: throughout the war and postwar years, people by the thousands had petitioned the government to allow them to use the IOUs to pay taxes, make mortgage payments to the old land bank, or deed new lands. All of those petitions had been rejected. As a result, most people had sold their IOUs for pennies on the dollar because they needed money.

Now that wealthy speculators had acquired the bulk of the IOUs, however, the state had developed a second system and had begun treating them as valuable commodities worth their full face value.[23]

The Plan proposed to rectify this unequal treatment and put everyone on the same footing by changing the official value of the IOUs to reflect the prices paid by speculators. The Plan's authors proposed calling in all of the old war debt certificates and issuing new ones bearing values that reflected the actual market prices for the IOUs—thereby acknowledging that they had never been worth the values printed on their faces. Rather than getting $100 for an IOU with $100 printed on its face, a speculator would be issued a new certificate closer in value to the $7–15 he had actually paid.

In fact, under the Plan, most speculators would actually get far more than they had paid. Out of concern that everyone be treated fairly, the Plan proposed setting the value of the new certificates at the highest price that the IOUs had reached in the Philadelphia market (which was about one-fourth of the face value). Even at this rate, most speculators still stood to make a tidy profit (they would receive about $25 for "$100" IOUs that probably cost them $7–15). However, they would not reap a phenomenal windfall. As Plan supporters put it, "The speculators have been actuated by the same motives which a man is who purchases a parcel of lottery tickets; if they draw prizes, he increases his fortune; if not he looses but little." And in this lottery, there would be no losers. The entire process would be accomplished "without injuring the property of any person." The Plan would provide "immense" advantages to the state by reducing the war debt and yet leave speculators with "no room . . . to complain of injustice." It was, according to the Plan's supporters, the best solution for rectifying past injustices and putting everyone back on equal ground.[24]

Supporters claimed that by revaluing the IOUs in this way, the Plan also ensured that the government treated all wartime paper equally by taking into account depreciation as it had done with every other slip of paper issued during the war. During the war, when currency or certificates had depreciated, the government had frequently called in the old paper and issued new papers that reflected market realities. "It has been the practice of the legislature at different periods since the revolution," the Plan's authors observed, "to establish the depreciation of our paper currency by law." The revaluation had often been extreme, sometimes knocking down the value of government paper by a rate of 150 to 1 or greater. The Plan's supporters said they were merely continuing this process. They asked: if it was proper to drop down to market value every other slip of paper the government had issued, "Why not establish the depreciation" of the last bits of paper? "I cannot imagine," wrote the Plan's authors, "that it would be either difficult or dishonest to establish a scale which would . . . put all public creditors upon the same ground." This was the hallmark of the Plan: consistency and equality.[25]

For taxpayers—many of whom had once held those IOUs—equality would come through a slashed tax burden for what would now be a much smaller war debt. The Plan promised to cut the war debt by more than half. The math was simple. The Plan's authors estimated that three-quarters of the war debt certificates in Pennsylvania were in the hands of "trading people" (a conservative estimate). The market for these certificates had topped out at about one-fourth of face value. Using those estimates, Pennsylvania's share of the war debt would drop from $4.5 million to approximately $1.9 million, cutting it by about 58 percent.

Moreover, under the Plan, taxpayers would only ever have to pay the interest on that $1.9 million: they would not have to pay a penny in taxes to retire the principal. Instead, supporters believed that the entire war debt could be retired—in just two years—by allowing people to use war debt certificates to pay any government tax, expense, or fee. No public transaction would be excluded. People could use the IOUs to pay back taxes, new taxes, state mortgages, or the cost of purchasing and patenting new land. (The Plan's authors said that Pennsylvania should handle the state-issued IOUs in the same way.) Thus, the objective was to retire the entire war debt—both state and national—purely by allowing people to use the certificates as cash for government transactions.

In the process, supporters said that the Plan would help to end the cash scarcity. It would cause millions of dollars in IOUs to flow through Pennsylvania and "become part of the circulating medium." This new "money" would ease the scarcity and allow people to get out from under the crushing weight of debt. They could keep their farms and businesses solvent, pay off mortgages, and even survey and purchase new lands.

For the Plan to work in this way—and especially for it to cut the tax burden—using the IOUs for government transactions had to be the only way for people to redeem them. No one would ever be able to walk into a government office and ask to be paid the principal of a war debt certificate in hard cash. Instead, all of the IOUs would be retired by people paying taxes, land-bank mortgages, land fees, etc.—and by that method alone. The Plan's supporters believed that this requirement would still be fair to certificate holders because public demand from people desperate to pay taxes and mortgages would ensure "the certificates would and in every respect" be "as valuable" as gold and silver.

In all of these ways, people thought the Plan would return the Revolution to the path of equality and justice. As supporters put it, the Plan rectified "the grievous and unequal burthens which have been imposed upon the citizens of this state" under the Morris plan. It provided some degree of promise that "our property may be protected and not wrested from us to answer improper purposes"—like paying taxes to benefit war debt speculators. It helped to ensure that "we who have born[e] the burthen in the heat of the day" and sacrificed for the nation's independence "may have some little property to assist us in the declivity of life." And most important, it left a legacy for the next generation: the Plan would keep the revolutionary generation from experiencing "the scorn of posterity in wondering what kind of clay their fathers were made of, to loose the benefits of a revolution purchased at the expence of so much treasure and blood." In all of these ways, the Plan was an attempt by ordinary Pennsylvanians to preserve the democratic inheritance of the American Revolution.[26]

It was an objective that enjoyed wide support. Within weeks of the Plan's publication in January 1786, ordinary Pennsylvanians flooded the state assembly with petitions calling for politicians to enact its primary reforms. The first petitions were printed on February 7 in the *Carlisle Gazette*, a newspaper that primarily served Cumberland and Franklin counties. Two weeks later, petitions began arriving from Cumberland denouncing the "inadequate . . . circulating medium" and insisting on the right to use certificates for taxes and other public fees. Days later, petitions signed by 494 people arrived from Northampton County; Westmoreland County sent petitions bearing 437 signatures. The following day, Berks County farmers sent in a stack of petitions with 1,610 signatures—a figure representing more than one-third of the county's households. In the following weeks, petitions arrived from the eastern counties of Lancaster and Chester, as well as another round from Cumberland. This was popular democracy at work. People were organizing themselves and expressing their views in ways that, if successful, could become ongoing routines of life in democratic America.[27]

Equal Rights for Debtors

For some people, promoting equality meant extending the idea of revaluing the war debt to all private debts. The idea was to restore some fairness for debtors who had been caught in a vise of wartime inflation and postwar deflation. Many people had gone into debt during the war when inflation was rampant, paying high prices for the goods they received on credit. During the postwar years, they were trying to pay back creditors at a time when money was desperately scarce. In effect, debtors lost on both ends. The popular remedy to this was to balance the burdens more equally between debtors and creditors by having the value of debts settled by arbiters rather than market forces.

The clearest push for a system of debt arbitration could be seen in York, Lancaster, and Cumberland counties. In these counties, people complained that, during the war, "Great numbers of the good people of this common-wealth" had "contracted debts and entered into contracts which they then conceived themselves fully able to pay." Due to the "almost total annihilation of private credit, the pressure of taxes, and the extreme scarcity of circulating specie" produced by the Morris plan, they were "now involved in difficulties and embarrassments, which no human foresight could have prevented and from which no industry or means within their own power can extricate them." By going into debt when prices were high and trying to pay out when they were low, the unfortunate debtor now faced a "merciless, rapacious cred-itor" determined "to sacrifice the property of his debtor by a public sale." As a result, ordinary folk across the state were "Robbed of their Property under Sanction of Law" and "reduced from a state of competency to beggary and [their] famil[ies] hurled into the depths of misery."

The popular solution was to let a jury of local men decide what a fair value for a debt should be. Petitions from these counties called for anywhere between three and twelve men to appraise a debtor's goods to reflect wartime inflation and the postwar cash scarcity. For example, if a debtor had borrowed money from his creditor when a horse sold for $40, then the jury would appraise the horse as worth $40 today—even if the actual market value for the horse had fallen to $20 or less. Under the proposed system, the creditor could either accept the goods at the appraised value, or he could wait and try a new apprais-al in the future. Petitioners argued that, in this way, creditors and debtors could reach a fair settlement that would keep both parties from being exploited.[28]

Equal Taxation

Popular notions of fairness were also at the heart of ideas about overhauling the tax system. As during the 1760s and 1770s, the complaint was about heavy and regressive taxes, and the solution centered on reducing the tax load and rewriting the tax code so that the wealthy paid more than everyone else. The push for equal taxation during the 1780s, however, was led by ordinary folk who wanted to make the system far more progressive.

Of course, given the heavy tax burden (and the fact that much of the money was going to war debt speculators), most people called for a reduction in taxes. In the words of York County farmers, due to the "grievous and insupportable load of taxes," they were "Struggling" to keep the "Independence" they had sacrificed their "Blood and Treasure to Secure." Other farmers were especially angry that the system tended to tax productive property, such as land under cultivation and livestock. "We are taxed for being employed in the cultivation of our fields," they petitioned state leaders. "Our farms, poor and exhausted, in many instances pay taxes to the amount of one half of their produce. Our cattle, and even horses absolutely necessary for tillage, pay taxes equally oppressive and impolitic." "This is by no means an exaggerated account," they said, "the frequent scenes of our property being exposed to sale may convince you that it is not." These farmers urged state leaders to follow "the spirit of the constitution" of 1776 and eliminate this regressive tax system. By doing so, they would "not only relieve the oppressed farmer, but you will give every encouragement to Agriculture, on which the prosperity and even the existence of your country, as an independent estate, must depend."[29]

To replace these taxes, many Pennsylvanians demanded that any new tax target what they called the "unproductive" wealth of the affluent. During the war, petitioners in several counties wanted to tax the money held by currency speculators. In the postwar years, many people demanded taxes on what they called the "two evils": war debt speculation and the "greedy" moneylenders at the Bank of North America. Numerous people proposed taxing the income from war debt certificates. Thousand of Pennsylvanians petitioned for taxes on bank stock, saying that "whilst their lands and occupations are highly taxd for public uses, the stockholders in the bank are enabled to exempt their enormous and accumulating property from any taxation whatsoever."[30]

The clearest carryover from the 1760s and 1770s was for taxes on "unoccupied lands"—the large speculative holdings usually held by the affluent. Part of the complaint was that, although the revolutionary government had enacted taxes on speculative lands, it had stopped trying to collect. In 1786, state leaders passed a law forbidding county officials from suing anyone who had not paid taxes on unoccupied lands; they renewed the ban every time it was set to expire. In 1788, one state legislator observed that giving such an obvious tax break to wealthy speculators seemed hypocritical at a time when the assembly was making it easier to foreclose ordinary farmers for unpaid taxes. He noted that, on one day, the legislature gave a break to speculators, and then, on the very next day, it cracked down on farmers who could not pay. To him, the double standard seemed obvious. "Shall the honest industrious hard working husbandman," he said, "receive less indulgence from the legislature than the gentlemen of *Philadelphia*, who hold large tracts of land unoccupied, and unproductive?" His colleagues were unmoved by the observation and voted to pressure collectors to speed foreclosures anyway.[31]

Aside from getting the state to enforce the collection of taxes on speculative lands, many people wanted to see the amounts increased on those they called "land jobbers." Many people undoubtedly saw such taxes as a way to free up land for ownership by small farmers by inducing speculators to sell to avoid paying the new tax. The idea became so popular that, by the 1790s, farmers made a new "land tax" part of their main platform, even emblazoning the slogan on signs and banners they carried during their protests.[32]

Land for Independence

The push for taxing unoccupied lands was part of a larger effort to assist those who worked the land for a living. Most ordinary folk believed that the current land system favored wealthy speculators, and they wanted to overhaul it to give more power to small farmers and tenants. By rectifying that imbalance, land reformers believed that they could promote democracy through widespread ownership.

Most of the struggle over land policy played out along the northern and western frontiers, where cash-poor settlers had carved out farmsteads but were finding it difficult to gain legal title. To own the land legally, farmers needed to have it surveyed and then make a journey of several days or weeks to the land office in Philadelphia to register the deed. In 1784, nearly 300 Westmoreland County farmers complained that "traveling to Philadelphia" entailed "enormous expenses" and that many people "cannot command money to pay such Expenses." They said the journey was a financial impossibility for "poor inhabitants" who could not get money "on acct. of the Scarcity of Cash." By contrast, speculators—many of whom tended to be Philadelphia gentlemen—had only to travel across town to fill out the paperwork. When farmers could not pay in time, these same "Land Jobbers" would then "buy the Lands" of "the real Owner" when they were "put to publick Sale for the Expences of Deeding."[33]

Other frontier farmers reported that their distance from the land office (and the easy access for Philadelphia gentlemen) allowed speculators to claim land out from under the people who were farming it. Frontiersmen denounced the "Evil disposed Persons" and "certain Scheming Men amongst us, who Steal thro the woods in the greatest privacy with the Surveyor at their back." Farmers claimed that these men used "fraudulent Schemes to take away our Lands" by entering the land in the Philadelphia office and then hitting settlers with "tedious litigation" to evict them, knowing that most rural folk did not have enough money to compete in the court system. Summing up their outrage, farmers in Washington County said they had "seen Scenes of cruelty exacted by the Savages; they have often been driven from their habitations; and often returned to those dreary homes." "But they never could have supposed that any Christian were capable" of something so oppressive as "an attempt to take away those Lands they have suffered so much for and have so nobly defended." In an echo of the accusations that Black Boy Jimmy Smith had once hurled at the British, frontiersmen said the speculators "treat us with more cruelty than the Indians were capable of, and have the affrontery to Stamp on their Proceedings the Sanction of the Law"— a gross violation of ideals "held Sacred by every free Citizen of the Commonwealth."[34]

To remedy this inequality, many farmers called for the state to open a land office in every county. Farmers saw local land offices as essential to ensuring that a farm's "real owner" gain title instead of wealthy gentlemen who were "busy in the Commercial Business." As one of the "inhabitants on [the west] side of the Allegheny mountain" put it in 1787, only a new system could preserve for ordinary farmers their "birth right of the richest tract of land in this continent." Only such a system could protect "the spirit of the late revolution from which every individual was to partake equally in the blessing of independence without any one being benefited at the expense of another."[35]

In the name of equality, farmers also demanded more time to pay for the lands they settled and a temporary reprieve from making mortgage payments to the old land bank. A group of western farmers said they wanted the state to "enable us to hold our small possessions by giving us time to pay." In effect, they asked for nothing different than what gentlemen in Philadelphia had long enjoyed. Those with connections to the land office did not have to pay within the timeframe mandated by law— or even pay the full amount. Farmers were merely asking for similar lenience.

To protect landless farmers against speculators, many Pennsylvanians wanted the state to adopt a new legal standard of ownership that gave preference to those who actually farmed the land. Under this new standard, cleared fields, farm buildings, and other "improvements" carried greater weight in evidence of ownership than a speculator's paper "Title" or a "Private Survey." As farmers in Northumberland County put it, they wanted the state to "give the Preference To those whose Lives have been Spent in Endeavouring To Procure an honest Livlihood on Lands"; "those only who have been Tillers of the ground & Livers on the Land" had a real "Right" to it. Under this standard, squatters too poor to pay for the lands they farmed had a greater claim to ownership than those who paid in cash. The idea was taken a step further by some tenant farmers in Bucks County (where the landless made up the majority of the population). These tenants wanted the state to give them the "Right of Purchasing from the Owners upon easy Terms the Lands that have been thus cleared improved and cultivated by their Labor and Industry." These were revolutionary claims: work meant more than money and paper titles in deciding who owned property.[36]

Equally revolutionary, many farmers called for the state to limit the amount of land that speculators could own. These people complained about "the evil Tendency of Engrossing Lands," due to which "many thousands of acres now lies uncultivated." Northumberland farmers said that the problem was wealthy men who bought up "large quantities" of land, which they wanted to turn into "Mannors" farmed by tenants, something these people saw as "not only Injurious to the poor, But also injurious to the Settling of Our New Country." To prevent speculation, farmers across Pennsylvania pushed for laws prohibiting the state from selling more than 400 acres of new frontier lands to any single individual or company. They also lobbied for laws requiring the purchasers to prove that they had actually settled the land themselves before they could patent it. To ensure that speculators did not get around the law by simply setting up a shack and planting some hay for a season, farmers demanded that settlers clear trees, build a house, put up fences, and cultivate at least two acres of land for every hundred acres—and occupy the land for the next five years—before it officially became theirs.[37]

In all of these ways, rural Pennsylvanians laid out a clear agenda for keeping land in the hands of small farmers and attempting to ensure that new lands remained open for future generations. Farmers attempted to turn taxation from something that burdened those who worked with their hands for a living into a tool for breaking up concentrated wealth. And through land policy reform, they sought to make it harder for gentlemen speculators to buy up the backcountry by making it easier for the "tillers of the soil"—and even the poorest squatters—to become independent yeomen farmers.

* * *

Taken together, the various calls for reform represented a renewed commitment to promoting equality and bolstering the power of ordinary folk. This slate of reforms—from the creation of a new land bank, to the Plan to revalue the war debt, to the overhaul of tax and land policy, to calls for a ban on for-profit corporations and land speculation—were all designed to reclaim a popular vision of the Revolution. Each program sought to protect democracy by promoting the wealth equality that many people believed was needed to defend their political rights. And each popular proposal attempted to extend those freedoms for future generations.

Pennsylvanians were far from alone in embracing such ideals. Throughout the new nation, ordinary Americans expressed similar notions of what they thought the Revolution was supposed to be about. They too conveyed their beliefs that the founding elite in their states was undermining the independence of the common people. The issues and circumstances were slightly different in each state, but the overall portrait was of ordinary folk outraged at what they saw as an attempt to concentrate wealth and stifle democracy. To counter the trend, people across America organized on behalf of their ideals and managed to get politicians to enact many reforms. In Rhode Island, popular forces swept elections, took control of the assembly, and put through an entire reform agenda.[38]

Could ordinary Pennsylvanians do the same? Could people of the middling and lower sorts also turn their shared idealism into collective action and make their reform agenda a political reality? The answer was complicated.

6

The Problem with Politics

WHY REFORM FELL SHORT

Why sleep our rulers?—Have we not appointed them to watch over our rights and our liberties and our interests, and are they not suffering us into bondage? Have we not expended our blood and our treasure to expel from the land a set of invaders who sought to rule over us as taskmasters, and shall we now become bondsmen to people of our own country?

—*Carlisle Gazette*, March 21, 1787

It was one thing to lay out an agenda for reform; it was quite another to make meaningful change happen. Reform-minded Pennsylvanians would soon discover that there was a big difference between dreaming up ideas like the Plan and getting politicians to enact them into law. Along the way, they discovered a gulf between "the people" as an abstraction and a majority mobilized to take power. In short, they found out that, even in a democracy, just because the majority of the public shared common ideals did not mean those beliefs would become the law of the land.

It also became clear that organizing "the people" was extremely difficult. Ordinary Pennsylvanians were divided across many lines: geography, language, religion and ethnicity, wartime loyalties, and a host of internal conflicts, which made it hard to bring them together politically—even for reforms that enjoyed widespread support. Reformers also faced a gentry-dominated political system where few of the elite candidates shared the reformers' values and policy positions.

Despite these obstacles, ordinary folk achieved some impressive victories during the 1780s. In several counties, regular folk managed to organize them-selves to take control of local politics: sometimes electing commoners to office, other times convincing the gentry to support their ideals. In 1784, the model spread, leading to a slate of reform candidates who captured a commanding majority in the state assembly. And, once in office, these new politicians enacted numerous popular reforms.

Real victory, however, proved to be elusive: many of those new politicians turned out not to be the reformers they had purported to be.

The People Divided

Of all the challenges reformers faced, perhaps the biggest was finding a way to make "the people" an organized reality. Pennsylvanians calling for reform leaned heavily on the concept of "the people." In petitions, they wrote about "the people" being oppressed by the "moneyed men" and spoke of bringing equal power to "the people." Given how often ordinary folk used the term, there can be no doubt that, at some level, those words had genuine meaning. The frequent use of the term, however, masked divisions among the people that made it difficult to organize for reform. Those divisions existed in neighborhoods, between townships, and across counties. They were often as deep as they were numerous, pitting farmer against farmer in confrontations that gave little hint that these people shared common ground. Although not insurmountable, the divides created serious problems for those hoping to gain the political power needed to stop the Morris plan and enact popular reforms.

Among the most imposing obstacles was geography. Pennsylvania covers a vast territory—about 280 miles east–west and 160 miles north–south—of often challenging terrain. During the 1780s, the main settlements ran along the southern tier of the state in what is now the I-76 corridor from Philadelphia, through Harrisburg, to Pittsburgh (an area of roughly 23,000 square miles). The eastern stretch of this route rolls through undulating hills filled with farms carved out of often-steep slopes. The foothills of the Appalachians begin in the center of the state and ascend as one heads west. Much of the land on the western side of the mountains is gouged by ravines that crisscross the landscape. Traveling this route is challenging enough on modern highways. Imagine the difficulties faced by farmers riding wood-wheeled wagons at a time when the "good roads" were bad and the "bad roads" were little more than glorified animal paths. Add snow, ice, mud, seasonal flooding, or trees downed by storms, and travel became all but impossible. In sum, little about the landscape encouraged popular mobilization.

Nor did the diversity of Pennsylvania's population. Those pushing for reform had to confront the legacy of William Penn's religious tolerance: a population scattered in ethnic and religious sects of Anglicans, Quakers, Baptists, and Scots-Irish Presbyterians as well as settlements built around Lutheran, Reformed, Mennonite, Moravian, Amish, and Dunker churches. Although these Protestant sects were not necessarily hostile toward one another, most were determined to retain cultural autonomy and some degree of isolation. This was especially true of German immigrants, most of whom continued to speak their native language and refused to learn English. Indeed, the language barrier would become one of the greatest impediments to popular organizing. The gap was not insurmountable; there were many examples of German and non-German unity. Nonetheless, the largely German-speaking counties of the east were in many ways clearly separate from the English-speaking central and western counties.

A more daunting problem was that the vote remained split along political fault lines that had opened during the war. Generally speaking, wartime loyalties shaped postwar political allegiances. Those who had supported independence and the revolutionary government (mostly Scots-Irish Presbyterians, Anglicans, and Germans, both Lutheran and Reformed) tended to vote for a political faction called the Constitutionalists, named for their support for the 1776 state charter. Those who opposed independence, the war, or the new government (a group that included most Quakers) generally voted for the Republicans—the party of Morris.[1]

Bitter wartime memories kept these political allegiances strong in the postwar decades. Quakers, Mennonites, and Moravians remembered the persecution they had faced at the hands of patriot neighbors and the Constitutionalist-controlled government. War supporters recalled that pacifists, in their opinion, had not done enough to secure American independence and had sometimes given comfort to the enemy. Even if farmers in both groups shared a dislike for the gospel of moneyed men, the cold stares these neighbors gave one another made it difficult for them to work together.[2]

The postwar years also saw new fault lines open over various issues, some seemingly as mundane as county boundaries or the location of a new courthouse. For example, blood was nearly shed in Chester County in 1785 when a state law moved the county courthouse from the town of Chester to a more central location. As soon as construction began, a militia major from Chester assembled a small army, raided the town armory, and confiscated guns and a cannon. He marched his men to the construction site intent on razing the walls of the new courthouse. Hearing of the army's approach, farmers living near the new courthouse raced with muskets in hand to protect the unfinished building. Nervous moments passed as the town square filled with anxious men facing off with hands on triggers. Thankfully, cooler heads prevailed, and the two sides dispersed without shots being fired. Nevertheless, this confrontation gives a sense of the challenges facing anyone trying to bring "the people" together.[3]

Other postwar divides pre-dated the war, most notably the conflict between settlers in Pennsylvania's Wyoming Valley, who battled over land claims. During the eighteenth century, the colonies of Pennsylvania and Connecticut had both claimed this territory in the north-central part of what is now the state of Pennsylvania. In turn, each colony had sold the land to its own speculation companies that, in turn, had sold it to settlers. Thus, a struggle between colonies turned into a fight (and even an actual war) between rival speculators and settlers. The so-called Pennamite War, which began in 1769, merged with the revolutionary conflict and spilled over into the postwar decade.[4]

In other cases, the divide wasn't old land claims but new immigrants who lacked a tangible connection to the Revolution. The postwar decade saw a steady stream of Europeans arriving in Philadelphia, and they soon headed into the countryside. Most passed through Pennsylvania on their way farther south or west. Thousands, however, settled in the Pennsylvania backcountry, sometimes blending into established communities, other times building their own new settlements. It's hard to say exactly how the new immigrants shaped postwar politics or if they participated at all. But it's clear that their arrival added yet another layer of diversity to "the people."[5]

Another set of travelers posed similar obstacles: the great number of Pennsylvanians who never settled into any one community. The state had a cohort of folks—usually poorer people—who tended to move in and out of counties in search of work or the chance to own land. These cottagers, tenant farmers, and farm laborers moved with the seasons. And their numbers were growing, augmented by the cash scarcity and the sale of land at sheriffs' auctions. As fewer farmers could pass down their property, their sons and daughters also joined the stream of drifters. Few of these people probably registered to vote. Most did not stay anywhere long enough to become part of a reform movement—even though many of them bore the heaviest grudges against the Morris plan.[6]

An urban-rural split also divided "the people." Although the lower sort of artisans, laborers, and sailors in Philadelphia shared much in common with ordinary farmers, the two increasingly lived in different worlds. It had not always been this way. During the 1760s and 1770s, the lower sort in Philadelphia had joined together with backcountry farmers to overthrow British and

Quaker rule and to design the 1776 state constitution. The war had shattered that unity. Part of the problem was that most city artisans and laborers had retreated from politics after the so-called Fort Wilson riot of 1779, when a militia of the lower sort was defeated by the gentry cavalry. This defeat effectively destroyed the political organizations of the urban lower sort and badly split the city vote. Indeed, when artisans, sailors, and laborers voted at all, they increasingly cast ballots for Republicans like Robert Morris, who promised to revive the badly slumping seaport and protect American manufacturing from foreign competition. Support for the party of Morris did not mean urban workers had abandoned their faith in democracy or shared his entire agenda (they would famously turn on Republicans during the 1790s, citing their aristocratic policies). Rather, such support was indicative of the division and desperation among working folk in the city.[7]

Gentry Politics

Reform efforts also faced a gentry-dominated political system where most of those who ran for office—especially in the eastern counties—opposed both democracy and popular ideas for change. Given the familiar problems of resources and connections, farmers were at a disadvantage in any attempt to oppose the gentry. And when ordinary folk challenged the system, they often found gentlemen willing to do whatever it took to retain their political power.

If the Revolution had changed much about the political landscape, it had not overturned gentry rule. County leadership remained primarily in the hands of local elites. There may have been a new set of political leaders in office; they may have been less wealthy than their predecessors; and they now represented a more ethnically and religiously diverse group than before the Revolution. But, on the whole, the men in office still tended to be lawyers, merchants, storekeepers, and gentlemen farmers.[8]

There were many practical reasons that political leaders tended to come from the local gentry. No doubt, the most important was resources. Although there were no property-holding requirements for the general assembly, wealth still mattered a great deal in determining who served. Given the meager finances of most people, it was simply not practical for them to hold office. Farmers struggling to get out from under a load of unpaid debts and taxes could not afford to leave the plow to spend months in Philadelphia debating laws. The salaries paid to assemblymen may have covered travel and room and board in Philadelphia. But the pay was not enough to get one's farm out of hock or to compensate for lost labor in the fields.

The fact that state assemblymen were chosen by an entire county (rather than, say, a group of townships) gave the gentry another advantage. As minister-farmer Herman Husband put it, a "County is too large a Bound" for ordinary people to win office. There were only "a few Men in a County who are generally known throughout the whole of it," meaning they were likely to get elected. According to Husband, these people were "generally the most unsuitable, they being chiefly Tavern-keepers, Merchants, &c. in the County Towns, with the Officers, Lawyers, &c."[9]

The gentry also continued to control the flow of information. Communications were built on the gentry-led committees of correspondence that had made the movement against Britain something more than isolated pockets of discontent (even if those pockets were seemingly everywhere). At the time, few farmers had appeared overly concerned about this control because these gentlemen had, more or less, supported popular policies. Indeed, given their lack of resources, most farmers had willingly ceded the task to local gentlemen. Recall, for example, the uncomfortable meeting in 1775 in York County, where farmers who had already formed militia companies pressured the local gentry to take a more aggressive stand against Britain. Perhaps these farmers did not entirely trust the gentlemen of York. But they deferred to the gentry—however symbolic that deference was—in order to connect their efforts to the wider resistance movement.

With the rise of the Morris plan, ordinary folk began to see the pitfalls of gentry control. When many of those gentlemen changed their minds about reform (or when new leaders took over), the communication networks transformed from tools to build up the vision of '76 into weapons aimed at cutting it down. Ordinary folk were suddenly cut off from one another, especially in rural areas. No doubt, many people were overwhelmed at the thought of replacing those connections. Whom should they contact? Should they reach out to other townships or counties? Who had the time and the money to undertake such a venture? Intimidating questions like these probably kept most farmers from even considering the idea of challenging the current political leadership.

At the same time, lack of a formal education likely dissuaded many farmers from considering a run at the state assembly. All one had to do to feel insecure about serving was to read a few laws the assembly passed, composed as they were of complicated legalese that read like another language to those educated for a life in the fields. The word-for-word reports of assembly debates printed in the newspapers must have been equally intimidating. Page after page was filled with verbal dueling by learned gentlemen trying to skewer one another with multisyllable words, references to classical history, and quotes in Latin. Debate in the general assembly sent a clear message that unless you knew something of Greek history, the works of Cicero, and the writings of Hume, Locke, and Adam Smith, you had best stay at home. Those debates also revealed the assembly as a minefield of parliamentary procedure, where novices could get ripped apart unless they understood how to manipulate the rules of order.

Challenging the local elite was not simply a matter of education or self-confidence, however; it was also potentially dangerous. After all, local leaders were among the wealthiest and most powerful men in the county. They often oversaw broad networks of patronage and credit. In this cash-scarce economy, openly defying men who could call in outstanding loans or refuse credit could prove to be financially perilous. The gentlemen did not have to make threats (that, after all, would be ungentlemanly). Instead, they relied on unspoken political and financial realities, which everyone understood.

When farmers mustered the courage to challenge such men, they often found that the local gentry would go to great lengths to maintain their positions. This lesson was learned the hard way by farmers from the mountain county of Bedford when, in 1783, they tried to oust a state assemblyman named George Woods whose tenure in office extended back to the years of British rule. The farmers had intended the 1783 election to be a popular referendum on Woods's support for Morris's policies. In campaign literature posted at meeting places throughout the county, insurgent farmers said that Woods was "no friend of the county," declaring that, due to his votes in the assembly, "Our county is almost ruined with . . . lawsuits and extravagant fees." They claimed that, if left to their own devices, Woods and his allies would do away with the democratic state charter. "If they are so elected," the letter warned, "we may readily conclude that the constitution will be altered and laws made to suit themselves." The farmers argued that the only solution was an alternative ticket: "Let us have a set of Farmers to serve us this year and no doubt but we shall be honestly represented."[10]

As tame as this letter was by modern political standards, in 1783, these few passages were all the evidence required to convict the authors of libel. The fines assessed by the county magistrate, although seemingly small, were large enough to silence the opposition. Without the financial resources to endure a lengthy court battle over the right of free speech, Woods's challengers backed off, and the electoral insurgency melted away. When Election Day arrived that fall, few voters went to the polls. Those who did returned Woods to his seat in the general assembly, where he continued to vote against policies supported by most of his constituents.[11]

Woods was not alone in using such tactics: county elections were rife with charges of fraud and intimidation. Evidently, some gentlemen brought in illegal voters from outside the county; they opened polling places late (or not at all) and closed them early, turning away farmers who technically had arrived on time. There were charges of ballot-box stuffing and stolen elections. All of this seemed to be relatively frequent: during a four-year period from July 1786 to July 1790, rural Pennsylvanians registered official complaints of election "irregularities" on forty-five separate occasions.[12]

Organizing Victory: 1784

Despite all of the obstacles, ordinary Pennsylvanians managed to pull off a stunning feat in 1784: they convinced politicians to adopt their agenda and elected a slate of candidates who promised to enact their reforms. When the new leaders started passing popular policies, many people began to believe that democracy had won after all.

The reform effort was led by several counties where ordinary people organized to take control of the county political system. What set these self-organized counties apart was not their geography: they could be found throughout the state, typified by Westmoreland in the west, Cumberland in central Pennsylvania, and Berks in the east. Nor was ethnicity the determining factor: Westmoreland was mostly English speaking; Cumberland was divided between Scots-Irish and Germans; Berks was perhaps 80 percent German.[13]

The clearest common denominator was that each of these counties had developed strong popular organizations during the 1760s and 1770s that served as training grounds for political mobilization. The struggle against the proprietors and the Crown had taught farmers in these counties the value of organization, showing them the power they could wield when they came together. As a result, these counties had been among the earliest advocates of independence and turned out a remarkable level of military support once the war started. They also proved to be far more united in favor of the new government. This is not to say the counties lacked dissent; far from it. But here the opposition to independence, the war, and the new government came in pockets that were far smaller than in counties like Chester and Bucks, which divided sharply over these issues.

Those early experiments paved the way for postwar organizing in these counties. Consider the case of Cumberland County, birthplace of the Plan and the county that consistently turned out the greatest number of voters on Election Days. Popular organization here could be traced at least as far back as the 1760s mobilizations of the Paxton Boys, who had slaughtered peaceful Indians, and the Brave Fellows, who had skirmished with royal soldiers. That organization continued through the 1770s and the war years and into the postwar decades. Popular mobilization created its own leaders: men like Black Boy Jimmy Smith and Robert Whitehill, a forty-year-old farmer who joined Smith in helping to draft the 1776 constitution. The leaders were not necessarily commoners: Whitehill, who would represent the county at the state and national level for the next thirty years, went by the gentleman's title "esquire," owned a slave, and built one of the first stone houses in the county (a true sign of gentility at the time). But with "the people" organized, county politicians remained responsive to the popular will. For example, in 1779, Whitehill led the effort that stopped Republicans from overturning the state constitution; later, he opposed every measure of the Morris plan—sometimes standing in dissent with only a few other representatives. Whitehill remained an advocate for tax relief, a new public land bank, a ban on for-profit corporations, and a revaluation of the war debt. In short, he was a product of popular organizing in Cumberland County and—no doubt, because that organization endured—he remained true to its goals.

The problem was that such organization generally stopped at the county border (which was the primary political unit in state politics). People in Cumberland, Berks, and Westmoreland may have been well organized, but they had not yet discovered a way to spread that organization to other counties or to the city. In fact, they seemed not even to have tried recruiting others or creating some kind of statewide political movement (apart from the Constitutionalist Party, which became the vehicle for reform efforts). That shortcoming ultimately proved decisive.

Despite the lack of overarching organization, the reform effort nonetheless spread in 1784, driven by widespread popular discontent with the Morris plan and a shared conviction about the kind of policies that people wanted to replace it. In nearly every county, new politicians emerged, saying they backed popular reforms; and many established leaders, who had opposed reforms in the past, seemed to change their beliefs overnight. Banding together behind the Constitutionalist Party, these men plucked phrases and ideas directly from popular petitions. They denounced Morris's bank and promised to revoke its corporate charter. They promised to bring back government paper money and the public land bank. And they spoke about reducing the costs of the war debt and ending the practice of taxing the public in gold and silver. In short, Constitutionalist leaders seemed to have adopted nearly the entire popular platform.

In the 1784 elections, the self-proclaimed reformers swept to victory, transforming the statehouse. Before the election, Morris's Republican Party controlled the assembly with 38 seats to 29 for the Constitutionalists. After the election, the Republicans held just 19 seats and the Constitutionalists had 57—three times as many as their opponents. It seemed like the advocates of the vision of '76 were back in power.[14]

And in many ways, it was true: over the next two years, the Constitutionalists enacted numerous popular policies and dealt the Morris plan several staggering blows. None was more damaging than taking away the Bank of North America's corporate charter. In September 1785, in a vote that went largely along party lines, the assembly took back the privilege of limited liability that shielded bank stockholders from being personally prosecuted for the bank's debts or financial mismanagement. The bank continued to function, but it did so without any of the protections of corporate status.[15]

Revoking corporate status posed a real threat to stockholders—especially because the directors had used the bank as a slush fund for war debt and land speculations (in violation of its bylaws) and thereby placed it on dangerous footing. The speculation problem was so serious that in October 1784 the bank's largest stockholder, Connecticut merchant Jeremiah Wadsworth, became "well convinced" that "the bank was on Slippery ground." He began to raise "great alarms" that Morris and the directors were gambling with the stockholders' money. When the assembly revoked the bank's charter, Wadsworth became panicked that he would be liable if the director's speculations failed, believing (along with Alexander Hamilton) that it was "too dangerous" to "leave *so considerable a sum* in a Company" that was "not incorporated." Consequently, he rode to Philadelphia in January 1786 to see if he could put a stop to the insider lending. At a stockholders' meeting, Wadsworth challenged the bank's directors, and James Wilson in particular, to explain why they had given themselves and their friends "great" loans "with out complying with ye usual forms." Unfazed by the accusations, Wilson "went into a detail of his schemes, disappointments and discounts which amounted to Near 100,000 dollrs"—which, against the bank's bylaws, he had obtained entirely through "Mortgages on Lands." After hearing such a candid admission of corruption, Wadsworth expected the directors to be contrite. Instead, bank president Thomas Willing reprimanded Wadsworth in a number of "*wise* Speeches & some *wiser* remarks" for questioning the directors' integrity. Five months later, the directors loaned Wilson another $66,000 to purchase his brother-in-law's foreclosed iron works and to fund a variety of related speculations.[16]

Despite their anger, Wadsworth and the other stockholders were left with few good options now that their personal finances were tied to the bank's success. They could not publicly reveal the bankers' indiscretions for fear of hurting its business. Likewise, they could not dump their massive stock holdings without taking huge losses—and no doubt they would not be able to unload it all anyway. Consequently, Wadsworth and the other investors held onto their stock and stayed quiet about the bank's troubles, gambling that the speculations would pay off.

In all these ways, the popular movement to retract the bank's corporate protections made this culture of speculation perilous. By making stockholders personally liable for bank debts, it tied their financial fate to the director's speculations in backcountry lands and in the war debt. If those speculations paid off, the bank and its stockholders would be fine. If they did not, the lack of a corporate charter could bring the entire Morris circle to their knees.

The Constitutionalists dealt another blow to the Morris plan with their changes to war debt payments. Responding to popular demands, Constitutionalists refused to enact any new taxes payable in gold and silver. And instead of paying the annual interest to speculators in hard money, they paid it in paper money, something Morris and the Republicans vehemently opposed. The Constitutionalists also passed a law that allowed people to use war debt certificates to pay part of their mortgages to the old colonial land bank.

To Morris's horror, the Constitutionalists also created a new land bank and revived government-issued paper money. Modeled after the colonial land bank, the new loan office gave long-term, low-interest loans to anyone who could offer property as collateral. As before, the land bank divided the money by county and population and let people go to offices in their counties rather than having to travel to Philadelphia. As before, the loans reached nearly every profession: farmers received 66 percent of the loans, artisans 17 percent, gentlemen 13 percent, and merchants 3 percent. In this sense, the new land bank brought equality and uplift to ordinary citizens across the state.[17]

This, however, was the extent of the popular triumph, and, in fact, most of the victories turned out to be rather hollow. For example, the new land bank was far less ambitious than even the one that had operated under British rule. The loan terms were worse: the 1785 land bank charged 6 percent interest (the colonial rate had been 5 percent) for loans of up to eight years (the old land bank had given borrowers sixteen years to repay). The new land bank was also woefully underfunded. Capitalized at only $130,000, the 1785 bank was three times smaller than the 1773 land bank the Penns had permitted that Pennsylvanians had uniformly condemned as being inadequate. Moreover, this paltry new bank was supposed to serve a much larger population; about 150,000 more people lived in Pennsylvania in 1785 than in 1773. Petitioners from Lancaster County said the sum was "too small . . . to give adequate relief to the several counties." One farmer estimated that, given Pennsylvania's population, the $130,000 was "not about quarter enough" to bring relief.[18]

To appreciate the problem, one need only compare the amount the land bank loaned out to each county with what that county owed in taxes. For example, Cumberland County received $8,000 to lend to its citizens at a time when the county owed back taxes of $59,000 in paper money and $140,000 in specie. Thus, while the land bank may have been a step toward what most people wanted, it was a tiny step.[19]

Constitutionalist war debt reforms were equally disappointing. Advocates of the Plan had wanted the state to revalue war debt certificates to reflect market realities; they also had called for people to be able to use certificates to pay any public fee. The Constitutionalists disappointed on all fronts. They did nothing to revalue the war debt and only allowed people to use certificates to pay old mortgages—refusing to accept certificates for taxes, land purchases, or fees at the land office. Even the seeming victory of taxes in paper money instead of specie was not much of a triumph. When Constitutionalists printed up $270,000 in new money to pay certificate holders, they also enacted $270,000 in new paper money taxes. Most people had trouble paying those taxes because little of the currency made it to the countryside. Since the vast majority of war debt certificates were held by wealthy Philadelphians, nearly all of the new money landed in the Quaker city. In fact, most of it ended up being deposited in the Bank of North America. In April 1786, Robert Morris observed that "the whole amount of the emission . . . has already passed through the bank." And, according to Morris, the new paper money was deposited in the accounts of just "sixty-seven persons." Such was the Constitutionalist plan to relieve taxpayers and end the cash scarcity: it brought relief to approximately sixty-seven wealthy families living in and around Philadelphia.[20]

What had happened? Why had seemingly dedicated reformers offered so little in the way of change? Why had they watered-down popular proposals, ignored them altogether, or exacted "reforms" that extended the public's misery?

The answer is that many of these Constitutionalist politicians either changed their minds about reform once in the state assembly, or else they were never the reformers they claimed to be when they ran for office.

Political Corruption: "a dinner of some stockholders fat beef"

In some cases, the problem was rural reformers seduced by the wealth and splendor of the city. The primary culprit was the corrupting power of money and a luxurious lifestyle. Put simply, the expensive ways of genteel Philadelphia seemed to cause some profarmer politicians to forget where they had come from and to lose sight of the people they were supposed to be representing.

The about-face was less a case of hayseeds being duped in the big city than it was a matter of lesser gentry from the countryside discovering that they wanted to be a part of high society. According to a Cumberland County tailor named William Petrikin, who was a reform organizer, Philadelphia was a "nursery of corruption," where moneyed men "converted" reformers into "the instrument of their intrigues." "The truth of these things are obvious," Petrikin wrote in a letter to a Philadelphia correspondent (who, unbeknown to him, was a speculator among those actively doing the converting). "And it is as obvious that they are produced by the influence of your overgrown Citizens and the Bank." The Cumberland man observed that when legislators from the countryside arrived in Philadelphia, they were courted with "a nod, a smile, a Bottle of wine or a dinner." The shower of attention and gifts overwhelmed "Many of the country Members." "A ticket to a play or admittance" to a ball hosted by a "Banker" and other "Enchanting alurements" were "honors too powerful for human nature to resist." Many gentlemen reformers grew accustomed to the finer things their hosts provided and began to "fancy themselves Men of some consequence." Not wanting the stream of honors and gifts to end, country legislators provided "their Benefactors . . . with their Vote." They surrendered campaign promises and, instead, cast their ballots as the moneyed men of Philadelphia "shall please to direct them."[21]

This seems to be exactly what happened to a Pittsburgh politician named Hugh Henry Brackenridge who, in a matter of weeks, transformed from an advocate of the Plan to an ally of Robert Morris. In a sense, Brackenridge was ripe for conversion. His entire life story was a tale of an outsider yearning for acceptance in genteel society. Born in Scotland in 1748, Brackenridge moved with his family to a rented farm in York County when he was five. His lucky break came when local clergy identified him as a bright lad and gave him an education more befitting a gentleman's son than the boy of a tenant farmer. At fifteen, he left home to teach at a school in Maryland. A few years later, Brackenridge was a student at Princeton, working his way through college by tutoring the sons of gentlemen. He graduated in 1771 with a class of young men born to wealth, including a Virginia planter's son named James Madison. With no landed estate awaiting him after Princeton, Brackenridge followed the path of many aspiring gentlemen, entered the ministry, and became a schoolmaster. When the Revolutionary War came, he served as a chaplain in the army. In 1778, he left the army and tried his hand at editing a literary magazine in Philadelphia. Few gentlemen were interested in what he had to say, however, and Brackenridge was forced to close shop within a year. His pride wounded, he fled the city. "I saw no chance of being anything in that city," Brackenridge later wrote, as "there were such great men before me." He headed to Annapolis, Maryland, where, in a career about-face, he studied law. When Brackenridge returned to Pennsylvania in 1781, he went as far away from Philadelphia as he could, settling in the frontier town of Pittsburgh. Here, Brackenridge thrived, developing a successful law practice, helping to establish the *Pittsburgh Gazette*, and moving to the center of what passed for genteel society in this backcountry outpost. But as high as Brackenridge rose in Pittsburgh, it was a far cry from the heights enjoyed by those in the inner circles of Philadelphia or the genteel circuits frequented by the rest of his class at Princeton.[22]

In 1786, Brackenridge decided to give Philadelphia another try. He ran for a seat in the general assembly and won based entirely on his promise to make his sole cause enacting the Plan. Specifically, Brackenridge pledged to sponsor a law to allow farmers to use war debt certificates to secure their lands and said that, if such a law wasn't passed in his first session, he would make sure it was "strongly urged at every session until it is gained." When he won the election, Brackenridge no doubt thought his return to Philadelphia would be his revenge: he would come back as an advocate for ordinary folk against the speculating gentlemen who had spurned him on his first stay in the city.[23]

Once in Philadelphia, though, Brackenridge began to change. The reason was clear: fawning attention from the same genteel men who had previously slighted him by refusing to subscribe to his magazine. Once ignored by Philadelphia society, Brackenridge now found himself embraced by it. He was invited to the most desirable balls and dinner parties. Robert Morris took him under his wing and personally shepherded him through the tricky routines of

FIG. 6.1. HUGH HENRY BRACKENRIDGE. A tenant farmer's son who managed to obtain a Princeton education, Brackenridge saw himself as an emissary of high culture in the backcountry. No doubt, he would have been pleased that this portrait accompanied several of his poems and essays in the *Cyclopaedia of American Literature*, giving him the literary success in death that so often eluded him during his life. (Reprinted from Evert A. Duyckinck and George L. Duyckink, *The Cyclopaedia of American Literature* 305 [Philadelphia, 1880], vol. 1.)

polite society. The attention from the "great men" was evidently too much for Brackenridge to resist. In a short time, his new social routine translated into a new political outlook. Having arrived in Philadelphia as a vocal critic of the gospel of moneyed men, he became one of its staunchest supporters. When the law to allow farmers to pay for land with war debt certificates came up for a vote, Brackenridge led the floor fight against it, and, then, he voted it down.

Back in western Pennsylvania, news of Brackenridge's transformation created a firestorm. Stories circulated that Brackenridge had "sold the good will of his country for a dinner of some stockholders fat beef." Even his dearest friends were enraged. "History, in my opinion, can scarcely produce a man so eminent for vanity, so prone to corruption and servility, as well as every other baneful quality proper to dignify a contemptible tool," seethed one of his closest allies. "On his appearance in this country I considered him as a man of virtue and was his friend," the man wrote. "I am not now his enemy, but I despise him, as I ever have and ever will engines of oppression."[24]

Defending himself in the local newspaper, Brackenridge insisted that he had merely changed his mind when he was "*struck by the power of reason*" in Morris's arguments. He recounted his conversion experience to his constituents. He said he had come to the conclusion that farm proposals were misguided and unnecessary. In fact, Brackenridge declared that "the people" were only getting in the way of the greatness of America. "The people were fools," Brackenridge announced. "[I]f they would let Mr. Morris alone he would make Pennsylvania a great people, but they will not suffer him to do it." Such was the transformation of the tenant farmer's son from a man of "the people" to a foot soldier for "Mr. Morris."[25]

The following fall, when Brackenridge went up for reelection, farmers in Westmoreland County turned him out of office. One observer reported that Brackenridge received only three votes in the entire county. Instead, Westmoreland voters turned to a proreform candidate whom they felt was less likely to be seduced by genteel Philadelphia. Unfortunately, as far as reform efforts went, the damage had already been done.[26]

Co-opting Reform

More common—and far more damaging to popular reforms—was the rash of Constitutionalists who posed as reformers in order to get elected and then enacted a series of self-interested policies once in office. These gentlemen—who dominated the Constitutionalist Party in Philadelphia and the eastern counties—never really supported popular ideals. They were new immigrants or "new money" gentry, who were less wealthy than their Republican counterparts, but who shared many of their ideals. Indeed, most of them joined Morris in wanting to limit democracy and to enrich the elite.

To get a sense of how closely many Constitutionalist leaders resembled their Republican counterparts, take the case of John Nicholson. Born in Wales, Nicholson emigrated to Philadelphia on the eve of the Revolution and bounced around between startup manufactories making iron, glass, and buttons. He rose to prominence during the war, primarily through a series of high-profile clerk positions with Congress and the Pennsylvania government. Like most of his Republican adversaries, Nicholson became a war debt speculator, amassing more than $13,500 in federal certificates (most of which he probably acquired from soldiers while he was in charge of settling army accounts at the end of the war). And like the Republican elite, Nicholson was a massive land speculator, gaining title to thousands of acres of lands, which he tried to fill with tenant farmers. In short, Nicholson—and many of his follow Constitutionalist leaders—had far more in common with Robert Morris than with the voters who elected him to office.[27]

Men like Nicholson only opposed the Republicans because Morris and his allies had continually tried to cut them out of plans to bring wealth and power to moneyed men. The Morris circle refused them credit at the bank, denied them lucrative government contracts, and refused to pass along insider information about war bond deals. The new men and their wives were not sent invitations to the balls and teas of polite society. Thus, many of these Constitutionalist leaders were driven by a desire for revenge against the Morris faction and an attempt to get their piece of the "moneyed men" pie.[28]

Vengeance was clearly the reason that many of these gentlemen worked to revoke the charter of the Bank of North America. Although Constitutionalist leaders publicly adopted the popular anticorporate stance in 1784, few of them embraced an ideological fear of corporate power. After all, earlier that year, many of these same men had tried to incorporate a rival private bank in Philadelphia. Those plans were scuttled when Morris co-opted many of the proposed bank's big-money backers by allowing them to purchase stock in the Bank of North America. The men left out of the deal became Constitutionalists and began calling for an end to all for-profit corporations—despite having tried to create just such a corporation only months before.[29]

Likewise, these Constitutionalists only supported paper money and war debt reform after the Morris faction tried to deny them a share of the war debt bonanza. The break began when a 1784 audit showed that the government had collected only 36 percent of specie taxes, creating a backlog of nearly $1.3 million. With only enough money to pay a portion of the interest on the war debt, certificate holders turned on one another. The first blow was struck by Republican bond holders, who attempted to pay themselves in gold and silver and leave the Constitutionalist war debt holders with nothing. Their plan was to reward only the so-called original holders, who held certificates acquired directly from Congress (these people were mostly army generals and friends of Morris who had used greatly depreciated Continental currency to buy war bonds for about one-fifth of their face value). The original holders attempted to deny interest payments to "secondary holders," who had purchased certificates from soldiers, farmers, or army suppliers (the category into which most of the new money Constitutionalists fell). Even though many of the original holders were also secondary holders, they were willing to forgo some of their interest so they could receive gold and silver for their original holdings.[30]

In response, the Constitutionalist elite, knowing there was no other way they would receive an interest payment, swallowed their antipathy for paper money and passed a law that paid all war debt holders with new currency.

(The new land bank was the price they had to pay to get the support of enough of the real reformers to get their payday.) Constitutionalist speculators like John Nicholson and Philadelphia merchant-lawyer Charles Pettit made no apologies for the "evils of speculation," insisting that they deserved "all the profit that can arise from" their investments. "We feel no apprehensions," they wrote, "of a few persons being suddenly raised into great wealth, while others are proportionately depressed." Of course, among those "raised into great wealth" was Pettit, who drafted the law that was rumored to have paid him $16,000 annually in interest (meaning he held over a quarter of a million dollars in certificates). Privately, Pettit spoke of the paper money law as "My funding Plan."[31]

Among those "depressed" by Pettit's plan were ordinary Pennsylvanians, who saw it as too high a price to pay for the pathetic new land bank. The anger at Constitutionalist leaders was palpable. "Do not mix this paper money in your schemes of obtaining 60 per annum for your own speculations," one farmer wrote in disgust. He said the small land bank was the equivalent of trying "to keep us quiet, and to get the money to pay your own certificate's interest." To him, the land bank was merely "a trick to obtain" the public's "consent to the taxes" for speculators. He told state leaders that if they had "designed in good earnest to help us," then they would have given the land bank "all the paper you propose making" instead of dishing out most of it to speculators.[32]

Many farmers also worried that Pettit's plan would end up discrediting paper money. Farmers had wanted all of the new money to be backed by land so it would hold its value. Instead, Constitutionalists had created a kind of hybrid currency. One-third of it (the $130,000 in the land bank) was backed by land and the other two-thirds (the $270,000 paid out to certificate holders) was backed by taxes, which was the system used during the war. Despite the different backing, the new currency looked identical and traded at the same value. Many farmers worried that the tax-backed money would sink in value and bring the land-backed money down with it. As one farmer put it, "The country want[s] money bad enough, but this very funding bill will be a means of destroying the paper money" rather than saving the public.[33]

In the end, most people were wildly disappointed by the faux reformers in the Constitutionalist Party. Their betrayal left voters with few real choices. No matter their party affiliation, most political leaders in Pennsylvania were dedicated to the goal of upward wealth redistribution. Elite Pennsylvanians differed over who qualified as moneyed men and how best to serve the interests of gentlemen. But each camp defined the public good in narrow ways,

seeing policies that benefited their own economic interests as the only proper course of action.

In the end, the sense of abandonment gave most Pennsylvanians little reason to go to the polls. As a result, in the next election, in 1786, most people
stayed home. In Philadelphia County and in nearby Bucks County, only 33
percent of the taxable population bothered to vote. In the counties of
Northampton, Dauphin, and York, only about 25 percent of voters went to the
polls. A mere 15 percent of Lancaster County voted. On average, only about 27
percent of eligible voters cast a ballot in 1786. In the face of disappointment
and elite opposition, most Pennsylvanians withdrew from electoral politics (or
continued to stay on the sidelines) and ceded the legislature to the gentlemen.

Not everyone retreated, however. While voters elsewhere stayed home in
1786, Cumberland County continued to produce a stunning turnout: that
year, Robert Whitehill earned the votes of 63 percent of the population.
Although no returns survive for the losing candidate, Whitehill probably
won with three or four times as many votes as his opposition. This model—
where most people voted even in an election where the outcome was never
in doubt—showed what was possible. If voting is a learned behavior,
Cumberland was the most effective school of democracy in the state.[34]

There were also hints that other counties were forming voter-education
societies. For example, in January 1787, in Washington County on the western
frontier, farmers formed a "Patriotic Convention" to give "instructions to our
representatives" who had disappointed them with their votes in the assembly.
Convention delegates demanded an end to the cash scarcity that was "daily
draining" the region, leaving them unable to pay "our taxes and debts" and
threatening "the fruits of our lands and labours." They called for laws allowing
people to pay taxes in produce or war debt certificates. The delegates even
organized a boycott of military contractors at Fort Pitt, saying that farmers
should not supply the fort with whiskey, flour, and meat unless the government
paid them in hard money instead of store credit. They demanded a law dividing the county into more election districts to make it easier for people to vote.
Finally, in hopes of expanding the reach of this new political organization, they
drew up an "instrument of association" to recruit "the people" in every township to attend subsequent conventions. In short, Washington County farmers
may have lagged behind counties like Cumberland in self-organization, but
they were determined to make up ground as quickly as possible.[35]

Elsewhere, however, this kind of formal organization was hard to find.
Ordinary folk in many counties—like Lancaster, York, and Chester—
continued to send petitions to the assembly calling for reforms similar to the

Plan (some arriving a few weeks after the election returns were announced). And petitioners still proclaimed that "the People" had the "Right of Governing and Regulating" their leaders so they could be "Restrained from Oppression." But these people either did not vote or else cast their ballots for candidates who shared their ethnicity or religion, which usually meant electing Republicans who were openly opposed to popular policies.[36]

In the end, popular organizing proved too sporadic or too preliminary to bring lasting change. It was not enough even to maintain the reforms that had been enacted. The 1786 elections returned the Republican Party to power, and Morris and his allies immediately began to reimpose their agenda, including reinstating the corporate charter of the Bank of North America.

*   *   *

Ultimately, the attempts of ordinary Pennsylvanians to work through the political system had mixed results. On one hand, those efforts demonstrated that regular people could organize and win political victories. On the other hand, they revealed that great obstacles stood in the way of broader change. Internal divisions, a gentry-dominated political system, speculators posing as reformers, and turncoat politicians—all blocked the path of reform. In some counties, people kept faith in the political system and continued to mobilize. Elsewhere, they abandoned voting altogether. This did not mean, however, that most people had given up on reform. To the contrary, nearly everywhere in Pennsylvania, ordinary folk renewed the strategies of the 1760s and 1770s and tried to achieve through protest what they could not achieve through the ballot box.

7

Rings of Protection

POPULAR RESISTANCE DURING THE 1780S

There seems to be almost a total stop in the Collecting of Taxes.

—Pennsylvania treasurer David Rittenhouse, April 27, 1784

The laws are eluded without being openly opposed.

—Fayette County treasurer Ephraim Douglass, July 11, 1784

During the 1780s, Pennsylvania politics tended to live on streets and country lanes. Thousands of Pennsylvanians who did not vote engaged in waves of protests that swept the countryside. The protests were as varied as they were ubiquitous, spanning a range of strategies from civil disobedience to armed resistance. Some were aimed at stopping foreclosures for unpaid private debts; most were directed at halting tax collection. The protests involved a great many people. They crossed lines of class and occupation, drawing together farmers, artisans, lawyers, gentlemen farmers, and county officials. Resistance also crossed lines of ethnicity, religion, and geography, involving Scots-Irish Presbyterians in central and western Pennsylvania, German Lutherans in the eastern counties, and even Quakers of English descent in the counties surrounding Philadelphia. These groups did not usually coordinate their protests; there was no central organization; they were not linked by committees of correspondence. Nevertheless, these people protested at exactly the same moment in precisely the same ways with at least some awareness of their common effort.

At stake in all of this was the meaning of democracy and the Revolution. The objective of all of the protest was simple: if state leaders were going to enact laws that hurt the public to reward moneyed men, then ordinary citizens were going to see that those laws did not come into operation. People would take it upon themselves to stop the gospel of moneyed men in its tracks.

At the same time, protesters were trying to preserve the practice of democracy. These people thought that the Revolution had given them the right to express their views in ways besides voting, petitioning, and lobbying. They took the words of the 1776 state constitution literally, believing that "the people" had the "sole, exclusive, and inherent right of governing and regulating" state policy. Many people were convinced that the constitution gave "the people" the authority to "take such measures as to them may appear necessary" to oppose policies like the Morris plan, which violated the constitution's stipulation that government must work for the "common benefit" of the "community" and "not for the particular emolument or advantage of any single man, family, or set of men who are only part of that community." People across the state believed that this right empowered them to use civil disobedience, crowd action, and, if necessary, even violent rebellion to oppose what they thought were unconstitutional laws. In practice, most people thought violence would be unnecessary and that they could regulate their government through more subtle forms of resistance.[1]

Indeed, during the 1780s, ordinary Pennsylvanians constructed elaborate resistance networks designed to shield themselves from the harmful effects of state policies. To envision these networks, it is perhaps best to see them as a series of concentric rings of protection that ordinary folk built around their communities. The outermost rings encircled an entire county, protecting everyone no matter where they lived; the inner ones protected individual neighborhoods and townships. Each ring also had a particular function and was staffed by a different set of people. For clarity's sake, let's say there were seven rings. Working from the outermost rings to the inner ones, the first was formed by county revenue officials who tried to thwart tax collection. The second ring was composed of county justices of the peace who refused to prosecute delinquent taxpayers and collectors. The third ring was formed by juries who acquitted those accused of not paying their taxes. The fourth ring was composed of sheriffs and constables who would not arrest non-paying citizens. The fifth ring involved ordinary folk attempting to stop tax collection and property foreclosures through nonviolent protest. Ring six was people trying to achieve those same goals through violent crowd action. Ring seven was composed of self-directed county militias that refused to follow orders to stop any of this protest. During the 1780s, these seven rings of protection—each a clear example of popular democracy in action—formed a barrier for defending both property and popular notions of a just society.[2]

Before we examine the rings in more detail, a word of caution is necessary: although the rings were powerful, they were neither all-encompassing nor impenetrable. Not every county treasurer, judge, or sheriff was an opponent of the Morris plan. Many of these officials and their allies supported the gospel of moneyed men. They were agents for eastern land speculators, large land holders who drew rents from tenant farms, holders of war debt certificates, shopkeepers who received credit from Philadelphia merchants, or simply people who considered themselves to be better than their neighbors. They were often the people who brought lawsuits in county courts and used their access to credit to purchase auctioned property at a fraction of its value.

Nor did ordinary farmers always oppose the actions of prominent community members. Countering the men who controlled access to money and credit, especially in a cash-scarce economy, meant risking the loss of future credit or having one's outstanding debts called in. Given the realities of economic dependence, many people remained silent, farming their land or hammering horseshoes, hoping that bad times would pass. Others tried to curry favor with local elites, hoping to gain an advantage over their neighbors in this moneyless economy. These realities also help to explain why rural people concentrated their anger at property foreclosures for public taxes rather than auctions for private debts. Many farmers undoubtedly reasoned that opposing the state entailed far fewer risks than directly confronting the local gentry.[3]

Despite such limiting factors, the rings of protection were impressive. They frustrated state and local elites and, ultimately, convinced many of them that they needed to develop new and more coercive ways of containing democracy. Thus, understanding the rings of protection is critical for comprehending why, at the end of the 1780s, so many elite Pennsylvanians dedicated themselves to radically restructuring the state and national governments.[4]

Ring One: County Tax Officials

The outermost ring of protection was formed by the men assigned to bring the Morris plan into their communities: county tax officers. Many county revenue officials delayed tax collection as long as possible—out of a sense of disgust with Morris's policies, compassion for the plight of their neighbors, or fear of retaliation for upholding an objectionable law. When state leaders handed down new tax quotas or sent menacing letters demanding immediate collection, these officials stalled. Instead of turning over money or ledgers to Philadelphia, they sent letters complaining about state policies and urging patience. This was the substance of the first ring: by refusing to do their jobs, many county tax officers delayed collection and protected those who could not pay.

Judging from the letters sent to Philadelphia, most county officers formed this protective ring because they believed that state policies were unworkable and unjust. In Bucks County, twenty miles outside Philadelphia, the tax commissioners said in 1783 that they would not compel payment because the "absolute scarcity of Money" made it "hard and impolitic to execute Rigours of the Law upon the Collectors." In nearby Chester County, officials claimed that collection was too "burthensome" and "utterly out of their power." On Pennsylvania's northeastern border, Northampton County officials said they were "not willing to distress the people" and tolerated delays because the "Scarcity" left "but few families that can much more than support themselves." "If they had the money they would pay their Taxes freely," these men declared. Along the state's southern border in York County, revenue agents refused to sue because doing so would be "ruinous to our County," allowing only a "few Individuals [to] escape the Gaol." Officials in neighboring Dauphin County demonstrated "Compassion" and would not sue taxpayers "who are willing, but not able to pay" due to "the Scarcity of Money."[5]

The most defiant statements came from the counties west of the Susquehanna River. Cumberland commissioners complained of the "severe" policy of "calling in all the Taxes due in a short or limited time" (which they said was an "impossibility"). Officials in Westmoreland County refused to prosecute because they too believed that "the payment of the present Taxes is an intolerable grievance & altogether beyond our power to comply with." In neighboring Washington County, the treasurer stalled collection to protect "a poor Distressed peepel That is Willing To Do Everything in Their power" to pay, but who had no money.[6]

Although county tax officials used strong words and made brave stands, they could only hold out for a limited time. Revenue laws made it relatively easy for state leaders to sue county tax officers for neglecting their duties. And the financial punishment could be severe. When revenue agents took office, state law required them to sign hefty bonds that mortgaged their property against the faithful performance of their duties. Since the law also required these bonds to be signed by two other propertied citizens, resistance threatened to punish an official's friends and business associates as well.

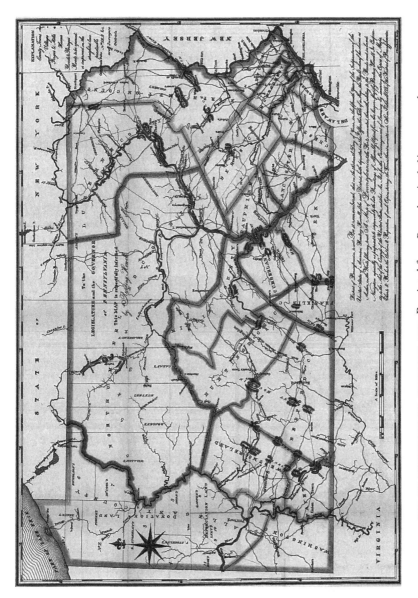

FIG. 7.1. PENNSYLVANIA COUNTIES, 1791. Reprinted from *Pennsylvania Archives*, ser. 2, vol. 4.

Thus, although many revenue officers viewed state policies with contempt, most of them eventually relented when state leaders threatened to sue.[7]

Sometimes, the lawsuits backfired, causing diligent tax officials to join the ranks of the disaffected. Such was the case with Robert Levers from Northampton County. If ever there was a dedicated county officer, it was Levers. During the 1780s, he made collecting taxes his personal mission, doing whatever he could to get the job done. But as Levers discovered time and again, it was nearly impossible to collect due to "the great scarcity of money in the County." His attempts to enforce the law merely prompted resistance by other county officials and angry neighbors. When he tried to get the names of those who had not paid their taxes, collectors refused to release their ledgers. When he tried to get the county sheriff to help him collect, the man refused. When Levers tried to get witnesses for lawsuits, no one would testify. "Few like to be deemed informers," he wrote to state leaders in frustration. Levers managed to assemble the lawsuits anyway, but, when he sent them to county justices, "no Prosecutions took Place." He found a justice willing to take the cases, but then the grand jury refused to indict "for want of evidence." None of this made Levers a popular man. His efforts brought hard stares and harsh comments from his neighbors. On one occasion, he was beaten by a crowd of farmers (including several "gentlemen") who broke into his home and punished him for his inability to take a hint.[8]

Levers received a more serious punishment from the state: a lawsuit for the money he could not collect. Given Levers's painstaking efforts, the suit came as a shock. "Little or no money has been paid into the treasury," he wrote, "but that has not been my fault." "I humbly trust that there is not a man of reflection & Virtue in the Honorable House of Assembly, in the Supreme Executive Council, or among the Public at Large that can think me criminal with respect to my delay of Payment of Taxes." Levers told state leaders that his only recourse was to sell off his own property, and he begged them not to drive his family into such a "state of wretchedness." "I have a wife and six children at home, all at present dependent on me for common support," he implored, adding that he had a "Sickly Son" who would never be able to live on his own.[9]

When state leaders ignored his pleas and sued him anyway, Levers felt a sense of betrayal that transformed him. No longer would he serve the state with unblinking loyalty. Never again would he sacrifice his body and property to uphold laws that could not be upheld. It was time for Robert Levers to think about his family. And if that meant finding a way around state laws, so be it. His path to safety was simple: while the lawsuit against him was "approaching to Judgment," Levers transferred all of his property to his children. He gave his farm to one of his sons; he gave his house in the town of Easton to his two eldest daughters; he gave bonds for money due from debtors to another daughter and to his "Sickly Son." State officials would win their lawsuit and earn the right to confiscate his property. But to collect, they would have to find a way to sue Levers's children—if they even could. Thus, in this roundabout way, Levers joined (albeit unintentionally) the defensive network he had once worked so tirelessly to dismantle.[10]

The state's get-tough policy also backfired by making it hard to fill vacancies for tax officials. For example, Bedford County leaders reported that no one would take the job of county treasurer for fear of being sued by the state. County officials explained the reasons: Bedford's yearly tax quota was $4,600, but officials could only collect about $2,700, meaning a $1,900 deficit each year. Add the expenses of the office, including two trips to Philadelphia every year to settle accounts, and the job was a sure money loser, if not a ticket to bankruptcy. "The present wages" of "Seven or Eight pounds will not bear the expence of the duty," Bedford leaders explained. In the eastern county of Bucks, it was also hard to find new tax collectors. Everyone knew the quotas could not be filled due to the "Poverty of the People" and that the state was suing collectors for the "Loss of any public Money." The only way to avoid a lawsuit was to sue one's neighbors, an act that would make collectors "liable to be carried off or destroyed by the Hand of Violence." It was a no-win situation. And so, Bucks officials explained, they could appoint collectors and fine those who refused to accept the job. But all of the "obvious Considerations . . . induce many to choose a Fine rather than the office." As a result, the offices remained vacant, and taxes went uncollected.[11]

In most cases, however, the state's hard-line policies eventually broke the ring formed by county tax officials. The state simply had too much leverage over them. Consequently, when state officials initiated lawsuits against them, tax officials sued their neighbors, who usually did not have the money to pay.

Rather than destroying the network, this breach in the outermost ring merely passed the burden of defense to another group of county officers. Quite often, county justices of the peace—perhaps the most powerful officers in county government—took it upon themselves to form a second ring of protection.

Ring Two: Justices of the People

Among the wealthiest and best-connected men in their counties, justices of the peace seemed unlikely candidates to oppose state authority. And to be sure, most justices actively followed state orders. But beginning in 1785, when a procedural change made justices responsible for enforcing tax collection, a surprising number chose to include themselves within the protective networks. Many undoubtedly joined the resistance out of sympathy for their neighbors or to support their own understanding of the Revolution. Others joined for pragmatic reasons: under the 1776 constitution, justices of the peace were elected. A justice who followed state orders too diligently could find himself voted out of office. As a result, even if they were unsympathetic to the plight of their neighbors, justices faced pressure to put their constituents' interests above unpopular state laws. This democratic system led to a situation where, as one state official put it, "people literally think that every justice of the peace is a justice of the people."[12]

During the 1780s, many justices lived up to that reputation by using their powers to create a formidable barrier. Some justices refused to hear tax-related lawsuits. Others let suits proceed, but stalled the process at every turn or would not rule on guilt or innocence. Justices who ruled against taxpayers or collectors sometimes "openly refused" to sentence the guilty or "carefully avoided issuing their warrants as the law directs" when it came to jailing collectors or holding property auctions. By the end of 1786, so many county justices were resisting in so many different ways that John Nicholson, the top state officer in charge of tax collection, threw up his hands in frustration. With little money coming into his office, Nicholson complained that justices across the state were doing all they could to "impede and protract the payment of the taxes."[13]

Perhaps the clearest example of the power that justices could wield came in the mountain county of Bedford. There, a justice named James Martin single-handedly stopped state policies because they violated his notions of how a democracy should function. Martin became an expert at stalling tactics. Throughout 1785 and 1786, he refused to prosecute anyone in his jurisdiction for nonpayment of taxes. Nor did he release the names of those who had not paid. To defend his neighbors, Martin was even willing to make himself appear to be a country bumpkin. He told revenue officials that he did not understand tax laws. He missed court appearances. He claimed to forget where he had placed tax ledgers.[14]

Beneath the veneer of a doddering judge, however, Martin shrewdly worked to find a solution for his constituents. He encouraged those who had cash to settle their accounts as quickly as possible. He collected the money and marked off the names and amounts in the official ledgers. When people could not pay in specie or paper money, Martin allowed them to pay in grain. If the system was unorthodox, no one complained of corruption. Martin had made it clear that he assumed responsibility for the money and the deficit.

When constituents came to him with fears about being foreclosed for unpaid taxes, Martin told them that he would continue to resist as best he could. In the summer of 1787, he was stopped by several worried neighbors, prompting an informal street-corner meeting, which was overheard by a county revenue official. As the eavesdropper reported, Martin "wondered what sort of Assembly we had got that made such Laws." "Lord have mercy on us," said Martin, wringing his hands, "the country will be ruined. I do not know what to do. The collectors all make returns of the Delinquents & I don't know what to do." He explained that he had "put one Township off" by telling officials "I did not understand the Law." "But I'll tell you what," the justice promised, "I will not sue one of you until I am sued." Martin did better than this. By stalling, he gave several taxpayers and collectors time to sell their property and flee the county. In these multiple ways, James Martin became a prime example of why so many Pennsylvanians considered their locally elected magistrate to be a "justice of the people."[15]

Once county justices like James Martin decided to obstruct the law, there was not much anyone could do to stop them. The 1776 constitution left county justices relatively autonomous. Unlike county tax officials, who were beholden to state leaders and who could easily be sued for failing to do their jobs, county justices enjoyed a degree of insulation from state authority. It was hard to coax them and even harder to sue them. "The justices . . . are Defective," complained commissioners from Bedford County, who could not get James Martin and his fellow justices to enforce tax laws. These men explained that no one seemed to have the power to stop judicial inaction: county tax collectors had "no Power to compel. The Treasurer has no Power to Compel. . . . The Commissioners has not the Power." And apparently neither did the state. "We would wish to know where the power is," the officials declared in exasperation. "Compel the justices and Constables to do their part, and I will do my part," wrote one frustrated Bedford officer whom the state had threatened to sue.[16]

State leaders could only make idle threats—and county justices knew it. In 1786, state tax official John Nicholson tried to get county justices to take action by sending out letters demanding prosecutions. His campaign had little success. "I showed the Magistrates your Letters at a court held here Last week," the treasurer of Franklin County reported in October 1786. "Their sentiments were that they would threaten the people as much as Possible but not proceed against them." Justices in several other counties gave Nicholson's letters the same cold reception. Despite his strongly worded reprimands, "no Prosecutions took place" in Northampton County; justices in Cumberland County remained "very Indifferent about Executing their authority"; in Northumberland County, magistrates continued to be "very baqward in giving Judgment"; in Huntingdon County, "justices refuse[d] to issue Executions" to foreclose property; and in Dauphin County, justices halted lawsuits, saying "the People are unable to pay [taxes] by reason of the Scarcity of Money."[17]

Although numerous, these examples should be kept in context. Despite the fact that judicial resistance touched nearly every county, it was never unanimous. For every justice who joined the rings of protection, there was another who enforced the law. After all, many justices were gentlemen who fully supported the gospel of moneyed men and its prescriptions for elite rule. And as these men demonstrated, if judicial power was an effective tool of resistance, it could also be a mighty weapon in support of state laws.

Ring Three: Resistance by the Jury; or, The Power of "Not Guilty"

When justices allowed lawsuits to proceed, it occasionally became clear that the judge's bench was not the only source of power in the courtroom. In a few cases, the jury or witness box demonstrated another kind of authority that was easily transformed into a new ring of protection.

The most common form of resistance by jurors and witnesses was letting off officials who were charged with not doing their jobs. Jurors and witnesses may well have played a broader role by acquitting debtors or taxpayers, but their resistance is difficult, if not impossible, to prove. When it came to cases involving county officials who refused to do their jobs, however, resistance is fairly clear—even if there were few actual instances where jurors or witnesses explained their decisions.

To get a sense of the scope of this resistance, consider these numbers. Of the fifty-four county officers prosecuted during the 1780s and 1790s, only two cases ever went to trial. Most of the cases were dismissed because witnesses would not testify or because grand juries would not bring charges after hearing the evidence. Although it is hard to prove that the witnesses and jurors saw themselves as part of the popular resistance, the fact that so few of these cases ever went to trial—just 4 percent—suggests that the dropped charges were not mere coincidence.[18]

There is also evidence of resistance in at least one jury decision in the trial of a tax collector. Unlike other county officers, tax collectors were tried in civil rather than criminal court, where they were sued as if they were debtors for the taxes they owed. These civil cases produced little in the way of paperwork that would give any sense of the jury's decision-making process. In fact, it is difficult even to distinguish most of these cases from all of the other debt cases the court handled. In one instance, however, the county commissioner who brought the case was so incensed by the verdict that he wrote down the entire story of the jury's unabashed resistance.[19]

The episode centered on a tax collector with the last name of Scott who lived in the southeastern county of York and who failed to submit his ledgers (an act that shielded his neighbors from lawsuits for unpaid taxes). That the case ever reached trial was a tribute to the determination of County Commissioner Richard McAlister. Like other county tax officials, McAlister had good reason to be diligent: state leaders had promised to sue him if the county's accounts were not settled. And so, with little help, he did his best to assemble an airtight case against Scott. For months, McAlister relentlessly pursued the collector, recording each of Scott's refusals to do his job and amassing a paper trail of incriminating documents. Of all the evidence he gathered, two items were critical: a receipt and a letter from the state treasurer. The receipt established the amount Scott owed and the letter set the final date for payment. McAlister asked the state treasurer to send a copy of each to Scott, and, because Scott could easily destroy this evidence, another copy to him. The receipt and letter set the stage for the lawsuit: when Scott missed the deadline, McAlister sued him.

The courtroom scene was dramatic. McAlister recounted his many travails attempting to compel Scott to settle up. He explained each incident and presented a document to back his version of the story. Before long, he stood before a tall stack of incriminating paper. McAlister ended with the most damning evidence: the letter and receipt from the state treasurer. When it was Scott's turn, he presented one of the shortest defenses in the history of American jurisprudence. He asked no witnesses to testify and presented no hard evidence; Scott merely stated that he had paid the money on time and then rested his case. When the jury retired to deliberate, the task seemed easy: they had to weigh a single statement of innocence against a mountain of evidence proving guilt.

When the jury returned a unanimous "not guilty" verdict, McAlister was understandably stunned. He returned home in despair and wrote to state officials to explain that the jury had voted to acquit despite overwhelming evidence of guilt. Weeks later, he received an astonishing reply: state leaders had decided to sue him for the deficits in Scott's tax accounts. McAlister would bear the burden of the jury's verdict. The commissioner went into a rage. He became so exasperated that he tracked down jurors from the trial to ask why they had acquitted Scott when all of the evidence had pointed to guilt. The one juror who would speak to him explained the jury's logic: "Scott said he had paid the money to the State, and it was a long time since. And Scott was but of low Circumstances and we thought it best to acquit him lest it might be wrong." For the jury, the most important fact had been that the amount of tax due from the collector was small enough that "the State would not miss it," but large enough so that "it was a great deal for the poor man to pay. And so we thought on the whole it was best to acquit him."

Dissatisfied with this answer, McAlister directed the juror to a discussion of the evidence. The juror replied that he could only remember two documents: the letter and receipt from the state treasurer. Encouraged, McAlister asked the juror to recall that these documents showed that Scott owed a large balance that was long overdue. The juror's reply shocked him: "he said he could not recollect seeing those things." The juror then repeated, "we thought it best to acquit him lest he should be wronged." The frustrated commissioner could take no more. McAlister explained that, because the jury had set Scott free, the state was going to sue him for the unpaid taxes.

Upon hearing this, the juror's tone instantly changed to one of shock: "*Good God, said he*, you are chargeable?" After a moment, the juror attempted to console the commissioner. As this man saw it, McAlister had nothing to fear. After all, he had the receipt from the state treasurer showing that Scott had not paid the money on time. "Surely this is sufficient for you," the juror replied reassuringly, "no person can hurt you or what the devil is Receipts for if not that." For the commissioner, the irony was flabbergasting. He stood listening to the juror touting with great conviction the incontrovertible strength of the very evidence that the juror himself had dismissed with ease during the trial. The message the juror sent was unmistakable: evidence was worthy of consideration when it saved someone from "hurt." It would be ignored when it undermined the independence of the citizenry. In this subtle way, the York County jury thwarted the ambitions of bond holders, bankers, and state assemblymen, replacing elite notions of justice with a distinctly different idea of how the rule of law should function.[20]

Ring Four: Law Un-Enforcement

When juries voted to convict, the defense network sometimes remained intact through the actions (or rather the inaction) of county law enforcement. This new ring was formed by county sheriffs and constables who, in varying ways and to varying extents, protected their communities by refusing to do their jobs.

County sheriffs—who were among the wealthiest officers in county government—joined the protective effort infrequently. The few who did join seemed to center their efforts on frustrating property foreclosures. For example, when a Northumberland County tax official requested that the sheriff hold property auctions, the sheriff refused, saying that "from the scarcity of money among the people, he cannot do anything." Likewise, the sheriff of Lancaster County caused "frequent disappointments" in property auctions for unpaid debts and taxes. One disappointed creditor alleged that the sheriff had made secret arrangements with debtors to spare their property by working together to "dupe" him.[21]

Since most sheriffs were reluctant to resist, the burden of defense generally fell to county constables, who were lower in rank. As tax officials from across the state complained, constables were far more likely to refuse to deliver warrants or to arrest taxpayers. Ironically, the constables' success in resisting was in many ways a function of their poverty. Typically, constables were the poorest officers in county government. And since most constables owned little property, the state lacked the financial leverage to punish them if they failed to perform their jobs. "Constables are generally chosen out of the Lowest Class of the people," explained the Bedford County commissioners. "What law can Compell a poor man that has Nothing to pay?"[22]

That lack of leverage led some constables to flout the law openly. In Washington County, the entire corps of constables boycotted the January 1786 court session—a session at the height of the foreclosure epidemic. In Northampton County, between 1785 and 1787, constables used the power of poverty to "Indulge their neighbors" by refusing to foreclose them for unpaid taxes. County officials thought about suing them, but they observed that constables "have no Real Estates," meaning the lawsuits would have been futile. "How the Collectors will Recover the money I know not," the treasurer said, wondering who would enforce the law now that the constables had refused.[23]

Once again, not all constables joined the resistance. But when they did, they made enforcing unpopular laws extremely difficult.

Ring Five: Nonviolent Protest

When the official channels of resistance failed—when tax officials collected, justices allowed lawsuits to proceed, juries convicted, and sheriffs held property auctions—ordinary folk throughout Pennsylvania built a fifth ring of defense that took the form of no-bid pacts aimed at stopping property auctions.

The strategy was time-tested and ingenious. Officials from Cumberland County explained how it worked: "Some townships have determined should their neighbors' property be Exposed to sale," they would turn out in great numbers at the auction site, but "not offer to purchase which defeats the Execution of the Law." Tax officials in Bucks County observed that crowds stopped auctions "especially where the Goods belong to the Persons who used to pay freely when they could." Elsewhere, farmers tried to halt all fore-closures, whether for unpaid taxes or private debts. This became clear to a storekeeper in Lancaster County who noted that the sheriff routinely had to "adjourn the sales for want of bidders." And when sheriffs adjourned such sales, the property usually remained in the possession of its original owner.[24]

As these comments suggest, the no-bid pacts were extremely effective. Across Pennsylvania, county officers were forced to declare: "it is in vain to expose the Goods of Inhabitants for Sale, for there are none to be purchasers." In at least nine counties (whose locations spanned the state), officials report-ed that they "could not get one single Shilling" from sheriffs' auctions, or that "no one would bid" on "goods taken by the collectors for the taxes," or that "when they seize goods no persons will buy them."[25]

Not surprisingly, the no-bid pacts became more pervasive as foreclosures became more common. In Westmoreland County, the rise in bidderless auc-tions mirrored the rise in property foreclosures. In 1783, Westmoreland expe-rienced 72 bidderless auctions. Each subsequent year, the number rose: in 1784, it was 155; in 1785, it was 267. In 1786, the year foreclosures reached their height, the number of bidderless auctions peaked at 300. Such was the scope of resistance: in 1786, people in Westmoreland County stopped auctions at a rate of nearly 6 per week.[26]

Needless to say, this kind of success depended on good organization. Farmers constructed their pacts, not on the county level, but rather within the townships that made up their counties. They assembled in local churches and taverns, at militia musters and meeting halls, to pledge their mutual sup-port toward stopping sheriffs' auctions. In Berks County, farmers from one township even put the agreement in writing. (This document later served as the primary evidence when the state prosecuted the farmers for treason— which helps to explain why no other written pacts have survived.) At least seventy-seven men from Bethel Township signed their names to a contract where they promised to "bind and engage themselves together as one man" to defeat foreclosures. The agreement included some serious enforcement provisions. The signers considered it a grave transgression if any of them failed to turn out "upon the first call" when another citizen needed assistance at a sheriff's auction. In such cases, the men of Bethel agreed that the violator would have his "goods seized without fail," and he would be "deemed an Enemy to the Liberties of this Country." So sacred did this community hold its agreement that simple passivity was considered grounds for retribution.[27]

The no-bid pacts were at their strongest in counties where townships worked in tandem. The treasurer of Fayette County explained how the networks functioned. "By a collusion of the inhabitants of any township, they may evade the payment of their taxes by refusing to bid at such sale," he reported. With the township united, no one who lived there was willing to bid for fear of reprisal. It was futile to send bidders from one township into a neighboring one because "an individual or a small number of them" would be "hardly enough" to make an auction successful in a township "where the inhabitants of it have threatened to punish such as will dare to bid for the property." Thus, the pacts were mutually reinforcing. Each township policed its own auctions and, by doing so, protected the whole. And since many townships participated, it was extremely difficult for county authorities to single out one for punishment.[28]

It needs to be emphasized that, although the pacts were usually upheld by threats of violence, they were effective because the protesters remained peaceful. Without violent outbursts (which would have overtly broken the law), state and local authorities had no one to arrest. "The laws are eluded without being openly opposed," observed the treasurer of Fayette County. And, as long as crowds refrained from violence, most officials had no idea how to defeat the no-bid pacts.[29]

Ring Six: Rough Music

This is not to say that violence never happened or that ordinary folk considered it beyond the pale. To the contrary, many Pennsylvanians believed that violence could be consistent with democracy—primarily when it was used to fight oppression (which should not be surprising, given that these people had just fought a long war to gain their independence). Violence was not the first choice for most people in dealing with their government. But when political channels were filled with obstacles, many people thought violence was an acceptable way to clear the path toward greater accountability.

Not everyone used violence in thoughtful and measured ways: clearly, some people swung first and worried about democracy later. Most often, this kind of violence consisted of outbursts by individuals. Men and women and sometimes entire households assaulted tax collectors who demanded payment, constables who served warrants, sheriffs who held auctions, or judges who ordered foreclosures. In these heated moments, some people were apt to hurl rocks, wield sticks, or throw punches at the county officials attempting to uphold state laws.[30]

Sometimes, this individual violence involved fights among county officers, with officials who were part of the resistance slugging it out with those who were not. For example, in Bedford County, Justice James Martin eventually came to blows with the county commissioner, who insisted that he prosecute recalcitrant tax collectors (they both claimed that the other one had started it, and each tried to get the other charged with assault). In Cumberland County, a tax collector named James Young who had refused to collect from his neighbors beat up the constable who came to foreclose his property for $1,210 in unpaid taxes. When the constable arrived at Young's home, the defiant collector said "he would not pay" and that, in fact, "he would never pay." When the constable attempted to seize his horse, Young choked him until he released the animal. Months later, the two scuffled again. In the spring of 1784, they tangled a third time when the constable planned to return to Young's home to confiscate property. Having heard of the impending visit, Young rode his horse to the constable's home and shouted for the man to come outside. When the constable opened the door, Young presented the horse and challenged the man to take it away. Not wanting to engage in another fight, the constable refused. Triumphant for the moment at least, Young mounted his horse and rode home, apparently satisfied that his show of force had convinced the constable to give up trying to collect from him.[31]

When violence took more collective forms, it usually followed traditional modes of crowd action. Here, the goal was to punish officials who violated community norms with ridicule and beatings in hopes of forcing them into compliance. The strategy was an old one, having roots deep in the European past and coming to America with each wave of immigrants. Whether taken from English "rough music" or French *charivari*, the effect was the same. Small groups of disguised men and sometimes entire communities (where unanimity meant that no one had to hide identities) participated in ritualized attacks aimed at getting officials to stop enforcing the law or to resign their posts entirely. The punishment was physical pain and, equally important, emotional humiliation.[32]

Usually, collective violence came with ample warning. Take, for example, the case of Manallin Township in Fayette County, where a tax collector was beaten in the spring of 1784. During the two years prior to the attack, crowds had gathered at the courthouse to protest Morris's specie taxes. Threats of violence made it hard for Fayette officials to find anyone willing to serve as a collector, noting that most appointees had chosen to pay a "high" fine rather than face "the terror of undertaking the duty of Collector." The first man brave (or foolish) enough to take the office was greeted in the night by a disguised crowd that demanded his tax ledgers and the money he had collected; they left without incident when the collector willingly turned them over. The same thing happened to the second collector, who also surrendered the money and ledgers. The third collector ran into trouble because he rebuffed the demands of the crowd that had broken into his home. The men were dressed in hunting shirts, with their faces streaked in black. As soon as the collector refused, one man beat him (rather lightly, the collector remembered) until he produced the money and documents. Before leaving, another man threatened him in a thick "Dutch" (probably German) accent, "if you go Collecting any more and Distressing for the tax you will be a Dead man and we will burn all you have, God Damn you." If the collector was surprised by this, he was probably the only one in the county.[33]

Elsewhere, ritualized violence involved an entire county and was performed without disguises. Such was the case in Washington County, where nearly every township took part in punishing a tax collector who violated county norms. In April 1786, an officer named Graham refused to heed his neighbors' warnings and, as a result, found himself accosted by a large group of men as he was collecting taxes during a break between spring rainstorms. Graham was beset in the middle of a country road by a crowd of farmers intent on teaching him a lesson. The men quickly subdued Graham, disarmed him, and broke his pistols into small pieces. They tore "his Commission and all of his papers relaiting to his Office" and threw them in the muddy road. Then the crowd ordered Graham to "stamp on them, and Imprecate curses on himself, the Commission and the Authority that gave it to him." Then, "they cut off one half of his hair" and made a pigtail on the other side. Then they "cut off the Cock of his Hat, and made him wear it in a form to render his [pigtail] the most Conspicuous." With this and "many other marks of Ignominy they Impos'd on him & to which he was obliged to submit," the men then "marched him amidst a Crowd." They walked him from township to township, collecting an ever-growing crowd and "calling at all the Still Houses in their way." At each site, the crowd was treated to a free round of drinks, and, as Graham downed his whiskey shots, they "expos'd him to every Insult, and mockery that their Invention could contrive." When the thoroughly intoxicated collector had completed his pub crawl of shame, the now-huge crowd "set him at Liberty at the entrance of Westmoreland [County] but with Threats of utter Desolation should he dare to return to our County."[34]

What most disturbed local officials (and state leaders) was that this ritualized attack seemed to reflect the democratic political culture in Washington County. According to the county treasurer, the thing that made this event the "most audacious . . . Insult that was ever offered to a Government" was that these people were so united, calm, and matter-of-fact about their proceedings. It would have been one thing, the treasurer noted, if this resistance had emerged "in a Gust of Passion." But it had not. This mass protest had unfolded "coolly, deliberately, and Prosecuted from day to day." And in the treasurer's opinion, it was precisely because such opposition had become a part of the political culture that it needed to be defeated quickly and decisively. Consequently, he urged state leaders to use "the most severe punishment" possible to destroy this resistance in a "speedy" way. He was not alone in this belief.[35]

The ranks of those who thought the rings needed to be shattered grew later that year, when, in December 1786, civil war nearly broke out in York County. The confrontation in York centered on the attempts of county farmers to halt a sheriff's auction for unpaid taxes. It began when county officials (themselves facing lawsuits from the state) attempted to defeat local no-bid pacts after a string of unsuccessful auctions. They tried to bypass the protective networks by moving all auctions to the courthouse in the town of York, where they thought potential bidders would feel safer.[36]

In response, at least 200 people from the surrounding townships assembled to enforce their no-bid pact. This group, which included a number of men of "good moral Carrectors, and of considerable Propperty," paraded through town "in good order," armed with guns and clubs. When the crowd arrived at the courthouse, a wagon had already been sold and the sheriff was taking bids on a cow. Farmers asked the sheriff to stop the auction. When he continued, three men stepped into the bidders' circle and led the cow away. The sheriff retreated and deputized ten men to arrest those who had taken away the cow. The deputies, however, were "opposed & pretty severely handled" by the crowd. Undeterred, the sheriff and his deputies went back to their homes and returned with swords and pistols to "attack" the 200 armed men. When it became clear that the sheriff and his deputies intended to use their weapons, people dispersed despite the fact that it was 200 against 11;

they obviously wished to avoid bloodshed. In the end, the officials arrested 3 men and issued warrants for several others.[37]

This did not end the resistance in York, however. At several subsequent property auctions, crowds assembled and stopped the bidding. In January 1787, county officials relocated an auction for unpaid taxes from a township with a no-bid pact to the home of a county justice, prompting a large crowd to rescue the cattle being sold. Such resistance continued to be so routine in York County that one official was forced to report, "this disorder I am nearly warranted to say is become epidemic."[38]

A decade earlier, when Pennsylvania was under British rule, the revolutionary elite considered this kind of protest to be highly patriotic. Indeed, rebellious patriots had closed courts throughout the colonies in similar ways. Much had changed in ten years. Gentlemen now considered such protests to be, as one official put it, an "infection" that "ought to be causiously as well as spirittedly treated" before it spread.[39]

And spreading it was. Following the incidents in York, revenue officials throughout the state reported threats of large-scale crowd action. The Washington County treasurer worried about the "Bad Consequences" of enforcing the law "Where the money is Not to be had." Another Washington County officer spoke of "danger from the hands of People in disguise, in dark Corners, etc. etc. etc." "I really doubt whether there is a man in the State who could Collect in this County," he concluded. In Berks County, tax officials who had initiated forty lawsuits against collectors feared that "strictly proceeding according to Law" would be the "Beginning of Troubles" because "many People have not the money & if their Effects are sold it might drive them to desperate measures." In Dauphin County, officials said the "rigorous" collection of taxes was having "dangerous consequences" among a "great many of the People" who were "unable to pay by reason of the Scarcity of Money." He reported that throughout the county "People threaten to rise and oppose the Constables" in "Commotions similar to those which lately happened in York County." Nearly everywhere, it seemed, the situation was about to bubble over, much as it had a decade before when Britain tried to use force to collect taxes from people without the money to pay.[40]

Ring Seven: The Delinquent Militia

Under such circumstances, what could the state do? Preventing this array of resistance was no simple matter. In most places, state leaders could not call out the militia to compel tax collection or to ensure the success of a sheriff's auction precisely because, as in York County, it was militiamen who were leading the protests.

State leaders also had good reason to worry that their orders would be ignored given the militia's lack of responsiveness when called out on several previous occasions. In these episodes, militiamen had rejected orders to march because they perceived the state's use of the militia to be a violation of revolutionary principles. The most noteworthy cases involved militiamen who rebuffed state orders to oust settlers from Connecticut who were living in Pennsylvania's Wyoming Valley (in the northeast portion of the state). Those orders were orchestrated by a powerful coalition of politician-speculators that cut across party lines: merchant-banker-politician Robert Morris, state comptroller general John Nicholson, banker-jurist James Wilson, and Philadelphia merchants William Bingham and Henry Drinker. These men had all heavily speculated in Wyoming lands and wanted the Connecticut settlers removed to protect their investments. Given the influence they wielded, these politicians easily convinced a majority of the Pennsylvania assembly to order militia units into Wyoming in 1784 to remove the so-called Connecticut claimants by force.[41]

In rejecting that call to arms, several county militias gave clear expression to popular ideals of the Revolution, complaining that they had been called to serve private, self-interested purposes rather than the public good. Thus, in August 1784, when the commander coordinating the Wyoming attack arrived in Northampton County, he discovered few soldiers willing to fight. "Upon our arrival at Easton," he reported, "we found neither the temper nor preparation of the militia such as we had expected to find them." He ordered Northampton County militia captains to call their companies together, but "not more than one third of the number . . . appeared at the place of Rendezvous & among these but very few declared themselves to be perfect-ly willing to go farther." Instead, "we everywhere met the following objec-tions: 'that it was the quarrel of a set of landjobbers—that the whole County was not worth the life of a single man, or the labor of the many who were now called out to quiet it.'" The militiamen claimed that they had been "drawn forth not merely to support the Laws but to extirpate the whole race of Connecticut claimants"—an objective they considered reprehensible and utterly inconsistent with the public good.[42]

In 1785, several militiamen in neighboring Berks County also refused to march. "To our Thoughts," the men said, the Connecticut settlers were "Not Being our Enimies" and so it was wrong to go. They also complained that

"the Poorer Sort of People were all ways Forced to Turn out" for militia service, while "the Wealthy of Good Estate" used their "Money" to exempt
themselves. The commanding officer later complained that he had called out
"two Classes of the Battallion" but "found the People so unwilling to go, and
so quarrelsome that it was not in my Power to do any Thing with them."[43]

Next door in Bucks County, militiamen made a far more serious stand
when called to march to Wyoming in 1785. Bucks County militiamen said
that they shared an "understanding that the Occasion of those Orders arose
from a dispute about private property." They said they were "Sensibly
touched with abhorrence of the Idea of Staining their hands with the blood
of their Countrymen & fellow Subjects, on such an occasion." In the event
that state leaders missed the reference to "subjects" and its implicit challenge
that politicians were using the government in aristocratic ways, the militiamen declared that they felt bound only to follow the 1776 constitution. And
since the orders from the state were not "Consistent with the Idea we have
of Justice & the Principles of Our Constitution," they "determined unanimously not to submit to those Orders." The militiamen also said that they
would refuse to follow any subsequent orders that "we apprehend to be
inconsistent with the Very Spirit of our Laws & [state] Constitution."[44]

So strong were their beliefs that the militiamen declared their willingness to
confront state authorities if pushed far enough. In a petition, they announced
that they would not pay any fines the state imposed on them for refusing to
attack the Connecticut settlers. And they promised that, if Pennsylvania leaders fined them, it would "Endanger the Peace & well being of this part of the
State." In a thinly veiled reference to armed resistance, they warned that, should
the state push the matter, it would "perhaps be attended with very serious
Consequences which we Sincerely wish may be avoided." If the state forced
things, these men from Bucks County were willing to fight their own government rather than march for the private gain of affluent speculators.[45]

State leaders must have been alarmed, not just by these words and actions,
but by their larger implications: militiamen framed their efforts in terms of
a larger struggle where ordinary people stood united against speculators and
government officials who worked for elite interests. The militia's stance
raised troubling questions for anyone who thought it would be easy to divide
and conquer "the people." Those expecting ordinary folk to be concerned
only about their own families and communities found instead people willing
to assist others living beyond their own networks of protection. It was a
shared sense of oppression and purpose that caused the militiamen to call the
Connecticut settlers "their Countrymen & fellow Subjects."

Moreover, it was clear by this protest—and all of the other forms of resistance—that ordinary people believed that they had the right to interpret laws and decide what was legal under the 1776 constitution and what was unconstitutional. Convinced that the legislature and judiciary were dominated by moneyed men, these people believed they needed to decide for themselves what was right and wrong based on the "Idea we have of Justice & the Principles of Our Constitution." They believed that they needed to follow a rule of law directed by their own understanding of "the Very Spirit of our Laws & Constitution." This kind of self-directed legal authority challenged the top-down ways that state leaders wanted the government and legal system to function. Many elite Pennsylvanians were deeply troubled that those whom they saw as "the masses" or "the rabble" felt so empowered. When that confident self-direction was displayed by the county militias, the elites found it positively alarming.

*   *   *

The sum effect of all this resistance is difficult to overstate. The clearest measure of its impact was the empty coffers at the state treasury. The combination of reluctant revenue officials, lenient judges, defendant-friendly juries, disobedient law officers, auction-halting crowds, and self-directed militias effectively immobilized the revenue system. "There seems to be almost a total stop in the Collecting of Taxes," reported the state treasurer in 1784. By 1785, there was a backlog of more than $1.2 million in unpaid specie taxes. By 1787, the counties had not paid 81 percent of their assessed taxes. For the man who presented the 1787 tax report—merchant, banker, bond holder, and politician Thomas FitzSimons—statewide taxpayer resistance was a "cause of alarm to all, more especially [to the retired army] officers and public creditors," men like himself, who counted on taxes to fund the yearly interest payments on their war debt certificates.[46]

The real significance of what happened in Pennsylvania was that it was part of a nationwide outbreak of popular opposition during the mid-1780s. Similar resistance emerged across the fledgling republic, started by ordinary people who believed that the revolutionary elite was attempting to dismantle democracy. They complained about a scarcity of money and unjust policies that left them unable to pay debts or taxes. In Maryland, Virginia, New Jersey, and South Carolina, protesters closed courthouses, halted sheriffs' auctions, and threatened violence if state officials continued to confiscate property for unpaid taxes. In Massachusetts, widespread popular resistance turned to civil war. After unsuccessfully petitioning for reform, people across Massachusetts, calling themselves Regulators who opposed an oppressive government, resorted to closing courts to save their possessions and farms. To put down the "Massachusetts Regulation," state leaders were forced to assemble a militia composed of merchants and former army officers, their sons and servants, and the poor of Boston, whom they paid to march. This army trudged to the countryside and, with force of arms, defeated the Regulators.[47]

The opposition in Pennsylvania, occurring as it did at the same time as these other resistance efforts, sent a chilling message to the gentlemen who governed Pennsylvania. This resistance—along with the attack on the Bank of North America, the Plan to revalue the war debt, and all of the other popular proposals—struck directly at the ideological beliefs and economic interests of the Pennsylvania elite. Fearing popular gains, these men—and others like them across America—concluded that they needed to remake state and national governments so that they would be less responsive to the popular will and more compliant with the interests and desires of moneyed men.

Part III

TAMING DEMOCRACY

(1787–1799)

8

"A Stronger Barrier against Democracy"

THE STRUGGLE OVER CONSTITUTIONS

Our chief danger arises from the democratic parts of our constitutions. It is a maxim which I hold incontrovertible, that the powers of government exercised by the people swallows up the other branches. None of the constitutions have provided sufficient checks against the democracy. The feeble Senate of Virginia is a phantom. Maryland has a more powerful senate, but the late distractions in that State, have discovered that it is not powerful enough. The check established in the constitution[s] of New York and Massachusetts is yet a stronger barrier against democracy, but they all seem insufficient.

—Edmund Randolph, Constitutional Convention, 1787

Threatened by popular political victories and widespread resistance, many elite Pennsylvanians launched an effort to remake the state and national governments so that they were less democratic. Their objective—which was shared by elite men in the other states—was to insulate critical government powers from popular control. In 1787 and 1788, these men, calling themselves Federalists, launched an aggressive—and at times ruthless—effort to create this "barrier against democracy" and get it ratified.

In response, many ordinary Pennsylvanians tried to stop these changes. This produced unprecedented attempts by rural Pennsylvanians to organize across the state to oppose the proposed federal Constitution and its limits on democracy. The culmination of this organizing was an effort by people of the middling and lower sorts to create a political party run by and for ordinary people, dedicated to enacting a popular vision of the Revolution.

The Popular Threat

By 1786, many gentlemen were convinced that, despite all of their political victories, their notion of the Revolution was falling apart. Such beliefs were ably summarized by Philadelphia merchant Stephen Collins, who declared in 1786, "The public have become theaves and pirates, entirely destitute of honour, honesty, or shame." In his mind, "the people" had taken control of the government and were now using it to unleash their "madness" upon gentlemen with a host of "abominable laws." The laws to repay the war debt were "gloomy and deplorable." "I should not wonder," he wrote in alarm, "if the public securities should be entirely annihilated." The 1785 law to print paper money was a "bad policy" that by itself had "almost destroyed" all "confidence in the public." He denounced any law that was remotely debtor-friendly as an attempt by "a rascally public" to "dissolve" contracts and escape paying creditors. As far as popular resistance was concerned, Collins was livid, calling protesting farmers "a pack of lazy, idle, lousing, whiskey-drinking, theaves."[1]

The venom behind those words came, in part, from the fact that popular policies and resistance—in short, democracy itself—threatened elite ideals. For those who believed that moneyed gentlemen understood "the public good" better than did ordinary folk, this upsurge of popular self-expression was disconcerting.

Equally alarming was how democracy threatened their personal finances. Popular calls for a revaluation of war debt certificates, bans on for-profit corporations, progressive taxation, limits on land speculation, and every other measure designed to make property more equal promised to take wealth away from the elite. The same was true of the popular resistance that halted tax collection or frustrated creditors in their attempts to foreclose on their debtors.

It was also threatening that popular politics frightened off potential European investors. Many genteel Pennsylvanians had based their ideas of personal wealth and national greatness on their belief that moneyed Europeans would purchase the investments they had to sell. Those ambitions were best captured by future Supreme Court justice James Wilson, who would become one of the chief architects of the 1787 federal Constitution. Wilson said that *"uniting the Land in America with the Capital and Labour brought from Europe"* would produce profits "greater than those which could be expected from any continued Series of mercantile Speculations—even those to the Indies not excepted." At a time when trade with the Orient represented the pinnacle of profitable investments, that was a bold claim indeed.[2]

Convinced that European money would flood into America at war's end, many gentlemen had speculated heavily in backcountry lands, war debt certificates, grist mills, timber stands, and iron foundries. They had wagered family fortunes on such ventures, using their own money and borrowing from Europeans and the Bank of North America (recall that the entire foundation of the bank itself rested on massive speculations in land and war debt certificates). Add to this the gentry's continued purchasing of luxury items to uphold their genteel status, and one can begin to appreciate the scope of the problem these men faced. By the mid-1780s, many genteel Pennsylvanians had overspent and overspeculated to such an extent that they needed Europeans to buy—and buy soon—to keep their finances from imploding.

Popular laws and protests—in Pennsylvania and across the new nation—scared off European investors who believed that democracy posed a threat to capital (and, indeed, to what many of them would have called "capitalism"). During the 1780s, moneyed Europeans said they would not yet invest in America because they were convinced that their money would not be safe in a country where economic and legal matters remained too responsive to the public will. A consortium of French and Swiss bankers made this clear in 1788 when it listed the reasons for holding out on an otherwise promising market. The bankers said they worried about the "chaotic state of the domestic debt" and the fact that tax collection was "not being carried out." They complained about the "dissension," "difficulty," and "disturbances" of popular resistance. They were repelled by protests to "impede the administration of justice," such as those by negligent county officers and farmers who stopped sheriffs' auctions. And they deplored laws that upset "normal commercial activities" by creating paper money and passing debtor relief.[3]

European investors were equally alarmed by the Pennsylvania legislature's 1785 annulment of the Bank of North America's corporate charter. Naturally, European financiers viewed private banks as "an extremely important part of a state." The same could be said of their support for profit-driven corporations in general. Consequently, moneyed Europeans, including financiers in Paris, London, Berne, and the Hague, expressed great concern when the Pennsylvania legislature repealed the bank's charter and issued strong statements against for-profit corporations. "The act of your Assembly for taking away the Charter of the Bank," wrote an American merchant in Holland, "has done more mischief to our country than you can conceive." According to the writer, "Hundreds of people . . .

in England," many of whom had "overgrown fortunes, were about to invest their cash in our lands" until "the tidings of the attack upon [the bank] reached London." After hearing of the Pennsylvania legislature's anticorporate stance, "they have all changed their minds, and consider nothing as secure in the new states."[4]

Pennsylvania gentlemen were forced to scour Europe to peddle their lands but came back empty-handed. In 1784 and 1785, William Bingham toured England, France, the Netherlands, and Italy but found few investors willing to buy. In March 1785, James Wilson's land proposals met a similar cold reception from Dutch investors. Two years later, Wilson booked passage to Europe to try to "extricate himself from his present difficulties by disposing of some of his lands" but found little success. Levi Hollingsworth faced similar troubles when he sent bundles of titles worth about $20,000 in land to England and Ireland in 1787. He reported, though, that his efforts "have all failed," leaving him "Loaded with expense." By 1788, Hollingsworth had only earned $1,100 from land sales—an amount that probably did not even cover the costs of the trip across Europe. His experiences and those of his speculating peers were ably captured by Stephen Collins, who observed, "It is a miserable time to dispose of real property in the country now."[5]

Indeed, by 1787 (and as early as the ending years of the war), the word "America" had become an epithet in European investment circles. As one agent reported, when Europeans talked about bad investments, it did not matter if they were talking about land or credit or war bonds or development deals, "The word *America* in the French language was applied to all." It was a painful reality for American gentlemen: in European investing circles, America had become synonymous with failure.[6]

With Europe refusing to invest, the speculative empires began to crumble. "We are next kin to ruin," Stephen Collins wrote to a friend in 1786. "I am almost ready to give out," Collins said, admitting that the only thing holding him up were "hopes that the abomination of these laws and times will be done away." This same sense of doom was conveyed by elite men throughout Pennsylvania who proclaimed, as one merchant put it in 1785, that "Bankruptcies are grown so familiar that they seem a thing expected."[7]

The close business connections of the late eighteenth century ensured that the peril spread even to those who had refrained from such high-stakes gambling. Speculators relied on family, friends, and business associates for loans or as cosigners who pledged to cover any losses. When speculators overreached, as they seem to have done with regularity, many a cosigner found himself hauled into court. Between 1785 and 1790, state bankruptcy files were filled with the names of the state's most notable men, who somehow found themselves tied up in the trouble: William Bingham, Stephen Collins, Clement Biddle, Blair McClenachan, and Tench Coxe.[8]

To get a sense of how far the problems spread, consider how speculation imperiled the new college at Carlisle (which later became Dickinson College). When college administrators went looking for funding to begin building the campus, they discovered that gentlemen mostly donated shares in backcountry lands or war debt certificates rather than money. As a result, by 1784, 90 percent of Dickinson College's startup money was composed of speculative investments. Even before a single building was constructed, the college's financial success was tied to the willingness of Europeans to buy American land and government securities.[9]

All was not lost for speculators and those bound to them, however. Many moneyed Europeans said they were willing to invest if the gentry could check democracy and protect investors. The Marquis de Chastellux started the list of proposed changes: "Till you order your confederation better, till you take measures in common to pay debts, which you contracted in common, till you have a form of government and a political influence, we shall not be satisfied with you on this side of the Atlantic." Englishman Samuel Vaughan added that "men of fortune" would have to see laws and a legal system that protected the "security of property" before they invested in America. Dutch bankers wanted to see taxes collected and the war debt repaid with gold and silver. They said that these changes were the only things that could "remove the prejudices of our money men and . . . accustom them again to such placings of their Capital" in America. Swiss and French bankers set the same conditions for investment—and they wanted to see a greater commitment to private banking. In short, these financiers said that the ability of the gentry to make America's government and legal system more like the ones in Europe would "decide Europe's confidence in the United States."[10]

Facing the prospect of financial ruin, elite Pennsylvanians could scarcely ignore such demands. Besides, it was not as if Europeans were asking Pennsylvania gentlemen to do something against their will: affluent Pennsylvanians had been trying since the end of the war to do much of what Europeans were requesting. Nevertheless, European demands—and the need of elite Pennsylvanians for European money—gave a new impetus to their efforts to scale back democracy.

There was, of course, a certain irony in all of this. Initially, the Revolution had been an attempt to free America from economic colonialism. But now, at the moment of freedom, America's elite founders dedicated themselves to remaking the new nation according to the demands of their former masters. In effect, they were trying to reestablish economic dependency by adopting rules of law that, during the 1760s and 1770s, they themselves had portrayed as Old World domination and oppression.

The Federal Constitution

Perhaps the most important element of this attempt to scale back democracy was replacing the Articles of Confederation with a new federal Constitution in 1787. The push for the Constitution was based in part on the belief that state governments across the new nation had been too democratic and, as a result, had produced policies—like paper money, land banks, and attempts to revalue the war debt—that threatened elite interests. Most of the men who assembled at the Constitutional Convention in Philadelphia in 1787 were also convinced that the national government under the Articles of Confederation was too weak to counter the rising tide of democracy in the states. Consequently, leading men in each state calling themselves Federalists decided to create a new national Constitution that barred states from passing popular economic policies and to establish a new federal government that would, in the words of Alexander Hamilton, contain "the amazing violence and turbulence of the democratic spirit," which had produced paper money, war debt revaluation, and debt relief and every other "popular" policy that had "spread like wild-fire" during the 1780s.[11]

Of course, this was not how the convention's sponsors pitched the idea to the Pennsylvania General Assembly. The convention was supposed to be about amending the Articles of Confederation to give the national government more power to protect shipping and to negotiate trade deals with foreign nations—which most people thought were good ideas. Had the true objectives of the convention been known, it is doubtful that the assembly would have approved the delegation it did, which, with the exception of Benjamin Franklin (a last-minute addition), consisted entirely of members of the circle surrounding Robert Morris: James Wilson, Gouverneur Morris (no relation to Robert Morris), Thomas FitzSimons, George Clymer, Jared Ingersoll, and Thomas Mifflin.

At the convention, the Morris group was joined by like-minded delegations from across the nation that were dedicated to containing democracy. Whatever differences the delegates brought to the convention (and there were many), most of them shared a core belief that democracy was to blame

FIG. 8.1. "WHAT THINK YE OF CONGRESS NOW? VIEW OF CONGRESS ON
THE ROAD TO PHILADELPHIA," ETCHING, CA. 1790, BY Y. Z. SCULP. In
this political cartoon, a giant Robert Morris (here called by his derogatory
nickname "Robert the Coffer") carries members of Congress with him to
Philadelphia. This satirical rendering captures Morris's larger-than-life persona and reveals how, at the time, he was presumed to be the most powerful
figure in the national government. (Collection of the New-York Historical
Society, negative number 44865.)

for the pains they suffered and needed to be scaled back. To be clear: the
objective was not to eliminate democracy. Rather, the idea was to create a
government where economic policy and other matters of state were better
insulated from democratic control. The objective was a government that was
less responsive to ordinary Americans and more compliant to the will of
moneyed men—something the founders believed that no state government
had done effectively during the 1780s.

Indeed, the belief that state governments had been captured by ordinary
folk caused the delegates in Philadelphia to strip from the states powers that
they believed had been used against them. Plank by plank, the new
Constitution obliterated popular policies. Consider how it killed the Plan for
the war debt. Article I took from the states control over the war debt and
vested it in Congress, thus preventing Pennsylvania from paying war debt
speculators the market worth rather than the face value for the certificates
they held. The Constitution paved the way for full payment in gold and

silver by vesting Congress with the power to tax citizens and giving it the coercive power to enforce tax collection. If farmers organized to resist those policies, the Constitution gave the national government the authority to break mass resistance in one state by bringing in militias from surrounding states.[12]

The Constitution also effectively outlawed most of the other popular reforms that ordinary Pennsylvanians had tried to enact. By itself, section ten of Article I left a host of popular policies in ruins—all in less than fifty words. It prohibited states from issuing their own paper currencies—effectively destroying state-run land banks and the system of public, long-term, low-cost credit. It barred states from enacting most forms of debt relief. Under section ten, states could not force creditors to accept anything other than "gold and silver" for the "payment of debts." It also made it illegal to enact any "law impairing the obligation of contracts." These provisions smothered calls for debt arbitration where local judges allowed debtors to pay with cows or produce instead of gold. They also stifled proposals calling for a moratorium on debt repayment. In just a few paragraphs, section ten created a tidal shift in power that favored the interests of moneyed Americans (and European financiers) over ordinary Americans.[13]

The Constitution's framers made it hard for ordinary folk to enact such policies on the federal level by building multiple checks against democracy into the structure of the new national government. Perhaps the most important check was the executive branch—where a president armed with veto power could stop popular ideas that threatened the gentry. Robert Morris's former underling in the Office of Finance, Gouverneur Morris, said the president needed the veto to keep Congress from enacting such policies as "Emissions of paper money, largess to the people, a remission of debts, and similar measures."[14]

Dividing Congress between the House of Representatives and the Senate provided another check. Specifically, the framers saw a "good Senate" as the best way to contain what Edmund Randolph called the "turbulence and follies of democracy." Alexander Hamilton explained that the Senate would "check the imprudence of democracy" by forming a "barrier against every pernicious innovation"—like the "torrent" of calls for paper money and debt relief that had flooded state assemblies.[15]

Finally, the framers believed that they could check the voice of the people in the most democratic branch of the federal government—the House of Representatives—by making it hard for ordinary folk to get elected to office. According to James Wilson, large election districts would ensure the selection of "men of intelligence & uprightness" (by which he meant members of the gentry). James Madison said that large election districts would provide a better "defence agst. the inconveniences of democracy." Madison explained that large districts would "divide the community" and make it difficult for ordinary citizens to "unite in the pursuit" of a "common interest" like paper money and other policies by which "Debtors have defrauded their creditors."[16]

Back in Pennsylvania, all of these changes bolstered the confidence of those whose fortunes and vision of America's future depended on narrowing democracy. Genteel Pennsylvanians across the state proclaimed that the Constitution would finally unleash the flood of foreign investment for which they had long been waiting. Many gentlemen were practically giddy over the ban on paper money and the requirement that debts be paid in gold and silver. Dr. Benjamin Rush gushed that the "eternal veto" on paper money would help to initiate "the beginning of a year of jubilee in Pennsylvania." Jasper Yeates, a merchant from Lancaster County, said the ban would make the nation "respectable in the eyes of all Europe" and cause "Foreigners" to "trust us" with their money. James Wilson—who had said that paper currencies and prodebtor laws threatened to overturn "peace with foreign nations"— believed that the paper money ban would usher in a wave of investment. Indeed, Wilson went so far as to say that if the Constitution consisted only of a single line of text banning paper money, "I think it would be worth our adoption."[17]

Land speculators believed that the Constitution would provide the same boost for real estate. Merchant Levi Hollingsworth believed the Constitution would save his skin by making a "favorable impression on the minds of Europeans" and would "induce men of fortune to Speculate in Lands in this Country." So too did Miers Fisher, who reported in October 1787 to his English creditor, the London banker Robert Barclay, that Europeans should have no worries about investing in America since the new form of government was practically like the one in England. The office of president may not be hereditary like that of the British king, "yet the Difference is not so great, as one would, at first, imagine." Fisher also insisted that the new Senate was just like the House of Lords: filled with the "most independent & wealthy Characters." What would foreign investors have to fear, he asked, from this government where the "Majority" of the American people could "never, upon any popular Convulsion, be put in to carry any improper Point"? Fisher insisted that, because the new government was so thoroughly insulated from democratic control, "before Long" the land market would become so hot that nearly everything "will become valuable."

In a not-so-subtle sales pitch, Fisher casually noted that the "Paper on which I write is manufactured at Our Mills in Brandywine," a venture which could earn any lucky investor a "very moderate Profit."[18]

Likewise, many of those who held war debt certificates believed that the new Constitution greatly increased their chances of getting paid at full face value in gold and silver. One man, who complained that the current situation in Pennsylvania was "very much against speculation," saw the Constitution as his salvation. "I know of nothing at present that makes for a Rise in Stocks, except the adoption of our New Constitution." Retired general Richard Butler (also a land speculator) was more to the point: "*I want the money*," he said emphatically, referring to the Constitution and his certificate collection.[19]

Ultimately, any number of reasons prompted gentlemen to favor the new federal Constitution. There can be no denying, however, that many of those reasons depended on narrowing democracy—whether for personal gain, to promote gentry rule, or to secure their vision of America's future greatness (or all three reasons at once).

The Rush to Ratification

To get the Constitution enacted, however, Pennsylvania Federalists needed to get their barrier against democracy past a public that, by the Federalists' own admission, was dedicated to democracy. In Pennsylvania, the solution was to use the element of surprise and get the Constitution ratified with as little public debate as possible. They would call for a state ratification convention before any opposition had a chance to organize.

The Federalists' ratification campaign was both masterful and ruthless. On September 28, just ten days after the first public reading of the new Constitution (and several hours before Congress called on the states to ratify it), Philadelphian George Clymer (a banker and war debt speculator) rose from his chair in the assembly and called for ratification elections—to be held just twelve days later. This was barely enough time for a rider to get copies of the Constitution to the western counties, let alone for serious debate over such an important matter. When representatives from the central and western counties stormed out of the assembly in protest, Federalists sent a "number of volunteer gentlemen" to bring them back by force. The posse was led by future admiral of the U.S. Navy John Barry (who was at the time captain of Robert Morris's ship *Asia*, a holder of many war debt certificates, and a partner in a $30,000 land speculation deal with James Wilson). They broke down the door of the boardinghouse where the representatives were staying, hauled them out of bed, and carried them through the streets to the state house. After literally dumping these men into their seats, Federalists called for elections. Their only concession was moving the date to three weeks later.[20]

During the month before the elections, Federalists launched an equally aggressive campaign to sell the Constitution. The strategy was worked out in advance by the leading Federalists (one opponent described them as "wealthy Men & Merchants, who have a continual Correspondence with each other"). The effort focused on framing the debate over ratification by controlling communications. In particular, the Federalists relied on the fact that they owned most of the state's newspapers—the only places people could get news beyond word of mouth. They used the papers to unleash a one-sided barrage of pro-Constitution editorials. Federalist newspapers— which is to say most newspapers—tended only to print editorials and news items that placed the Constitution in the best possible light or those undermining the opposition (branded "Antifederalists").[21]

Federalists also attempted to stifle the opposition. The few newspaper editors who came out against the Constitution received swift retribution: merchants pulled advertisements and Federalist readers "withdrew their Subscriptions." In some places, "violent Threats were thrown out against the [Antifederalist printers] & Attempts were made to injure their Business." Meanwhile, Federalist gentlemen, who owned most of the printing shops and the taverns that served as unofficial post offices, turned the mail system into a weapon against the opposition. They "stopped & destroyed" Antifederalists' "Pamphlets & Newspapers." Federalist postmasters "frequently intercepted" Antifederalist mail and "detained" it "till they Judged what it contained would be antiquated" or else "suppressed" it altogether. They also "broke" open letters and "selected & published" excerpts of people's mail in newspapers to embarrass them.[22]

Federalist leaders took things to such extremes that they astonished even those who favored the new Constitution. "If you were only here to see and hear those people, to observe the means they are using to effect this purpose," wrote Pennsylvania vice president David Redick. "To hear the Tories declare they will draw their sword[s] in its defense, to see the Quakers running about signing declarations and petitions in favor of it before they have time to examine it, to see gentlemen running into the country and neighboring towns haranguing the rabble"—all of this was for Redick "strong evidence that these people know [the Constitution] will not bear an examination and therefore wishes to adopt it first and consider it afterward."[23]

Part of that "haranguing" involved presenting the Constitution as a democratic document that would solve every imaginable problem. Despite privately bashing democracy, Pennsylvania Federalists portrayed the Constitution as being, in James Wilson's words, "purely democratical." As far as cures went, Dr. Benjamin Rush prescribed the Constitution for everything from economic ruin to the decline of religion to the spread of immorality and vice—including "the numerous instances of conjugal infelicity and divorces, etc. among the lower classes of people."[24]

Federalists also offered reassurances that, just because the Constitution gave the federal government great power, it did not mean that Congress or the president would use it. "The good sense of the citizens of the United States is not to be alarmed by the picture of taxes collected at the point of a bayonet," James Wilson promised. He used the same argument to deflect criticism about the lack of a bill of rights. Wilson said the Constitution was so democratic that a bill of rights was "not only unnecessary, but preposterous and dangerous." Federalist Thomas McKean, chief justice of the Pennsylvania court system, stated that a bill of rights was "an unnecessary instrument, for, in fact, the whole plan of government is nothing more than a bill of rights."[25]

Those arguments were evidently convincing to large pockets of ordinary folk across the state. Promises of economic revival certainly convinced the lower sort in Philadelphia to vote for ratification in hopes that the new government could revive shipping and enact a new tax on imports that would encourage people to buy American-made goods. Many farmers in the southeastern counties believed the Constitution would open foreign markets for their grain. Most Quakers believed that Federalist leaders, as undemocratic as they were, would protect their rights better than Constitutionalists who had once barred them from voting and who were now mostly Antifederalists. In the western counties, the Constitution had the support of an influential group of merchants, lawyers, and farmers who believed ratification would open trade down the Mississippi River.[26]

There was, however, considerable opposition throughout the state. In the northern and western counties, discontent was rampant. "I am exceedingly surprised how this matter is forcing on against a great majority of the people," declared an official from Northumberland County. "I'm sure four-fifths of the people here are against" the Constitution. Another observer was "very confident that on the West side of the Susquehanna in this state there is at least nine out of every ten that would at the risk of their lives & property be as willing to oppose the new constitution as they were the British in their late desighns." The aristocratic Charles Nisbet, president of Dickinson College, shared the assessment, stating, "the counties on this side of the Susquehanna are averse" to the new Constitution, believing it would "take away what they falsely call liberty." Farmers "beyond the Allegany Mountains" were said to be "enraged at it." In Pittsburgh, a merchant reported that the "Majority of the People in this Country except in this depraved place Pittsburgh are perfectly opposed to our new consolidated Govt." He said Hugh Brackenridge had held a celebration for the federal Constitution in Pittsburgh, but only a "*dozen* or *fifteen*" people turned out, and they were "discharged officers" from the army who "embrace dispotick principles."[27]

Given the short time frame, however, this opposition could not mobilize quickly enough. Antifederalists were unable to overcome the one-sided newspaper campaign and the mail theft that often made it impossible to coordinate any kind of opposition. Their efforts also foundered on the same weaknesses that had plagued popular politics in the past: the lack of resources and the many divisions among "the people." As a result, the ratification contest produced a narrow Federalist victory in Pennsylvania.

In the end, though, it is difficult to say anything about what the ratification elections really meant because so few people actually voted. Antifederalist leaders estimated that only about 13,000 of the state's 70,000 eligible voters had gone to the polls—meaning that about 82 percent had stayed home. Moreover, by Antifederalist calculations, Federalists had carried only 6,800 votes statewide—or less than 10 percent of the electorate. Federalists did not dispute the figures. Rather, they argued that low voter turnout was a "very unfair mode of determining the strength or number of friends of the new government." Thus, whatever the ratification vote signified, it was hardly a popular endorsement of the Constitution.[28]

Indeed, support may have been even weaker than the vote totals suggest. Federalists reported strong opposition in several of the counties that elected proratification candidates. In York County, where the delegation was completely Federalist, "great numbers of the people" were said to be "much dissatisfyd" with the Constitution. Likewise, after traveling through the German-dominated eastern counties, one Federalist reported that the Constitution enjoyed little support among the people he met. "The Germans are all against the New constitution," the man explained. "The better sort" were "much afraid of the Foederal constitution in its present form without a bill of rights," and "the inferior class are totally against it, from their current Sentiment against proud & Lordly Idea's."[29]

In Luzerne County, the choice of a Federalist candidate in the ratification election had nothing to do with the Constitution; instead, as strange as it may seem, the selection of Federalist Timothy Pickering was part of an elaborate plot to kidnap him. The ratification vote had come at an especially tense moment in the long-standing dispute over the Wyoming Valley. Shortly before the election, Pickering (whose titles derived from a Pennsylvania speculation company) had ordered the arrest of John Franklin, one of the settlers who had purchased land from the Connecticut-based company. Fearing retribution, Pickering had fled to Philadelphia. Weeks later, in what seemed a shocking turn of events, Luzerne voters elected Pickering to the ratification convention. Pickering interpreted the vote as a sign that the "Connecticut settlers" had come to their senses. Exuberant, he made immediate plans to ride home to be among (those he thought were) his adoring constituents. Pickering's wife, however, warned him to stay away, saying the vote had been a sham. "Whatever may be the general opinion," Rebecca Pickering wrote to her husband, the Constitution's supporters in Luzerne were "few in number." She told him most people had voted for Pickering solely to heighten his importance so they could take him hostage to force the state to free Franklin. Rebecca pleaded with him not to come home because she was "convinced you will be taken prisoner." "They will use you," she said, to "compel the state to release him, or you must suffer." Pickering, flush with confidence from the ratification victory, dismissed his wife's letter as paranoia. It turned out he should have listened. As soon as Pickering arrived home, a large crowd took him by force and held him captive until the state released Franklin. Thus, although Luzerne technically voted for ratification, it was hardly a reliable center of support for the Constitution or for the Federalists.[30]

Organizing the People

The shaky support for the Constitution convinced many of its opponents that they could organize ordinary folk across the state to stop ratification despite the vote. That effort began in Cumberland County in late 1787 and by the next spring had spread throughout much of the central counties. The attempt to bring people together revealed the potential of popular mobilization: it showed how ordinary people could self-organize, develop ways to recruit others, and coordinate resistance. In short, this mobilization started to create a democratic political network that could, if expanded, revolutionize state politics.

Organizing efforts in Cumberland County began on the day after Christmas 1787 at a Federalist ratification celebration in the town of Carlisle. At five o'clock on the evening of December 26, Carlisle Federalists rang bells and beat on drums to call a meeting in the public square to praise the new Constitution. They had paid men to haul a cannon from the armory along with enough powder to fire it thirteen times, each shot a salute to one of the states they hoped would ratify. As the ceremony got under way, a large crowd of Carlisle Antifederalists arrived to stop the proceedings. They declared the celebration to be an illegal assembly because the Federalists had not gotten public approval to use the town square and cannon. The protesters stated that these violations made the gathering of Federalists an "unhallowed riotous mob"—the very charges that gentlemen in the town usually made against crowds of the middling and lower sorts. The Carlisle Federalists laughed off the charges and ordered the protesters to disperse. The gentleman loading the cannon said he would "blow them up in the air" if they did not leave. Angered at the threat, the crowd began pelting the Federalists with staves from a broken barrel. A fight broke out between the two sides, and the Federalists, who were far outnumbered, retreated.

The following day, December 27, Carlisle Federalists tried once again to conduct their celebration. This time, they were met by an even larger crowd carrying effigies of Federalists James Wilson and Thomas McKean. The crowd burned the effigies and, before the flames had died, threw a copy of the federal Constitution onto the pyre.[31]

The push to organize came the next day, when word spread that Federalist judges in Carlisle planned to ask the state supreme court for arrest warrants against the protest organizers. From what we can tell, the main organizers were a mixed group. The core included many farmers, a tailor, and a judge. The vast majority were from the middling sort. They were literate, land-owning yeomen who possessed slightly more taxable property than the average Cumberland citizen. A few, like county judge John Jordan, carried the gentleman's title "esquire." Some of the organizers owned a slave or several slaves, including farmer-politician Robert Whitehill. On the whole, however, even the most propertied of them was, as John Jordan put it, "not of the richest sort." Several could trace their lineage in Cumberland County back a few generations. Some, like Whitehill, had come from eastern counties such as Lancaster before the war. Others hailed from Scotland, arriving in the decades before the war with Britain or, like tailor and yeoman William Petrikin, as the conflict drew to a close. No doubt, more than a few had been born in Protestant settlements in Ireland. One organizer said he "belonged to a Volunteer Company in Ireland" and "bravely espoused the cause of liberty" against Britain both there and in America—a fight for liberty he promised never to "desert."[32]

Organizers saw themselves as patriots defending the Revolution and, consequently, they modeled their organizing after the efforts of the 1760s and 1770s. To the chagrin of John Montgomery, a Federalist town official, the "rioters" quickly set about "forming combinations" and creating a "correspondent Committee" (now run by middling folk rather than the gentry) to communicate with other parts of the county and beyond the borders of Cumberland. They also used express riders—the tactic that had made Paul Revere famous. Montgomery said they "made the best of it, by riding, and sending their emissaries through the country inflaming the minds of the people." Express riders took the "cause of liberty" to distant townships, calling on others "to lift up their voices against the most detestable system of tyranny and arbitrary power that was ever devised for the total and final destruction of freedom."[33]

In February 1788, Cumberland organizers began recruiting in the neighboring counties. They sent waves of riders south into Franklin and York counties and east across the Susquehanna River into Dauphin County. By late February, William Petrikin reported, those efforts had achieved success. "The people here in this County and Franklin County are forming Societys for the purpose of opposing this detastable Fedrall conspiracy: we almost every day here of some new society of this nature being formed." And, like during the conflict with Britain, the committees organized militia companies, where the privates were allowed to vote on nearly everything, as they had during the heady days in 1775.[34]

The fruits of this organizing became clear on February 23 when Federalist officials in Carlisle finally arrested the men who had disrupted their ratification celebrations back in December. Twenty-one protesters—a group that included county judge John Jordan—were brought to the courthouse. Federalist justices offered to free the men on bail until their trials. Seven of the protesters, including tailor William Petrikin, refused bail and instead went to jail. That jail-instead-of-bail strategy became the basis of a new protest that flexed the network's power.

In response to the jailings, the political organization sprang to action. "Immediately the drum beat to arms and the bell was rung," Federalist John Montgomery reported. "In consequence of a preconcerted plan, riders had gone out to all quarters warning the friends of freedom to collect and rescue their persecuted brethren." In the days that followed, "A party consisting chiefly of such boys and fellows of dissolute character went through town every night afterwards beating the drum" and giving out "information" to the public. Riders were dispatched "from time to time" to the countryside to provide "Very exact intelligence . . . of their proceedings."[35]

On March 1, "the people" descended on Carlisle. Montgomery watched it all unfold: "At break of day, according to appointment and expectation, the bell began to ring," whereupon "the militia armed and under their officers, from all parts of the county" entered the town. The Cumberland farmers who had marched into Carlisle were soon joined by several militia companies "from Dauphin County and from the Redlands of York County." Next came a committee of "five persons with delegated power from the people of Dauphin County" (they had decided to send militia representatives rather than full companies). Estimates of the number of troops assembled in Carlisle varied: John Montgomery set the total at 500; the Federalist-run *Carlisle Gazette* reported "About 1500 men." One Federalist called the crowd filling the town square a collection of "dirty rag-a-muffin-looking black-guards" such as he had "never beheld." The newspaper portrayed the troops as being "generally men of property and good characters," an assessment shared by Montgomery, who noted that the protesters included "many respectable characters" and that "they seemed upon this occasion as anxious to preserve peace and good order."[36]

When the last company arrived at ten o'clock that morning, the militias "marched to the jail and demanded the prisoners; upon which they received them, placed them in their front, and marched through the town huzzaing, singing, hallooing, firing, and the like." Meanwhile, the Dauphin County delegation brokered a deal with the town's Federalists to drop all charges. After representatives from each militia company accepted the deal (the farmers emphasized order and democracy to the end), the militiamen declared victory and huzzahed again. They assembled in rank and fired their guns in a salute that cascaded down the line "from right to left of the companies." Finally, they all "marched out of town in good order, without injuring any person or property, except two balls which was fired through a tavernkeeper's sign who is said to be a warm Federalist."[37]

Those musket ball holes at the tavern frequented by Federalist gentlemen revealed the class tensions that underlay the whole proceedings: these farmers shared a belief that the federal Constitution—and the various other policies of the new government—represented victories for wealthy gentlemen and losses for the interests and ideals of ordinary folk. Those tensions were obvious to John Montgomery, who reported that many of the militiamen believed that elite Federalists in Carlisle "are enemies to equal liberty, and that they are in favor of the Constitution, because they expect to be enabled under it to make dependents of the farmers, who will be reduced to a sort of vassalage."[38]

There was a considerable anti-elite sentiment to the proceedings. For example, the militia companies marched into town singing a song they called "Federal Joy," which recounted the day-after-Christmas showdown in Carlisle. The lyrics spoke of how Federalists—"Lawyers, doctors and store-keepers"—with their "powdered heads" and "Soften'd hands" had "march[ed] with curls flying." The song sarcastically recalled the great tragedy of the conflict: how the gentry's ensuing fight had "Despoil'd the work of their hair-dressers." The song concluded in a far more serious vein, though, warning gentlemen that "Liberties sons" would not "by fed'rals be controul'd." The last rhyme threatened that "if those harpies seek preferment" and tried to enrich themselves under their new government, they would end up digging "graves for their own internment."[39]

Weeks later, a similar protest erupted in nearby Huntingdon County after Federalists publicly destroyed petitions against the Constitution. In response, a group of protesters made effigies of two local Federalists and paraded them to the courthouse "upon the backs of old *scabby* ponies." A Federalist justice, who was caricatured by one of the effigies, "thinking his dignity wounded, ordered the officers of the court to assist his partisans in apprehending the effigy-men." After they threw the men in jail, "Immediately the county took the alarm, assembled," and militia companies "liberated the sons of liberty." The freed prisoners "passed down the jail steps, under loud huzzas and repeated acclamations of joy from a large con-course of people." With the prisoners free, the militias "retired from the town" peacefully. On their way out, they declared their intention to "*duck*" Federalists in a pond if they "repeated their insults." Months later, the militia returned when local Federalists tried to prosecute the men arrested for the effigies. Several companies of militia forcibly stopped the court proceedings, destroyed all records of the arrests, and then marched back home.[40]

The Harrisburg Convention: Lost Opportunities

These successes encouraged organizers to try something truly remarkable: they attempted to expand their network across the state to organize "the people" to overturn the state's ratification vote. The idea was hatched at a

1788 "general meeting" held "in the spring, consisting of delegates from the sevral township[s] and societys in the Countys of York, Dauphin, Cumberland, and Franklin." The delegates planned a statewide "General Conference" to be held in Harrisburg that September to "unite the opposition in the different parts of the state that they might act in concert to form committees and associations." Delegates envisioned the Harrisburg conference opening "a Chanel of communication through-out the united states" to pave the way toward a nationwide popular organization. They imagined that this new political network would create a voting bloc "so formidable to the Federalists that they durst not have refused us our demands."[41]

Many Federalists were, indeed, terrified by the prospect of the convention. One Federalist was so worried that Cumberland organizers would defeat the Constitution (and enact "very alarming" policies like revaluing the war debt) that he predicted that this emerging popular movement would soon engulf the state in "Blood and slaughter" between the gentry and ordinary folk. He went so far as to say that the only solution was "sending a sufficient body of militia instantly to remove the sinews of war from Carlisle."[42]

Unbeknown to Federalists, however, the Cumberland organizers had their hands full trying to get ordinary Pennsylvanians to participate in the Harrisburg conference. The biggest enemy was time. If they were going to stop the federal Constitution, organizers needed to strike before enough states had ratified it. Thus, they only gave themselves a few months to pull off an unprecedented organizing feat. In the end, organizers managed to have their convention. But the concessions they made on the road to Harrisburg ultimately doomed their larger goals.

The central problem for the Harrisburg conference was figuring out how to contact the largely German-speaking eastern counties. Although organizers had mobilized the central counties, they still felt isolated and worried about how they would reach people to the east. "We are at a great loss here for Inteligence," Petrikin confessed in February 1788. By May, the questions had become more serious: "Do you hear how the people is affected in other States and in other parts of this State?" Petrikin asked a correspondent. "Do you think opposition is in vain?" Will the proposed Constitution "be established in Spite of all we can do?" Knowing they were "in a great measure Shut out from inteligence that can be credited," leaders in central Pennsylvania concluded that they could not organize the east fast enough by themselves to stop ratification.[43]

Consequently, they ceded the task to Philadelphia gentlemen known to oppose the Constitution. It was a risky gamble: many of these elite

Antifederalists were the same Constitutionalist politicians who had disappointed them so badly in the past. Almost to a man, they were large land and war debt speculators who had worked against popular policies. Even now, most of them only opposed the Constitution because the Morris circle had threatened to cut them out of wealth and power, just as it had done during the 1780s. Nevertheless, given the time constraints, conference organizers felt they had no choice. And so they asked the gentlemen of the Antifederalist "Society in the City" to organize Philadelphia and "the lower Counties" to attend the Harrisburg convention in September. The decision would backfire badly.[44]

The pitfalls of relying on elite Antifederalists should already have been apparent: in January 1788, these same men flubbed an attempt to mount a petition campaign to overturn the state's ratification vote. Philadelphia Antifederalists drafted a petition demanding that the assembly reject the state's ratification vote because the Constitutional Convention in 1787 had only been empowered to revise the Articles of Confederation, not create a new form of government. The task of distributing this petition fell to John Nicholson, a leading Constitutionalist politician and one of the biggest land and war debt speculators in the state.[45]

Nicholson's failures with the petition drive foreshadowed how eastern Antifederalists would undermine the Harrisburg convention: he was afraid to send the petition to ordinary folk. Nicholson only mailed the petition to gentlemen and avoided contacting the actual leaders of the grassroots opposition because he knew they opposed speculators like himself. He sent the petition to tax officials, land agents, and elite business contacts, who were generally not excited about stirring up opposition to the Constitution. Some of them opposed the Constitution but believed "an appeal" to the "people at large" was "dangerous." Elsewhere, Nicholson's contacts turned out to be staunch Federalists. In York County, he mailed the petition to a business associate who thought "the People" were bent on "total Anarchy" and who believed that the Constitution would "quiet the minds of the People here after the Riot in York" in 1786. In Cumberland County—where opposition to the Constitution was overwhelming—Nicholson somehow found two of its few supporters: a minister in Carlisle described as an "insignificant tool of the mock gentry here," who took to the pulpit to preach that the Constitution was the work of God, and another man whom local Antifederalists called "our most Malicious enemy." Needless to say, none of these correspondents did much to increase the petition's circulation.[46]

In fact, the petition only circulated at all because Cumberland organizers managed to get a hold of one. They immediately copied it by hand and sent it out through their correspondence network. It took less than three weeks for them to collect signatures on stacks of petitions, which they sent to Philadelphia. The results from Cumberland and Franklin counties were impressive. By February 22, they had sent over 100 separate petitions to the general assembly. Cumberland County produced 2,321 signatures, about 59 percent of the taxable population. In Franklin County, 1,884 people signed—approximately 84 percent of the county's adult male population.[47]

Despite the achievements of Cumberland and Franklin counties, the statewide petition campaign was a failure. Due to Nicholson's selective mailings, the petition never circulated in most counties or only reached a few townships. In other counties, the drive was derailed by local Federalists. In Northumberland County, the petition campaign initially had great success, causing one Federalist to complain that "there is no News here only them d[a]mned antifeoderal Petitions are Signing here very fast." To defeat the campaign, Northumberland's representatives (who were Federalists) simply refused to submit them to the assembly. In Huntingdon County, Federalists were less subtle in their opposition: they confiscated signed petitions and then held a public ceremony where they ripped them to pieces. All of this opposition and mismanagement left the final statewide tally at just over 6,000 signatures—about 70 percent of which came from Cumberland and Franklin counties. Even if the total had been much greater, however, the Federalist-controlled assembly no doubt would have voted to table them without any debate—just as it did with the petitions that were sumbitted.[48]

Despite this failure, Cumberland organizers would turn to the Philadelphia gentlemen for help in organizing the Harrisburg convention. The Cumberland men even toned down their objections to the Constitution and did not mention paper money or the war debt in hopes of finding common ground with the eastern elite. Just months before, the Cumberland network had petitioned for paper money, land banks, and a revaluation of the war debt. Now it was silent on these issues to appease the eastern gentlemen and convince them to organize the German-speaking counties in the east.[49]

The concessions were probably not worth it: for whatever reason, the eastern Antifederalists never contacted any Germans. When the Harrisburg convention met, none of the German townships was represented—a fact Federalists later trumpeted in newspaper editorials.[50]

Nor did the Antifederalist elite recruit ordinary folk, who frightened them more than the Morris circle and its Constitution. In fact, leading Antifederalist Charles Pettit (who may have owned more war debt certificates than anyone else in the state) organized delegations specifically to stifle the opposition from the central and western counties. He only recruited easterners willing to make a "peaceable acquiescense" to the Constitution. And he urged "the leading men in those counties" to do the same.[51]

That objective was shared by most of the eastern Antifederalist elite. For example, the chief organizer in Bucks County was a man named James Hanna, who thought it was "madness and folly" to continue opposing the Constitution. To ensure that the county delegation would stop the opposition Hanna told his associates to abandon the idea of democratic elections in favor of simply selecting people who shared their views. He told them that, if they did not think "the people" would vote for representative who would "acquiesce" to the new Constitution, then they should simply "write or call on a few of the most respectable people of your township, to attend at the general meeting." This way, Hanna was certain he could produce a majority large enough to "swallow" any townships pushing a "more injurious" opposition. (Philadelphia Federalists somehow got hold of Hanna's letter and published it in the *Pennsylvania Gazette*; they used it to portray the Antifederalists as antidemocratic elitists who were trying to oppose the democratic federal Constitution.)[52]

The elite effort to "swallow" the opposition proved to be successful. The bellwether of the convention was the Philadelphia delegation, headed by two of the state's largest war debt speculators: Pettit and Blair McClenachan. When the delegates subsequently appointed McClenachan to be chairman of the meeting, the conference was effectively finished as a tool of reform. The eastern counties pushed through a statement of support for the Constitution, calling only for the addition of a limited bill of rights. Then, McClenachan used the meeting to lobby for himself and Pettit as candidates for the upcoming congressional elections. They allowed Cumberland organizers to pass a resolution calling on delegates to organize new committees of correspondence across the state, and then promptly ignored it once the meeting had adjourned.[53]

In the end, the convention was so tepid that many Federalists reported its results with enthusiasm. One Federalist writer praised the meeting's "moderation" and "*acquiescence*." Another told George Washington that "no harm" had come from the convention; to the contrary, it seemed that elite Antifederalists had switched sides. "Our Antifederalists have changed their battery," he wrote. "They are now very Federal."[54]

He was right: many elite Antifederalists now joined hands with their former enemies. One Federalist leader put it this way: Antifederalist gentlemen had decided to "let themselves down as easy as possible and to come in for a share of the good things the new government may have to bestow."[55]

Many elite Antifederalists did indeed attempt to "come in for a share of the good things"—none more so than Charles Pettit and John Nicholson. For his part, Pettit quickly disavowed his work as a Constitutionalist and Antifederalist. In 1791, seeking appointment to the newly proposed Bank of the United States, he told George Washington that his opposition to the party of Morris had been "misrepresented." Pettit said that it only appeared he had been working against the Morris faction; in reality, he was secretly "leading the people into due order and submission."[56]

Nicholson's conversion was even more dramatic. After spending the better part of a decade in the opposition—and even attempting to prosecute Morris for embezzling government monies—Nicholson soon formed a land partnership with the financier. Their past disagreements behind them, Morris and Nicholson united to launch one of the most audacious land-speculating ventures the continent had ever seen. Between 1792 and 1795, Morris added to his holdings approximately 3.3 million acres of land on the state's northern and western frontiers. Nicholson acquired another 4 million acres of Pennsylvania land and millions of acres in other states (accumulating over $12 million in debts in the process). It was said Nicholson owned one-seventh of Pennsylvania on his own and in partnership with Morris. For Nicholson, the "good things" the government bestowed had softened his feeling about those he had once denounced as an "Aristocratic Junto."[57]

For Cumberland organizers who remained determined to oppose this "Junto," the Harrisburg convention was a disaster. "I am Clearly of [the] opinion our Harrisburgh conference did more injury to our cause than all the stratagems of our advarsaries," William Petrikin wrote to Nicholson. "Our friends throughout the state expected something decisive from us and we spent our whole time Canvassing for places in Congress." He had intended for these new networks to energize the citizenry to political action. Instead, "some of our leaders" had "defeated every salutary measure." To Petrikin, the betrayals at the convention had destroyed the chance to build a statewide organization. "We will perhaps never find the people in the same spirit again," he lamented. "Opportunitys once lost is not easily recovered."[58]

Ever the optimist, William Petrikin continued to hope that a new meeting could be organized to "unite the Friends of Liberty in the different counties." He persisted in writing to Nicholson, urging that "our friends in the city must take the Lower counties in their own hand." And he continued to prod Nicholson to mobilize eastern farmers according to the same democratic "Spirit" that had become standard "Business in these Back Counties." Petrikin even dreamed that, with a little financial support, he could start a newspaper to serve as a source of reliable political information for central Pennsylvania's farmers. Nicholson showed no interest in any of Petrikin's ideas.[59]

Unlike Petrikin, others descended into hopelessness, dropping their plans to organize the state and even retreating from electoral politics altogether. Most ordinary folk had given up on the Constitutionalist Party, which many of them had once seen as a promising vehicle for reform. Just as Federalist Tench Coxe had predicted in 1787, the "former cordiality" between the elite and ordinary Constitutionalists had given way to "bitter" animosity that tore "the Constitutionalist Party to pieces."[60]

Having lost faith in the two main political options, voter turnout fell to new lows in many of the counties that were Antifederalist strongholds. For example, in the fall 1788 elections, the average turnout in Pennsylvania was about 21 percent. As usual, Cumberland County offered the best showing in the state, with 47 percent voter turnout (85 percent of whom voted for Antifederalist candidates)—a steep decline from previous elections. The turnout was anemic in virtually every other county where popular protests had traditionally shown strength. In Bedford County, 264 people voted, or 10 percent of the electorate. Only 9.8 percent of Berks County's 4,700 voters went to the polls; in Washington County, the turnout rate was just 8.6 percent. In Fayette County, 80 voters cast their ballots. In Luzerne County, just 18 people voted.[61]

In the face of that retreat, Pennsylvania Federalists attempted to secure a long-awaited prize: overturning the democratic 1776 state constitution. Although many ordinary folk were angered by the effort to revoke their beloved constitution, they were too defeated to take action. "The people as far as I know are grown callow to an extreme," reported rural politician William Findley, who had led the political fights against the Morris circle during the 1780s. "The people here condemn the Calling of a Convention by the Assembly very generally yet will not exert themselves to oppose the measure." "We have circulated petitions," he noted, "and many I know have signed, but I am doubtful of there being returned to send down" to Philadelphia. He observed that "some leading men amongst us who could have promoted petitioning to advantage, in a kind of sullen fit, refused to sign themselves or promote the signing by others, though heartily adverse to the measure." The only real opposition came from the central Pennsylvania network. According to a hostile newspaper report, people in "Cumberland and Franklin County" attempted to use "the same arguments and stratagems to prevent the alteration of our State Constitution that they did to prevent the adoption of the federal government." With little popular organizing elsewhere, those efforts went nowhere.[62]

Facing no organized opposition, Federalists in 1790 pushed through a new state constitution—without even allowing the new document to come up for a popular vote. In the end, even Findley caved in to the plan for the new constitution, which was both drafted and ratified in a single backroom conference. He even yielded to Federalist plans to prohibit a popular vote on its ratification. Perhaps Findley hoped to gain concessions from Federalists; maybe his spirit had been broken. Whatever the reason, he joined the all-Federalist constitutional committee in pushing through a document that repudiated many of the ideals for which he had fought during the 1780s. Despite this surrender, Findley would remain a bitter opponent of Robert Morris and, later, Alexander Hamilton. He would continue to curse the Federalists. But something had clearly changed. State politics was not the same after the ratification of the federal Constitution. Nor was William Findley the same kind of political leader he once had been.[63]

The state government was certainly not the same under the 1790 Pennsylvania constitution, structured as it was with new barriers against democracy that were modeled after the new federal Constitution. The single-house assembly gave way to a divided legislature with a senate to check democracy in the lower house. The 1790 constitution replaced the toothless office of president with a powerful governor who could veto any law passed by the assembly. Finally, the new constitution established a top-down legal system with governor-appointed judges replacing the locally elected justices of the peace.

The 1790 constitution did not eliminate all of the democratic advances of 1776. The 1790 charter continued to allow 90 percent of adult men to vote and did not include any property requirements for office holding. It also largely preserved the bill of rights from the 1776 document. Most white Pennsylvanians now considered these things—the vote, the absence of property requirements to hold office, and the protection of civil liberties—to be their rights (even if most white adult men did not vote and most offices were held by wealthy gentlemen). Federalists knew better than to risk waking the public from its sullen political slumber by revoking "rights" that ordinary folk held sacred. Nevertheless, the 1790 constitution was a stinging defeat for popular ideals.[64]

* * *

In terms of scaling back democracy, the two new constitutions were a remarkable Federalist victory. By itself, the federal Constitution placed formidable barriers in the path of popular reformers. Before its adoption, ordinary

Pennsylvanians only had to organize across the state to get their agenda put into law. Now, they would have to organize a majority of the states. Even then, popular reforms could be vetoed by the Senate or president or else overturned by the new Supreme Court. The one democratic victory in the saga of the Constitution, and it was a big victory, came later, when widespread popular opposition led the founding elite to concede to adding a Bill of Rights—a set of amendments that not even James Madison had originally wanted.

Meanwhile, the new Pennsylvania constitution signaled but the beginning of wide-ranging efforts to tame democracy within the state.

9

Roads Closed

DESPERATE OPPOSITION TO THE NEW ORDER

Rouse then my fellow citizens before it be too late; act with a spirit becoming freemen; convince the world and your adversaries . . . who wish to become your tyrants—That you are not insensible of the invaluable blessings of liberty—That you esteem life and property, but secondary objects; when your liberty comes to be attacked.

—"The Scourge" [William Petrikin], *Carlisle Gazette,* January 23, 1788

Something strange happened in the Pennsylvania countryside in the years following the federal Constitutional Convention of 1787: large numbers of farmers closed the main roads that led in and out of their communities. During an eight-year period, dating from the fall of 1787 through the fall of 1795, rural Pennsylvanians obstructed roads at least sixty-two times. The road closings were not confined to any particular county or region. The closings were more frequent in the central and frontier counties, but barriers also appeared in roads just twenty-five miles outside Philadelphia.[1]

The obstructions were formidable. Throughout Pennsylvania, people constructed six-foot-high fences that stretched fifty feet across the highway. Some people felled trees across roads or hauled timber into log piles that sometimes measured thirty feet wide and forty feet long. Others blocked roads with heavy stones, decaying logs, and scrub brush. More often, they dug eight-foot-wide and five-foot-deep ditches in the road, imposing enough to halt any wagon or coach. One group in the southeastern county of Chester shoveled enough dirt out of the main highway to Philadelphia to create an impassable crater measuring fifty feet in circumference and seven feet deep. People in two other eastern counties flooded roads by carving out canals that redirected streams and rivers to flow across the highway. Along a narrow passage that cut through the western frontier, people dug into a hillside, causing an avalanche of earth and rocks. And in the central county of Cumberland, farmers dumped fifteen wagonloads of manure on a highway, creating a four-foot-high wall of stink.[2]

The barriers usually proved to be long lasting. Once the ditches, stones, and log piles appeared on the roads, few people were willing to remove them—not even the county road supervisors responsible for keeping the highways free from debris. In several counties, entire corps of road supervisors (sometimes as many as twenty-three individual officers) were hauled into courts and ordered to hire men to remove log piles and fill in ditches. The supervisors usually ignored the orders and accepted fines; some even served jail terms for contempt of court. For example, in the summer of 1792, judges in Lancaster County ordered road supervisors to widen county roads to make them passable for wagons. In August, the judges had the supervisors arrested because, rather than widening the roads, the supervisors had narrowed them.[3]

This disobedience did not stop with the officers in charge of the public highways: road closings were a community affair. Crews of men hired to unclog highways often stood guard over the fences rather than dismantling them. In Cumberland County, a team of workers hired to remove a log pile actually added more lumber to the road and then went home. In August 1788, Dauphin County justices ordered one road closer to tear down a twelve-foot-long fence he had built across the main road leading to Harrisburg. In November, they arrested him again, this time because he and his neighbors had extended the fence to thirty feet. In Chester County, when judges arrested a man for digging a fifty-foot crater in the middle of a road, forty-two others signed a petition saying he should be released because the road was passable despite the huge crater.[4]

The citizens of Woodberry Township in Huntingdon County tried to keep roads closed at the ballot box. After the county court levied a string of fines on road supervisors for failing to reopen blocked highways, not a single vote was cast for the office of road supervisor in the fall election, leaving the court with no one to sue to clear the blockades.[5]

Why were so many Pennsylvanians closing roads in the years after ratification? Roads, after all, were lifelines for rural communities. They brought wagons bearing spices, salt, kettles, and plows to places where such necessities were not produced. They brought rural neighborhoods news of grain prices, state and national politics, wars in Europe, and the happenings of distant relatives. Roads allowed farmers to take their flour, whiskey, and livestock to market. They brought in the money farmers needed to repay their mortgages and to purchase the tools of their trade. The numerous petitions that rural folk drafted during the 1790s pleading for the construction of new roadways (even as they closed local highways) stand as a testament to the importance people placed on roads.

Given their significance, why did farmers throughout Pennsylvania obstruct so many roadways and keep them closed for long periods of time? Why would rural people sever lines of communication and jeopardize their ability to get their goods to market? In short, why did people who were so dependent upon the world outside their neighborhoods take such extreme measures to isolate themselves?

This chapter argues that the road closings were part of the new and desperate rural politics that emerged after the ratification of the federal Constitution, when, between 1788 and 1793, the state elite attempted to dismantle the rings of protection that rural folk had used to defend their communities. Through the powers of the 1790 state constitution and a host of new laws, Pennsylvania Federalists attempted to outlaw each ring. And as they fell, ordinary Pennsylvanians were forced to develop new and more creative ways to defend their vision of the Revolution. These strategies—which included the road closings—represented a new kind of isolationism in

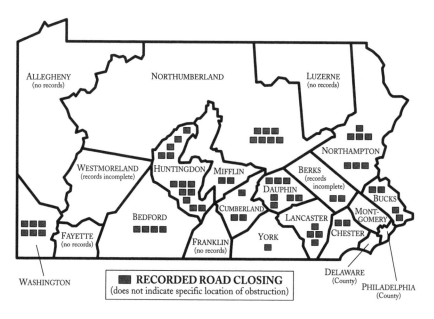

FIG. 9.1. ROAD CLOSINGS IN PENNSYLVANIA BY COUNTY, NOVEMBER 1787–NOVEMBER 1795.

popular politics. Rather than trying to reach out and organize, ordinary folk increasingly walled themselves off from one another in an attempt to shut out a hostile new political and legal system.

Forcing Tax Collection

The first ring that came under attack was the one formed by county tax officials. Before 1787, many tax officers had tried to protect their communities by delaying collection. That resistance, which had limited success during the 1780s, would now have even less. After the ratification of the federal Constitution, emboldened state Federalists began demanding immediate payment and preparing lawsuits against county officials who had not fulfilled their quotas. The new attack was announced in law proposed in March 1788 that increased the financial penalties on collectors who refused to do their duties. The new law would give the state the right to imprison collectors and sell their property if they did not settle immediately. It also empowered tax collectors to sell taxpayers' property without having to go through the court system. The law even gave collectors the authority to imprison taxpayers and hold them without bail but not have to go before a judge. In effect, the new law made collectors the judge and jury in revenue cases. Without a trace of irony, Federalists said they designed the law to relieve "the distresses of the people."[6]

On the same day this bill was introduced, John Nicholson, the chief tax official in the state, sent out a circular that warned county officials "who have to pay" that lawsuits and foreclosures would soon follow. He encouraged officials to "sell their property" quickly because they would undoubtedly get "a higher price" now "than they will be able in the future to do" when the federal Constitution's ban on state paper money took effect.[7]

Initially, county tax officials responded to the circular with angry letters explaining that it was impossible to collect large sums of money in a cash-scarce economy. "We can hardly Live in the frequent Scarcity of money," protested an official from Cumberland County whose neighbors were "very poor and generally in debt." In his opinion, forcing the collection of $115,600 in taxes that the county owed would cause them to "Loose the morsel they have to give thire Wives and Children." The treasurer of neighboring Dauphin County registered the same complaint: "the people are unable to pay" due to the "great Scarcity of Money." Washington County's treasurer would spend the next three years expressing his conviction that "the people is doing what they can to raise the money" but could not pay because "money is not to be had." One tax official from Huntingdon County was so distressed by the prospect of being compelled to inflict "great cruelties" on his neighbors that he attempted to resign, declaring himself "an unfit person for such business" as bringing "ruin on their poor families."[8]

State leaders responded to this resistance by passing a new law in 1791 that increased the state's power over county tax officers. The new law required county officials to file monthly reports, and it appointed outside auditors to look over their books. The law empowered the auditors to prosecute officials who refused to hand over county books or who delayed notifying the state of the names of delinquent tax collectors and taxpayers.[9]

In fear of being sued, many county treasurers and commissioners ended their resistance and began prosecuting county tax collectors. Across the state, they took out newspaper advertisements and printed broadsides to nail to trees throughout their counties, listing the names of tax collectors who owed money and promising to sue "without further delay" unless they settled immediately. These lists contained anywhere between 50 and 100 names; one broadside posted in Cumberland County in 1791 listed 112 "Delinquent Collectors." Anyone reading those lists knew that when the collectors were sued, they would be forced to use their new powers to collect by force from their neighbors, many of whom did not have the money to pay.[10]

Treasurers and commissioners took little solace when their enforcement of the law produced little money. Several officials even wrote I-told-you-so letters that placed blame where they knew it belonged: with the cash scarcity. The Washington County treasurer reported that lawsuits had been "very tedious" and merely confirmed that most of the collectors were "insolvent." He said his efforts had driven some collectors into poverty and induced others to flee the county, never to return. The treasurer of neighboring Mifflin County said his county was "poor in a general way," which rendered lawsuits "next to impracticable." A York County official reported that lawsuits had failed, ensuring that collection "does not go on at any rate but stands still."[11]

State leaders proved to be unsympathetic to such pleas—even from county officers whose diligence had brought them the scorn of their neighbors. They sued one collector who had refused to back down when challenged by a crowd of angry taxpayers intent on destroying his ledgers and reclaiming the tax money he had gathered. After suffering a beating for doing his duty, the collector was forced by the state to sell all of his property to compensate for the tax money the crowd had taken from him. In another county, the state jailed an official after the sale of all his possessions (even his clothes) failed to produce enough money to pay his quota, driving his "wife and seven small children" "to the lowest ebb of misery & distress." State leaders also sued a "very clever & honest" tax official after fire destroyed his home, possessions, and the tax records he had been keeping at his house for safety. The lawsuit drove him so "Out of his reason" that county officials cuffed him in irons and "confined him as mad." He remained imprisoned for the next "two or three years" because he never quite "recovered." As stories like these circulated, they lent credence to the popular belief that state leaders were willing to sacrifice anyone—even those who worked hardest to enforce the laws.[12]

In many cases, collectors fled rather than wait to be foreclosed, some taking whatever tax money they had collected with them. In 1790, the state treasurer reported that collection efforts were being badly undermined by "Collectors, many of whom, after getting considerable Sums into their Hands, have died, failed, ran away, or other ways eluded Payment." Instead of ensuring diligence, the get-tough policy had prompted an unprecedented outbreak of corruption.[13]

The problem ran far deeper than this: the new policies caused many taxpayers with long-outstanding balances to flee as well. When collectors began prosecuting taxpayers, many of them—unable to acquire the money needed to pay—sold or abandoned their farms and drove away. Some county officials reported that so "many of the people ran away" that collection efforts were in disarray. With large segments of the population gone, how would the county ever fill its outstanding quotas? The only remedy left to county officials was to tax new inhabitants for old taxes. But, as many officials said, new settlers refused to pay taxes dating back to the war, and most people (including the officials) thought the practice was both unethical and illegal.[14]

In the end, the attempt to shatter this ring of protection had mixed results. On one hand, it compelled county tax officials to do their jobs. On the other, it did not fill government coffers as state leaders imagined it would. In many ways, the state's attempts at severity did little more than expose the fundamental flaws in the get-tough plan. Federalists had taken great pains to end collection delays but had done nothing to alleviate the cash scarcity. In fact, they had made it worse. As a result, their efforts were destined to fall short. Federalists, however, did not blame their policies; instead, they cited the remaining rings of protection. And so, dissatisfied with the initial results, they set out to destroy the other rings.

Bypassing Justice

The next assault began with an angry Benjamin Franklin fuming about county justices of the peace. In November 1787, Franklin, who was serving as president of the state, complained that too many justices were "not prosecuting delinquents" for unpaid taxes. To remedy the situation, he urged the general assembly to begin "either removing the Magistrates guilty of such neglect, or subjecting them to some penalty that may compel them to a faithful discharge of their duty." Franklin's views were shared by state legislators, who decided in early 1788 to crush the resistance of county justices.[15]

Their first step was enacting a new law that removed justices entirely from tax collection. Under this 1788 law, justices no longer oversaw the cases of delinquent taxpayers and collectors and, thus, were unable to delay lawsuits or withhold ledgers. The new law also set heavy fines for justices who refused to immediately surrender ledgers or lists of delinquent taxpayers that were currently in their possession.[16]

In explaining why they wanted to bypass county justices, state legislators offered an array of often-conflicting reasons. On one hand, they said the justices were too "popular." They were too much like the common folk and too responsive to the whims of their constituents. As one legislator put it, they were ordinary men who were "the bosom friend[s] and boon companion[s] of these people at the ale-houses." On the other hand, legislators portrayed the justices as "mean and rapacious wretches, pursuing every infamous means that can be devised to prey upon their neighbors." It was a contradictory picture: legislators painted justices as being too responsive to the public and yet, somehow, unresponsive overlords.[17]

No matter the contradictions, Federalist leaders portrayed themselves, rather than the justices, as saviors of ordinary citizens. They said the new law would free the public from financial "distresses" by removing justices from the process. Now, indebted taxpayers could jump straight to having their property foreclosed without delaying the process and racking up legal fees.[18]

Many justices did not give up easily, however. In fact, the new law seemed to increase their efforts to avoid becoming, as one justice put it, a "Minister of Misery" to his neighbors. Opposition by justices became so widespread during 1788, 1789, and 1790 that the state treasurer was forced to issue a report in November 1790 saying that judicial resistance had spread to nearly every part of the state. The most serious opposition was in the central and western counties. In Cumberland and Washington counties, justices refused to surrender lists of delinquent taxpayers and collectors—thus preventing the state attorney general from initiating lawsuits. In Huntingdon County, a number of justices refused to issue writs of foreclosure. In Mifflin County, several justices shut down the legal system by refusing to attend court for several months. Elsewhere, justices appeared but provided "little or no support" for collection efforts. Rather than suing delinquent collectors, they merely "admonished some, excused others, and where they assessed fines, they were so small" that the money was almost not worth collecting. In Bedford County, Justice James Martin continued his campaign of frustrating local tax officials and actually recruited other justices to adopt his habit of neglect. Needless to say, the initial attempt of state leaders to get the justices to do their jobs did not work well.[19]

The 1790 state constitution proved to be far more effective in curbing resistance by county justices—because it completely reorganized the legal system to remove their power. The new constitution broke the judicial ring of protection by transforming Pennsylvania's bottom-up legal system into one that ran from the top down. It was a dramatic change from the 1776 state constitution. Under the 1776 constitution, locally elected justices retained considerable power to shape how laws were interpreted and enforced. The 1790 constitution tried to make the judiciary far less responsive to the popular will. First, it ended the practice of local election of justices and instead made them appointed by the governor. Then, it took most of the authority away from county justices and lodged it in the hands of new state-appointed judges. Finally, it increased the power of the state supreme court to overrule local courts and compel the new judges to follow its direction. In all of these ways, the 1790 constitution produced a judicial system where the magistrates were far more likely to uphold unpopular laws.[20]

In a few places, the transfer of judicial power met resistance. In York County, many jurors failed to show up for the opening of the court. The story of their absence was told in two notices that ran side by side in the local newspaper. In the left-hand column of the paper was a report on the opening of the state court "for the first time under the new Constitution of this Commonwealth" that observed that things had not gone smoothly because most of the "Jurors who were summoned by the Sheriff" had refused to attend. The adjoining notice in the newspaper's right-hand column suggested the reason that they had stayed home: it listed the names of sixty tax collectors who had outstanding balances along with a statement that "the law will be put in force" against them (that is, the grand jury would decide which cases were indictable).[21]

In the western counties, the new judges were greeted with several attempts to set up extralegal courts to mediate debt cases. The most serious effort was the creation of "the Association" by farmers in Washington County. These farmers, it was said, had been "harassed with suits from justices and courts, and wished a less expensive tribunal." They organized their association around militia companies and brought together "near 500 persons" who agreed to settle debt cases before judges who received a small fee in exchange for determining the fair value of a debtor's property.[22]

It appears that the court functioned as intended. Beginning with the arrival of the new judges in the late fall of 1791, numerous creditors dropped debt suits—and paid stiff penalties for doing so—no doubt to comply with the new extralegal court. That pattern repeated in neighboring Westmoreland County, the home of another popularly organized "society."[23]

The transition was not as peaceful in Mifflin County, where the arrival of the new judges triggered a mass protest that lasted four days. The target of the protest was one of the new judges, Samuel Bryson, of whom it was said "nine-tenths of the people of his acquaintance in Mifflin County" believed him to be "very unfit for any civil office in a republican government." Evidently, Bryson had proclaimed publicly that he and the Society of the Cincinnati (an organization of former military officers) would "rule the people of America independent of their consent." As one protester put it, "the people were generally of [the] opinion [that] such a man should have no such power." And they intended to force Judge Bryson out of office.

The protest began on September 12, 1791, the day the new court under the 1790 constitution was set to open. The court remained closed that day because one of the three new judges refused to show, saying "he would not sit with such a rascal" as Bryson. The next day, several hundred farmers marched into town, led by the brother of the county sheriff and the nephew of the judge who had refused to show up the previous day. Two militia colonels on horseback led the way, along with the sheriff's brother, who was, as one witness recalled, "well dressed, with a sword, and I think two pistols belted round him, cocked hat, and one or two feathers in it." Most of the men marching beside them were said to be without weapons, except for a few who "imprudently took arms." Even without weapons, the military precision, fife playing, and chants of "liberty or death" let it be known the crowd meant business. And that business was to "take Judge Bryson off the bench, and march him down the Narrows to the judge's farm, and make him sign a written paper, that he would never sit there as a judge again." Before the troops arrived, however, Bryson went into hiding. When the militia discovered that he had fled, they left a list of demands in a letter signed "the people," and then marched back home.[24]

The following day, the protest started again in an unlikely way. Judge Bryson, determined to take his office despite the threats, was walking to the courthouse with an armed escort that included the county sheriff. On the way, Bryson and the sheriff got into a heated argument. Before anyone could separate them, the two men were punching and kicking one another. The rest of the escort subdued the sheriff and, at Judge Bryson's request, locked him in his own prison.

When news of the sheriff's arrest reached the countryside, a group of seventy farmers assembled and marched to the prison. As evening fell, they entered the town chanting "liberty or death," surrounded the jail, and demanded the sheriff's release. They only departed when the sheriff shouted from his cell that he did not wish to be released and urged his rescuers to return home. The farmers complied and filed out of town without incident.

The next morning, 300 militiamen returned to the courthouse to demand the sheriff's release and Judge Bryson's resignation. Before the militias reached town, local Federalists decided to concede. Judge Bryson released the sheriff from prison and dropped the charges against him. Later that day, he resigned from the new court.

Although the farmers in Mifflin won the battle to chase Judge Bryson from office, they lost the war over the reorganization of the court system. If it were not Bryson on the bench, it would be another gentleman appointed by the governor and taking orders from the state rather than a man elected by the citizens of the county who was, comparatively speaking, beholden to his neighbors. Ordinary Pennsylvanians continued to complain about the system—sending hundreds of petitions to the assembly that called for judges to be removed or replaced. But that system remained in place.[25]

Forcing Law Enforcement

From the perspective of state leaders, the problems with justices of the peace were equaled only by the resistance of county law enforcement. And, according to most Federalists, the chief problem in the years after ratification was local constables. Like other county officers, constables seemed to increase their resistance after the ratification vote. Take, for example, the situation in Fayette County, where constables were said to be the "principal deficiencies" that prevented tax collection. The county treasurer reported that most constables were consistently in "neglect of duty," showed little "industry in collecting," and boycotted court appearances—a pattern that started in 1787, when state Federalists began their get-tough policy. That resistance continued through January 1789, when the Fayette treasurer implored the general assembly to find "some summary way of calling the Constables to account."[26]

Fayette constables were not alone in opposing the new order. A similar boycott developed in Cumberland County, where constables missed several court sessions and refused to process any legal papers from February to July 1788. In Huntingdon County, constables had no need to boycott: county leaders were "unwilling to put" property executions "into the Hands of the Constables" because they were afraid that the court orders would be "treated with Contempt."[27]

While constables continued their previous resistance, many county sheriffs who had upheld the law in the years before ratification now decided to join in. The rise in resistance by sheriffs became so extreme across Pennsylvania that the state treasurer issued a report raising grave concerns that "County Treasurers . . . uniformly complain of the Sheriffs not doing their Duty." To get a sense of what sheriffs were up to, consider the sheriff of Lancaster County, who simply sat on warrants. "Time after time I have issued Executions for the sale of [tax collectors'] Estates," wrote the widow of a tax commissioner who was trying to clear her late husband's accounts. "But I cannot get the sheriff to do his duty." In February 1790, she had foreclosure orders against thirteen collectors; by May, the sheriff had acted on only three of them.[28]

Equally galling to Federalist leaders was how sheriffs were being complicit in neighborhood no-bid pacts. In the years after ratification, the number of bidderless auctions was multiplying. With the state tearing down the other rings of protection, many communities reintensified their attempts to thwart property auctions by agreeing to "combine together and not give a single bid." In 1788, state Comptroller General John Nicholson reported that some county sheriffs were exploiting loopholes in state tax laws and allowing the pacts to continue. State law required sheriffs to advertise property auctions. Nicholson observed that several county sheriffs wrote those ads to intentionally mislead potential bidders by leaving out critical details: "the time of the sale and the place of the sale of the land [was] not mentioned," nor was the name of the person whose property was being foreclosed. The announcements simply listed the items to be sold without telling potential buyers where and when the auction was going to be held.[29]

A similar kind of protection was sometimes offered by county jail keepers. Theirs involved perhaps the greatest level of inactivity: they simply allowed imprisoned debtors and taxpayers to walk away. In most cases, the jailer's guilt was hard to prove because friends and relatives arrived at the jail to break their loved ones out of prison. In other cases, it seems clear that jailers unlocked cell doors and looked the other way.[30]

Frustrated by resistance from all levels of law enforcement, state leaders attempted to break this ring of protection. They began by increasing the financial pressure on sheriffs and constables. A 1788 law established high fines on constables who did not help when a tax collector asked for assistance. When the fines did not generate enough compliance from constables, legislators passed a law in 1789 that gave the state the right to imprison them and sell their property. Another law increased the dollar amount of the bonds that sheriffs had to sign before they took office, forcing them to surrender more property if they resisted. This same law prevented sheriffs from transferring their property to relatives during their tenure to ensure they could not get around a lawsuit.[31]

The 1790 Pennsylvania constitution tried to make county sheriffs more responsive to state leaders by changing how they were elected. Under the 1776 constitution, voters elected county sheriffs, with the winner being the person who received the most votes. The 1790 constitution still allowed people to vote, but it gave the governor the power to select the winner from the top two vote getters. Now, the candidate for sheriff who received the vast majority of votes could be rejected in favor of the one whom the governor preferred.[32]

At the same time, state leaders devised new procedures to break the no-bid pacts. John Nicholson ordered tax collectors and sheriffs to hold auctions as far away from the owner's neighborhood as possible. "If the Collectors should not get bidders in the same townships," he informed county officers, "they must take the property to some more public place" in a different township.[33]

If this didn't work—if people followed the sheriff's wagon or if no one bid at the new auction site—Nicholson instructed tax collectors either to bid on the property themselves or else to bring someone with them who would buy the auctioned goods. In this way, even if the property sold "at a cheap rate," it would still bring money into the state treasury. Nicholson believed that this would cause people to back down because it would show them that the state meant business about trying to "destroy or prevent" the no-bid pacts. Until that time, Nicholson was willing to use his own money to buy auctioned goods. "If after all they will not sell," Nicholson informed one county tax official, "I will be a bidder myself at a low rate rather than that the law should be defeated." Of course, Nicholson did not emphasize that, in the process of assisting the state, he also augmented his personal fortune by acquiring property for a fraction of its usual value.[34]

Finally, to remedy the rash of jail breaks, some county judges and commissioners attempted to tighten prison procedures. For example, in Lancaster County, Federalist judge Michael Hubley ordered the local jailer to place a new prisoner in irons to prevent him from escaping. The jailer, who had no intention of following the order, airily replied: "tell old Squire Hubley the damned old rascal to mind his own business and not mine, and tell the old bougre the damned rascal that he may kiss my arse." The jailer's refusal landed him in court and brought a sizable fine for neglecting his duty and insulting the judge.[35]

The combined effect of all of these changes was to bring new discipline to law enforcement. Some constables continued to resist (stiffer penalties had less effect on men who lacked property). And, as the Lancaster jailer's indelicate reply showed, many of those forced to follow orders were not happy about the changes. Nonetheless, the state's new leverage made any officer think twice about resisting again and, thereby, withered this ring of protection by compelling local officers to enforce the law.

Crowd Control

Probably the clearest sign of the deteriorating rings was the rise in violent outbursts across the state. After the ratification vote, Pennsylvania was swept by a wave of violence that encompassed the whole state. The violence took many different forms, and not all of it was overtly political. Indeed, the variety of violence raised great concerns for state leaders and sent them scurrying for ways to tame it.

Part of the problem had to do with the rise in crime that accompanied the hard economic times of the 1780s and 1790s. In the decades after the war, the state saw a dramatic rise in the kinds of crimes generally associated with a bad economy: burglary and armed robbery. These years also saw an explosive outbreak of riots. In Chester County, the number of riots tripled between the 1780s and 1790s, a pattern repeated in the central counties of Dauphin and Mifflin.[36]

Some of this crime was undoubtedly retribution from the mass sheriffs' auctions that spread across the state in the postwar decades. That was surely the case with an arson in Cumberland County, in which the records office in Carlisle was "set on fire by some malicious persons, and entirely consumed." (If the arsonists had been hoping to destroy the files for debt cases, they were no doubt disappointed that the "greatest part of the records were saved.") The most numerous incidents of retribution came with the rise in the crimes of forcible entry and rescue—both categories referring to people claiming (or reclaiming) property held by others. Surviving records reveal 875 prosecuted cases of forcible entry or rescue between 1781 and 1800. Although it is impossible to say why so many people were forcibly claiming their neighbors' property, the dramatic rise in this kind of crime occurred precisely during the years when sheriffs' auctions were most prevalent. It is probably safe to assume that much of this crime was committed by desperate individuals trying to reclaim furniture, livestock, or tools that had been sold at auction for unpaid debts or taxes.[37]

Another kind of violent crime was undeniably a form of resistance: the significant increase in attacks on constables, sheriffs, tax collectors, and judges. Before 1787, such violence had formed only a small part of defensive efforts. Indeed, from 1781 through 1787, surviving court records reveal only twenty-three cases of violence against county officials. By comparison, in the seven years after the ratification vote—when state leaders broke through the rings of protection—the number of attacks on public officials nearly tripled, with sixty-three separate incidents of violence. Nearly half of those cases involved individuals or groups trying to rescue incarcerated debtors or foreclosed property.[38]

Threats of violence were on the rise as well. For example, in Fayette County in 1788, one officer attempted to move property auctions away from the defendants' neighborhoods and also tried to plant bidders in the crowd to ensure that property sold. His attempts were quickly thwarted by promises of retaliatory violence from citizens of different townships who "threatened to punish such as will dare to bid for the property of any of them." In Huntingdon County, officials reported in August 1788 that "Threats have been sent from all parts of the county that death—or what is to a man of feeling worse—cropping, tarring, etc., should be inflicted on us or any other officer of the county who should attempt to put the laws in force."[39]

As menacing as all of this was, state leaders were especially alarmed by what they saw as the growing unruliness of the militias. Federalists were well aware that most popular actions were organized along militia lines. The evidence was abundant: the incidents in 1786 and 1787 at York County sheriffs' auctions, protests against the federal Constitution in Carlisle and Huntingdon, the central Pennsylvania Antifederalist networks, and the ouster of Judge Bryson in Mifflin County—all of these efforts were organized primarily through county militias. Officials were equally worried that, in most cases, the militias marched with officers leading the way, on horseback and in uniform.

Federalist leaders were concerned—with good reason—that the decentralized militia system would become the biggest threat to their new order. To understand their worries, take, for example, the new militia companies formed in Cumberland County as an extension of the popular political network. In 1788, William Petrikin, the tailor from Carlisle who was one of the chief Cumberland organizers, explained, "We have made up a volunteer company, all antifederalists." The members of this company had signed a pledge to "oppose the establishment of the new Constitution at the risque of our lives and Fortunes." They had even designed their own uniform: "blue Coats faced with white edges with scarlet applets on each shoulder, Cocked Hatts, White Jackets & Breeches & black getters." By May 1788, the company counted seventy members and were "daily increasing" in number. Despite opposition from Federalist leaders, "the Colonel who is a Federalist was obliged to admit us tho with great reluctance into the Battalion." The only stumbling block was weapons. "All we want is arms," Petrikin reported, "and I am afraid this will be difficult to procure" since the local armory was under Federalist control.[40]

A year later, Petrikin's militia company had increased in size and fashioned itself into a formidable corps. "Our Volunteer company is very large, well armed and Equipted, parades often and exercises very well," Petrikin said. At the same time, a number of other like-minded militia companies had formed across the county. He noted that, while these militias were spreading rapidly and drilling consistently, the "federal company" composed of gentlemen "is retired to the land of forgetfulness." "Gentlemen," Petrikin concluded, were "not made for fighting." Indeed, he crowed about how on "saint Patricks night one of our Volunteers almost killed four stout young Feds without receiving the least damage." He bragged that "the night following another volunteer floged six Federal soldiers of a recruting party and left one of them under the care of the docters." The Federalists "got a state warrant for him the next day," and "the whole party with a Constable at their head went to take him." The posse rumbled into the rural hamlet where the man lived and "scared some women with their swords and pistols." But, according to Petrikin, this "was all the damage they did": the militiaman defended himself "so gallantly that they returned as they went except a little of their Blood which adhered to the Volunteers Hickery Bludgeon."[41]

Accurate or not, Petrikin's recollections reveal the extent to which his ideas of politics now centered on the militia. In the wake of the disastrous Harrisburg convention, which had derailed Petrikin's idea of a statewide political network, and amid the election defeats that followed, Petrikin and his associates threw themselves into remaking the militia so that it would defend their ideals. No doubt, given Petrikin's boasting and fiery language, the militia also served to salve his wounded pride. Without the stomach to continue organizing to win at the polls, Petrikin and others evidently tried to rescue their self-esteem and sense of manhood by playing soldier and fighting Federalists with a "Hickery Bludgeon" instead of the vote.

No matter the ultimate futility of relying on the militia to defend one's community from political and economic change, the rise of opposition-minded companies like those in Cumberland worried state Federalists, who turned their attention to regaining control over the militia. In Cumberland County, Federalist leaders tried to shut down the militia by refusing to appoint officers or muster the troops. As John Jordan, a local justice and militia officer, put it: "everything is done to prevent the Militia from being in a State of defense even against a common enemy if they should have occasion." Federalist officers would not call the men to drill. Nor would they approve the slate of company officers the men elected. When a battalion officer died, Federalists "refuse[d] to grant an Election," fearing the companies would choose an insurgent. "The Major of Our Battalion has been Dead upwards of fifteen months," Jordan reported, but state Federalists rejected "any application" to elect a replacement.[42]

It was largely the same story farther west in Huntingdon County. There, local Federalists tried to keep the militia from meeting after nearly a battalion had marched against them in the spring of 1788. This was the march in retaliation for Federalists destroying petitions against the Constitution. The militia companies did not fall back into line after that initial confrontation. "This ferment was kept up for better than a year," reported the officer responsible for calling musters of the county militia. As a result, this officer refused to let the militia drill because he "had it not in my power to git the Malitia of this County Properly Organized." When he finally called out the militia in October 1789, an entire battalion refused to come. This officer pleaded with the new state governor to strengthen the militia law to increase the fines on officers who would not follow orders. He said the present law did not "answer the Purpose with a Number of the Present Malitia Officers, who are men, perhaps, that have a very Contemptible opinion of the Word Honour." He also urged the governor to change how militia officers were selected to ensure that battalions were staffed with leaders who would try to control the unruly companies.[43]

Evidently, the governor listened: in 1793, the state passed a new law that completely overhauled the militia system to make it more difficult for officers and privates to act independently. Although the new law preserved much of the traditional structure where militiamen elected their officers, it strengthened the militia's top-down hierarchy. In the new system, the governor appointed all officers above the rank of lieutenant colonel. The governor also appointed a new set of brigade inspectors with the power to review militias and to levy fines on those they felt were not performing properly. And the law spelled out what neglecting one's duty meant for officers and enlisted men, thereby closing loopholes in the old law. The new law also increased fines from $20 to $200 for each offense of noncompliance. Finally, the law streamlined the court-martial process and included fines for any militiaman who refused to testify against his officers or fellow soldiers. Taken as a whole, it was a serious step toward keeping militias in line.[44]

None of these changes fully ended crowd violence or ensured that militiamen remained obedient. In fact, in 1794, a year after Federalists passed the new militia law, they faced the greatest outbreak of crowd action and the largest episode of militia disobedience in the postwar decade. For the moment, though, the new law seemed to have ruptured the militia's ring of protection.

Closing Roads

All of this brings us back to the mysterious road closings. Seen in the context of the rings of protection being dismantled, the road closings begin to make sense. They appear to have been a new and desperate strategy by people who felt they were quickly running out of options. In short, ordinary Pennsylvanians took the drastic step of blocking roads with fences, log piles, avalanches, and deep ditches as a way of constructing a new (and, as it turns out, literal) ring of protection around their communities.

To appreciate the meaning of the road closings, consider their timing. Farmers tended to block roads at the precise moments when state leaders launched new efforts to prosecute taxpayers and collectors. Although people closed roads at varying times, there appear to have been two dominant waves. The first began in 1788, when the state attorney general initiated lawsuits against tax collectors; this was also the year that John Nicholson began ordering county tax officials to move sheriffs' auctions and to plant bidders. The second wave came in 1792, following the passage of the law allowing state officials to prosecute tax officials who had not fulfilled their quotas. This law also expanded the range of "delinquent" accounts to include land payments and money due to the land bank, making it the equivalent of calling in all outstanding mortgages. For citizens in the heavily mortgaged countryside, the law was alarming, to say the least.[45]

While these factors help to explain why ordinary Pennsylvanians closed roads, a closer look at where people placed the barriers reveals how the tactic was supposed to work. Most of the roads people closed were ones that surrounded county courthouses or that linked rural neighborhoods to nearby commercial centers. During the road closings of 1788 and 1792, barricades could be found in the roads leading to and from the courthouses in the county seats of Harrisburg, Reading, Easton, Carlisle, Bedford, Washington, Sunbury, and Huntingdon. In other places, people obstructed roads leading from ferry stations. In some neighborhoods, they felled trees across the main routes that connected one county to another. In the eastern counties, inhabitants obstructed the main highways that led to and from Philadelphia.

Targeting these particular roads protected the community in a number of ways. Barricades on roads to courthouses slowed the court's operation or

FIG. 9.2. ROAD FROM YORK TO CARLISLE. This spot in the highway linking York and Cumberland counties would have made an inviting target for road closers. To obstruct such a passage, people elsewhere dug into the base of the cliff to cause an avalanche that made the road impassable. *View of a Pass over the South Mountain from York Town to Carlisle*, reprinted from *Columbian Magazine* (May 1788). (Courtesy American Antiquarian Society.)

stopped it altogether. They prevented jury members and constables from attending court, or at least gave them an excuse for missing a required appearance. For example, in Northumberland County in 1792, inhabitants dug ditches and erected fences on at least five of the main roads that led to the courthouse at Sunbury. At the April session of the county court, twenty-three of thirty-five jurors failed to appear. At the next session, held in August, the story was roughly the same—except now the absent jurors were joined by eleven missing constables.[46]

As effective as such actions were, the real power of road closings came when they made county highways impassable to the wagons of the sheriff and outside bidders. Even if the court sat and judges ordered auctions, blocked roads made removing property an arduous task. With county roads filled with trees and fences, sheriffs could not relocate auctions to courthouses or commercial centers. Indeed, since the county seats were often surrounded by barricades, many sheriffs probably found themselves unable to move their wagons beyond the courthouse steps. Barriers in roads also foiled attempts to plant bidders at auctions. With so many roads blocked, it made little difference that someone from outside a no-bid pact purchased furniture, grain, or livestock at low prices. They would be unable to get their wagons to the ferry station or the main highway that led back home. In this way, the road closings were a new way of producing the same result as the old rings: keeping property in the hands of its owners.

*　　*　　*

On final reflection, the road closings were also symbolic of the long-standing shortcomings of popular politics—communication and political organization—and how those problems had worsened. In this hostile new environment, ordinary folk who wanted to uphold their vision of the Revolution urgently needed to find ways to work together. Instead, in the face of political setbacks, they retreated rather than redouble their efforts. Rural Pennsylvanians abandoned the hard work of organizing beyond their neighborhoods and even let their local and regional societies languish. Instead, they closed roads and isolated themselves from one another.

Like the barriers in the roads, however, this retreat from politics was temporary. Several years into the new federal and state governments, ordinary people across Pennsylvania would once again try to organize and work together to oppose the new order. Those attempts ultimately led to two violent showdowns that would change America.

10

The Pennsylvania Regulation of 1794

A REBELLION OVER WHISKEY?

It is only a well regulated republican government that can secure the native dignity and equal rights of the citizens and provide for their happiness.

—William Findley, *A Review of the Revenue System,* 1794

On August 1, 1794, a nervous Federalist judge and whiskey merchant from Pittsburgh named John Wilkins, accompanied by several colleagues, rode his horse up a steep bluff that overlooked the Monongahela River. The men were making the climb to see if the rumors were true: they had received "certain intelligence" that thousands of militiamen from across the region were marching to "take the garrisons" at Fort Pitt and then head to "Pittsburgh (or Sodom as they called the town) and destroy it by fire." Wilkins had been so worried that, at 2:00 a.m. on the night before this climb, he had decided "to hide or bury property, the county books and treasury, the books belonging to my office as justice, my private books, and money left in hand." Without much sleep, he was now heading up the bluff to "see the length of the line" when "the people" arrived.[1]

Nothing could have prepared Wilkins for what he saw when he looked down into the valley. Below him was a sea of men, who "marched in files and in good order leaving a small space between each battalion." The militias flowed down the opposite side of the river, pooled at the ferry station, flooded boats crossing the Monongahela, and gushed out in torrents that ran down the road to Braddock's Field. Wilkins guessed this human river ran "upward of two and one half miles long." He estimated that by "the space of ground they took up there might be between 5 & 6 thousand." Some of his friends standing on the overlook "said 7 or 8 thousand." Others thought even more. The best estimate may be that of the Federalist *Pittsburgh Gazette*, which placed the number at around 9,000 men: 5,400 in the assembly Wilkins saw, another 1,500 who arrived later in the day, and an additional 2,000 who marched halfway to Pittsburgh and then returned home when they received a muddled order, which suggested that the meeting had been called off. None of these estimates included the many women who had accompanied their fathers, husbands, sons, and brothers on the march. Whatever the actual figure, it was an astounding assembly.[2]

Wilkins was equally shocked to see gentlemen alongside the common folk. "The people engaged in the present opposition to government," he wrote in alarm, were not "an inconsiderable mob"; rather, "they are a respectable & powerful combination" composed of "some of the most respectable people in the country." This was truly a movement of "the people" in the western counties, regardless of class, ethnicity, or religion.[3]

Why did an estimated 9,000 militiamen march to Pittsburgh? What could have mobilized so many people to take such drastic action? What did they hope their march would achieve? Who had organized the assembly, and how did they manage to pull off the largest protest to date in the history of Pennsylvania, surpassing even the greatest incidents of mass resistance against Britain?

For more than 200 years, historians have mischaracterized this protest because they have examined it within too narrow a context to reveal the motives of those who marched and to understand the full meaning of what they were trying to do. As a result, this insurgency has generally been seen as the product of a federal excise tax, problems specific to the frontier, or some kind of generic fear of centralized government. Historians have portrayed the protesters as acting out of base self-interest, ignorance, an intense commitment to "localism," or paranoia. They usually do not see the protest as having especially deep roots and often depict it as being spontaneous and ephemeral and ending as quickly as it began.

Rural protest is also generally portrayed as outbursts on the edges of society. Pennsylvania's various "rebels" nearly always appear as marginal folk: frontier settlers who felt abandoned in a violent, austere backcountry; poor landless men frustrated in their attempts to scratch out a raw subsistence; Scots-Irish Presbyterians consumed by a hatred of taxation and government; or German sectarians undermined by a cultural and language gap that caused them to misperceive reality. Whatever the case, the protesters come across as outsiders, not "normal" people. Although historians have tended to sympathize with the "rebels" and to find substance in some of their grievances, the overall picture is one of people whose experiences and/or ideals set them apart from the majority of Americans—and even from the typical Pennsylvanian. As a result, the story of farm unrest in Pennsylvania has become a tale told beyond the Revolution's main narrative. It exists, as one account of the 1794 uprising puts it, as little more than a "frontier epilogue to the American Revolution."[4]

Worse than this, the events of 1794 have become the "Whiskey Rebellion"—a label that historians borrowed from Alexander Hamilton, who played a leading role in provoking the uprising and who personally led an army to put it down. The term implicitly ridicules the protest, much as Hamilton intended. By adopting that label, historians have, intentionally or not, perpetuated the derision, ensuring that the first image that pops into the heads of schoolchildren in a history lesson on the subject is drunken, gun-wielding hillbillies, frightening but too comical to be taken seriously.

The time has come for a new title that allows the 1794 uprising (and its 1798 counterpart in the eastern counties) to be seen as part of the broader effort by ordinary farmers in the political mainstream of Pennsylvania (and, indeed, the mainstream across the new nation) to defend their vision of the Revolution.

The most appropriate renaming would be to call these uprisings the Pennsylvania Regulations. Although less theatrical than Whiskey Rebellion, the term "regulation" offers a more accurate depiction of what the farmers were trying to do. Few of those who rose up in 1794 and 1799 thought they were engaged in "rebellions." Instead, they believed that they were trying to "regulate" their government to act on behalf of the ordinary many rather than the wealthy few. As William Findley explained in 1794 (just a few months before federal troops marched west), the goal of popular protest was not to overthrow the government but to find new ways for citizens to get their voices heard by political leaders. In his words, the objective was to make society more "democratical" by empowering "the people" so that "every man feels his own importance and asserts his privileges" in creating "a well regulated republican government." Findley believed that "the body of the people" working to "regulate" their government was the only way to "secure the native dignity and equal rights of the citizens and provide for their happiness."[5]

By acting to regulate their government, these people were following a well-worn path of popular regulations in their age. The term "regulation" reached back to the previous century in England, used by men who attempted to gain more control over their political leaders. The phrase was employed frequently during the revolutionary era, with the closest parallels coming in the North Carolina Regulation during the 1760s and 1770s and the Massachusetts Regulation of the 1780s. In pre-independence North Carolina, rural folk—reeling from the cash scarcity and suffering from land policies and a legal system that favored wealthy speculators—demanded paper money, tax reform, an overhaul of the legal system, and new land laws that favored settlers over speculators. When their attempts at political reform failed, farmers from the Piedmont protested and eventually closed courthouses. In response, the royal governor (and the future revolutionary elite) marched an army into the countryside to put down the regulation and hang its leaders.[6]

About fifteen years later, in the mid-1780s, Massachusetts farmers organized an even more widespread regulation, which opponents would call Shays's Rebellion. The issues were similar to those that had roused North Carolina farmers and nearly identical to the situation facing rural Pennsylvanians in the 1780s. They complained about a government ban on paper money and high taxes to pay war debt speculators. They blamed greedy elites for creating a dire cash scarcity that resulted in mass property foreclosures. Like rural Pennsylvanians, Massachusetts farmers pushed for paper money, a land bank, tax and debt relief, a revaluation of the war debt, and a host of reforms to land laws and the legal system, which they said were needed to preserve equality. When their attempts at political reform failed, they organized protests and eventually shut down courts. In response, the state government organized a 1,200-man army to suppress the Massachusetts Regulation.[7]

The 1790s uprisings in Pennsylvania fit seamlessly into this pattern of popular regulation. In fact, one of the leaders of the 1794 uprising had also been a primary organizer of the North Carolina Regulation. Herman Husband, a farmer and preacher, had fled to Pennsylvania in 1771 to avoid the hangman's noose. Husband had settled in the backcountry where he continued to preach against "designing and ambitious men" who enacted "self-interested" policies to "tyrannize over others and oppress them." When tensions rose in 1794, Husband represented Bedford County at meetings that decided the fate of the 1794 regulation, a fate that would closely resemble its predecessors.[8]

This chapter recounts the story of the Pennsylvania Regulation of 1794, focusing on how it represented a continuation of popular attempts to regulate government that had begun with the resistance against Britain during the 1760s and 1770s.

Opposing the Speculator's Revolution

Although the 1794 uprising is usually portrayed as a protest over a 1791 federal excise tax on distilled alcohol (which is, in part, why historians use the name Whiskey Rebellion), the stakes were far higher. This protest was about popular beliefs that the state and national governments were undermining equality and democracy to enrich and empower a handful of moneyed men. In particular, many people were convinced that Federalists at both the state and national levels were working to reward wealthy speculators at the expense of those who worked for a living (or, as westerners put it, creating a government that was "subversive of industry by common means").[9]

The biggest complaint of those who marched in 1794 was Congress's plan to pay war debt speculators. Specifically, many people were enraged at the way Alexander Hamilton's Funding Act of 1790 gave speculators the fantastic windfall of which they had been dreaming since they had bought war IOUs nearly a decade before. Under Hamilton's plan, the federal government redeemed the war debt certificates at their full face value, no matter how little speculators had paid for them, creating a domestic national debt of about $28 million. Next, Hamilton's law paid all the uncollected interest on those IOUs, adding another $13 million to the debt. Then, it threw in all of the IOUs still in circulation that state governments had issued during the war, paying them all off at face value—even though they had depreciated far more than the IOUs issued by Congress; this added as much as $21.5 million. The sum total of all these payouts was a domestic war debt of about $62.5 million, most of which was pure profit for war debt speculators.[10]

Hamilton did make a few concessions, hoping to quell popular opposition. He lowered the annual interest rate paid on some of the certificates from 6 percent to 3 percent and spread out payments over many decades rather than trying to collect the tax monies all at once. Hamilton also placed most of the new tax burden on imported items rather than on farms, livestock, and land as state governments had done during the 1780s.

In a sense, such provisions represented a victory for the popular protests of the 1780s. During this decade, Federalists had learned that any attempt to wrest all of the money from the public at once only produced unrest. Their lesson was patience: in order to get the full amount, they would have to wait a little longer and take a little less each year. For most Americans, this meant a decrease in the yearly taxes they paid.

Of course, there was a catch (several actually). Although Hamilton's plan lowered taxes in any given year, it also stretched out the burden over a longer time, meaning that, in the end, Americans would pay more in taxes because it would take many more years to retire the debt. Likewise, while import taxes were less unpopular, they raised the prices of many goods that people purchased. And, although Federalists promised to tax only luxury imports, in practice, the impost spread to necessities like salt—a tax that most people found "oppressive," because, in the words of Mifflin County citizens, it fell "mostly on the poor" who needed salt for livestock and to preserve food. Finally, in 1791, when it became clear that revenue from the impost would not be sufficient, Hamilton added an excise tax on distilled alcohol, which many people saw as a regressive tax on small farmers.[11]

The western folk who marched on Pittsburgh in 1794 were explicit that the whole funding program—not just the excise tax—was what angered them. Shortly after the passage of the Funding Act, people in the four western counties (Westmoreland, Washington, Fayette, and Allegheny) convened a series of meetings to express their belief that "in a very short time," Congress had made "hasty strides" toward "all that is unjust and oppressive." They assailed the payout to war debt speculators as "unreasonable" and "unconscionable." They said it took "undue advantage" of the "ignorance or necessity" of soldiers and civilians who had sold certificates for pennies on the dollar. Taxing these same people so speculators could "make fortunes" struck them as being "contrary to the ideas of natural justice."[12] Guided by this sense of injustice, westerners declared that any federal tax—not just the excise—was immoral because it funded a windfall for war debt speculators. To them, the taxes were the "base offspring of the funding system" for speculators and, therefore, were "oppressive," no matter how progressive they were.[13]

Westerners also said that the excise was especially "obnoxious to the feelings and interests of the people" because it was a regressive tax. They proclaimed the whiskey tax "unjust in itself" because it taxed ordinary folk heavily and was "oppressive upon the poor," especially in a countryside still struggling with an acute "scarcity of a circulating medium." Without cash and with few markets for their produce, western farmers relied on whiskey as a form of money. The Constitution and Federalist laws had stripped the state of paper money; now, the Federalist excise tax promised to take the only form of cash they had left and "bring immediate distress and ruin on the Western Country."[14]

At these meetings, westerners also denounced another key part of Hamilton's financial program: the creation of a new private national bank in 1791, the Bank of the United States. Westerners complained that this new bank magnified all of the problems of Robert Morris's Bank of North America. They said the bank's "capital of nearly eighty million dollars" lodged too much power in the "hands of a few persons," who could dominate the economy and buy political "influence." Westerners called the Bank of the United States "an evil" even "greater" than Hamilton's war debt and tax policies.[15]

As angry as they were about federal policies, westerners made it clear they were equally upset with how the state government had also become a vehicle for rewarding speculators, especially land speculators (who also happened to be the leading politicians). To get a sense of what bothered them, consider the star-studded venture called the Pennsylvania Population Company, which was run by the biggest names from the Constitutionalist and Republican parties. The company controlled a 483,000-acre tract in the northwest corner of the state called the Erie Triangle. It united leading Constitutionalists John Nicholson, Charles Pettit (now a director of the Bank of the United States), and retired army general William Irvine with leading Federalists Robert Morris, James Wilson (now a U.S. Supreme Court justice), John Nixon (president of the Bank of North America), and Pennsylvania governor Thomas Mifflin. These high-placed officials gave their company the rights to the entire Erie tract before the public even had an opportunity to place a bid. Many people complained of corruption, but hardly any effort was put into investigating the scheme. No doubt, it helped that U.S. Attorney General Edmund Randolph was among the company's largest shareholders.[16]

Such duplicity was symptomatic of the unabashed self-interest that state leaders now routinely applied to their public duties. In the name of amassing huge amounts of land, state leaders bent rules and scuttled procedures that hindered their ambitions. They shamelessly used their offices to cut special deals and to avoid complying with laws that governed the lives of ordinary citizens. The examples were as glaring as they were numerous. The most obvious came in the ways that state leaders avoided paying for lands by exempting themselves from rules they applied to everyone else. As a result, by 1794, Pennsylvania speculators had amassed approximately 10 million acres of new lands on the state's northwestern frontier but had only paid for 720,000 acres—scarcely 7 percent. The same state leaders who were cracking down on land payments from ordinary farmers failed to meet payment requirements on 93 percent of the lands they bought.[17]

Nor did speculators have to pay taxes on these lands. At the same time that state leaders were foreclosing on ordinary citizens for nonpayment of taxes, they gave exemptions to land speculators (in effect, giving themselves sizable tax breaks). This pattern began in 1786 with a law that prohibited counties from selling speculative tracts for nonpayment of taxes; the assembly renewed the law each time it was set to expire. As late as 1793, county officials wrote heated letters to state leaders wondering why land speculators were being excused from paying taxes while everyone else was being prosecuted.[18]

As controversial as all of this was, it was surpassed by the prospeculator rulings of the new Pennsylvania Supreme Court. To appreciate its zeal, consider the court's questionable ruling in a case about a 1792 law designed to make it more difficult for speculators to acquire large tracts of land. On its face, the 1792 law appeared to be a dramatic victory for small land holders: it limited those buying land to 400-acre tracts and required them to provide evidence of physical settlement before receiving title. Despite the law's seemingly clear intent to limit speculation, the state's supreme court effectively nullified it. First, the justices dispensed with the residency requirement by giving a generous ruling on a section of the law that gave extra time to families who had been driven from their homes by Indian attacks. Under the court's interpretation, everyone qualified as a victim of Indian attack, even if they had never set foot on the property. The court dispensed with the 400-acre limit in a similar manner. It ruled that those who settled the land "by means of labor" could only claim 400 acres, while those who paid cash could purchase "any quantity whatever." Thus, the court transformed a law restricting speculators into one that restricted ordinary farmers.[19]

All of this angered westerners (and many other Pennsylvanians) who condemned the state's favoritism and corruption. These people called for genuine limits on land speculation and demanded that, if there were to be new taxes, they should be laid on the "Men of fortune" who "have engrossed immense tracts of land." Many people believed that a tax on speculative real estate would cause the "rich and opulent" to sell their holdings, thereby opening the land for settlement by small farmers—which, they said, was much fairer than "The *happy* excise law." Even backcountry aristocrat Hugh Brackenridge declared his preference for ditching the excise in favor of "a direct tax with a view to reach unsettled lands which all around us have been purchased by speculating men who kept them up in large bodies and obstructed the population of the country."[20]

Although upset at a wide array of state and federal policies, the physical protests concentrated on the excise tax. The reason was obvious: only the excise reached into their communities in a tangible way. As upset as people were about the payout to war debt speculators, the impost, the court decisions, and the new bank, none of these policies offered an easy target. Impost collectors, war debt speculators, land speculators, congressmen, assemblymen, bankers, and judges all generally resided in and around Philadelphia. By contrast, the new excise collectors were stationed in their neighborhoods and physically entered their homes. Aside from land surveyors (who faced frequent attacks on the deepest frontiers), none of the other potential targets ever set foot in the backcountry. It was actually a repeat of what had happened during the 1760s and 1770s: although people were angry about a range of British policies, popular protest focused on taxes because there was no one to "punish" for the Currency Act or trade restrictions.

As a result, excise collectors bore the full brunt of popular anger, especially in the cash-scarce western counties. In the backcountry, excise collectors were assaulted by large crowds—sometimes 150 strong—in disguises or with blackened faces. Most crowds offered collectors the chance to avoid punishment by resigning their commissions and turning over their tax ledgers and the money they had collected. If the collector submitted reluctantly or refused altogether, pain followed. One crowd tarred and feathered an excise collector, cut off his hair, and took his horse; when local authorities sent a constable to make arrests, a crowd whipped the officer, then tarred and feathered him, blindfolded and tied him up, and left him in the woods for five hours. Another crowd pulled a collector from his bed, marched him several miles, stripped him naked, and burned his clothes; then they tarred and feathered him and tied him to a tree. A different crowd did the same thing to a collector, except rather than tie him to a tree, they branded him with a hot fireplace poker. One crowd burned a collector's barn; another torched a collector's house.[21]

Westerners were not alone in roughing up collectors: similar protests happened throughout the state. Federal excise collectors faced violent attacks in the eastern county of Bucks and the central county of Northumberland. In Chester County, just outside Philadelphia, in June 1792, a group of men with blackened faces attacked an excise collector, taking his horse and papers and then tying him to a fence. When the local constable came to arrest the men involved, another group, who were painted black and dressed in overalls, chased him from the township. In Philadelphia County, people in Germantown tore down the sign a federal tax collector had hung outside his office and replaced it with a drawn and quartered animal as a warning. In Northampton County, threats against collectors caused considerable "delays and impediments" in the collection of excise taxes. In Cumberland County, an excise collector had a run-in with "a party of twelve men provised with clubs." Opposition even appeared in the heart of Philadelphia when "about three hundred of the lower class of people" assembled to condemn a proposed excise tax on tobacco as "oppressive and dangerous" and pledged to oppose it. In sum, people everywhere in Pennsylvania protested against the excise.[22]

And, as during the 1780s, so many people were involved that it was hard to prosecute anyone to stop the protests. In the western counties, grand juries

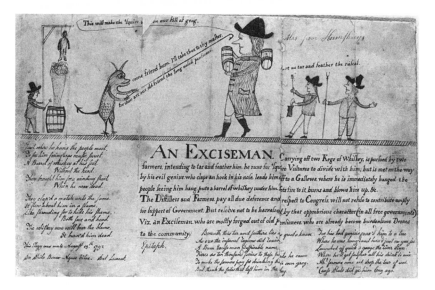

FIG. 10.1. AN EXCISEMAN, AUG. 13, 1792. This drawing, thought to have been done by a participant in the western uprising, shows an excise man pursued by farmers intending to tar and feather him. He is apprehended by an "evil genius" who hooks him through the nose and hangs his lifeless body from a tree. "The people" then blow up the corpse by exploding a cask of whiskey beneath it. The passage below implicitly links the excise protest with war debt payments by noting that excise men are the most "opprobrious character (in all free governments)" who "are mostly forged out of old Pensioners, who are already become burdensome Drones to the community." The word "Pensioners" is one of the many terms that ordinary Pennsylvanians used to denounce war debt speculators. Courtesy of the Atwater Kent Museum of Philadelphia.

refused to indict attackers, and witnesses routinely failed to show up for court (leading one official to proclaim that it was "impossible to get any person now living here to give testimony"). Many judges refused to help, saying "it was not our duty to hunt after prosecutions." If cases went to trial, officials reported that "no jury could be found in the counties of Washington, Westmoreland, or Fayette" that would convict, because "the people in these counties were equally opposed to the excise."[23]

There was nothing really new in any of this. The grievances that Pennsylvanians raised were largely the same ones they had expressed during the 1780s (if not the 1760s and 1770s). The forms of protest were essentially the same ones that had been used against British and, then, against state officials who had tried to impose policies that ordinary Americans found to be oppressive. Consider, for example, the connections between the multicounty meetings in western Pennsylvania to protest the Funding Act and the road closings that swept the state at about the same time. The leaders of those meetings were also among the chief road closers in the region. In fact, the purported mastermind of the 1794 uprising, a lawyer named David Bradford from the town of Washington, was arrested several times for closing roads. In March 1791 (the same month that Congress enacted the federal excise tax), Bradford was arrested along with fourteen other supervisors for failing to remove obstructions from the road. At least three of his codefendants would go on to play prominent roles in the 1794 drama. In 1792—only ten days after he had supervised a meeting against the Funding Act—Bradford again stood before the court, this time for creating a barricade of timber and brush in the main highway leading out of Washington. Another man who attended this meeting had been arrested the day before for erecting "edifices" across a different public highway, and in 1794, he was charged with treason for marching on the home of a federal collector. In sum, the protests against the Funding Act fused seamlessly with all of the other popular attempts to reclaim the Revolution.[24]

"'Tis time to assume a different tone"

Ultimately, however, the efforts against the Funding Act were different because, now, it was no longer just a Pennsylvania matter. People were resisting a federal law, administered by national leaders who were determined to compel the public to submit—and who now had the power to enforce their will. As a result, Federalists singled out the opposition in Pennsylvania, and the western counties in particular, to make it a test case of their new federal authority.

The key figure in all of this was Treasury secretary Alexander Hamilton, who had designed the Funding Act and was tasked with enforcing tax collection. When opposition to the excise emerged in Pennsylvania (and across America), Hamilton took it personally. In light of the revolution brewing in France, he also saw the opposition as a grave threat to the republic. Paris was in turmoil as crowds of commoners seemed to have taken over the government; in 1793, Parisians lopped off the head of the king, and nearly every month saw another prominent royal or aristocrat dispatched at the guillotine. For men like Hamilton, the news from France cast the American protests in a new and dangerous light, convincing him that the government needed to come down hard in one place to crush dissent before it spread out of control. "Decision successfully exerted in one place will, it is presumable, be efficacious everywhere," he wrote to President George Washington. The only question was: where to make the stand?[25]

By 1792, there were many viable possibilities beyond Pennsylvania. In Kentucky, popular resistance had brought excise tax collection to a near standstill, and many officials refused to prosecute those who would not pay. In Virginia, protests by distillers in one county stalled collection efforts. In Georgia and the Carolinas, threats of violence and sporadic attacks persuaded many excise collectors to abandon their commissions. Crowds in North Carolina locked one collector in a distiller's home for three days and threatened to grind off his nose at the local mill.[26]

Given the widespread opposition, why did Hamilton single out Pennsylvania (and the western counties in particular) to be his test case? The answer is twofold. First, Congress was located in Philadelphia, making Hamilton especially sensitive to opposition "in the State which is the immediate Seat of the Government." If the federal government could not uphold the law in Congress's backyard, what chance did it have to compel compliance in Maine, Kentucky, or Georgia?[27]

Second, western Pennsylvanians were better organized and more ambitious than any of the other protesters: they were intent on forming a national resistance movement against Federalist rule. That goal and the beginning of unprecedented organization in the region led Hamilton to perceive them as the biggest threat.

The organization in the western counties began in July 1791, when men from Westmoreland, Washington, Fayette, and Allegheny counties organized a multicounty meeting to protest the Funding Act. Any Federalist who knew the men in attendance would have been shocked. The meeting brought together leaders of the 1780s protests and their former enemies (the lawyers, judges, and large land holders who had tried to stifle those protests). Here were Constitutionalists and Republicans, Antifederalists and Federalists united against what they called the "evil" of Hamilton's policies.[28]

Supporting these meetings was a series of local organizations, each dedicated to regulating the "audacious and corrupt administrations" in the state and national governments. They went by many names: there was the Association, the Society of United Freemen, the Republican Society of the Yough (a reference to the Yough River in southwestern Pennsylvania), the General Committee, and numerous "patriotic" societies. Many of them had drafted formal constitutions that pledged members to reverse the current situation where "the people" were "but the shadow of a name" in "their own governments." Instead, the new societies said they would do their "duty" to preserve "our Liberties" and ensure "a more perfect union to ourselves and our posterity." Those pronouncements led Hugh Brackenridge to say that these organizations (and the United Freemen in particular) were "more democratic" than any institution he had ever seen. Brackenridge would call the United Freemen the "cradle of the insurrection" of 1794.[29]

These organizations were also intent on coordinating their efforts. Westerners spoke of forming a "cordial union of the people west of the Allegheny Mountains" and overcoming the many "divisions among our citizens here." The new societies created "committees of correspondence" to "form a speedy communication between ourselves" and to ensure that resistance was "carried out with regularity and concert." If needed, westerners wanted to be able to instantly "call together either general meeting[s] of the people in their respective counties or [a] conference of the several committees."

More than this, the societies were intent on spreading their model of organization and recruiting a nationwide network of "the people." Westerners used their committees of correspondence to try to connect their efforts with the rest of Pennsylvania and with people "in other parts of the United States." And they actually made inroads toward that goal, managing to link up with like-minded people in western Maryland, Virginia, and Kentucky— a remarkable feat given the organizing problems of the past.[30]

All of this organizing—and the attempt to form a nationwide movement in particular—set western Pennsylvanians apart. In other states and in eastern Pennsylvania, resistance may have been endemic, but it did not reach out like it did in the western counties. As a result, it did not frighten Federalist leaders to the same extent.

Thus, Hamilton and his Federalist associates perceived the movement in Pennsylvania for what it was: a serious, if embryonic, political threat. Western Pennsylvanians did not merely want to repeal the excise tax: they intended to create a national movement to oppose Federalist rule. They wanted to dismantle Hamilton's entire financial system: the federal revenue laws and infrastructure, the war debt funding program, and the Bank of the United States. They were not yet powerful enough to challenge Federalist policies on the state level, let alone the national level. But their organization was intent on growing. These people had taken only a few months to mobilize four of the state's largest counties in a region where travel was made difficult by poor roads. Who knew how successful they might be if their efforts gained momentum?

Alexander Hamilton, undoubtedly guided by such thoughts, treated the petition of the 1792 multicounty meeting as a declaration of war. As soon as he received news of the meeting, Hamilton asked President Washington to send troops against the people of western Pennsylvania. "'Tis time to assume a different tone," Hamilton announced to the president on September 1. It was time to "exert the full force of the Law against the Offenders." The delegates at the multicounty meeting had crossed the line by promising to work for the "undoing" of the Funding Act and to "obstruct the operation of the Law." For Hamilton, those objectives made "a vigorous exertion of the powers of government indispensable" to halt the movement in its tracks.[31]

To Hamilton's disappointment, however, few members of Washington's cabinet shared his belief in the legality or advisability of sending troops. Attorney General Edmund Randolph said that, from a legal standpoint, public meetings and petitions were not, in and of themselves, sufficient justification for military intervention. John Jay, chief justice of the U.S. Supreme Court, worried that using the army against Americans would "render the operations of [the] administration odious" and make it hard to get anything done. In the end, the most important opinion was that of Washington himself, who believed that sending in troops would give weight to long-standing popular fears that Federalists had only wanted the power to raise an army so that they could enforce tax collection. Consequently, although Washington would issue a proclamation condemning opposition to the excise, he would not yet consent to sending an army against American citizens.[32]

While Hamilton accepted the decision, he did not relent in his efforts to suppress the growing political movement in western Pennsylvania. He ordered the federal supervisor of collection in Pennsylvania, George Clymer (a Philadelphia bank official who possessed nearly $10,000 in war debt certificates), to go to the western counties to collect information on the people involved in "obstructing the law" and to obtain depositions from as many witnesses as he could. Hamilton insisted that Clymer must pay careful attention to the people's "language and conduct," noting anything that could lead to an "indictable offense." Hamilton even admitted to Washington that his goal was to provoke an uprising. "If the processes of the Court are resisted, as is rather to be expected," Hamilton explained, it would behoove Washington to "employ those means, which in the last resort are put in the power of the Executive."[33]

Hamilton's desire to provoke the western counties was evidently not a well-kept secret. William Findley, now a U.S. congressman, quickly caught wind of the secretary's intention and, just as rapidly, penned warnings in 1792 that "Something serious is brooding respecting the excise law in our county."

"The wrongful Secretary wishes to make us examples," Findley asserted. "Him and others of the same stamp urge the President on in that business." "The scene of operation will be Washington County," he declared. "I believe the Secretary wishes either to subdue Washington County; or else to provoke them to such conduct as will destroy their character in the public opinion." The information was accurate: Hamilton had, indeed, selected Washington County as the place to make his test case.[34]

Findley also observed that Hamilton seemed to be doing everything in his power to instigate an uprising. Hamilton had Clymer publish provocative accounts of his trip to western Pennsylvania which, in Findley's words, contained "an unprovoked attack in the news-papers on the magistrates, clergy, and all the other inhabitants of the whole western counties." Findley thought that it was like poking westerners in the chest, hoping they would take a swing.[35]

It is noteworthy that Hamilton was less than evenhanded in enforcing the tax laws. At the same time that he was insisting on collecting the excise, Hamilton was being especially lenient with merchants who cheated on paying the import taxes. For example, Hamilton reprimanded an impost collector in Providence, Rhode Island, who tried to stop widespread tax evasion by merchants. The collector explained to Hamilton that the merchants were "strangers to an honorable payment" and that they "paid but little regard to the law when it clashed with their Interest." He complained about rampant corruption among his fellow tax collectors, saying they were "perfectly under" the "control" of the merchants and allowed them to cook their books to avoid payment. Rather than support the effort to rout corruption, however, Hamilton scolded the collector for being "too *punctilious* and not sufficiently accommodating" to the merchants. He said that maintaining the "good will of the Merchants is very important" and that, in the Treasury Department, "it is a rule, in a doubtful case, to lean in favor of Merchants."[36]

By contrast, western farmers experienced little of this "favor." Instead, Hamilton was determined to push them to submit either voluntarily or, as he anticipated, forcibly through the power of a federal army.

The Showdown

Hamilton got his showdown. It began on July 15, when a federal marshal delivered a warrant to a farmer named William Miller, ordering him to appear in a Philadelphia court. Like many of his neighbors, Miller had protested against the excise by refusing to register his still or pay taxes on the whiskey he produced. The marshal had come to collect the price of that protest: $250. It was a steep sum for anyone to pay and especially for a man whose fortunes had taken a downturn during the postwar cash scarcity. Things had gotten so bad for Miller that he had already planned on selling his farm and moving to Kentucky to make a new start once he got the fall crops in. Now, with a $250 warrant staring him in the face, even those plans were over. Miller's face grew red. "I felt myself mad with passion," he recalled. "I thought 250 dollars would ruin me." When he read the part of the warrant saying he had to appear in federal court hundreds of miles away in Philadelphia, Miller crumpled the paper in disgust.

Then he looked up. And when Miller saw that the man who had led the marshal to his home was his neighbor John Neville, one of the wealthiest men in the western counties, he snapped. Miller had long detested Neville and considered him to be a traitor to the cause of liberty. He believed that Neville, a whiskey merchant and former politician, had continually betrayed his neighbors, and Miller would not let another act of disloyalty pass.

It had not always been this way. At one time, Miller had admired Neville, a war hero who had been a brigadier general in the Continental Army and the former commandant at Fort Pitt. After the war, Neville emerged as a strong voice for profarm reform, which gained him a reputation as a man of the people. In 1786, when farmers in Westmoreland County accosted a tax collector, chopped off the hair on half of his head, and then forced him on a punishing pub crawl, Neville had said the crowd was too restrained. "I heard general Neville himself say," Miller recalled, "they ought to have cut off the ears off the Rascal." In 1787, Neville had helped to organize the "Patriotic Convention" of Washington County that worked to support the Plan. He also helped to organize a boycott of Fort Pitt, calling for everyone to stop selling whiskey or grain to the fort until the government paid cash-strapped farmers in hard money. Soon after, Neville had won a seat in the state assembly and counted Miller among his strongest supporters. "I was always for general Neville, in his elections," said Miller, who also liked how Neville had stood up for his constituents once in office. Neville had spoken out against the Funding Act. And Miller remembered him having been "against the excise law as much as any body." Neville had even taken to the floor of the state assembly to demand that Congress repeal the excise tax and the other objectionable parts of the Funding Act.[37]

Then, just a few days after delivering this speech, Neville seemed to change. The reason was clear: Alexander Hamilton had offered him a job as an excise

tax collector, and he had accepted. Western Pennsylvanians were dumbfound-
ed by the reversal. As one observer put it, people could only conclude that
Neville was "giving up his principles for a bribe, and bartering the confidence
they had in him for money." "The people were more irritated against him," the
observer noted, "on being informed that when he was told that he would for-
feit the good opinion of his neighbors" by taking the appointment, Neville had
replied that "he did not regard their good will" because "he had got an independent salary of 600 a year." Indeed, Neville soon had more than that. Using
his connections at Fort Pitt, he monopolized the whiskey trade, which
Hamilton's policies concentrated in the hands of large distillers and traders
who had paid the excise. Neville grew so wealthy that he gave his son his
"mansion" and built a new luxurious estate, which he called "Bower Hill" and
filled with imported finery from Europe. Neville lived there in frontier ele-
gance with eighteen slaves who waited on him night and day. Reclining in one
of his many Windsor chairs, he dropped all talk about the virtues of the people. Now, he spoke only of his neighbors as "the rabble."[38]

Knowing the disdain Neville felt for him, Miller exploded when he saw
that his ruin was being delivered with the help of a man he considered to be
an unprincipled turncoat. "I felt my blood boil," he recalled, "at seeing general Neville along, to pilot the sheriff to my very door." Unable to contain his
fury, Miller unleashed a verbal tirade, shouting for Neville and the marshal
to get off his property. He made such a ruckus that between ten and thirty
of his neighbors came running. These men had been harvesting that week,
taking turns bringing in the crop on each other's farms. They were hot and
tired and in no mood for small talk. Hearing Miller's shouts and then seeing
the marshal and the hated Neville, they quickly surmised what was afoot.
The farmers formed a circle around Neville and the marshal, who were on
horseback, and began cursing them. One man shot a gun in the air, causing
the horses to rear in fright and prompting the two men to gallop off.[39]

From here, it was a blur of dramatic scenes. News of the confrontation at
Miller's house swiftly reached a militia company of the United Freemen who
had been drilling at nearby Mingo Creek in anticipation of heading to the
Ohio Valley to join the war against the Indians. Now, they changed their
plans and, instead, called for "the people" to march to Neville's estate the next
morning to compel the marshal to head back to Philadelphia. (No one knew
that the marshal had gone back to Pittsburgh rather than with Neville.)
Meanwhile, at Bower Hill, Neville got wind of the plan and started preparing for a siege. He lodged thick planks in the windows and doled out guns to
his slaves, ordering them to hide in their quarters until the militia arrived.

The next morning, militiamen numbering anywhere from 37 to 100 (the estimates vary widely) marched on Bower Hill. They shouted for Neville and the marshal to come out of the house. Neville shouted back that the marshal was gone and yelled at them to stand off. When some men hesitated, Neville fired his gun into the crowd. William Miller remembered that, in the next moment, Neville's slaves "fired out of their cabins upon our backs, and shot several." A man fell. Someone grabbed the dying body and, with lead balls flying, Miller and the rest "got off as well as we could."[40]

News of the death spread through the county and, the following day, between 500 and 700 militiamen marched to Bower Hill to demand Neville's resignation. One gentleman reported that it made him "afraid" when he saw gentry officers leading the way: "Here I beheld justices of the peace, officers of the militia and in a word the most respectable characters in the county commanding an armed banditti in opposition to the law and in opposition to that Constitution which they had sworn to support." The militiamen had signed a pledge promising that, if Neville would give up his commission, "no harm should be done to his person or property"—precisely as Stamp Act protesters had done in 1765.[41]

To get a sense of the crowd's restraint, consider that, on their way to Bower Hill, the militia stopped in mid-march to debate the wording of the pledge demanding Neville's resignation. Some of the militiamen thought the statement on taxes was unclear and made it seem like they opposed all taxation. These men wanted to discuss the wording before they got to Neville's. And so, in the middle of the road, the militiamen debated how best to reframe the statement to avoid any misperception of their intentions. It was decided to add the phrase "the people did not refuse to pay a proportional part of the revenue" to make it clear that they did not want to throw off the war debt altogether; they just did not want to pay a regressive tax that would go to funding an enormous windfall for speculators. The matter settled, the men reformed their ranks and continued the march, no doubt fully expecting Neville to resign his commission peacefully.[42]

Little did they know that Neville intended to fight back. After the shootout, he had requested help from every authority around. Local leaders refused to intervene, saying it was a federal matter. The new commandant at Fort Pitt was more supportive and sent a detachment of eleven soldiers led by an army major. The soldiers took up strategic positions inside Neville's house, while the major sent Neville to hide in the woods behind Bower Hill. For reasons that remain unclear, he kept Neville's wife and children inside.

Soon after, the militia arrived, marching in good order to fifes and drums. They formed lines in front of Neville's house and when they had come to attention, the militia commander, James McFarlane, announced his intention to search the house and destroy Neville's excise commission. When McFarlane and the major from Fort Pitt could not agree on terms for a search, McFarlane ordered the house evacuated. The major replied that the soldiers would stay and defend Bower Hill and sent Neville's family out of the house. As soon as the children were out of harm's way, gunfire erupted. At some point during the battle (some said fifteen minutes after the shooting began, others said an hour), the soldiers in the house stopped shooting. A voice called out from inside. And McFarlane, who thought it was a call for negotiations, ordered his men to hold fire. When the air was silent, he stepped out from behind a tree and began approaching the house. A single shot rang out. McFarlane fell, perhaps dead before his body hit the ground. Silence returned.

An instant later, the militia, enraged by what they saw as murderous deception, trained their guns on the house and unleashed a furious hail of musket balls. Soon after, one militiaman set fire to straw in the barn. Others spread the fire to the main house. As flames licked around them, the soldiers knew the battle was lost. They surrendered and left the house, greeted by angry militiamen who yelled that this battle should never have taken place because the soldiers, being so badly outnumbered, should have surrendered before anyone was hurt. Despite their rage, the militiamen let all of the soldiers return to Fort Pitt unharmed. With the house now empty, they took out their wrath on Bower Hill, torching buildings throughout the estate and smashing Neville's Windsor chairs and expensive finery. Everything went up in smoke, including $4,600 in war debt certificates. The militiamen only left a few buildings that Neville's slaves had begged them to spare. (Neville managed to escape and moved back into the mansion he had given to his son; he would file an enormous claim with the federal government for all the burned property.)[43]

Organizing for Independence

In the weeks that followed, the nature of the protest changed dramatically. As word spread about what had happened, most westerners stopped talking about regulating their governments and, instead, began making plans to form their own independent government. Convinced that their governments had abandoned the principles of the Revolution, westerners began planning secession from either the state or the new nation (their exact intentions remain unclear). They met at militia musters, in township assemblies, and at county conferences. County committees wrote to one another and to committees in Virginia. A regionwide gathering was set for the beginning of August at Braddock's Field on the outskirts of Pittsburgh to plan their secession.

The intentions for independence were clear. A committee created a flag that would soon appear everywhere: a standard with six stripes that represented the four western counties of Pennsylvania (Washington, Westmoreland, Fayette, and Allegheny) and two northwestern Virginia counties (Ohio and Monongalia). This six-stripe flag would fly before the procession to Braddock's Field, and farmers would plant it at the center of the meeting there.[44]

The choice to assemble at Braddock's Field was also tied to the push for independence. Braddock's Field was near the federal armory at Fort Pitt. The committees intended to raid it for weapons to counter any force that might be sent against them. (This was precisely what patriots had done at the outbreak of war with Britain and what Massachusetts Regulators had attempted to do in 1787.)

Two days before the scheduled meeting at Braddock's Field, however, march organizers decided to cancel the raid. They did not want to send the "brave sons of war" against the federal armory because, as the chief organizer, lawyer David Bradford, explained, "We have been informed that the ammunition which we were about to seize was destined for General Scott who is just going out against the Indians." "We therefore have concluded not to touch it." For these men, fighting Indians took precedence over their plans for independence. Indeed, for most westerners, removing Indians was just as fundamental a part of their vision of independence as their notions of good governance.[45]

Neither was there the attack on Pittsburgh that John Wilkins and his neighbors had feared. Although the militias marched through Pittsburgh, it was generally a peaceful protest. A few guns went off, and some marchers shouted and cursed. But the militia came and went without serious incident. Several observers even reported that they paraded through in surprisingly good order.

In the end, the purpose of the march seems to have been to send a message that "the people" were strong and united and to pave the way for a formal vote on independence. The militias returned home to discuss the matter and to hold elections for delegates to a regional meeting two weeks later. The committees also exerted "much industry" in writing to "relations & friends" elsewhere to muster support for what they undoubtedly believed would be their declaration of independence.[46]

War or Peace?

The objective of that meeting soon changed profoundly. When President Washington heard about the march through Pittsburgh, he decided to call out the army to put down what he called an "insurrection." Federal troops would march on western Pennsylvania, perhaps by month's end. The meeting to decide on independence suddenly became a vote for war or peace.[47]

The debate over whether or not to go to war was fueled by a decade of dissatisfaction with the direction the Revolution had taken. In talking about war, westerners—and those in the eastern counties who sympathized with them—were explicit that what bothered them was how the new state and national governments had undermined democracy. Whether they ultimately voted for war or peace, these people made it clear that they wanted the same kinds of dramatic changes for which many of them had been calling since the earliest days of the struggle again Britain.

In this sense, the debate at the August 14 meeting over whether to fight ranged over everything that stood in the way of giving "industrious men of a middle and low class an equal privilege with those of the rich." Of course, delegates cited the excise tax. But they also condemned government policies that promoted the "engrossing of large quantities of land in the state by individuals." They blasted the judges of the new court system for discriminatory rulings that favored land companies over settlers. They called for replacing the excise with a "direct tax on real property" (by which they meant speculative land holdings), which would keep "men of wealth from engrossing lands profusely." They complained about "the use of [state-appointed] judges in courts" rather than elected justices of the peace. And they denounced "the high salaries of officers both in the general and state governments." Some delegates reported that "the people" were "outrageous to do something" about problems like "the costs on the suits before justices" and "court expense[s]." All of these policies, they said, worked against the equality that "ought to be the true object of a republican government."[48]

Those same ideals infused resistance in other parts of Pennsylvania. The first reports of sympathetic protest came from the mountain county of Bedford. In early September, Attorney General William Bradford noted, "The disaffection seems to have spread in Bedford County, where about ten days ago, near two-hundred men assembled, & in the very view of the court which was then sitting, erected a liberty pole." Similar liberty poles had been raised in the 1760s and 1770s by patriots, who cut down ship-mast-like trees and then planted them in town centers; atop the poles, they attached banners and flags bearing revolutionary slogans and symbols. In Bedford, the pole bore the "six striped flag" of western independence and included "the inscription that is the common one among the insurgents" (which was undoubtedly something like "LIBERTY, LAND TAX, and NO EXCISE"). To Bradford's chagrin, the pole was "still standing" nearly two weeks after it was put up, which he took as a sure sign that Bedford County stood in opposition to the federal government.[49]

Soon after the pole raising in Bedford, protests broke out in the central counties. When news arrived that Washington had called out an army, the old networks returned to life. Farmers called meetings and began speaking out and drafting petitions. They raised liberty poles in the counties of Cumberland, Franklin, Dauphin, Mifflin, and Northumberland, often placing them at several different locations.[50]

Like farmers in the west, protesters in central Pennsylvania said they were doing all of this because they believed that the new government had violated the ideals of the Revolution. Petitions drafted in Cumberland, Mifflin, and Dauphin counties declared that the government seemed only to work for the "class" of man who was a "speculator in the funds" of the war debt, a "stockholder in the Bank of the United States," or a "landjobber." "These are a class of men," they wrote, "who seem to have a separate interest from the mass of the people." Thus, they said, "the Funding Act ought to be repealed, or at least so altered as to prevent the unprincipled class of mankind called speculators from drawing out of the treasury what they never were justly entitled to." They also called for the repeal of the "excise law," which was "oppressive on the poor people." "And least we may be thought by some to be enemies to all taxation and good order," the petitioners noted, "we unanimously resolve that we will be ready at all times to support government by the payment of taxes common with our fellow citizens." They only stipulated that the taxes target the wealthy and not enrich speculators.[51]

Farmers in the central counties saved some of their strongest language to condemn land speculation. In petitions, they called for an end to the "unjust and improper" policy of "selling Back Lands in great quantities to companies." Northumberland County pole raisers complained that "the officers of government and the land jobbers were engrossing all the property of the country" and called for a new tax to be "laid on the land and not on our own produce and that the land jobbers should pay the taxes." At a Franklin County pole raising, farmers condemned land speculation "in a great rage" and said that "any man who surveyed" land for speculators was "a damned rascal." Farmers' petitions said that allowing wealthy men to buy up so much real estate was "destructive of an essential principle in every republican government: the equal division of landed property." Their objective, they said, was regulating a "tyrannical and unjust" system so that "the common people" could be placed "upon the same terms with the favorites of government."[52]

People in the central counties also expressed their democratic ideals in the ways that they organized their protests. For example, in Franklin County, 500 men marched in a militia battalion without officers. They paraded alongside a wagon filled with timber to set up liberty poles throughout the county. Along the way, they intended to force an excise tax collector "to give up his books and papers." In response, several county judges rode out to stop the procession. When they caught up to the militia, they asked to speak to the officers. The farmers said "they had not officers they were all as one." When the judges replied that the assembly was illegal, the men marched on anyway, telling the judges "they would set up the pole if the Devil stood at the door."[53]

As far as democratic standards went, no one topped the farmers at a pole raising in Northumberland County in early September. At the town of Derrs, between 200 and 300 neighbors (including the county sheriff) came together and talked about how people throughout the county were setting up a "number of Liberty poles" and then discussed whether they should put one up too. The men stood in a circle and debated. Then, they voted on *everything*: whether to raise a pole, what the flag attached to the pole should say (they agreed on "Liberty, Equality of Rights, a Change of Ministry, and no Excise"), who should go to the woods to cut down a tree, and who would stay and dig so they could plant the pole. They voted on who would go door to door to get people to sign a petition and on who would ride to neighboring townships to get the "support [of] the people." When a county judge came out to read them the riot act (literally), the men proclaimed that they were an orderly assembly following the rule of law. One man shouted that they were not in opposition to the government and that the whole point of the pole raisings was to support *"Liberty and Government"* for "the people" against the "land jobbers." As soon as he finished speaking, "immediately the whole company huzzaed for *Liberty and Government*." In their minds, they were not rebels; instead, these people saw themselves as the defenders of democracy and good government.[54]

Those beliefs led many central county farmers to refuse to muster when they were ordered to march against the western insurgents. The most dramatic scene came in Franklin County, where a militia captain called his company together and told them "that he had received orders to draft a party." The captain told his men that "he did not know for what purpose but he supposed they could all guess it was to fight against the back country rioters." He said "he would take the sense of the company whether they thought it was proper to go to fight against the back counties or not." The captain then "directed all those who were for turning out to stand fast and those who were not for opposing the rioters to ground their arms," whereupon the captain, signaling his support for the western insurgents, "drew his sword and laid it on the ground and set his foot on it." Moments later, "the whole company" took their guns from their shoulders, "ground their arms," and "set their feet on their guns." When one man refused, the captain said "he was very sorry this company was not all of one mind" in opposition to the march.[55]

It was the same story elsewhere in central Pennsylvania. Observers in Cumberland County reported that "the militia would rather pay their fines than march," noting that many people had backed a resolution stating, "We depreciate those measures arming one part of the citizenry against the other." Many of these people thought "the people on the West had better separate themselves from the government of the United States than undergo such hardships as they were subjected to." They said it would be "better" for westerners to form a new "government for themselves" that "had no President, no King." The opposition was so united that U.S. Attorney General William Bradford proclaimed, "I am apprehensive that the militia of this state west of the Susquehanna is not to be depended on."[56]

Many Federalists were worried that people across Pennsylvania might actually fight against the army they sent. Those fears were heightened by a report from backcountry Federalist Hugh Brackenridge saying that the people were ready to rise up in opposition to the entirety of Hamilton's financial program. "The excise law is a branch of the funding system, detested and abhorred by all the philosophic men and the yeomanry of America, those who hold certificates excepted," he said. "There is a growling, lurking discontent at this system that is ready to burst out and discover itself everywhere." "Should an attempt be made to suppress these people," Brackenridge warned, "I am afraid the question will not be whether you will march to Pittsburgh, but whether they will march to Philadelphia, accumulating in their course, a swelling over the banks of the Susquehanna like a torrent, irresistible and devouring in its progress." Brackenridge reported that ordinary folk saw an impending conflict between the people and the moneyed men in Philadelphia whom they believed were oppressing them. "There can be no equality of contest between the rage of a forest and the abundance, indolence, and opulence of a city," he warned his fellow Federalists.[57]

There was reason to take such claims seriously. For example, in Northumberland County, one man said "he could raise one hundred fifty men to join them the insurgents," predicting that "the insurgents could beat any force to pieces that could be sent against them." In Franklin County, there was talk that it would take "six hours [to] raise 500 men" to fight against the speculators and every other "damned rascal" in government. Others announced that the government "might as well turn the Susquehanna" River than send an army against the protesters, saying that "there was more men engaged in the present opposition than was at the beginning of the Revolution between Britain and America." Those sentiments were even more widespread in Cumberland County, where some people talked about marching "out with the army" but, then, once in the western counties, turning "against them and join[ing] the other party."[58]

There was also reason to be concerned about the eastern German-speaking counties. In Chester County, militia officers resigned rather than march to subdue their fellow countrymen. In Lancaster and Northampton counties, several militia officers condemned the United States and the use of troops against American citizens. At a militia muster in Northampton, one militia captain announced he was "under marching orders but he would be damned if he would go and every man that did go was a damned fool."[59]

Nor was it easy for the government to recruit in neighboring states. In western Virginia and Maryland, large numbers of people opposed the draft, raised liberty poles, and declared themselves "in favor of a Revolution." In Norfolk, Virginia, "Small parties of the lower order" refused to enlist "upon a plea of serving against their countrymen, who were oppressed and could no other way obtain redress but by resort to arms." Summarizing the opposition, Edmund Randolph, who was now secretary of state, said he "was alarmed at the strength of the insurgents, at their connexion with other parts of the country, [and] at the extensiveness of the prevailing discontents with the administration."[60]

Attorney General Bradford was worried that all of this opposition would cause western Pennsylvanians to vote for war. He knew many westerners were convinced that, even if they voted for war, the federal army would not march. Bradford reported that most westerners had "strong hopes that many will advocate their cause—that few will join the government & that even the

[Pennsylvania] assembly itself may favor their endeavors." He said this idea was strengthened by envoys from the central counties who were "continually coming" to the west carrying "tales" that bolstered the "too prevalent" belief "in the insurgent country that the militia will not march." One letter from Cumberland County promised that "the militia will not come against us and if formed will come and be in our favour and that it is the case all over this state." Another letter proclaimed, "There is Not one Company [that President Washington] can get to go in full," and most of the troops who did march had said "they will turn [against the federal army] as soon as they are in your country."[61]

This was precisely the argument that backcountry lawyer David Bradford made in what one observer called "a violent speech" before the final vote on war or peace. Bradford made the case "for open resistance, stating the practicability of it." He declared that western forces could "easily defeat" the small federal army, which he said would have no stomach for battle.[62]

In the end, however, the ones without the stomach for war turned out to be "the people" themselves. Despite all of the talk of rising up, when faced with the actual choice, most Pennsylvanians voted to submit once it became known that a 10,000-man army was headed their way. It was a strange army, composed largely of gentlemen cavalry units and an infantry made up of the urban poor who had negotiated high wages in exchange for their service. Nevertheless, the force was large enough to convince most westerners to vote for submission. At the final multicounty meeting, it was close. But when the final votes were counted, twenty-three delegates voted for war and thirty-four to submit. With that vote, the resistance was effectively over.[63]

People continued to protest, but did so in small ways. In many townships, people refused to sign their names to formal submissions. In other places, people tore the declarations to pieces; and many of those who did sign changed the language of the document to make their submission far less docile. Others protested by leaving the state. As many as 2,000 people headed to Kentucky or to the Ohio country. A few, like David Bradford, relocated to Spanish territory in the Mississippi Valley.[64]

Many people east of the Appalachians quietly protested against the army as it marched. Protesters in the central counties raised liberty poles along the roads the army took westward. Officers reported that, in Cumberland County where the federal militias rendezvoused before marching west, many people refused to supply the army and that "the farmers in this neighborhood reluctantly thresh oats or refuse even to dispose of it when threshed." To "pro-cure an ample supply" of grain to feed his men, the officer was forced to use wagon trains to cart in food from far away.[65]

It was the same in the eastern counties. Several towns in southeastern Pennsylvania gave a cold reception to the federal army as it passed through. A captain from New Jersey complained that in Norristown in Montgomery County, "we found many people very much in favor of the rioters." He reported that the town of Reading in Berks County was also "full of prejudice against our happy government, and very unfriendly to our cause." In both cases, the captain dismissed the opposition as the "most ignorant and uninformed part of society." Whatever the case, the army met hard stares and symbolic resistance, but encountered no armed opposition.[66]

The only real violence came in Carlisle, where two protesters were killed. The first death came when federal troops shot a boy who had helped to raise a liberty pole. The second occurred when a drunken tavern scuffle ended with a soldier running a local man through with his bayonet.

The only other death was the former North Carolina Regulator—and now Pennsylvania Regulator—Herman Husband. When troops came to arrest him, Husband did not flee like he had in 1771. At seventy-three, he no longer felt capable of running. Federal authorities marched him across the state to a Philadelphia jail. "A prison," Husband wrote to his wife from his cell, "seems to be the safest place for one of my age and profession." The wry tone masked his profound disappointment that yet another regulation had ended in defeat. A millenarian who thought the end of days was near, Husband had been convinced that the "labouring industrious people, the militia of freemen" would "prevail over the standing armies of kings and tyrants that only rob them and live upon their labour in idleness and luxu-ry." Now, he was forced to admit that, once again, his prophecy had not come to pass. Instead, Husband watched as those he considered greedy men "whom our Lord called vipers" were victorious once again. Sitting in that cell for nearly a year, Husband had plenty of time to ponder the theological implications of the defeat of God's army.[67]

When the government dropped the charges against him in May 1795, Husband started to make the long journey back home to Bedford County, Bible in hand. Perhaps when he arrived home, he would start preaching again. Maybe he could finally lead his flock to the promised land of equality and independence. If those were the thoughts in Husband's head as he traveled, they were his last. Suffering from pneumonia, he collapsed on his way home and never regained consciousness.

* * *

The loss in 1794 was only the first attempt at regulation in Pennsylvania. In 1798 and 1799, ordinary folk in the eastern counties, most of whom had been silent during the 1794 protests, rose up in their own attempts to regulate the government. Those efforts would once again reveal the possibilities and limits of popular democracy in the new republic.

11

The Pennsylvania Regulation of 1799

JOHN FRIES'S REBELLION?

If a war should break out, we would show them who were "The People."

—Jonas Hartzell, brigadier general of the Northampton County militia, 1798

In 1799, ordinary Pennsylvanians engaged in another regulation of their government, this time centered in the German-speaking counties in the eastern part of the state. For the last 200 years, this uprising has been seen as being entirely distinct from the one in 1794: historians tell us that 1799 was caused by conditions unique to the German population in the eastern counties and involved issues separate from those that had inspired westerners. To be sure, there were differences between the two. But those disparities have been exaggerated to the point where they mask the stunning similarities. In both regions, people rose up for fundamentally the same reason: because they believed that their governments were undermining equality through policies that favored land and war debt speculators and because they opposed how the governments were attempting to stifle democratic self-expression.

By separating the two events, we have missed the important lesson that they collectively tell us about the importance of organization to the success of popular movements. Despite the fact that most people across Pennsylvania supported the vision of '76, they never managed to organize in ways that allowed them to adequately defend that ideal in the postwar decades. Placing the Regulations of 1794 and 1799 side by side, it becomes clear that, in particular, ordinary Pennsylvanians never found a way to bridge the cultural divide that had long separated the German- and English-speaking parts of the state. Moreover, they didn't really even try. In 1794, westerners never contacted the German-speaking east. And in 1799, German easterners never approached like-minded folk in the central and western counties. Instead, each side believed that shared ideals would always lead to shared action—without any common organization. As a result, they were both proven wrong in tragic ways.[1]

Familiar Troubles

Despite differences in time and place, the Regulation of 1799 was in many ways a replay of what had happened in 1794. The heart of the 1799 opposition was in Bucks and Northampton counties, eventually spreading to Montgomery, Berks, Dauphin, and parts of York County—in short, it encompassed the heart of the German-speaking east. Like the earlier regulation, the 1799 protest was fundamentally about people who believed that their government was undermining the accomplishments of the Revolution by working for the interests of moneyed men and making it harder for ordinary folk to reverse the trend—or even to complain about it.

The trigger for the 1799 Regulation was Federalist preparations for what the administration of President John Adams believed was an impending war with France. Relations with France had soured with the rise of the French Revolution and had taken a serious downturn in 1794, when President Washington stopped repayment of the money France had loaned to the United States during the War for Independence (Washington had argued that the rise of the new French regime voided the loans). In retaliation, France dispatched privateers to disrupt American shipping. The conflict reached a crisis point in 1798, when President Adams pulled the United States out of its 1778 treaty with France and sent American naval ships against French privateers. Amid escalating tensions, the Federalists launched a massive military buildup of about $10.5 million.

To pay for this buildup, Congress passed a host of new taxes. To appease the public, most of the taxes targeted the wealthy more than ordinary folk. The best example of such a progressive tax was the "house tax," or "window tax," as it was popularly called. These taxes rated people based on the size of their houses and the number of rooms and windows they contained. At a time when the vast majority of the population—even the middling sort— lived in what modern Americans would consider small hovels, the gentry paid far more under the house tax than did the average farmer or artisan. Moreover, the gentry were also taxed for interior features like wallpaper or a tiled chimney—expensive decorations usually found only in the most affluent homes. Finally, the new law taxed slave owners for each person they held in bondage, which, again, was a tax largely on prosperous families.[2]

Not all of the new taxes were so progressive, however. The "direct tax" assessed land in ways that ordinary farmers had long complained were unfair. The law rated the cultivated farmland of small holders at a higher rate than the unoccupied land held by speculators. Perhaps unwisely, Federalists also enacted a new stamp tax on legal documents that was remarkably similar to the one Britain had enacted in 1765.

At the same time, Federalists also passed the infamous Alien and Sedition Acts to clamp down on political dissent. Arguing the need to enhance national security during wartime (even though the United States was not officially at war with France), Federalists put new limits on free speech and immigration. The Alien Acts—passed to quell fears about revolutionary-minded French and Irish transplants—made it easier to deport immigrants and harder for foreign settlers to become U.S. citizens, extending the residency requirement from five to fifteen years. Meanwhile, the Sedition Act made it a crime to "write, print, [or] utter" anything "false, scandalous and malicious" against the government. It was a crime even to say or write anything that might bring Congress or the president "into contempt or disrepute" or "excite" the "hatred of the good people of the United States" against them. This vague law also outlawed any public "assembly" to "impede the operation of any law" and criminalized any attempt at "resisting any law of the United States, or any act of the President."[3]

These laws instantly triggered protests among many German-speaking Pennsylvanians in the eastern counties, who saw them as a renewal of old injustices. Not surprisingly, the Stamp Act was especially unpopular. Protesters—most of whom were either veterans of the Revolutionary War or their sons—"damned" the Stamp Act at meetings and pole raisings and accused anyone who supported Federalist policies of being a "Stampler," "Stamper," or "Stamp Act man." Several people said they had "fought against the Stamp Act [once], and would fight against it again." No doubt, the new Stamp Act also prompted declarations that no one was "in favour of those laws but tories" (the derogatory named used for loyalists during the Revolutionary War) and induced farmers to begin "huzzaing for liberty and democracy, [and] damning the tories."[4]

Many people also condemned the new taxes—despite their generally progressive nature—because they were angry that Federalists had, yet again, taxed farmland at higher rates than speculative holdings. "It is now well known," declared a petition from farmers in York County, "that the owners of houses in Pennsylvania will pay much more in proportion to the value of their property than the holders of uncultivated lands" (a tax on which they said would be "more equal"). Many eastern farmers were already convinced that elite Federalists were trying to "oppress the people" by turning them into serfs and tenants like in manorial Europe. These people claimed that the new taxes were part of a larger effort by rich Federalists to buy up "all their lands" and then "lease" them back to "the people" in contracts that lasted "for their life or perhaps two lives." It was said that if the "people did not oppose the laws they would certainly loose their lands," and the countryside would be governed by "great Lords and the people would be slaves."[5]

Fueling those beliefs was the growing stratification of wealth and land in the eastern counties. During the postwar decades, wealth had accumulated at the top of society and decreased among ordinary citizens. In Chester County, in 1799, the top 10 percent held about 46 percent of the wealth; the lowest 60 percent held just 16 percent. More than half of southeastern families did not own land. Things were somewhat better in the counties that were home to this new regulation: there, a great majority still owned the farms they worked. Nevertheless, farm size was shrinking, and many people worried that they or their children might join the expanding ranks of the landless.[6]

Moreover, a new economic downturn that hit as the decade drew to a close convinced many southeasterners that they could not bear any new taxes. Although the French Revolution and war in Europe had ushered in a few years of prosperity by forcing the Atlantic world to buy its flour from America, the conflict with France had caused the economy to sour once again. The downturn was nowhere near as bad as the grim postwar years. Still, in the late 1790s, farmers once again complained of a money scarcity, and courts were busy with debt cases and foreclosures. All of this helps to explain why southeastern farmers proclaimed the government was trying to "rob the people" and leave them "as bad off as they were in Europe" or else "famished like the Irishmen."[7]

The new downturn also helps to explain their opposition to the current military buildup—which many of them viewed as yet another boon for the same moneyed speculators who had profited from the Revolutionary War debt. One target of popular ire was $5 million in new war bonds that Congress was selling (mostly to wealthy men), which paid a steep annual interest of 8 percent. Many people felt the government had no business offering what some called a yearly "tribute to the amount of 100,000 dollars" in interest payments to "*usurious nabobs*" and "*Harpies*" who hoped to increase their wealth through "the House and Land Tax" on ordinary citizens. They blamed the "increase of heavy taxes" on "characters amongst us . . . who care not what becomes of the public good so that they can make their own fortunes." And they identified those "characters" as "the rulers of the people, speculators, swindlers, and traders." According to protesters, this was yet another attempt to bathe the gentry in "luxury" through "flattering" rewards doled out by the government and paid for by taxes on "the fruits of [the] industry" of ordinary farmers. "These gentry ought to be ashamed," concluded protesters. "So much for Tory disinterestedness, and love of country."[8]

Likewise, many easterners pointed out the similarities between Federalist attempts to limit dissent and the way Britain had curbed free speech and assembly during the 1760s and 1770s. Many people were especially angry that the limits on criticizing the government were so closely timed with the new heavy taxes. A federal assessor observed that people in Northampton County "connected" the new taxes with "the Stamp Tax & Alien and Sedition Acts and said they had fought against such laws once already and were ready to fight for it again." York County petitioners said the Sedition Acts promoted "disunion" and wore "the face of persecution." A crowd in Bucks County said Federalists were attempting to "bring us into bondage and slavery" like Britain had done and then "damned" the house tax, Congress, and the president and then "damned the alien law and sedition law."[9]

Many easterners made it clear that they were also protesting against earlier Federalist policies—especially the Funding Act that had rewarded war debt speculators. For example, a writer calling himself "Joe Bunker" proclaimed that, rather than taxing houses and farms, the government should enact new taxes on those who had made a killing speculating in the Revolutionary War debt. "It was a hard case," he wrote, that the farmer had to "pay a Tax on his hard earned property" while the war debt speculator "paid no tax on 10,000 dollars which he bought off a number of Soldiers." "These are strange times," Joe Bunker observed, "when the Speculator goes free and the industrious farmer is become the object of Taxation."[10]

Likewise, many protesters said they were still angry about the 1791 federal excise tax. At a Northampton County meeting in early 1799 to prepare a petition to Congress, one resident entered the room and asked if the document contained anything "against the excise upon spirituous liquors." When the men framing the petition answered no, the man replied, "then throw the petition into the fire and erect a Liberty Pole and let us fight." The man left the meeting and, along with his neighbors, cut down a tree and put up a liberty pole. In Berks County, the inhabitants of one township told a federal excise officer that if he continued to collect, "they would tie him fast to the liberty pole and keep him there till he gave an account of the money on duties they had paid on stills."[11]

Many easterners also renewed complaints about the taxes on imported goods to pay the interest on the Revolutionary War debt, saying the impost raised the prices of necessities. "*Who* pays these taxes?" asked one writer. "The merchant . . . ? No—he lays the tax upon the freight. The merchant importer? No—he lays it upon the articles he sells. The retailer? No—he imitates the merchants" and raises the prices of goods at his store. This writer concluded, "The consumer—the farmer, the mechanic, the laborer, they and *they alone* pay." The only ones who benefited from the impost, according to this man, were "the unproductive classes of the community, the merchants, the factors, the agents, the counting house clerks, and revenue officers" who either held war debt certificates or made their living collecting taxes for speculators.[12]

In all of these ways, easterners placed their grievances within the traditions of the Revolution. From complaints about the Stamp Act to anger over war debt speculation to worries about favoritism toward land speculators, eastern protesters made it clear that they were merely continuing the stand for good government they had begun in the 1760s and 1770s.

The Regulation

As threatened as Federalists were by such pronouncements, what drove them to attempt to subdue the opposition were the protests—and especially popular attempts to obstruct the law. Like the 1794 Regulation, the forms of protest repeated the kinds of resistance ordinary folk had displayed throughout the revolutionary era.

Given the context, the eastern protests seem especially daring. It took considerable courage to denounce state and national leaders at a time when any criticism of the government could lead to jail. Likewise, collective protest sent a powerful statement of ideals when it was done by people who had watched an army march through their neighborhoods to subdue similar protest in 1794.

And the physical protests of 1799 were indeed similar to the ones that preceded them. Like westerners in 1794, eastern protesters formed local "Associations" and agreed to oppose the law. They signed pledges, promising to support one another in resistance. They hoisted liberty poles adorned with flags bearing slogans like "The Constitution Sacred, No Gagg Laws, Liberty or Death." And, like the crowds of the 1760s and 1770s, the pole raisers sometimes held mock funerals where they burned and buried copies of the Alien and Sedition Acts and the new tax laws.

As before, the most serious acts were the attempts to compel collectors and tax assessors to stop doing their jobs. Southeasterners pressured federal tax officials to refuse their commissions. If the officials resisted, crowds chased them off with promises of beatings or death if they returned. The protests were communal and ritualized. They involved both men and women: men did most of the threatening and attacking; women were said to have dumped buckets of boiling water over the heads of assessors who attempted to rate their homes—the reason that some historians have derisively called the uprising the "Hot Water War."[13]

Federalists, obsessed with stopping any political dissent, viewed these actions as sedition and treason. Some Federalist leaders—paranoid about the reach of revolutionary France—actually believed that resistance in Pennsylvania was the handiwork of French spies, who were goading the protesters into overthrowing the government. Consequently, as in 1794, the Federalists worked to suppress the protests and to enforce the law as quickly as possible.[14]

As in 1794, the confrontation between protesters and federal authorities began with the arrival of a federal marshal to deliver warrants to arrest those who had obstructed tax collection. On March 1, 1799, a federal marshal rode into the town of Bethlehem in Northampton County, near the border with Bucks County, and set up an office at the town jail. Armed with several dozen federal warrants, he rode out each day to the surrounding countryside to arrest protesters and bring them back to the Bethlehem prison. He intended to hold the men there until he had captured everyone on his list and then cart the lot down to Philadelphia for trial. But the marshal did not have great luck in his quest. He only arrested about half of the men for whom he came. In some places, hostile crowds formed when he arrived and demanded that he leave their neighborhoods. Worse yet, when the marshal began locking protesters in the Bethlehem jail, he got word that several hundred men were coming on March 7 to free the prisoners.

The marshal was determined to stop that march. He asked four men from Bethlehem to ride out on the morning of March 7 to meet the militia at the toll bridge on the outskirts of town and plead with them to turn back. Hoping to appear bipartisan, the marshal asked for two volunteers from each political party: two Federalists and two men from the newer Democratic-Republicans, the party that had formed around Thomas Jefferson and James Madison (which, in Pennsylvania, was essentially the old Constitutionalist Party). It was easy to find four volunteers, since Bethlehem gentlemen from both parties did not want to see trouble enter their town.

The four men were not at the toll bridge long before the sound of distant trumpet blares could be heard coming down the road leading from the countryside. Soon after, they could just make out a line of militiamen on horseback heading toward them, followed by troops on foot. There appeared to be about 100 men. As the force drew closer, an alarming detail emerged: most of the uniformed militiamen wore liberty caps adorned with red, white, and blue badges made of feathers or ribbon—the exact kind of caps and emblems worn by revolutionaries in France. This was not good news. In France, the men who wore the tricolored cockade had guillotined the heads of aristocrats, gentlemen, and just about anyone else who had stood in their way.[15]

Given the violent talk that had been circulating through the region, the four men no doubt thought they had reason to worry. Many people had promised beatings and made death threats when chasing away collectors and the federal marshal. One man talked of raising "Troops to cut the Stampler's Heads off." Another said he would "cut" an assessor "to pieces and make sausages of him."[16]

In the rough-and-tumble world of late eighteenth-century America, threats like this were not uncommon—even gentlemen sometimes spoke in such coarse and violent language. It was nearly always just words, however, and when action did follow, it invariably took the form of fisticuffs rather than gunplay. Nevertheless, the men from Bethlehem also knew that such encounters could boil over as they had in western Pennsylvania five years earlier. Pennsylvania was not France during "the Terror"; there was no guillotine there. But anger, guns, and frayed nerves meant that this time around things might not end like they usually did. Perhaps this time, tensions would explode into another Bower Hill.

When the militia approached the toll bridge, violence seemed likely. The militiamen came toward the four gentlemen with drawn swords, and a rifleman aimed his weapon at the heads of the men from Bethlehem. (His companions quickly forced him to lower his gun and pushed him to the back of the line.)

There was another problem: it wasn't clear who the militia commanders were. All of the men were dressed the same. When the Bethlehem men asked for the officers to step forward to negotiate, no one moved. Instead, the militiamen replied "they were all the commanders." Not good, thought the four townsmen.

Thankfully, the militiamen agreed to negotiate—as a whole. They said they had no intention of harming anyone and that they had only come to free the prisoners. To reassure the townsmen, the militia elected a three-man delegation to ride into Bethlehem while the rest of them waited at the toll bridge. The militiamen also voted that, if the marshal refused to release the prisoners, they would all march to the jail.

The meeting between the delegation and the marshal went badly. The marshal's only concession was releasing two militiamen who had mistakenly arrived in Bethlehem that morning, thinking they were supposed to rendezvous in town rather than at the bridge. The marshal flatly refused to release the other prisoners, saying that to do so would violate federal laws. Consequently, the delegation mounted up and rode back to fetch the others.

They did not get far: long before they got to the bridge, they heard the sound of fifes and drums coming toward them; the militia had decided to march anyway. And it was a much larger force than the one they had left at the bridge—now perhaps as many as 400 men strong. The 100 or so Northampton militiamen waiting at the bridge had been joined by about 30 or 40 militiamen from Bucks County. Behind them was a huge crowd of hundreds of country folk, most of them armed. A single militia officer led the force, wearing a black feather in his cap—a symbol that identified him as a Federalist and an opponent of the French Revolution. Anyone who took comfort in seeing that black feather, however, soon discovered that the man wearing it was not a typical Federalist.[17]

The black feather was worn by John Fries, a forty-eight-year-old farmer, cooper, and auctioneer from Bucks County, who had been a war hero in the local militia during the conflict with Britain. Fries was, indeed, a Federalist. In 1794, he had even marched with the army to put down the regulation in the central and western counties. But he was also incensed with his party, believing that most of the laws that Federalist leaders had passed in the last several years were both dangerous and unconstitutional. Fries was no fan of revolutionary France—the black cockade announced his disdain for the Jacobins and the Terror. But he thought that talk of a French invasion was bunk, as were claims that opposition to Federalist policies was the work of French spies. In his opinion, Federalist leaders were rushing into a pointless war and using national security as an excuse to trample civil liberties at home. He was infuriated at how the Alien Acts made it harder for immigrants, like the young German men in his neighborhood, to become citizens and how it made it easier to deport them on trumped-up charges. He railed against the Sedition Acts that labeled nearly any criticism of the government a crime and allowed law enforcement to silence critics with heavy fines and long jail terms. He saw the arrest and impending extradition of his neighbors to Philadelphia as yet another breach of protected rights. Fries declared that "bringing people charged with crimes to Philadelphia" instead of trying them "in their own courts and by their own people" was "an oppressive thing" that violated the right to trial by a jury of one's peers (the same argument that colonists had made against British vice admiralty courts during the 1760s and 1770s).[18]

Fries was equally angry about the huge amounts of money Federalists were throwing into the military buildup. He believed that the government had spent too much money on the military with too little purpose. He also thought the new taxes to fund the buildup were unfair and unequal, placing too heavy a burden on hardworking ordinary folk and letting off the wealthy too easily. In fact, Fries had come to the conclusion that Federalist leaders were using the government to enrich themselves at public expense. Ultimately, he decided that Federalist leaders needed to be stopped. "If we let them go on so," he told his neighbors, "things would be as in France," where the people were "as poor as Snakes." In short, although Fries wore the black feather of federalism, he was a far different Federalist than most state and national leaders.[19]

When Fries and the militia he led had initially reached the bridge, the four men from Bethlehem rode out to meet them and begged him to turn the army around. Fries continued the march. As the lines passed, the four men shouted that they hoped "they would not hurt anybody." Fries shot back "No!" the militia would not hurt anyone. But he added that, if someone in Bethlehem shot first, all promises were off. He also said that, if the marshal did not "let the prisoners clear," there would probably be a "skirmish."[20]

When the militia arrived in Bethlehem, Fries entered the tavern unarmed to negotiate with the marshal. As before, the meeting did not go well. Fries called for the release of the prisoners and even offered to pay their bail, but the marshal refused. Two hours passed while occasional huzzahs, shouts, and curses could be heard from the crowd outside. It was now late afternoon, and Fries decided to leave the tavern to consult with the men outside. The militiamen voted to take the prisoners by force. As one man put it, they had "come so far, it was a damned shame not to have them." And so, Fries entered the tavern one last time accompanied by an armed guard. Before they passed through the entrance, Fries implored his men to hold their fire. "Please, for God's sake," he said, "don't fire *except* we are fired on first." Seeing the armed men with Fries, the marshal finally relented. He released the prisoners but would not accept the offer of bail. Instead, the marshal returned to Philadelphia to report that an armed militia had taken the prisoners by force.[21]

Suppression

Like his predecessor, George Washington, President John Adams greeted the news of the courthouse showdown as a declaration of war and began assembling an army to march to the southeastern counties. He issued a proclamation demanding that the "insurgents of Northampton, Montgomery, and Bucks counties" end their "treasonable proceedings," and he gave them a deadline of March 18 to "disperse and retire peaceably to their respective abodes." In the week that followed, people in these counties held meetings and planned a "committee of the three counties" to meet on March 18 to vote on whether to submit to or to fight the federal army.[22]

As in 1794, it was not entirely clear which way the counties would vote. In the previous weeks, many southeasterners had made strong statements about their willingness to fight a federal army. A Northampton County man had proposed that rural militias "storm" Philadelphia, prompting a neighbor to offer seven swords he had stored at home as a contribution to the "fight against the law." Others in Northampton had pledged that they would "rather die than submit" to Federalist rule, stating that "they had fought against such laws" in the Revolution and that they would fight again. One man in Bucks County had claimed he could "raise 10,000 men if they should be wanted to oppose the sedition and alien laws . . . and fifty other damned laws." Crowds in Berks County had promised that, if troops marched, "the army" would be "shot like flies because [Berks County] had ten men against the law to one who is in favor of it."[23]

Even much of the gentry from the region wanted to fight. A captain of an elite cavalry company in Northampton County urged his men to "take up arms and oppose the law." The brigadier general of the entire county militia (who was also a state assemblyman) declared flatly, "if a war should break out, we would show them who were 'The People.'" A state senator from the region advised militia captains to "collect their Companies" and amass "Plenty of Powder and Balls," since "a great many Pidgeons" would soon "be up from Philadelphia" for them to shoot.[24]

Even some of the local clergy urged violence. A minister named Jacob Eyermann told his parishioners "not to suffer the direct tax law to be put into execution that it was too hard." He preached that "Congress and the government only made such laws to rob the people, and that they were nothing but a parcel of damned rogues." He told his congregants that if they allowed the law to be implemented, the people of Pennsylvania "would be as bad off as they were in Europe." Eyermann then clutched his minister's robe and swore that, if it came to it, he would hang his "black coat on a nail and fight the whole week and preach for them Sundays." For uttering these words, Eyermann would later be thrown into the Bethlehem jail by the federal marshal.[25]

Many of those who preached armed resistance did so because, like the western farmers in 1794, they were convinced that the army would not march or that ordinary folk from across the state (or nation) would grab guns and come to their assistance. One man predicted that "if the army should come up from Philadelphia against the people here," another "army from the back country" would assemble and "come to support" them. One group "said they could raise 10,000 men" between "Quaker town and [the] Delaware River." Elsewhere, men "went about to collect money to go to Virginia to raise troops." In one of the most bizarre developments, a letter said to be from George Washington circulated through Bucks County, convincing many people that "General Washington" had "20,000 men ready to assist them in this undertaking to oppose the laws."[26]

Federalist leaders were certainly convinced that the eastern counties intended to fight. The commanding general sent to scout the situation reported back that "the people" seemed "ripe for anything" and that it appeared to be the "intention on the part of the Insurgents to make some stand." The general concluded that the federal army had better march soon, because "nothing but a display of force would reform them."[27]

In the end, however, the conclusion of the 1799 Regulation was as anticlimactic as the one in 1794. Despite all of the talk of "the people" rising up against the federal government, most easterners voted to submit. The protesters wanted to regulate their government, not overthrow it. And when John Adams sent out an army, the easterners laid down their guns.

Nor had anyone come to their assistance: the rumored army of the west never appeared or even mobilized. In fact, the western counties were largely silent during the entire 1799 Regulation. Having been defeated in 1794, fear seemed to have replaced democratic self-confidence. So pervasive was public caution that westerners refused to speak their minds on even mundane public issues. For example, in the winter of 1795, Federalist Hugh Brackenridge published an editorial in the *Pittsburgh Gazette* declaring that a Federalist candidate for the state assembly was ineligible to hold office because he currently served as a state surveyor (multiple-office holding was forbidden by the state constitution). Upon reading the editorial, a neighbor worried that Brackenridge would be arrested for criticizing a political leader (and this was *before* the Sedition Act). "Oh! You will be ruined now," the man exclaimed to Brackenridge. "Can't they make that out treason?" "No no," replied Brackenridge, a lawyer. "I know what treason is, and what it is not." The man was not relieved by such unflappable self-assurance. "It is well for you that you do," he replied, "for our part . . . we are afraid to say anything."[28]

Frightened into submission in 1794, the sole statement of support from westerners during this later regulation was the raising of a single liberty pole in Westmoreland County in 1799. Unlike the boisterous public pole raisings in the past, this one was put up in secret. And the sign on the pole carried a strange message, which few people understood: "The Father is gone to the Grandfather, and will come again and bring with him 70,000 men. In the year 1799. Tom the Tinker." This obscure protest represented the sum total of western support. Westerners—and their counterparts in the central counties—may have sympathized with the eastern insurgents, but their response in 1799 was mostly silence.[29]

In the end, the only real drama to the conclusion of the 1799 Regulation came in the trials of John Fries for treason, which became national news events. After two trials—the complete transcripts of which were published and widely sold at the time—Fries and his fellow protesters were convicted and sentenced to be executed. Hoping to send the message that the government was tolerant and generous, John Adams later pardoned the men, officially ending the Regulation of 1799.[30]

*   *   *

The story of the 1794 and 1799 Regulations is not simply a tale of people who believed that the Revolution had been betrayed. The story is also about the difficulties that ordinary Pennsylvanians had in making "the people" into something meaningful. The biggest gap separating the two regulations ended up being the cultural and language gap that split the English-speaking central and western counties from the German-speaking east. Instead of trying to organize to bridge that gap—a task made more difficult and dangerous by hostile federal laws—ordinary folk in both west and east assumed that "the people" all believed the same thing and would rise up as one. As before, however, shared grievances did not translate into united action. As a result, they continued to think alike, but could not find a way to work together to gain the political power needed to counter a government they all believed was putting their vision of the Revolution beyond reach.

Conclusion

It is rebellion in this Country to fight for liberty, tho' it is highly meritous everywhere else. The Government of the Country had given the most decided approbation to the French Doctrines and often drank whole hogsheads to their success. And yet when these Doctrines were reduced to practice by their own countrymen, they treat them as pernicious and subversive of all government.

—Charles Nesbit to Alexander Addison, March 4, 1795

This story of democracy and the Revolution in Pennsylvania has been a complex tale, filled with triumph and tragedy and riddled with irony. Its high points are the things we rightly celebrate about the Revolution: the overthrow of British rule, the opening of the political system, and the empowerment of ordinary Americans (even though it was mostly white men who were empowered). Its low points are the parts of the story that have been removed from public memory: the scaling-back of democracy and the dramatic defeat of a popular vision of the Revolution. This book has been an attempt to reconcile those two sides of the story, to put together what the public celebrates with one of the many stories from the Revolution's darker side. Ranging over the period from the 1760s through the 1790s, I've tried to explain how, for many ordinary Pennsylvanians, the Revolution was a tale of sweet victories that ended in a string of bitter defeats that left many people feeling that their ideas of democracy had been betrayed.

There remains much to celebrate in this story—a point even those who marched in 1794 and 1799 would have conceded. During the 1760s and 1770s, ordinary people in Pennsylvania had pushed the Revolution to become not simply about overthrowing British rule but, in a larger sense, about empowering ordinary white men both politically and economically. They had framed the Revolution around opening the political system to regular folk and restructuring government to make it more responsive to the will of the many. During the 1760s and 1770s, those ideals had been shared even by many of the gentry who originally supported the democratic 1776 state constitution. Together, ordinary folk and gentlemen made great strides toward universal male suffrage—which at the time even included free black men. They removed checks against democracy in government by creating a powerful unicameral legislature. They allowed people to vote for most political offices (including those in the judiciary). And they made it so that any white man—or at least any white male Christian—could hold most political offices.

Likewise, before 1776, elite and ordinary folk united behind the belief that only an equal distribution of wealth would protect freedom and keep democracy healthy. Even many of the state's most genteel men pushed for things like progressive taxation, easy access to currency and low-cost credit through a government-run land bank, and bans on for-profit corporations. Gentlemen also supported popular calls to protect a wide array of civil rights and to sanction an idea of participatory democracy that went far beyond voting in annual elections. They even condoned the idea that the common people had a right to regulate their government to follow the popular will—especially when the government enacted policies that undermined liberty by making wealth more unequal.

After 1776, ordinary Pennsylvanians tried to build on those achievements by deepening their commitment to economic and political equality. They continued to denounce as a threat to democracy any attempt to concentrate wealth and power. At the same time, they extended their ideas of democratic self-expression and expanded the range of issues about which they believed ordinary citizens had a right to express their views. They added stronger calls for equal land ownership and for policies that would make the common people economically independent—all in the name of keeping democracy healthy and strong.

In all of these ways, most ordinary Pennsylvanians saw themselves as upholding the mainstream understanding of the Revolution. They did not see themselves as radicals or outsiders or as people trying to take the Revolution in a new and different direction. They believed that their notions of democracy were rights they had secured through the struggle with Britain and the overthrow of the provincial government. And those who shared these ideals believed—with good reason—that most people in the state (and, indeed, across the nation) supported them too.

To most Pennsylvanians, the only "radicals" were the gentry who had so dramatically changed their minds about what constituted good government.

And changed they had. In the waning years of the War for Independence, many of the gentry began embracing ideals and policies that they had once denounced as British "oppression." Frightened by the upheavals of war and spurred by a heightened sense of social status, many of Pennsylvania's self-styled gentlemen abandoned their commitment to extending political and economic power to ordinary folk. Instead, they adopted a new ideal of "good government" based on concentrating both political and economic might in the hands of the elite. They launched a prolonged attack on popular ideals and the democratic achievements of the Revolution, attempting to undo reforms that many of them had helped to create. In this sense, the postwar period was essentially a replay of the 1760s and 1770s, with the revolutionary gentry playing the role of Britain.

And, like Britain had done earlier, the gentry's effort to narrow democracy created an economic crisis and provoked an intense political struggle. Elite policies strangled the economy and led to mass property foreclosures across Pennsylvania. Many people from the middling and lower sorts initiated a powerful defense of popular ideals. They launched a barrage of petitions and tried to elect reformers to office. When those efforts fell short, they used mass civil disobedience and crowd protests to advance their ideals. In this way, the postwar years became a struggle to define whose vision of the Revolution—and whose definition of democracy—would reign in Pennsylvania and the new United States.

During the 1780s, that contest more or less played to a standoff. Despite legislative victories, the elites had trouble enforcing their plan to redirect wealth and power to moneyed men. And by far their biggest problem was mass popular opposition. Ordinary folk mobilized on the local level and proved adept at preventing elite policies from going into effect. Those efforts benefited from a decentralized legal system and a government that lacked the coercive power to enforce its will over popular opposition. At the same time, there were clear limits to popular power. Ordinary Pennsylvanians proved unable to organize at the ballot box to secure the power they needed to push through their agenda. Their efforts remained frustrated by the gentry opposition, the difficulties of organizing across county lines, a belief that shared ideals would lead to common action, and a political culture that valorized petitions and crowd protests over electoral politics.

Ultimately, those weaknesses led to critical defeats for popular democratic ideals. Genteel Pennsylvanians joined with elite men from the other states to create a new national government designed to be a stronger barrier against democracy. The new federal Constitution removed many economic powers from the states (like the ability to print paper money) and imposed new demands (like requiring debts to be paid in gold and silver), which effectively outlawed most popular reforms. At the same time, the Pennsylvania gentry replaced the 1776 state constitution with a new 1790 charter that mirrored the checks on democracy in the federal Constitution. State leaders then directed this new government toward enhancing the wealth of the elite and dismantling the rings of protection that ordinary Pennsylvanians had built to protect their communities. Ordinary folk continued to resist, even going so far as to close roads across the state. But they remained unable to mobilize in ways that would bring the changes they wanted. In 1794, when western farmers finally began organizing the state to oppose the new order, Federalist leaders became so threatened that they provoked a conflict to prevent ordinary folk from uniting. The final defeats came when armies marched in 1794 and 1799, solidifying a victory for the elite founders' vision of the Revolution.

It would be an enduring victory for the elite. Although the Federalists fell both politically and personally, the system they created to check democracy has lasted. Many of the key players in the drama, including Robert Morris, James Wilson, and John Nicholson, ended their days in debtors' prison—victims of their own greed and a land speculation bubble that burst when the French Revolution diverted the European investment on which they had gambled their fortunes. But their fall and the rise of the Jeffersonians in 1800 merely confirmed the victory rather than repudiating it. Although the Democratic-Republicans rode to power in Pennsylvania and across the nation by promising to restore the popular vision of the Revolution, once in power they offered little more than a shadow of the vision of '76. They did make important changes by trimming back Federalist excesses: the Jeffersonians repealed the excise tax and the Alien and Sedition Acts, protected free speech, and eventually lowered the price of new frontier lands to make it easier for small farmers to purchase them. Most Democratic-Republican leaders, however, were content to leave the bulk of the Federalist system in place. They ended up being much like the elite Constitutionalists and Antifederalists of the 1780s, who used popular rhetoric but shunned popular reforms (in fact, most of the key Jeffersonian leaders in Pennsylvania were exactly the same Constitutionalist land and war debt speculators, businessmen, and bankers who had thwarted popular initiatives in the past). To these men, "reform" meant pruning around the edges of the political, economic, and legal system. It did not mean pulling down the barriers to democracy that they had helped to create. Nor did it mean dismantling a financial system that rewarded moneyed men and land speculators like themselves.[1]

It was far from a total victory for the founding elite, however. Even the most antidemocratic founders understood that ordinary people would revolt if the gentry usurped too many popularly held "rights." Thus, in Pennsylvania, even as the 1790 state constitution included new checks on democracy, most white men remained eligible to vote and to serve in the legislature; most political offices remained elected rather than appointed; and the state continued to uphold most of the civil rights protected under the 1776 constitution. On the national level, fears of sparking popular revolts had convinced the men who sat in the 1787 convention to back off from the more extreme checks on the people called for by serious antidemocratic crusaders like Alexander Hamilton. And it was clearly popular pressure during and after the ratification struggle that produced a strong Bill of Rights, which not even James Madison had originally wanted. No doubt, if ordinary folk in Pennsylvania and elsewhere had simply sat on their hands during the 1780s, the new federal and state governments would have contained far higher barriers against democracy and become far greater tools for enhancing the wealth and power of the elite.

Nevertheless, despite this "triumph" of democracy, we should not lose sight of how that concept was greatly narrowed by the defeats of the 1780s and 1790s. The democracy that survived had been drastically changed from the ideal that ordinary Pennsylvanians—and many of the Pennsylvania gentry—had embraced in 1776. Make no mistake: the founding elite constricted the meaning and practice of democracy in fundamental ways that continue to shape our government and society today.

In terms of the practice of democracy, the defeat helped to confine democracy to forms of political self-expression that did not overtly threaten elite interests. The Revolution had convinced many ordinary Pennsylvanians—and common folk across the colonies—that they had a right to monitor the government, to shape policy, and to regulate the government if they believed that their leaders were not responding to the popular will. For these people, politics was not just about casting ballots—indeed, politics was not even primarily about voting. To them, regulating the government to act on behalf of the governed happened mostly outside the polling place. And "the people" expected to participate not just on Election Day but 365 days a year. Indeed, many Pennsylvanians believed they had a sacred right to regulate their government and that it was their duty to exercise that right to preserve democracy.

The founding elite attempted to obliterate that idea of politics during the 1780s and 1790s and to confine political self-expression within an electoral system replete with barriers against democracy. Undoubtedly, the most powerful barrier was the new federal system that placed a tremendous organizing burden on anyone pushing reforms opposed by the ruling elite. In the 1780s, ordinary Pennsylvanians could have enacted the array of policies they wanted by organizing across the state—itself a daunting goal. Thereafter, to achieve those reforms, they needed to organize across the nation. Reformers needed majorities in the U.S. House and Senate—and probably the support of the president too, if they hoped to avoid a veto. They also needed to organize for the long haul, since terms for national office were staggered at two, four, and six years. To get a majority, it was not enough to win during one election cycle; securing sweeping reform meant victories over many cycles. And in the new system, even winning Congress and the presidency was not enough since any reform could be swiftly nullified by a Supreme Court decision. Indeed, the elite founders had given Supreme Court justices lifetime appointments in part to defend the interests of the few against popular reform. In sum, this revamped political system posed an enormous challenge for ordinary people attempting to enact any kind of change that threatened the interests and ideals of the elite—whether the old revolutionary elite or the new elite who displaced them.

This was one of the most important legacies of the popular defeats of the 1780s and 1790s: federal and state governments designed to impede popular reform. In the more than two centuries that have followed the Revolution, the barriers against democracy put in place by the founding elite have frustrated countless movements intent on enacting changes opposed by the ruling elite. Indeed, the frustrations in getting change through the federal system helps to explain why so many reform movements—from the Jacksonians to the Populists to the Progressives to the modern labor, civil rights, and women's movements—have placed removing (or at least minimizing) those barriers at the center of their efforts. The difficulties these movements have faced also explains why elites from nearly every generation have tried fervently to keep the checks on democracy in place—or else put up new barriers to replace the ones the movements have taken down.

Along with radically scaling back the practice of democracy, the defeats of the 1780s and 1790s also weakened democracy's meaning—primarily in the way the elite founders attempted to eradicate the idea that concentrations of wealth pose a threat to the republic. In Pennsylvania, the Revolution had been forged by elite and ordinary folk who insisted that a free government could only survive in a society with a relatively equal distribution of wealth. That belief had pushed the revolutionaries of the 1760s and 1770s to make wealth more equal—or at least to repeal laws that made wealth more unequal. When many of the gentry decided during the war that concentrations of wealth were a blessing rather than a curse, they attempted to divorce wealth equality from the public's understanding of the Revolution. That effort was not entirely successful: well into the nineteenth century many ordinary Americans—and even some political leaders—continued to embrace the belief that government should oppose policies that concentrated wealth (in the case of politicians, at least they paid lip service to that ideal). Nonetheless, governments—with a few brief exceptions, like the Progressives at the beginning of the twentieth century or the New Deal of the 1930s Roosevelt administration—have done little to counter the growing disparities of wealth or even to denounce the trend. Instead, the governments that emerged from the Revolution often fostered massive inequalities of wealth. At the same time, they redefined "democracy" as an ideal that could be reconciled with those disparities. By transforming democracy into a concept that encouraged uninhibited wealth accumulation rather than wealth equality, the founding elite (and subsequent generations of elites) tamed what they could not defeat. They turned democracy from a threat into an asset by making it into a concept that supported their own ideals and interests.[2]

The result of that transformation was a largely unimpeded concentration of wealth across the nineteenth and early twentieth centuries. It was an ironic turn. Even as more ordinary white men voted—producing many of the highest voter turnout rates in American history—political leaders seldom put policies to promote wealth equality on the ballot. Each time that ordinary folk attempted to support such policies, elite leaders tried either to crush the opposition or to co-opt the rhetoric and water down the reforms. As a result, the century and a half after the Revolution saw wealth and power concentrate to such an extent that it would make the revolutionaries of 1776 shudder. No doubt many of them would have been equally alarmed at the extreme concentration of wealth in America that has occurred over the last three decades, which has eroded the (relatively speaking) more egalitarian wealth distribution created at mid-century in part by progressive taxation, government programs that redistributed wealth and income to ordinary Americans, and the rise of organized labor.[3]

If ordinary white men were the primary losers in the scaled-back version of democracy that emerged from the Revolution, they were not the only ones who saw democracy narrow. Indeed, as ordinary white men found themselves living with a more limited version of democracy, they in turn tried to narrow the concept to exclude others. In recent decades, historians have charted those exclusions and the rise among ordinary white men in the

FIG. C.I. THE BURNING OF PENNSYLVANIA HALL, 1838. The destruction of this abolitionist meeting house reveals how far ordinary white men had moved from the vision of '76. No doubt some of the perpetrators were the sons and grandsons of men who had supported a gradual emancipation law and allowed free black men to vote. Reprinted from Samuel Webb, *History of Pennsylvania Hall, which was Destroyed by a Mob, on the 17th of May, 1838* (Philadelphia, 1838).

decades after the Revolution of virulent racism, which was directed against African Americans, Native Americans, and new immigrants. They have also chronicled how democracy was limited by gender, as men placed increased emphasis on keeping women in the "domestic sphere." Neither of these unflattering trends can be understood apart from the frustrations that white men (and their sons and grandsons) experienced as the gap widened between their notions of what they thought the Revolution should be and what it had become.

Each decade after 1776 seemed to expand the gap between the rich and nearly everyone else, and the "independence" of previous generations became increasingly untenable for many, if not most, people. As economic independence and equality moved further out of reach, many ordinary white men worried about their position as citizens, as men, as fathers and husbands. Haunted by the specter of dependency and besieged by insecurities about themselves and their ability to provide for their wives and children, many men tried to bolster their flagging sense of self-worth by degrading and excluding others. These unsavory attributes, which had always been a part of the world view of ordinary white men from the revolutionary generation, now assumed paramount importance. The crowd protests that had once been directed against haughty officials and tax collectors were redirected at black neighborhoods and immigrant communities. Having lost so much, many white men clung to their identities as citizens, believing that if they had nothing else, they at least could vote when others could not. And without much else on which to stake their sense of self-worth, these people became fixated on ensuring that all white men had the vote and that everyone else was disenfranchised.

In Pennsylvania, this more vicious brand of democracy was on clear display during 1838. In May, white Philadelphians burned to the ground Pennsylvania Hall, an abolitionist meeting house, to protest calls for immediate emancipation and the fact that it was hosting female speakers at the Anti-Slavery Convention of American Women. In the following days, whites attacked a black church and torched the Shelter for Colored Orphans and then stood guard around the burning building so that fire companies could not reach the flames. That same year, state leaders rewrote the Pennsylvania constitution to confine the vote to "white freemen"—continuing to deny women the franchise and purging black men from the voter rolls. As all of these incidents reveal, by 1838, the revolutionary vision of hopeful uplift had, in many ways, been replaced by a new democratic ideal in which white men identified their standing as free citizens based largely on patriarchy and white supremacy.[4]

Notes

Abbreviations

AHP	*The Papers of Alexander Hamilton*, ed. Harold C. Syrett (26 vols., New York, 1961–1979)
Brinton Papers	Jasper Yeates Brinton Papers, Historical Society of Pennsylvania, Philadelphia
Collins Papers	Stephen Collins Papers, Library of Congress, Washington, DC
Debates and Proceedings	*Debates and Proceedings of the General Assembly, on the Memorial Praying a Repeal or Suspension of the Law Annulling the Charter of the Bank*, ed. Mathew Carey (Philadelphia, 1786)
DHFFE	*The Documentary History of the First Federal Elections, 1788–1790*, ed. Merrill Jensen and Robert A. Becker (4 vols., Madison, WI, 1976)

DHRC	*The Documentary History of the Ratification of the Constitution: Ratification of the Constitution by the States: Pennsylvania,* ed. Merrill Jensen et al. (21 vols., Madison, WI, 1976–), vol. 2
DHRCM	*The Documentary History of the Ratification of the Constitution: Ratification of the Constitution by the States: Pennsylvania,* ed. Merrill Jensen et al. (21 vols., Madison, WI, 1976–), vol. 2, microfiche supplement
Drinker Papers	Henry Drinker Papers, Historical Society of Pennsylvania, Philadelphia
GC	General Correspondence
James Hamilton Papers	James Hamilton Papers, Cumberland County Historical Society, Carlisle, PA
HSP	Historical Society of Pennsylvania, Philadelphia
Irvine Family Papers	Irvine Family Papers, Historical Society of Pennsylvania, Philadelphia
Mitchell Papers	*The Sequestered John Mitchell Papers, 1762–1781* (Harrisburg: Pennsylvania Historical and Museum Commission Microfilms)
Morris Papers	*The Papers of Robert Morris,* ed. E. James Ferguson et al. (9 vols., Pittsburgh, PA, 1973–)
Nicholson Papers	*Sequestered John Nicholson Papers, 1765–1852* (Harrisburg: Pennsylvania Historical and Museum Commission Microfilms)
Pennsylvania Archives	*Pennsylvania Archives,* ed. Charles F. Hoban (9 series, Harrisburg, PA, 1857–1935)
PHMC	Pennsylvania Historical and Museum Commission, Harrisburg
PHMCM	Pennsylvania Historical and Museum Commission Microfilms
Pollard Papers	William Pollard Papers, Historical Society of Pennsylvania, Philadelphia
QS	Quarter Sessions
Rawle Papers	"Insurrection in Western Pennsylvania," Rawle Family Papers, Historical Society of Pennsylvania, Philadelphia

RCG	Records of the Comptroller General, Pennsylvania Historical and Museum Commission, Harrisburg
RGA	Records of the General Assembly, Pennsylvania Historical and Museum Commission, Harrisburg
RPRG	Records of Pennsylvania's Revolutionary Government, Pennsylvania Historical and Museum Commission Microfilms
RTD	Records of the Treasury Department, Pennsylvania Historical and Museum Commission, Harrisburg
SALP	*The Statutes at Large of Pennsylvania from 1682 to 1801,* ed. James T. Mitchell and Henry Flanders (17 vols., Harrisburg, PA, 1896)
Waln Papers	Richard Waln Papers, Historical Society of Pennsylvania, Philadelphia
WRLC	Pennsylvania Whiskey Rebellion Collection, Library of Congress, Washington, DC

Introduction

1. Linda K. Kerber, *Women of the Republic: Intellect and Ideology in Revolutionary America* (New York, 1980); Mary Beth Norton, *Liberty's Daughters: The Revolutionary Experience of American Women, 1750–1800* (Boston, 1980); Benjamin Quarles, *The Negro in the American Revolution* (New York, 1961); Gary B. Nash, *Forging Freedom: The Formation of Philadelphia's Black Community, 1720–1840* (Cambridge, MA, 1988); Sylvia Frey, *Water from the Rock: Black Resistance in a Revolutionary Age* (Princeton, NJ, 1991); Colin Gordon Calloway, *The American Revolution in Indian Country: Crisis and Diversity in Native American Communities* (New York, 1995); Claudio Saunt, *A New Order of Things: Property, Power, and the Transformation of the Creek Indians, 1733–1816* (New York, 1999); Daniel K. Richter, *Facing East from Indian Country: A Native History of Early America* (Cambridge, MA, 2001), 189–236.
2. Gordon S. Wood, *The Radicalism of the American Revolution* (New York, 1991), 8.
3. For example, the political histories of Pennsylvania tend to either end or begin at 1776: Theodore Thayer, *Pennsylvania Politics and the Growth of Democracy, 1740–1776* (Harrisburg, PA, 1953); Robert L. Brunhouse, *The Counter-Revolution in Pennsylvania, 1776–1790* (New York, 1971); Richard Alan Ryerson, *The Revolution Is Now Begun: The Radical Committees of Philadelphia,*

1765–1776 (Philadelphia, 1978); Owen S. Ireland, *Religion, Ethnicity, and Politics: Ratifying the Constitution in Pennsylvania* (University Park, PA, 1995). The essays in John B. Frantz and William Pencak, eds., *Beyond Philadelphia: The American Revolution in the Pennsylvania Hinterland* (University Park, PA, 1998), largely treat the Revolution as the War for Independence, as does Francis S. Fox, *Sweet Land of Liberty: The Ordeal of the American Revolution in Northampton County, Pennsylvania* (University Park, PA, 2000). Historians who examine popular movements generally make a pre- and postwar break, with studies of Philadelphia artisans and laborers concentrating on the prewar period and rural studies focusing on the postwar period. See Gary B. Nash, *The Urban Crucible: Social Change, Political Consciousness, and the Origins of the American Revolution* (Cambridge, MA, 1979); Charles S. Olton, *Artisans for Independence: Philadelphia Mechanics and the American Revolution* (Syracuse, NY, 1975); Steven Rosswurm, *Arms, Country, and Class: The Philadelphia Militia and the "Lower Sort" during the American Revolution, 1775–1783* (New Brunswick, NJ, 1987); Ronald Schultz, *The Republic of Labor: Philadelphia Artisans and the Politics of Class, 1720–1830* (New York, 1993); Thomas P. Slaughter, *The Whiskey Rebellion: Frontier Epilogue to the American Revolution* (New York, 1986); Paul Douglas Newman, *Fries Rebellion: The Enduring Struggle for the American Revolution* (Philadelphia, 2004).

4. Robert J. Dinkin, *Voting in Provincial America: A Study of Elections in the Thirteen Colonies, 1689–1776* (Westport, CT, 1977); and Dinkin, *Voting in Revolutionary America: A Study of Elections in the Original Thirteen States, 1776–1789* (Westport, CT, 1982).

5. Pennsylvania Constitution (1776).

6. Pennsylvania Constitution (1776); Roberdeau quoted in Rosswurm, *Arms, Country, and Class*, 180; *Debates and Proceedings of the General Assembly, on the Memorial Praying a Repeal or Suspension of the Law Annulling the Charter of the Bank* [hereafter *Debates and Proceedings*], ed. Mathew Carey (Philadelphia, 1786), 65, 125; Thomas Crossan to John Nicholson, Aug. 22, 1787, file 6, box 5, General Correspondence [hereafter GC], Records of the Comptroller General [hereafter RCG], Pennsylvania Historical and Museum Commission [hereafter PHMC], Harrisburg, PA; Petrikin to Nicholson, *The Documentary History of the Ratification of the Constitution: Ratification of the Constitution by the States: Pennsylvania* [hereafter DHRC], ed. Merrill Jensen et al., 21 vols. (Madison, WI, 1976–), vol. 2, microfiche supplement [hereafter DHRCM]; Husband quoted in Dorothy Elaine Fennell, "From Rebelliousness to Insurrection: A Social History of the Whiskey Rebellion, 1765–1802" (Ph.D. diss., University of Pittsburgh, 1981), 208, 219–220.

7. "Observations on the Present State of Affairs," Jan. 13, 1783, in *The Papers of Robert Morris* [hereafter *Morris Papers*], ed. E. James Ferguson et al., 9 vols. (Pittsburgh, PA, 1973–), vol. 7, 306; Morris to John Jay, July 13, 1781, *Morris Papers*, vol. 1, 287; Morris to Thomas Jefferson, June 11, 1781, ibid., vol. 1, 143; Morris to the President of Congress, July 29, 1782, ibid., vol. 6, 59. For

the founders as losing, see Wood, *Radicalism of the Revolution*. For an alternate synthesis focusing on popular ideals and discontent, see Gary B. Nash, *The Unknown American Revolution: The Unruly Birth of Democracy and the Struggle to Create America* (New York, 2005).

Chapter 1

1. "A Citizen," *Pennsylvania Chronicle*, Nov. 9, 1767; "Another Farmer," *Pennsylvania Chronicle*, Dec. 21, 1767.
2. James S. Lemon, *The Best Poor Man's Country: A Geographical Study of Early Southeastern Pennsylvania* (Baltimore, MD, 1972); Allan Kulikoff, *From British Peasants to Colonial American Farmers* (Chapel Hill, NC, 2000).
3. Dinkin, *Voting in Provincial America*, 44, 49.
4. Ibid., 38–39, 44, 52, 64, 80–83, 155–161.
5. Billy Gordon Smith, *The "Lower Sort": Philadelphia's Laboring People, 1750–1800* (Ithaca, NY, 1990), 86.
6. Lemon, *Best Poor Man's Country*, 94; Lucy Simler, "Tenancy in Colonial Pennsylvania: The Case of Chester County," *William and Mary Quarterly* 43 (Oct. 1986): 542–569; Simler, "The Landless Worker: An Index of Economic and Social Change in Chester County, Pennsylvania, 1750–1820," *Pennsylvania Magazine of History and Biography* 114 (Apr. 1990): 163–199; Jack D. Marietta, "The Distribution of Wealth in Eighteenth-Century America: Nine Chester County Tax Lists, 1693–1799," *Pennsylvania History* 62 (Oct. 1995): 532–545.
7. R. Eugene Harper, *The Transformation of Western Pennsylvania, 1770–1800* (Pittsburgh, PA, 1992), 28–35.
8. Fred Anderson, *Crucible of War: The Seven Years' War and the Fate of Empire in British North America, 1754–1766* (New York, 2000); Matthew C. Ward, *Breaking the Backcountry: The Seven Years' War in Virginia and Pennsylvania, 1754–1765* (Pittsburgh, PA, 2003).
9. Anderson, *Crucible of War*, 557–564, 811n5.
10. On the tax burden, see Gary B. Nash, *The Urban Crucible: Social Change, Political Consciousness, and the Origins of the American Revolution* (Cambridge, MA, 1979), 252–253.
11. Gregory Dowd, *War under Heaven: Pontiac, the Indian Nations, and the British Empire* (Baltimore, MD, 2002), 191–200; Ward, *Breaking the Backcountry*, 60, 67, 91, 94–95, 102–104, 236–240.
12. Dickinson, "The Late Regulations Respecting the British Colonies on the Continent of America Considered, 1765," in *The Writings of John Dickinson: Vol. 1. Political Writings, 1764–1774*, ed. Paul Leicester Ford (Philadelphia, 1895), 219. For paper money and the colonial economy, see John J. McCusker and Russell R. Menard, *The Economy of British America, 1607–1789* (Chapel Hill, NC, 1985), 338–339; Kulikoff, *From British Peasants*, 203–226; E. James Ferguson, *Power of the Purse: A History of American Public Finance, 1776–1790*

(Chapel Hill, NC, 1961), 3–24; Nash, *Urban Crucible*, 26–53, 76–101, 129–157, 198–232, 264–384; Leslie Van Horne Brock, *The Currency of the American Colonies, 1700–1764: A Study in Colonial Finance and Imperial Relations* (New York, 1975); Mary M. Schweitzer, *Custom and Contract: Household, Government, and the Economy in Colonial Pennsylvania* (New York, 1987), 115–167.

13. Joseph Albert Ernst, *Money and Politics in America, 1755–1775: A Study in the Currency Act of 1764 and the Political Economy of Revolution* (Chapel Hill, NC, 1973).

14. Ibid. Britain had punished the New England colonies in 1751 with a similar act.

15. "The PETITION of the Representatives of the Freemen of the Province of Pennsylvania, in General Assembly met," Jan. 14, 1766, in *Pennsylvania Archives*, ed. Charles F. Hoban, 9 series (Harrisburg, PA, 1857–1935), ser. 8, vol. 7, 5826. For estimates of Pennsylvania currency in circulation, see Ernst, *Money and Politics*, 368; "Another Farmer," *Pennsylvania Chronicle*, Dec. 21, 1767.

16. Paton Wesley Yoder, "Paper Currency in Colonial Pennsylvania" (Ph.D. diss., Indiana University, 1941), 307–322.

17. "Three Petitions from the County of Bucks signed by a considerable Number of the Inhabitants," Jan. 4, 1769, *Pennsylvania Archives*, ser. 8, vol. 7, 6293–6296, and listing of subsequent petitions on 6299–6320; Richard Waln to Nicholas Waln, Mar. 10, 1764, Letter Book, 1762–1766, Richard Waln Papers [hereafter Waln Papers], Historical Society of Pennsylvania, Philadelphia, PA [hereafter cited as HSP].

18. Arthur Meier Schlesinger, *The Colonial Merchants and the American Revolution, 1763–1776* (New York, 1918); John Tyler, *Smugglers and Patriots: Boston Merchants and the Advent of the American Revolution* (Boston, 1986); Dickinson, "Late Regulations," 218.

19. Dickinson, "Late Regulations," 228.

20. "A Remonstrance and Petition from the Commissioners, Assessors, and Freemen of the City and County of Philadelphia," Jan. 25, 1773, *Pennsylvania Archives*, ser. 8, vol. 8, 6921–6922.

21. Thomas Clifford to Thomas Pennington & Sons, Nov. 23, 1765, quoted in Harry D. Berg, "Economic Consequences of the French and Indian War for the Philadelphia Merchants," *Pennsylvania History* 13, no. 3 (July 1946): 192–193.

22. Scholars whose studies center on urban centers such as Philadelphia have identified two long periods of hardship: the first spanning the years 1764 to 1769 (quite possibly beginning as early as 1760) and the second from 1772 until the outbreak of the Revolution. Marc Egnal, *A Mighty Empire: The Origins of the American Revolution* (Ithaca, NY, 1988), 129; Nash, *Urban Crucible*, 246–263, 317–322; Ernst, *Money and Politics*, 94–96, 102, 207–209; Yoder, "Paper Currency," 209–219, 331–333; Berg, "Economic Consequences"; Schlesinger,

Colonial Merchants, 50–90, 240–242. The economic situation after 1772 remains less clearly documented. For pioneering work, see Nash, *Urban Crucible*, 317–325; Ernst, *Money and Politics*, 307–308; Richard B. Sheridan, "The British Credit Crisis of 1772 and the American Colonies," *Journal of Economic History* 20 (June 1960): 161–186. Compare with the argument that "Philadelphia's economy was not especially disordered or depressed between 1760 and 1775," in Thomas M. Doerflinger, *A Vigorous Spirit of Enterprise: Merchants and Economic Development in Revolutionary Philadelphia* (Chapel Hill, NC, 1986), 167–180, and the general portraits of prewar prosperity in Frantz and Pencak, *Beyond Philadelphia*, 5, 26, 72, 89.

23. Richard Waln to Haliday & Dunbar, Oct. 12, 1768, Letter Book, 1766–1800, Waln Papers; Stephen Collins to Nathanael and Robert Dennison, June 8, 1770, Letter Books, Stephen Collins Papers [hereafter Collins Papers], Library of Congress; Collins to Benjamin and John Bowen, Mar. 23, 1773, ibid.; Collins to William and Neate, Apr. 28, 1773, ibid.

24. Richard Waln to Nicholas Waln, Mar. 10, 1764, Letter Book, 1762–1766, Waln Papers; Waln to Barclay & Sons, June 13, 1766, ibid.; Owen Jones to David Barclay & Sons, July 8, 1766, Owen Jones Letter Book, 1759–1781, Jones Papers, HSP; Benjamin Marshall to Dr. James Tapscott, Oct. 22, 1764, "Extracts from the Letter-Book of Benjamin Marshall, 1763–1766," *Pennsylvania Magazine of History and Biography* 20 (1896): 208; James & Drinker to Neate & Pigou, Feb. 27, 1764, Letter Book, 1762–1764, Henry Drinker Papers [hereafter Drinker Papers], HSP; Thomas Clifford to Thomas Pennington & Sons, Nov. 23, 1765, quoted in Berg, "Economic Consequences," 192.

25. James & Drinker to John Oseland, Oct. 20, 1764, Letter Book, 1764–1766, Drinker Papers; James & Drinker to Kendrick Pecky, Mar. 14, 1764, ibid.; James & Drinker to Robert Levers, June 11, 1765, ibid.; James & Drinker to James Read, Aug. 26, 1773, Foreign Letters, 1772–1785, Drinker Papers; James & Drinker to Lancelot Cowper, Aug. 4, 1772, ibid.; James & Drinker to Thomas Pearsall, Dec. 5, 1772, Letter Book, 1772–1786, ibid.; James & Drinker to Parvin & James, Mar. 28, 1766, Letter Book, 1764–1766, ibid.; James & Drinker to Dennis Wheeler, Dec. 13, 1769, Letter Book, 1769–1772, ibid.

26. William Pollard to Benjamin and Jonathan Bower, Manchester, Apr. 28, 1773, Letter Book, 1772–1774, William Pollard Papers [hereafter Pollard Papers], HSP; Pollard to Peter Holme, Liverpool, June 22, 1772, ibid.; Pollard to Thomas Earle, Liverpool, May 6, 1773, ibid.; Pollard Jonathan Swine, Yorkshire, Sept. 13, 1773, ibid.

27. "Mercator," *Pennsylvania Journal*, Sept. 14, 1769, quoted in Ernst, *Money and Politics*, 213–214.

28. Dickinson, "Late Regulations," 227; Moses Montgomery to Thomas Wharton, Apr. 27, 1764, box 5, Wharton-Willing Papers, HSP; David Lewis, Thornbury Township, Chester County to William Barrell, Feb. 12, 1773, Correspondence, Collins Papers; William Keene to John Steinmetz, Mar. 25,

1770, folder 10, box 1, Domestic Correspondence, Steinmetz Section, Jasper Yeates Brinton Papers [hereafter Brinton Papers], HSP; Benjamin Lightfoot, Reading, PA, to John Reynell, Nov. 24, 1766, Correspondence, Coates & Reynell Papers, HSP.

29. John Sheppard to Stephen Collins, Philadelphia, June 19, 1765, Correspondence, Collins Papers; Joseph Musgrave, Chester County, to Collins, May 5, 1772, ibid.; Edward Parrish to Collins, Aug. 12, 1764, ibid.; James Partridge to Hollingsworth & Rudolph, Oct. 14, 1766, Correspondence, Hollingsworth Family Papers, HSP; William Nelson, Providence, to John Steinmetz, May 23, 1774, Brinton Papers; Forbes Patton to John Mitchell, Apr. 17, 1775, in *The Sequestered John Mitchell Papers, 1762–1781* [hereafter *Mitchell Papers*] (Harrisburg: Pennsylvania Historical and Museum Commission Microfilms [hereafter PHMCM]); Dickson McMillan to Mitchell, May 4, 1775, ibid.; William Kelso to Mitchell, Cumberland County, Nov. 6, 1775, ibid.

30. Edward Parrish to Stephen Collins, Mar. 21, 1767, Correspondence, Collins Papers; Joseph Musgrave, Kennett Square, Chester County, to Stephen Collins, Nov. 9, 1772, ibid.; William Moore, Reading, to John Mitchell, Oct. 21, 1775, *Mitchell Papers*; John Barclay to Mitchell, Sept. 20, 1775, ibid.

31. William Barrell to Robert McGraw, York County, July 28, 1773, Correspondence, Collins Papers; James Armstrong, Juniata, to William Barrell, Jan. 3, 1775, ibid.; Richard Waln to Nicholas Waln, Mar. 10, 1764, Letter Book, 1762–1766, Waln Papers; *Pennsylvania Chronicle*, Nov. 11, 1767.

32. William Moore, Reading, to John Mitchell, Oct. 21, 1775, *Mitchell Papers*; Peter Schuck to Stephen Collins, May 4, 1765, Correspondence, Collins Papers.

33. For quote, see Peter Schuck to Stephen Collins, May 4, 1765, Correspondence, Collins Papers. Philadelphia County Execution Docket, 1769–1771, City Archives, Philadelphia, PA; Northampton County Execution Dockets, 1766–1775, County Archives, Northampton County Courthouse, Easton, PA; Berks County Execution Dockets, 1769–1775, Berks County Courthouse, Reading, PA; Northumberland County Execution Dockets, Northumberland County Courthouse, Sunbury, PA; Bedford County Execution Dockets, 1772–1775, Bedford County Courthouse, Bedford, PA. For Northumberland, see also Peter C. Mancall, *Valley of Opportunity: Economic Culture along the Upper Susquehanna, 1700–1800* (Ithaca, NY, 1991), 117–118. Philadelphia had 2,120 executions for a taxable population of 10,455 (6,700 in the county), Northampton had 1,170 executions for a taxable population of 2,793; Berks 2,011 executions for a taxable population of 3,642; Northumberland 553 executions for a taxable population of 2,111; and Bedford 687 executions for a taxable population of 1,201. For estimates of the taxable population, see *Hazard's Register of Pennsylvania* 4 (July 1829): 12–13.

34. Dickinson, "Late Regulations," 228; William Pollard to Jonathan Swine, Sept. 13, 1773, Pollard Papers.

35. Samuel Allison to Stephen Collins, May 6, 1767, May 21, 1768, Correspondence, Collins Papers; John Ashbridge, Lancaster, to John Steinmetz, Aug. 9, 1770, Brinton Papers. For a range of selling prices at auction, see "Mercator," *Pennsylvania Journal*, Sept. 14, 1769, quoted in Ernst, *Money and Politics*, 213–214; Peter Schuck to Stephen Collins, Sept. 23, 1767, Correspondence, Collins Papers; James Pemberton to Samuel Fothergill, Dec. 17, 1765, Nov. 11, 1766, Pemberton Papers, vol. 34, 130, 32, HSP; Joseph Musgrave, Kennett Square, Chester County, to Stephen Collins, Aug. 2, 1773, Correspondence, Collins Papers.

36. "A Petition from a number of the Inhabitants of Chester County," Jan. 23, 1769, *Pennsylvania Archives*, ser. 8, vol. 7, 6328.

37. Dickinson, "Late Regulations," 228.

38. James & Drinker to Neate, Pigou & Booth, June 19, 1765, Letter Book, 1764–1766, and May 23, 1769, Letter Book, 1769–1772, Drinker Papers; James & Drinker to Dennis Wheeler, Dec. 13, 1769, ibid.; Stephen Collins to Neate and Pigou, July 28, 1769, Letter Books, Collins Papers; William Pollard to Thomas Hodgson, May 6, 1773, Pollard Papers.

39. Stephen Collins to Benjamin and John Bowen, Mar. 23, 1773, Letter Books, vol. 57, Collins Papers; William Pollard to Jonathan Swine, Sept. 13, 1773, Pollard Papers.

40. Daniel Roberdeau to Meyler & Hall, Sept. 19, 1764, Oct. 21, Nov. 9, 1765, Mar. 15, 1766, Jan. 2, 1767, Daniel Roberdeau Letterbook, 1764–1771, Buchanan Roberdeau Papers, HSP; Roberdeau to Woodson & Trevanion, Nov. 26, 1767, Dec. 9, 1768, ibid.

41. Stephen Collins to William, Tibbs, & Williams, Aug. 3, 1773, Letter Books, Collins Papers; Richard Waln to Crafton & Colson, June 19, 1765, Letter Book, 1762–1766, Waln Papers; William Pollard to John Woolman, Sept. 13, 1773, Pollard Papers; Daniel Roberdeau to Meyler & Hall, Oct. 21, 1765, Roberdeau Papers. For the importance of their reputation to merchants, see Doerflinger, *Vigorous Spirit of Enterprise*, 18, 48–57, 141–146.

42. William Pollard to Jonathan Swine, Sept. 13, 1773, Pollard Papers; James & Drinker to Peter Hasenclever, Nov. 15, 1764, Letter Book, 1764–1766, Drinker Papers; Benjamin Rush to Ebenezer Hazard, Nov. 8, 1765, *Letters of Benjamin Rush*, ed. L. H. Butterfield, 2 vols. (Princeton, NJ, 1951), vol. 1, 18.

43. Anon., *Whereas the Number of Poor in and around This City . . .*, quoted in Gary B. Nash, "Up from the Bottom in Franklin's Philadelphia," *Past and Present* 77 (Nov. 1977): 71; Committee on the proposed House of Employment, Jan. 16, 1766, *Pennsylvania Archives*, ser. 8, vol. 7, 5829–5831; Gary B. Nash, "Poverty and Poor Relief in Pre-Revolutionary Philadelphia," *William and Mary Quarterly* 3rd ser., 33, no. 1 (Jan. 1976): 28; Nash, "Urban Wealth and Poverty in Pre-Revolutionary America," *Journal of Interdisciplinary History* 6, no. 4 (Spring 1976): 545–584; Smith, *Lower Sort*, 94–125, 150–175.

44. *Pennsylvania Chronicle*, Feb. 23, Apr. 6, Nov. 9, 1767; Petition from the Overseers of the Poor for the City of Philadelphia, Jan. 14, 1766, *Pennsylvania Archives*, ser. 8, vol. 7, 5823–5824; "Report of the Contributors to the Relief

and Employment of the Poor," quoted in Nash, "Urban Wealth," 545. For poor relief in Philadelphia, see Nash, "Poverty and Poor Relief"; and John K. Alexander, *Render Them Submissive: Responses to Poverty in Philadelphia, 1760–1800* (Amherst, MA, 1980), 64–66.

45. Dickinson, "Late Regulations," 233, 221; "Old Trusty," *Pennsylvania Evening Post,* Apr. 30, 1776.

46. "A Watchman," *Pennsylvania Packet,* June 24, 1776; "Independent," *Pennsylvania Packet,* Mar. 18, 1776; "The Examiner," *Pennsylvania Evening Post,* Oct. 15, 1776; "Pennsylvanicus," *Pennsylvania Chronicle,* Sept. 20, 1773.

47. *Pennsylvania Chronicle,* Apr. 6, 1767; "A Lover of Pennsylvania," *Pennsylvania Chronicle,* Jan. 4, 1768; *Pennsylvania Packet,* Sept. 25, 1775, quoted in Rosswurm, *Arms, Country, and Class,* 48.

48. Nash, *Urban Crucible,* 202–232.

49. John Reynell to Noah Parker, Nov. 2, 1770, Letter Book, May 1769–Nov. 1770, Coates & Reynell Papers.

Chapter 2

1. The point here is not to dismiss the important differences in ideology that separated elite and common folk and that divided various groups of ordinary people. Instead, it is to recognize that there was considerable common ground that is often masked by concentrating on the differences. For a perceptive attempt to understand the variety of ideologies at work, see Gary B. Nash, *The Urban Crucible: Social Change, Political Consciousness, and the Origins of the American Revolution* (Cambridge, MA, 1979), 339–351.

2. *Pennsylvania Packet,* Sept. 25, 1775, quoted in Steven Rosswurm, *Arms, Country, and Class: The Philadelphia Militia and the "Lower Sort" during the American Revolution, 1775–1783* (New Brunswick, NJ, 1987), 48; *Pennsylvania Evening Post,* Apr. 27 and 30, 1776; "Queries," *Pennsylvania Packet,* Mar. 18, 1776. For expressions of similar ideals elsewhere in the colonies, see Michael Bellesiles, *Revolutionary Outlaws: Ethan Allen and the Struggle for Independence on the Early American Frontier* (Charlottesville, VA, 1993); Richard L. Bushman, "Massachusetts Farmers and the Revolution," in *Society, Freedom, and Conscience: The American Revolution in Virginia, Massachusetts, and New York,* ed. Jack P. Greene et al. (New York, 1976), 77–124; Edward Countryman, *A People in Revolution: The American Revolution and Political Society in New York, 1760–1790* (Baltimore, MD, 1981); Countryman, "'Out of Bounds of the Law': Northern Land Rioters in the Eighteenth Century," in *The American Revolution: Explorations in the History of American Radicalism,* ed. Alfred F. Young (DeKalb, IL, 1976), 37–69; Marjoleine Kars, *Breaking Loose Together: The Regulator Rebellion in Pre-Revolutionary North Carolina* (Chapel Hill, NC, 2002); Allan Kulikoff, *The Agrarian Origins of American Capitalism* (Charlottesville, VA, 1992); Allan Kulikoff, *From British Peasants to Colonial American Farmers* (Chapel Hill,

NC, 2000); Staughton Lynd, "Who Should Rule at Home? Dutchess County, New York, in the American Revolution," *William and Mary Quarterly* 18, no. 3 (July 1961): 330–359; Brendan McConville, *These Daring Disturbers of the Public Peace: The Struggle for Property in Early New Jersey* (Ithaca, NY, 1999).

3. Robert E. Shalhope, "Toward a Republican Synthesis: The Emergence of an Understanding of Republicanism in American Historiography," *William and Mary Quarterly* 29 (Jan. 1972): 49–80; and Shalhope, "Republicanism and Early American Historiography," *William and Mary Quarterly* 39 (Apr. 1982): 334–356.

4. "The PETITION of the Freeholders and other Inhabitants of the Massachusetts-Bay, Rhode-Island, and Providence Plantations, New-Jersey, Pennsylvania, and Government of the Counties of New-Castle, Kent, and Sussex, upon Delaware, and the Province of Maryland," Jan. 7, 1766, *Pennsylvania Archives*, ser. 8, vol. 7, 5808; Dickinson, "Late Regulations," 228. For debates over taxation, see Robert A. Becker, *Revolution, Reform, and the Politics of American Taxation, 1763–1783* (Baton Rouge, LA, 1980), 42–61.

5. Dickinson, "Late Regulations," 228–230.

6. "The Address of a Number of Freemen of the County and City of Philadelphia," *Pennsylvania Chronicle*, Oct. 17, 1772. For artisan opposition, see Nash, *Urban Crucible*, 376.

7. *Pennsylvania House Journal*, Mar. 1764, quoted in Becker, *Revolution, Reform*, 55; Dickinson, "Late Regulations," 230. For tax debates and policies in Pennsylvania, see Becker, *Revolution, Reform*, 49–56, 176–188.

8. The Pennsylvania General Assembly only printed the full text for the first petition from Bucks County: "Three Petitions from the County of Bucks signed by a considerable Number of the Inhabitants," Jan. 4, 1769, *Pennsylvania Archives*, ser. 8, vol. 7, 6293–6296. Assembly minutes noted that subsequent petitions followed the wording of the first Bucks petition in "setting forth the Distress of the people from the Present Want of Paper-Currency as a circulating medium of commerce." Those petitions arrived over the next two weeks from both the city of Philadelphia and Philadelphia County (twenty-two petitions) and the counties of Bucks (seven more), Chester (two), Berks (six), Lancaster (ten), York (seven), and Cumberland (five). See entries for Jan. 5–19, 1769, ibid., 6299–6320. For a similar petition sent a year earlier, see "A Petition from a Number of the Inhabitants of the Counties of Philadelphia and Chester," Feb. 16, 1768, ibid., 6160. See also "Petition from the County of Lancaster for an Emission of Paper Money for a Public Loan Office," Jan. 5, 1769, Society Miscellaneous Collection, box 4B, folder 4, County Petitions, 1736–1799, PHMC.

9. "Petition of the Representative[s] of the Freemen of the Province of Pennsylvania to House of Commons," Jan. 14, 1766, *Pennsylvania Archives*, ser. 8, vol. 7, 5824–5827; Richard Waln to Nicholas Waln, Mar. 10, 1764, Letter Book, 1762–1766, Waln Papers; James Pemberton to Samuel Fothergill, London, Nov. 11, 1766, Pemberton Papers. For similar complaints, see "The Petition of the

Representatives of the Freemen of the Province of Pennsylvania, in General Assembly met," Jan. 14, 1766, *Pennsylvania Archives*, ser. 8, vol. 7, 5825; Dickinson, "Late Regulations," 219–221; Pennsylvania House of Representatives, Instructions to Richard Jackson and Benjamin Franklin, Oct. 20, 1764; Oct. 18, 1766; Oct. 17, 1767; Sept. 22, 1768, *Pennsylvania Archives*, ser. 8, vol. 7, 5678–5682, 5945–5947, 6069–6071, 6277–6280.

10. Kulikoff, *From British Peasants*, 203–226.

11. Mary M. Schweitzer, *Custom and Contract: Household, Government, and the Economy in Colonial Pennsylvania* (New York, 1987), 114–167.

12. Ibid., 147–161.

13. For petitions, see note 8 above.

14. Becker, *Revolution, Reform*, 48; E. James Ferguson, *Power of the Purse: A History of American Public Finance, 1776–1790* (Chapel Hill, NC, 1961), 6.

15. James Logan to Henry Gouldney, Feb. 9, 1722; Logan, *The Charge Delivered from the Bench to the Grand Inquest* (Philadelphia, 1736); Isaac Norris to James Pike, May 7, 1723, Isaac Norris Letterbook, 1716–1730, all quoted in Nash, *Urban Crucible*, 149–150.

16. Pennsylvania House of Representatives, Instructions to Richard Jackson and Benjamin Franklin, Oct. 17, 1767, *Pennsylvania Archives*, ser. 8, vol. 7, 6069–6071.

17. "A Lover of Pennsylvania," *Pennsylvania Chronicle*, Jan. 4, 1768.

18. "Remonstrance from a great Number of the Inhabitants of the City and County of Philadelphia," Jan. 12, 1767, *Pennsylvania Archives*, ser. 8, vol. 7, 5952–5953; *Pennsylvania Chronicle*, Oct. 12, 1768; *Philadelphia Gazette*, Dec. 11, 1766; Jonathan Bayard Smith, Philadelphia, to Alexander Hill, Dec. 13, 1766, Letterbook, Jonathan Bayard Smith Papers, reel 67, ser. 8D, Peter Force Collection, Library of Congress, Washington, DC; General Assembly, Feb. 4, 1767, *Pennsylvania Archives*, ser. 8, vol. 7, 5980–5981. On the proposed bank, see Joseph Albert Ernst, *Money and Politics in America, 1755–1775: A Study in the Currency Act of 1764 and the Political Economy of Revolution* (Chapel Hill, NC, 1973), 122–124.

19. Dickinson, "Late Regulations," 220; "Another Farmer," *Pennsylvania Chronicle*, Dec. 21, 1767.

20. Dickinson, "Late Regulations," 220; "Another Farmer," *Pennsylvania Chronicle*, Dec. 21, 1767. See also petitions in note 8.

21. Joseph Galloway to Benjamin Franklin, June 21, 1770, quoted in Ernst, *Money and Politics*, 282–283; Pennsylvania House of Representatives to Richard Penn, Provincial Governor, Mar. 18, 1772, *Pennsylvania Archives*, ser. 8, vol. 8, 6838–6840. For land-bank proposals, see Ernst, *Money and Politics*, 128–129, 207–215, 313–315; Paton Wesley Yoder, "Paper Currency in Colonial Pennsylvania" (Ph.D. diss., Indiana University, 1941).

22. Dickinson, "Late Regulations," 234; William Allen to D. Barclay & Sons, Oct. 29, 1768, in *Extracts from Chief Justice William Allen's Letter Book*, ed. Lewis Burd Walker (Pottsville, PA, 1897), 74–76; Waln to Nicholas Waln,

June 25, 1764, Letter Book, 1762–1766, Waln Papers; Waln to Haliday & Dunbar, Oct. 12, 1768, Letter Book, 1766–1800, Waln Papers.

23. For a range of ways of thinking about the relationship between the gentry and the crowd, see Edmund S. Morgan and Helen M. Morgan, *The Stamp Act Crisis: Prologue to Revolution* (Chapel Hill, NC, 1953); Pauline Maier, *From Resistance to Revolution: Colonial Radicals and the Development of an Opposition to Britain, 1765–1776* (New York, 1972); Nash, *Urban Crucible*; and T. H. Breen, *The Marketplace of Revolution: How Consumer Politics Shaped American Independence* (New York, 2004).

24. "Pacificus," July 16, 1768, quoted in Richard Alan Ryerson, *The Revolution Is Now Begun: The Radical Committees of Philadelphia, 1765–1776* (Philadelphia, 1978), 23; J. Paul Selsam, *The Pennsylvania Constitution of 1776: A Study in Revolutionary Democracy* (Philadelphia, 1936), 66–67.

25. The following paragraphs on the Black Boys are based on Gregory Dowd, *War under Heaven: Pontiac, the Indian Nations, and the British Empire* (Baltimore, MD, 2002), 203–212; and Wilbur Nye, *James Smith: Early Cumberland Valley Patriot* (Carlisle, PA, 1969).

26. Dowd, *War under Heaven*, 203–212; Nye, *James Smith*.

27. "A Brother Chip," *Pennsylvania Chronicle*, Sept. 27, 1770; "Committee of Tradesmen," Nov. 1, 1771, quoted in Rosswurm, *Arms, Country, and Class*, 42; Clement Biddle to Thomas Richardson, July 24, 1770, quoted in Rosswurm, *Arms, Country, and Class*, 41. For organizing during the 1760s and 1770s, see Charles S. Olton, *Artisans for Independence: Philadelphia Mechanics and the American Revolution* (Syracuse, NY, 1975), 41–63; Nash, *Urban Crucible*, 374–377; Peter Thompson, *Rum Punch & Revolution: Taverngoing & Public Life in Eighteenth-Century Philadelphia* (Philadelphia, 1999), 145–181.

28. David Ammerman, *In the Common Cause: American Response to the Coercive Acts of 1774* (Charlottesville, VA, 1974).

29. Ryerson, *Revolution Is Now Begun*, 39–115; Rosswurm, *Arms, Country, and Class*, 43–46; Nash, *Urban Crucible*, 377–379.

30. Ryerson, *Revolution Is Now Begun*, 77–115.

31. Phineas Bond quoted in Rosswurm, *Arms, Country, and Class*, 51. For organizing after 1775, see ibid., 46–108; Ryerson, *Revolution Is Now Begun*, 117–175.

32. The following discussion of the February meeting in York County is based on "Minutes of meeting at York," Feb. 14, 1775, in I. Daniel Rupp, *History of York County: From One Thousand Seven Hundred and Nineteen to the Present Time* (Lancaster, PA, 1845), 604–605; and Thomas Hartley to John Mitchell, Feb. 23, 1775, Correspondence, *Mitchell Papers*. Rupp claims that Hartley had organized the militia for the town of York in December 1774. Hartley's own letter contradicts this claim, indicating that the town of York did not mobilize its militia until after the Feb. 1775 meeting.

33. For the provincial convention, see Ryerson, *Revolution Is Now Begun*, 100–102.

34. "Minutes of meeting at York," Feb. 14, 1775; Thomas Hartley to John Mitchell, Feb. 23, 1775, *Mitchell Papers*, PHMCM.

35. Frantz and Pencak, *Beyond Philadelphia*, 93, 51, 74, 122–123; for the taxable population, see *Hazard's Register of Pennsylvania* 4 (July 1829): 12–13.

36. Selsam, *Pennsylvania Constitution*; Eric Foner, *Tom Paine and Revolutionary America* (New York, 1976), 71–144.

37. Resolution of Congress, May 10, 1776, quoted in Ryerson, *Revolution Is Now Begun*, 211–212; also see ibid., 149–246.

38. "To the Several Battalions of Military Associators in the Province of Pennsylvania," June 22, 1776, quoted in Rosswurm, *Arms, Country, and Class*, 101–102; "Conversation between CATO and PLAIN TRUTH," *Pennsylvania Packet*, Mar. 25, 1776.

39. Pennsylvania Constitution (1776).

40. "Andrew Marvell," *Pennsylvania Packet*, Nov. 26, 1776; Thomas Smith, quoted in Selsam, *Pennsylvania Constitution*, 149. For the claim of Franklin's authorship, see Walter Isaacson, *Benjamin Franklin: An American Life* (New York, 2003), 315.

41. Committee of Privates, Sept. 28, 1775, quoted in Rosswurm, *Arms, Country, and Class*, 70; Dinkin, *Voting in Provincial America*, 44; and Dinkin, *Voting in Revolutionary America*, 36, 41–43.

42. Pennsylvania Constitution (1776).

43. *Pennsylvania Gazette*, Mar. 31, 1779; Foner, *Tom Paine*, 71–144.

44. Pennsylvania Constitution (1776).

45. Anne M. Ousterhout, *A State Divided: Opposition in Pennsylvania to the American Revolution* (Westport, CT, 1987); Francis S. Fox, *Sweet Land of Liberty: The Ordeal of the American Revolution in Northampton County, Pennsylvania* (University Park, PA, 2000).

46. Gary B. Nash and Jean R. Soderlund, *Freedom by Degrees: Emancipation in Pennsylvania and Its Aftermath* (New York, 1991).

47. For petitions to stop the overturning of the 1776 constitution, see "Memorials Against Calling a Convention, 1779," *Pennsylvania Archives*, ser. 2, vol. 3, 299–332. For petition totals, see Feb. 17–Mar. 13, 1779, *Minutes of the Third General Assembly* (Philadelphia, 1778–1779). (All of the minutes of the general assembly as well as much of the other published material from the late eighteenth century cited in this book are available on *Early American Imprints, Series I: Evans, 1639–1800*. The assembly minutes and journals can be found under the heading "Pennsylvania. General Assembly Journals.")

48. William Shippen to Edward Shippen, July 27, 1776, quoted in Gordon S. Wood, *The Creation of the American Republic, 1776-1787* (Chapel Hill, NC, 1969), 87; "Sully," *Pennsylvania Packet*, Feb. 2, 1779.

Chapter 3

1. Robert Morris to John Jay, July 26, 1783, in *The Papers of Robert Morris* [hereafter *Morris Papers*], ed. E. James Ferguson et al., 9 vols. (Pittsburgh, PA, 1973–), vol. 8,

342–343; "A Citizen of Philadelphia," *Pennsylvania Gazette*, Dec. 13, 1780; Thomas Smith quoted in J. Paul Selsam, *The Pennsylvania Constitution of 1776: A Study in Revolutionary Democracy* (Philadelphia, 1936), 149.

2. "Andrew Marvell," *Pennsylvania Packet*, Nov. 26, 1776; Alexander Graydon, *Pennsylvania Evening Post*, Oct. 19, 1776; Peter Grubb, Sept. 14, 1776, all quoted in Selsam, *Pennsylvania Constitution*, 149, 206–209. For elite opposition, see ibid., 205–254; Robert L. Brunhouse, *The Counter-Revolution in Pennsylvania, 1776–1790* (New York, 1971), 18–155.

3. On the rates of depreciation, see E. James Ferguson, *Power of the Purse: A History of American Public Finance, 1776–1790* (Chapel Hill, NC, 1961), 32; Anne Bezanson, *Prices and Inflation during the American Revolution: Pennsylvania, 1770–1790* (Philadelphia, 1951), 345, appendix, table 4.

4. Morris to Jacques Necker, June 15, 1781, *Morris Papers*, vol. 1, 150–151.

5. Joseph Reed, President of Pennsylvania, to Morris, July 27, 1781, *Morris Papers*, vol. 1, 408.

6. Rush to Jeremy Belknap, Feb. 28, 1788, DHRC, DHRCM.

7. Brunhouse, *Counter-Revolution*, 18–155.

8. Arthur Lee to James Warren, Dec. 12, 1782, *Warren-Adams Letters: Being Chiefly a Correspondence among John Adams, Samuel Adams, and James Warren*, 2 vols. (Boston, 1917–1925), vol. 2, 181; Stephen James Brobeck, "Changes in the Composition and Structure of Philadelphia Elite Groups, 1756–1790" (Ph.D. diss., University of Pennsylvania, 1972), 194–248; Robert James Gough, "Towards a Theory of Class and Social Conflict: A Social History of Wealthy Philadelphians, 1775 and 1800" (Ph.D. diss., University of Pennsylvania, 1977), 127–610.

9. Charles B. Royster, *A Revolutionary People at War: The Continental Army and American Character, 1775–1783* (Chapel Hill, NC, 1980).

10. Alexander Graydon to Joseph Reed, Oct. 5, 1780, *Pennsylvania Archives*, ser. 3, vol. 3, 437–438.

11. Thomas M. Doerflinger, *A Vigorous Spirit of Enterprise: Merchants and Economic Development in Revolutionary Philadelphia* (Chapel Hill, NC, 1986), 20–36; Richard L. Bushman, *The Refinement of America: Persons, Houses, and Cities* (New York, 1992), 46–58. I converted costs from pounds to Pennsylvania dollars.

12. Lee to Warren, Dec. 12, 1782, *Warren-Adams Letters*, vol. 2, 181; Samuel Vaughan to Richard Price, Jan. 4, 1785, ser. 9, reel 108, Peter Force Collection; Arthur St. Clair to Thomas FitzSimons, Jan. 21, 1783, quoted in Royster, *Revolutionary People at War*, 344.

13. Vaughan to Price, Jan. 4, 1785, Force Collection; John Jay, Paris, to Gouverneur Morris, Sept. 24, 1783, *Morris Papers*, vol. 8, 541; J. P. Brissot de Warville, *New Travels in the United States of America, 1788*, ed. Durand Echeverria (Cambridge, MA, 1964), 256.

14. Vaughan to Price, Jan. 4, 1785, Force Collection.

15. "A Planter," *Pennsylvania Evening Herald*, Aug. 27, 1785; Pennsylvania president Joseph Reed, Nov. 1, 1781, in *Life and Correspondence of Joseph Reed*, ed.

William B. Reed, 2 vols. (Philadelphia, 1847), vol. 2, 373; John Vaughan quoted in Doerflinger, *Vigorous Spirit of Enterprise*, 243.

16. Stephen Collins, Philadelphia, to Zach Collins, July 5 and 19, 1784, Letter Books, Collins Papers.

17. St. Clair to the Officer of the Pennsylvania Line, Mar. 29, 1783, in *The St. Clair Papers: The Life and Public Services of Arthur St. Clair*, ed. William Henry Smith, 2 vols. (Cincinnati, OH, 1882), vol. 1, 576.

18. Officers' petition quoted in Steven Rosswurm, *Arms, Country, and Class: The Philadelphia Militia and the "Lower Sort" during the American Revolution, 1775–1783* (New Brunswick, NJ, 1987), 52; Richard Peters quoted in Selsam, *Pennsylvania Constitution*, 85.

19. Carl Van Doren, *Mutiny in January* (New York, 1943); Royster, *Revolutionary People at War*, 302–308; Kenneth R. Bowling, "New Light on the Philadelphia Mutiny of 1783: Federal-State Confrontation at the Close of the War for Independence," *Pennsylvania Magazine of History and Biography* 101, no. 4 (Oct. 1977): 419–450.

20. Daniel Roberdeau and "Come on Warmly" quoted in Rosswurm, *Arms, Country, and Class*, 180, 205–206. For price regulation and the crowd's response in Philadelphia, see ibid., 172–227.

21. Rosswurm, *Arms, Country, and Class*, 203–227.

22. Silas Deane, July 27, 1779, quoted in Rosswurm, *Arms, Country, and Class*, 191.

23. "A PENNSYLVANIAN," *Pennsylvania Gazette*, Sept. 11, 1782; "THE PETITION of the Committee of Public Creditors of the City and Liberties of Philadelphia," ibid., Dec. 15, 1784; "LEONIDAS," ibid., July 10, 1782; "A CITIZEN OF PHILADELPHIA," ibid., Jan. 31, 1781.

24. Morris to Matthew Ridley, Oct. 6, 1782, *Morris Papers*, vol. 6, 512; "Observations on the Present State of Affairs," Jan. 13, 1783, ibid., vol. 7, 306.

25. As central as Robert Morris was to the revolutionary period, no complete modern biography of his life exists. The most thorough accounts, including Ellis Paxson Oberholtzer, *Robert Morris: Patriot and Financier* (New York, 1903), and William Graham Sumner, *The Financier and the Finances of the American Revolution*, 2 vols. (New York, 1891), were written before a complete set of Morris's papers had been compiled. Modern scholarship treats only a portion of Morris's life: Clarence L. Ver Steeg, *Robert Morris: Revolutionary Financier* (Philadelphia, 1954); Barbara Ann Chernow, *Robert Morris, Land Speculator, 1790–1801* (New York, 1978); Eleanor Young, *Robert Morris: Forgotten Patriot* (New York, 1950).

26. Morris to Philip Schuyler, May 29, 1781, *Morris Papers*, vol. 1, 92.

27. Morris to [William Hooper], Jan. 18, 1777, quoted in Ver Steeg, *Robert Morris*, 38; Morris to the President of Congress, July 29, 1782, *Morris Papers*, vol. 6, 63.

28. Morris to Alexander Hamilton, Aug. 28, 1782, *Morris Papers*, vol. 6, 271.

29. Ferguson, *Power of the Purse*, 74–83.

30. Joseph Reed to Nathaniel Greene, Nov. 1, 1781, Mar. 14, 1783, in *Life and Correspondence of Joseph Reed*, vol. 2, 374, 393. According to one historian:

> The power [Morris] held in the 1780's may be compared to that of the House of Morgan in the early twentieth century, which means that no one knows exactly how great it was. Probably J. P. Morgan would have had to add the secretaryship of the treasury and the control of Tammany Hall to match Morris' power.

Forrest McDonald, *We the People: The Economic Origins of the Constitution* (Chicago, 1958), 54.

31. Morris to John Jay, July 13, 1781, *Morris Papers*, vol. 1, 287; Morris to Thomas Jefferson, June 11, 1781, ibid., 143; Morris to the President of Congress, July 29, 1782, ibid., vol. 6, 59.

32. Morris to Benjamin Franklin, Sept. 27, 1782, *Morris Papers*, vol. 6, 449–450; "Observations on the Present State of Affairs," Jan. 13, 1783, ibid., vol. 7, 306.

33. Catherine Drinker Bowen, *Miracle at Philadelphia: The Story of the Constitutional Convention* (Boston, 1966), 21; James Thomas Flexner, *George Washington and the New Nation: 1783–1793* (Boston, 1970), 130, 270.

34. Morris to President of Congress, July 29, 1782, *Morris Papers*, vol. 6, 61.

35. Morris to Philip Schuyler, May 29, 1781, *Morris Papers*, vol. 1, 92.

36. Morris to Benjamin Franklin, July 13, 1781, *Morris Papers*, vol. 1, 283.

37. Brunhouse, *Counter-Revolution*, 150–152; M. L. Bradbury, "Legal Privilege and the Bank of North America," *Pennsylvania Magazine of History and Biography* 96, no. 2 (Apr. 1972): 142–143; and Janet Wilson, "The Bank of North America and Pennsylvania Politics: 1781–1787," *Pennsylvania Magazine of History and Biography* 66, no. 1 (Jan. 1942): 4.

38. Morris to Thomas Jefferson, June 11, 1781, *Morris Papers*, vol. 1, 143; Lawrence Lewis, Jr., *A History of the Bank of North America* (Philadelphia, 1882), 152, 133.

39. Alexander Hamilton to Morris, Apr. 30, 1781, *Morris Papers*, vol. 1, 43–44.

40. Morris to Hamilton, May 26, 1781, *Morris Papers*, vol. 1, 79; "Plan for Establishing a National Bank with Observations," ibid., 70.

41. Hamilton to Morris, Sept. 21, 1782, *Morris Papers*, vol. 6, 413.

42. Morris to Hamilton, Oct. 5, 1782, *Morris Papers*, vol. 6, 499–500; Morris to the Governor of Rhode Island, Jan. 4, 1782, *Morris Papers*, vol. 4, 20.

43. Diary, Feb. 18, 1782, *Morris Papers*, vol. 4, 249; Morris to Edward Carrington, Apr. 25, 1782, ibid., vol. 5, 57; Pierre Guillaume De Peyster, May 1782, ibid., vol. 5, 377n5.

44. George David Rappaport, *Stability and Change in Revolutionary Pennsylvania: Banking, Politics, and Social Structure* (University Park, PA, 1996), 235.

45. For interest rates, see Sept. 6, 1785, *Minutes of the First [–Third] Session of the Ninth General Assembly* (Philadelphia, 1784–1785); *Morris Papers*, vol. 6, 79n51.

46. "The Petition and Remonstrance of a Number of the Inhabitants of the County of Philadelphia," 1782, misc., reel 4, Records of the General Assembly [here-

after RGA], PHMC. For a listing of the petitions, see the entries for Feb. 25–Mar. 2, 1782, *Minutes of the First [–Third] Session of the Sixth General Assembly* (Philadelphia, 1781–1782); *Freeman's Journal*, Mar. 12, 1783. For tax quotas, see *State of the Accounts of the Several Counties for their Taxes, from the 1st of October, 1782 to the 1st of January, 1785* (Philadelphia, 1785).

47. Deposition of John Robinson, June 20, 1782, *Pennsylvania Archives*, ser. 1, vol. 9, 572; Dorsey Pentecost to President Moore, 1782, ibid., 546; Alexander McClean to President Moore, June 27, 1782, ibid., 565.

48. Morris to John Wendell, Mar. 25, 1782, *Morris Papers*, vol. 4, 453; Morris to Comte de Grasse, May 16, 1782, ibid., vol. 5, 193.

49. "The Petition of the Inhabitants of the County of Westmoreland," 1779, reel 2, RGA; Deposition of John Robinson, June 20, 1782, *Pennsylvania Archives*, ser. 1, vol. 9, 572.

50. Morris to the Governor of Connecticut, July 31, 1782, *Morris Papers*, vol. 6, 112.

51. Morris to the Governor of Maryland, July 29, 1782, *Morris Papers*, vol. 6, 84; Diary, July 26, 1782, ibid., 26.

52. The following paragraphs are based on Correspondence of James Finley, Apr. 28 and Mar. 18, 1783, *Pennsylvania Archives*, ser. 1, vol. 10, 40–42.

53. Ibid.

54. Morris to the President of Congress, July 29, 1782, *Morris Papers*, vol. 6, 63.

55. Morris to Nathanael Greene, Jan. 20, 1783, *Morris Papers*, vol. 7, 326; Ferguson, *Power of the Purse*, 155–176, 188; William H. Glasson, *Federal Military Pensions in the United States* (New York, 1918), 49.

56. Aug. 29, 1783, *Minutes of the First Session of the Seventh General Assembly* (Philadelphia, 1782–1783).

57. William Findley, *A Review of the Revenue System Adopted by the First Congress under the Federal Constitution* (Philadelphia, 1794), 6; "A Letter from a respectable farmer in York County," Mar. 5, 1785, *Pennsylvania Evening Herald*; Ferguson, *Power of the Purse*, 279. Ferguson's estimate of a 60 percent transference rate for certificates in Pennsylvania greatly undercounts the degree of transference: the sources he used only indicated transfers that occurred after 1786. In those records, anyone who obtained their certificates before 1786 appears as an original holder.

58. Ferguson, *Power of the Purse*, 179–180, 202, 278, 321. While the actual size of the Pennsylvania war debt was approximately $4.8 million in certificates, records have survived for only about $3.6 million. This sum did not include the mass of state certificates that were issued during the war. For individual certificate holdings of the war debt in Pennsylvania, see Certificate Exchange Proposals, 1789–1793, RCG, PHMC.

59. Certificate Exchange Proposals. The 234 certificate holders who could be identified as customers, directors, or shareholders of the Bank of North America held $2.4 million in war debt certificates.

60. "A Friend to Truth," *Independent Gazetteer*, Feb. 15, 1783; Ferguson, *Power of the Purse*, 35–40, 53–55, 59–69, 251–286. For the market value of securities in Pennsylvania, see *Independent Gazetteer*, Feb. 15, 1783; Feb. 12, 1784; Jan. 8, 1785; *Carlisle Gazette*, Feb. 22, 1786; Dec. 4, 1784; Mar. 16, 1785, *Minutes of the First [–Third] Session of the Ninth General Assembly*.

61. Morris to the President of Congress, Aug. 28, 1781, *Morris Papers*, vol. 2, 134; Certificate Exchange Proposals; Ferguson, *Power of the Purse*, 37–44.

Chapter 4

1. For the basic form of the petitions, see "The Humble Petition of the Subscriber Inhabitants of the Said State," 1784, frame 186, reel 21, and frames 501–505, reel 22, Records of Pennsylvania's Revolutionary Government [hereafter RPRG], PHMCM.

2. Robert Galbraith, Pittsburgh, to George Woods, Dec. 4, 1787, document 253, frame 1167, DHRCM; "Meeting of the Patriotic Convention," *Pittsburgh Gazette*, Feb. 17, 1787.

3. *Debates and Proceedings of the General Assembly, on the Memorial Praying a Repeal or Suspension of the Law Annulling the Charter of the Bank* [hereafter *Debates and Proceedings*], ed. Mathew Carey (Philadelphia, 1786), 129, 123.

4. William Gray, Northumberland County, to John Nicholson, Feb. 20, 1788, folder 16, box 5, GC, RCG; John Armstrong, Carlisle, to William Irvine, Aug. 16, 1787, vol. 9, Irvine Family Papers, HSP; William Nelson, Lancaster County, to Stephen Collins, May 12, 1788, Correspondence, Collins Papers; Adam Hubley, Lieutenant of Lancaster County, to John Nicholson, Mar. 1784, Letter Book, RCG; Robert Levers, Northampton County, to John Nicholson, Jan. 25, 1783, folder 9, box 1, GC, RCG; Andrew Boyd, Chester County, to John Nicholson, Aug. 14, 1787, folder 5, box 5, ibid.

5. Stephen Collins, Philadelphia, to Jinks & Forrester, Dec. 11, 1782, Letter Books, Collins Papers; Collins to Knox & Cowan, July 15, 1783, Jan. 8, 1784, ibid.; Collins to Harrison & Ansley, Oct. 29, 1785, Stephen Collins Letter Book, 1782–1793, Daniel Parker Collection, HSP; Collins to Charles Wright, Sept. 7, 1787, Letter Books, Collins Papers.

6. Terry Bouton, "A Road Closed: Rural Insurgency in Post-Independence Pennsylvania," *Journal of American History* 87, no. 3 (Dec. 2000): 864.

7. John J. McCusker and Russell R. Menard, *The Economy of British America, 1607–1789* (Chapel Hill, NC, 1985), 373–374. The figure of 46 percent for 1790 followed several years of improvement over the depths of the downturn during the mid-1780s. There are few economic studies of the period after the American Revolution. These figures are the best guess of economic performance based on the evidence presently available. Stanley L. Engerman and Robert E. Gallman, "U.S. Economic Growth, 1783–1860," *Research in Economic History* 8 (1982): 1–46; Alice Hanson Jones, *Wealth of a Nation to Be: The American Colonies on the Eve of the Revolution* (New York, 1980), 79–85.

8. These relationships are clearly displayed in county execution dockets. The names of the "old" debtors are recorded in parentheses to the right of the "new" debtor's listing.

9. Bouton, "Road Closed," 859, 862. These figures represent orders processed, not the actual number of people foreclosed. Since the sheriff typically made several visits to the home of a debtor before the legal action was brought to a close, each case typically generated multiple foreclosure orders.

10. Bouton, "Road Closed," 859–860, 862.

11. Smithson and Greaves, Leeds, to Stephen Collins, Philadelphia, May 29, 1786, Correspondence, Collins Papers; William and John Sitgreaves Letterbook, 1783–1794, Thomas A. Biddle Papers, HSP; Stephen Collins to Minton Collins, Sept. 13, 1787, Correspondence, Collins Papers.

12. Westmoreland County Execution Dockets (Westmoreland County Courthouse, Greensburg, PA). This figure was calculated from a pool of 1,580 cases where the amount of debt could be determined.

13. For the per capita income estimates in 1774, see Jones, *Wealth of a Nation*, 61–64, 369–374. I adjusted Jones's figures (£11.5–13.4 for the middle colonies) to Pennsylvania currency values using the tables provided in Anne Bezanson, *Prices and Inflation during the American Revolution: Pennsylvania, 1770–1790* (Philadelphia, 1951), 346. I further adjusted them to reflect the national decline in income by 46 percent over the course of the 1780s. Finally, I converted the figure to dollars using a 2.66 multiplier. I derived yearly household income using the average household size in Pennsylvania, 5.5 people, from James S. Lemon, *The Best Poor Man's Country: A Geographical Study of Early Southeastern Pennsylvania* (Baltimore, MD, 1972), 239n71.

14. The various fees are typically itemized beneath the case listing in Appearance, Continuance, and Execution dockets. For a complete accounting of specific rates, see "Mode of Taxing in Fayette County," Thomas Hamilton Papers, folder 5, box 1, Westmoreland County Historical Society, Greensburg, PA.

15. Apr. 1782, 1786, 1790, Westmoreland County QS Dockets (Westmoreland County Courthouse, Greensburg, PA). To get an estimate of typical court expenses, I sampled costs from the April session of three years, producing a mean of £6.1 and a median of £5.3 (N = 347). While based on specific docket entries, these estimates undercount the actual mean and median court costs. In suits that lasted for a considerable length of time, court fees were sometimes added to the debt, so that the cost figure printed in the docket book only reflected the last round of fees rather than the costs for the whole case. Additionally, defendants often paid their fees—particularly the sheriff's and attorney's fees—when they could not pay any other part of their debt. This meant that, as the case progressed, the court fees printed in the docket failed to account for the money paid on different occasions to court officials.

16. Petition from Cumberland County, Sept. 3, 1784, frame 560, reel 21, RPRG; Petition to General Assembly, Westmoreland County, Feb. 19, 1789, frame 227, reel 24, ibid. Of the 2,206 separate cases of foreclosure that Westmoreland

County courts processed in a decade, 614 resulted from legal costs. The fraction of foreclosures arising from costs was 27.8 percent.

17. This detailed portrait of the activities of a county sheriff is made possible due to the elaborate inventories included in most county execution dockets. These inventories list the basic items foreclosed and provide descriptions of the property, noting such things as color, number, quality, make, patterns, markings, and, when appropriate, an estimate of work potential. Unfortunately, a complete quantitative survey of foreclosed goods is impossible since county clerks only listed the itemized possessions in a fraction of the cases where property was attached. That said, crops and livestock appear to have been by far the most common goods foreclosed.

18. In the moneyless economy of the backcountry, the importance of whiskey as a cash crop took on heightened significance, causing stills to be the most likely manufacturing tool taken on execution. Likewise, the practical utility of flour in the backcountry caused sheriffs to seize grinding stones from county mill owners. The tools of blacksmiths, cobblers, and weavers required specific training to use and, therefore, were less desirable and less often included among sheriffs' inventories.

19. Household items were usually only taken from the homes of gentlemen debtors. The utensils in the homes of ordinary citizens typically were not of high enough quality to draw a bid. In some cases, the sheriff took dressers and desks with the contents included. In one case, the sheriff actually auctioned off a desk and the personal papers it contained. Over the decade 1782–1792, the Westmoreland dockets list thirty-two slaves taken on execution. The slaves who were sold ranged in age from young children to the elderly.

20. Beds, particularly feather beds, were popular items on sheriffs' inventories. Blankets, bed covers, and quilts made fewer appearances, while linens were a rare inclusion found only at the homes of especially well-to-do debtors.

21. Stephen Collins, Philadelphia, to Jeremiah Brooks, Dec. 26, 1787, Letter Books, Collins Papers.

22. The specific procedures varied with the kind of debt and changed as regulations were modified over time. Placing advertisements at two or three meeting places was the minimum notification in all cases. Tax sales and auctions for defaulted mortgages typically required the most publication.

23. The time between the first visit of the sheriff and the actual auction date varied considerably. Some goods were auctioned during the same week that the sheriff made the inventory; others required a month's waiting period.

24. It is difficult to determine the percentage of auctions in which no one bid on property. In most cases, no docket entry was used to record the sale of attached property, making it impossible to estimate the actual number of auctions performed. What is clear is that, between 1782 and 1792, Westmoreland County auctions failed to produce bidders more than 1,650 times.

25. Alexander Boyd, Treasurer of Chester County, to John Nicholson, Aug. 14, 1787, folder 5, box 5, GC, RCG. The range of sale prices for auctioned goods

varied by place and what was being auctioned. Delinquent excise collector for Lancaster County William Hay had his land sold for one-third of its value and his possessions for one-fifth. Petition of William Hay, Aug. 26, 1785, frame 385, reel 22, RPRG. The lands and property of collectors in Bedford County would "not sell for one Eight part of their value." James Gilmore to John Nicholson, Feb. 16, 1788, folder 18, box 5, GC, RCG. Property sold for taxes in Bedford County sold for only "one-tenth part of the value." Thomas Crossan to John Nicholson, July 27, 1787, folder 5, ibid.

26. The story of the plight of William McKinney that follows is drawn from William McKinney Deposition, 1786, folder 3, box 33, James Hamilton Papers, Cumberland County Historical Society, Carlisle, PA.

27. The sale price of property was listed in only a fraction of the cases. Of these, sixty-one sales out of a total of sixty-six did not cover the cost of the debt. In two of the five cases where the sale price surpassed the debt, there was not enough money left to pay the court costs.

According to the tax officials in Bucks County, the scarcity of money often prevented many buyers from paying for their goods. As they noted, "the Purchasers themselves are often unable to make immediate Payment, though Owners of considerable Estates." Commission[er] of Taxes of Bucks Co. to Pres. Dickinson, July 31, 1783, *Pennsylvania Archives*, ser. 1, vol. 10, 75.

28. Thomas Cheyney to John Nicholson, Sept. 16, 1785, folder 1, box 3, GC, RCG. Cheyney was later a delegate from Chester County who voted for ratification of the federal Constitution.

29. Anthony Butler to James Hamilton, Oct. 20, 1791, folder 2, box 33, James Hamilton Papers. For worries about land being stripped of timber, see Edward Byrd, Philadelphia, to Jasper Yeates, Lancaster, Sept. 7, 1784, Yeates Family Papers, HSP.

30. As the execution docket books do not always list the action taken by the court, the figure derived here undoubtedly undercounts the number of people who lost their land.

31. Leilin & Snyder to Stephen Collins, Philadelphia, Jan. 13, 1789, Correspondence, Collins Papers; Execution Dockets, Westmoreland County.

32. Docket entries in such cases shift among "nulla bona," "no goods," and "nei." The first two terms meant that the defendant had nothing of value to attach or that the property was already claimed in another legal action. Nei was used when the defendant could not be located. Not surprisingly, defendants in poverty often dodged the sheriff or constable when they came to town.

33. It is unclear whether those imprisoned for longer terms served continuously or were released at some point each term. From the few annotations beside the case entries, it appears that both scenarios occurred.

34. Westmoreland County Execution Dockets, 1782–1789.

35. Thomas M. Doerflinger, *A Vigorous Spirit of Enterprise: Merchants and Economic Development in Revolutionary Philadelphia* (Chapel Hill, NC, 1986), 246–247, 262–265; for Hollypeter, see *Carlisle Gazette*, May 30, 1787.

36. Stephen Chambers to James Hamilton, Dec. 4, 1784, folder 2, box 33, James Hamilton Papers (emphases in original).

37. William Findley, Westmoreland County, to George Bryan, Philadelphia, Aug. 3, 1789, folder 13, box 3, George Bryan Papers, HSP; Findley to William Irvine, May 23, 1790, vol. 10, Irvine Family Papers.

38. Billy Gordon Smith, The "Lower Sort": Philadelphia's Laboring People, 1750–1800 (Ithaca, NY, 1990), 228.

39. Jack D. Marietta, "The Distribution of Wealth in Eighteenth-Century America: Nine Chester County Tax Lists, 1693–1799," Pennsylvania History 62 (Oct. 1995): 537–538; R. Eugene Harper, The Transformation of Western Pennsylvania, 1770–1800 (Pittsburgh, PA, 1992), 28–35, 55–56; "Nestor," Independent Gazetteer, July 1, 1786.

40. Daniel Mifflin to Stephen Collins, Philadelphia, Mar. 2, 1788, Correspondence, Collins Papers; John Wilkins, Jr., Pittsburgh, to William Irvine, Feb. 3, 1791, vol. 10, Irvine Family Papers; William Findley, Westmoreland County, to Irvine, May 23, 1790, ibid. Peter C. Mancall provides a clear description of the influence that landlords and other propertied men wielded in the backcountry economy: "Thus, though families remained the basic economic unit, they found themselves increasingly bound into an elaborate system of debt, mortgages, or tenancy. Economic security in this rural hinterland, all valley residents knew, meant living in the landholders' commercial world." Peter C. Mancall, Valley of Opportunity: Economic Culture along the Upper Susquehanna, 1700–1800 (Ithaca, NY, 1991), 202.

41. "An infallible Cure for Hard Times," Pennsylvania Herald and York Central Advertiser, Feb. 16, 1791.

42. McCusker and Menard, Economy of British America, 373–374; Engerman and Gallman, "U.S. Economic Growth"; Louis Maganzin, "Economic Depression in Maryland and Virginia, 1783–1787" (Ph.D. diss., Georgetown University, 1967), 177–202, 265–268; John H. Flannagan, Jr., "Trying Times: Economic Depression in New Hampshire, 1781–1789" (Ph.D. diss., Georgetown University, 1972), 76–132; David P. Szatmary, Shays' Rebellion: The Making of an Agrarian Insurrection (Amherst, MA, 1980), 27–31; Jerome J. Nadelhaft, The Disorders of War: The Revolution in South Carolina (Orono, ME, 1981), 155–172; Michael Bellesiles, Revolutionary Outlaws: Ethan Allen and the Struggle for Independence on the Early American Frontier (Charlottesville, VA, 1993), 246–248, 278; James Leamon, Revolution Downeast: The War for American Independence in Maine (Amherst, MA, 1993); Jean B. Lee, The Price of Nationhood: The American Revolution in Charles County (New York, 1994), 228–258.

Chapter 5

1. Unfortunately, quantitative analysis of the petitions is impossible since only a fraction of them have survived. The petition listings in the minutes of the state assembly generally do not include every petition submitted, nor do they repro-

duce the whole text of petitions nor indicate the number of signers. The editors of the printed volumes of the *Pennsylvania Archives* excluded many petitions. The petition files at the Pennsylvania State Archives are spotty at best: although they contain petitions that can be found in neither the minutes nor the published archives, many documents have evidently been lost, and there are numerous partial petitions and pages of signatures not attached to any petition.

2. John Caldwell, *William Findley from West of the Mountains: Congressman, 1791–1821* (Gig Harbor, WA, 2002).

3. *Debates and Proceedings of the General Assembly, on the Memorial Praying a Repeal or Suspension of the Law Annulling the Charter of the Bank* [hereafter *Debates and Proceedings*], ed. Mathew Carey (Philadelphia, 1786), 65, 130.

4. Ibid., 65–66.

5. "The Remonstrance of the Subscribers, Yeomen, and Citizens of Pennsylvania," House Files, 1793–1794, and misc., RGA.

6. Ibid.

7. Ibid.; *Debates and Proceedings*, 126, 129. Those who wish to see Findley as the mouthpiece of economic liberalism and of an idea of democracy that equated with the unrestrained pursuit of one's own self-interest have quoted selectively from Findley's pronouncements and often taken his words out of context. In particular, they have cited a passage where Findley says "I love and pursue" wealth, which to these scholars is an admission of favoring aggressive individualism. These historians, however, ignore all of the other instances where Findley elaborated a vision of political economy predicated on self-restraint and the need for government to limit accumulations of wealth.

8. *Debates and Proceedings*, 66, 69, 129.

9. "Aristocratis" [William Petrikin], *The Government of Nature Delineated*, 4, 21–24, 31, document 661, frames 2513, 2530–2533, 2540, DHRCM. At least 1,400 copies of this pamphlet circulated through the state. John Jordan to John Nicholson, Jan. 26, 1788, DHRC, 693.

10. *Pittsburgh Gazette*, Feb. 10, 1787; "Political Sentinel IV," ibid., July 14, 1787; *Debates and Proceedings*, 69; *Independent Gazetteer*, Feb. 23, 1787.

11. *Pennsylvania Evening Herald*, Feb. 23, 1785. For other petitions sent, see Mar. 21–28, 1785, *Minutes of the First [–Third] Session of the Ninth General Assembly*; *Debates and Proceedings*. See also the assembly debates during Sept. 1785, *Minutes of the First [–Third] Session of the Ninth General Assembly*.

12. *Pennsylvania Evening Herald*, Feb. 23, 1785; Feb. 10, 1786; *Debates and Proceedings*, 65, 123, 125, 130.

13. *Pennsylvania Evening Herald*, Feb. 23, 1785; Feb. 10, 1786; Apr. 1, 1782; *Minutes of the First [–Third] Session of the Sixth General Assembly*.

14. *Debates and Proceedings*, 65–66, 69.

15. Mar. 28, 1785, *Minutes of the First [–Third] Session of the Ninth General Assembly*; *Debates and Proceedings*, 24, 62; William Barton, *The True Interests of the United States and Particularly of Pennsylvania Considered* (Philadelphia, 1786), 21–22.

16. "The Remonstrance of the Subscribers, Yeomen, and Citizens of Pennsylvania," House Files, 1793–1794, and misc., RGA; "The Remonstrance and Petition of the Subscribers, Landholders, and Citizens," Sept. 29, 1791, House Files, 1790–1791, RGA.

17. For quotes, see "Petitions of the Sundry Inhabitants of the County of Bucks," Mar. 1781, reel 2, RGA; "The Humble Petition of the Subscriber Inhabitants of the Said State," 1784, frame 186, reel 21; frames 501–505, reel 22, RPRG. For other petitions, see R. Terry Bouton, "Tying Up the Revolution: Money, Power, and the Regulation in Pennsylvania, 1765–1800" (Ph.D. diss., Duke University, 1996), 176–177.

18. For quotes, see "The Petition of the Subscribers," *Pennsylvania Evening Herald*, Feb. 26, 1785; "Petition from Westmoreland County," 1784, reel 3, RGA. The seven types of state paper in circulation during the war were commonly referred to as "provincial money" (issued by provincial authorities), "resolve money" (issued in 1775 and 1776 by the revolutionary government), "commonwealth money" (issued in Mar. 1777), "state island money" (issued in Mar. 1780), "dollar money" (issued in June 1780), "shilling money" (issued in Apr. 1781), and the money issued in Mar. 1783.

19. "A Letter from a respectable farmer in York County," *Pennsylvania Evening Herald*, Mar. 5, 1785; "Petition from Westmoreland County," 1784, reel 3, RGA; "The Humble Petition of the Subscriber Inhabitants of the Said State," 1784, frame 186, reel 21; frames 501–505, reel 22, RPRG; "Petition from Philadelphia County," Dec. 5, 1783, *Minutes of the First [–Third] Session of the Eighth General Assembly* (Philadelphia, 1783–1784).

20. John Armstrong, Carlisle, to William Irvine, Aug. 16, 1787, vol. 9, Irvine Family Papers.

21. "A Citizen," Franklin County, *Carlisle Gazette*, Feb. 22, 1786; "A Respectable Farmer from York County," *Pennsylvania Evening Herald*, Mar. 5, 1785. The figure "two shillings and six pence in the pound" represented the price at which Philadelphia brokers sold certificates when they first came on the market. The amount is the equivalent of purchasing a certificate at approximately one-ninth of its face value—a figure considerably greater than the actual amount many speculators had paid when they purchased the certificates from their original holders.

22. For petitions from 1781–1785, see Bouton, "Tying Up the Revolution," 203–205. "The Plan" was spelled out in a newspaper exchange between a farmer named James R. Reid from Cumberland County and a writer from Franklin County identifying himself as "A Citizen." *Carlisle Gazette*, Feb. 1, 21, 22, 1786.

23. For petitions calling for the government to accept IOUs in payment of taxes and fees prior to the Plan, see Bouton, "Tying Up the Revolution," 203–205.

24. *Carlisle Gazette*, Feb. 22, 1786. As James Reid concurred, the Plan "preserves the faith of the state by doing what every impartial man must call justice in giving an ample compensation for the certificates in the hands of the trading people." *Carlisle Gazette*, Jan. 11, 1786.

25. *Carlisle Gazette*, Feb. 1 and 22, 1786.
26. *Carlisle Gazette*, Feb. 1, 1786.
27. "The following petition is now in circulation . . . ," *Carlisle Gazette*, Feb. 7, 1786; for subsequent petitions, see Bouton, "Tying Up the Revolution," 213–215.
28. "Petition of the Subscribers in behalf of the Freemen of the Commonwealth of Pennsylvania," *Carlisle Gazette*, Apr. 2, 1788; "Petition from the Inhabitants of York County respecting the present mode of enforcing the payment of debts," 1787, reel 3, RGA; "Petition from Lancaster County," Jan. 29, 1783, *Minutes of the First Session of the Seventh General Assembly*.
29. "The Remonstrance of the Farmers of the township of Bristol," *Pennsylvania Evening Herald*, Mar. 8, 1785; "York County Petition," 1784, reel 3, RGA; *Carlisle Gazette*, Apr. 2, 1788.
30. Sept. 9–21, 1779, *Minutes of the Third General Assembly*; "A FARMER," *Independent Gazetteer*, Feb. 14, 1787; *Pennsylvania Evening Herald*, Feb. 23, 1785. For other petitions, see Mar. 21–28, 1785, *Minutes of the First [–Third] Session of the Ninth General Assembly*.
31. Sept. 19, 1788, *Debates of the General Assembly . . . Volume the Fourth* (Philadelphia, 1788).
32. For the calls for a land tax, see chapters 10 and 11 below.
33. "The Humble Petitions of the Frontier Inhabitants of Westmoreland County and State of Pennsylvania" [295 signers], Jan. 5, 1784, reel 3, RGA; "A Farmer," *Pittsburgh Gazette*, Jan. 20, 1787.
34. "The Petition of the Subscribers [and] Inhabitants of the County of Northumberland," 1784, reel 3, RGA; "The Petition of the Frontier Inhabitants of Washington County," Feb. 5, 1785, reel 3, RGA.
35. "The Humble Petitions of the Frontier Inhabitants of Westmoreland County and State of Pennsylvania," Jan. 5, 1784, reel 3, RGA; Michael Lacassagne to William Irvine, Apr. 1, 1787, vol. 9, Irvine Family Papers.
36. "The Petition of the Subscribers [and] Inhabitants of the County of Northumberland," 1784, reel 3, RGA; "The Petition of a Number of Inhabitants of the Township of Buckingham in the County of Bucks," n.d., misc., reel 4, RGA. The Land Act of 1792 gave squatters just such a right over speculators. Like the caps on speculation, those rights were often ignored by the courts and the men who ran the state land office (who were usually speculators themselves).
37. "The Petition of the Subscribers [and] Inhabitants of Northumberland County," 1781, frame 1019, reel 18, RPRG; "The Remonstrance of the Principal Inhabitants of Northumberland County," Aug. 4, 1784, reel 3, RGA. For popular attempts to limit land speculation in Pennsylvania, see Norman B. Wilkinson, *Land Policy and Speculation in Pennsylvania, 1779–1800: A Test of the New Democracy* (New York, 1979); Donna Bingham Munger, *Pennsylvania Land Records: A History and Guide for Research* (Wilmington, DE, 1991), 145–173; and James F. Dinsmore, "Courts and Western Pennsylvania Lands: The Origins of the Attack on Pennsylvania's Courts, 1790–1810" (Ph.D. diss., Temple University, 1990), 69–77.

38. For examples, see Barbara Karsky, "Agrarian Radicalism in the Late Revolutionary Period," in *New Wine in Old Skins: A Comparative Study of Socio-Political Structures and Values affecting the American Revolution*, ed. Erich Angermann et al. (Stuttgart, 1976), 97–114; David P. Szatmary, *Shays' Rebellion: The Making of an Agrarian Insurrection* (Amherst, MA, 1980); Ruth Bogin, "Petitioning and the New Moral Economy of Post-Revolutionary America," *William and Mary Quarterly*, 3rd ser., 45 (July 1988): 391–425; Rhys Isaac, *The Transformation of Virginia, 1740–1790* (Chapel Hill, NC, 1982); Alan Taylor, *Liberty Men and Great Proprietors: The Revolutionary Settlement on the Maine Frontier, 1760–1820* (Chapel Hill, NC, 1990); Michael Bellesiles, *Revolutionary Outlaws: Ethan Allen and the Struggle for Independence on the Early American Frontier* (Charlottesville, VA, 1993); Michael Merrill and Sean Wilentz, *The Key of Liberty: The Life and Democratic Writings of William Manning, "A Laborer," 1747–1814* (Cambridge, MA, 1993); Robert A. Gross, ed., *In Debt to Shays: The Bicentennial of an Agrarian Rebellion* (Charlottesville, VA, 1993); Jean B. Lee, *The Price of Nationhood: The American Revolution in Charles County* (New York, 1994); Barbara Clark Smith, "Food Rioters and the American Revolution," *William and Mary Quarterly*, 3rd ser., 51 (Jan. 1994): 3–38; Michael Merrill, "Putting 'Capitalism' in Its Place: A Review of Recent Literature," *William and Mary Quarterly*, 3rd ser., 52 (Apr. 1995): 315–326; Thomas J. Humphrey, *Land and Liberty: Hudson Valley Riots in the Age of Revolution* (DeKalb, IL, 2004); Woody Holton, "An 'Excess of Democracy'—or a Shortage? The Federalists' Earliest Adversaries," *Journal of the Early Republic* 25, no. 3 (Fall 2005): 339–382.

Chapter 6

1. For ethnic divisions in politics, see Robert L. Brunhouse, *The Counter-Revolution in Pennsylvania, 1776–1790* (New York, 1971); Owen S. Ireland, "The Ethnic-Religious Dimension of Pennsylvania Politics, 1778–1779," *William and Mary Quarterly* 30 (July 1973): 423–448; Ireland, "The Crux of Politics: Religion & Party in Pennsylvania, 1778–1789," *William and Mary Quarterly* 42 (Oct. 1985): 453–475.

2. Anne M. Ousterhout, *A State Divided: Opposition in Pennsylvania to the American Revolution* (Westport, CT, 1987), 279–303; Francis S. Fox, *Sweet Land of Liberty: The Ordeal of the American Revolution in Northampton County, Pennsylvania* (University Park, PA, 2000).

3. Henry G. Ashmead, *Historical Sketch of Chester on Delaware* (Chester, PA, 1883), 55–57.

4. Paul Benjamin Moyer, "Wild Yankees: Settlement, Conflict, and Localism along Pennsylvania's Northeast Frontier, 1760–1820" (Ph.D. diss., College of William and Mary, 1999).

5. The effect may have been tempered by the fact that many fewer immigrants came than before the war. See James S. Lemon, *The Best Poor Man's Country: A Geographical Study of Early Southeastern Pennsylvania* (Baltimore, MD, 1972), 224.

6. For geographic mobility, see ibid., 71–97; Lucy Simler, "Tenancy in Colonial Pennsylvania: The Case of Chester County," *William and Mary Quarterly* 43 (Oct. 1986): 542–569; Simler, "The Landless Worker: An Index of Economic and Social Change in Chester County, Pennsylvania, 1750–1820," *Pennsylvania Magazine of History and Biography* 114 (Apr. 1990): 163–199; R. Eugene Harper, *The Transformation of Western Pennsylvania, 1770–1800* (Pittsburgh, PA, 1992).

7. Steven Rosswurm, *Arms, Country, and Class: The Philadelphia Militia and the "Lower Sort" during the American Revolution, 1775–1783* (New Brunswick, NJ, 1987), 203–247; Ronald Schultz, *The Republic of Labor: Philadelphia Artisans and the Politics of Class, 1720–1830* (New York, 1993), 37–139.

8. The best chronicle of the changing faces in the assembly during the 1780s remains Brunhouse, *Counter-Revolution*.

9. Husband, "Proposals to Amend and Perfect the Policy of the Government of the United States of America," 1782, quoted in Woody Holton, "'Divide et Impera': Federalist 10 in a Wider Sphere," *William and Mary Quarterly* 62, no. 2 (Apr. 2005): 187.

10. Oct. 1783, Bedford County QS Papers, Bedford County Courthouse, Bedford, PA.

11. Ibid.

12. For election complaints, see Minutes of the Supreme Executive Council, July 1786–July 1790, *Pennsylvania Archives*, Colonial Series, vols. 14–16.

13. John B. Frantz and William Pencak, eds., *Beyond Philadelphia: The American Revolution in the Pennsylvania Hinterland* (University Park, PA, 1998), 69, 108.

14. Brunhouse, *Counter-Revolution*, 156–165; Roger H. Brown, *Redeeming the Republic: Federalists, Taxation, and the Origins of the Constitution* (Baltimore, MD, 1993), 63–64. Both Brown and Brunhouse suggest that this election caused a dramatic transformation in the general assembly that led to prodebtor policies, a portrait at odds with the one presented here.

15. *Debates and Proceedings of the General Assembly, on the Memorial Praying a Repeal or Suspension of the Law Annulling the Charter of the Bank* [hereafter *Debates and Proceedings*], ed. Mathew Carey (Philadelphia, 1786), 132.

16. Jeremiah Wadsworth to John Chaloner, Oct. 24 and Dec. 21, 1784, quoted in John D. Platt, *Jeremiah Wadsworth: Federalist Entrepreneur* (New York, 1982), 152–153; Wadsworth to Alexander Hamilton, Jan. 9, 1786, in *The Papers of Alexander Hamilton* [hereafter AHP], ed. Harold C. Syrett, 26 vols. (New York, 1961–1979), vol. 3, 645–646; Hamilton to Wadsworth, Oct. 29, 1785, ibid., 625; Janet Wilson, "The Bank of North America and Pennsylvania Politics: 1781–1787," *Pennsylvania Magazine of History and Biography* 66, no. 1 (Jan. 1942): 11; Charles Page Smith, *James Wilson, Founding Father, 1742–1798* (Westport, CT, 1973), 150, 369.

17. John P. Kaminski, *Paper Politics: The Northern State Loan-Offices during the Confederation, 1783–1790* (New York, 1989), 77–78.

18. "Petition from Lancaster County," Feb. 23, 1785, *Minutes of the First [–Third] Session of the Ninth General Assembly*; "A Letter from a respectable farmer in York County," *Pennsylvania Evening Herald*, Mar. 5, 1785. This writer suggested that the loan office should have been capitalized at £200,000.

19. For the 1773 loan office, see Paton Wesley Yoder, "Paper Currency in Colonial Pennsylvania" (Ph.D. diss., Indiana University, 1941), 317–318. For the 1785 loan office, see "An Act for Erecting and Opening a Loan Office for the Sum of Fifty Thousand Pounds," Apr. 4, 1785, in *The Statutes at Large of Pennsylvania from 1682 to 1801* [hereafter SALP], ed. James T. Mitchell and Henry Flanders, 17 vols. (Harrisburg, PA, 1896), vol. 11, 560–572. The bill allocated £3,000 to Cumberland County; the county's debts were £22,000 in paper money and £52,000 in specie. "State of the Accounts of the Treasury . . . from 1782 . . . to 1785," *Pennsylvania Archives*, ser. 3, vol. 5, 373.

20. *Debates and Proceedings*, 119; Wilson, "Bank of North America," 10.

21. William Petrikin to John Nicholson, Apr. 14, 1789, in *The Documentary History of the First Federal Elections, 1788–1790* [hereafter DHFFE], ed. Merrill Jensen and Robert A. Becker, 4 vols. (Madison, WI, 1976), vol. 1, 410. Petrikin alleged that the bank directors in the general assembly who purchased support were Thomas FitzSimons, George Clymer, and Mordecai Lewis.

22. Brackenridge quoted in Claude M. Newlin, *Life and Writings of Hugh Henry Brackenridge* (Princeton, NJ, 1932), 57.

23. *Pittsburgh Gazette*, Sept. 9, 1786.

24. "A Farmer," *Pittsburgh Gazette*, Jan. 20, 1787; Alexander Fowler, DHRC, 287.

25. *Pittsburgh Gazette*, Apr. 21, 1787 (emphasis in original); *Pittsburgh Gazette*, May 26, 1787. For Brackenridge's elaborate defense of his actions, see *Pittsburgh Gazette*, Mar. 24, Apr. 21, 28, May 5, 12, 19, June 9, Aug. 3, 11, 1787. See also the rebuttals by William Findley, *Pittsburgh Gazette*, July 21, 28, Aug. 18, Sept. 1, 15, 22, 1787.

26. William Shippen, Jr., to Thomas Lee Shippen, Nov. 18, 1787, DHRC, 236.

27. Robert D. Arbuckle, *Pennsylvania Speculator and Patriot: The Entrepreneurial John Nicholson, 1757–1800* (University Park, PA, 1975), 46–74.

28. For the social, economic, and political divisions among the elite, see Brunhouse, *Counter-Revolution*; Roland M. Baumann, "Democratic-Republicans of Philadelphia: The Origins, 1776–1797" (Ph.D. diss., Pennsylvania State University, 1970); Stephen James Brobeck, "Changes in the Composition and Structure of Philadelphia Elite Groups, 1756–1790" (Ph.D. diss., University of Pennsylvania, 1972), 194–248; Robert James Gough, "Towards a Theory of Class and Social Conflict: A Social History of Wealthy Philadelphians, 1775 and 1800" (Ph.D. diss., University of Pennsylvania, 1977), 127–610.

29. Robert Morris to Thomas Jefferson, Apr. 8, 1784, *Morris Papers*, vol. 9, 240. On the proposed new bank, see George David Rappaport, *Stability and Change in Revolutionary Pennsylvania: Banking, Politics, and Social Structure*

(University Park, PA, 1996), 160–165; Brunhouse, *Counter-Revolution*, 150–152; M. L. Bradbury, "Legal Privilege and the Bank of North America," *Pennsylvania Magazine of History and Biography* 96, no. 2 (Apr. 1972): 142–143; and Wilson, "Bank of North America," 4.

30. For specie deficits, see Dec. 16, 1784, *Minutes of the First [–Third] Session of the Ninth General Assembly*. For how holders acquired certificates, see E. James Ferguson, *Power of the Purse: A History of American Public Finance, 1776–1790* (Chapel Hill, NC, 1961), 37–44, 278–280. For calls to cut out secondary holders, see "A Worn Out Soldier," *Independent Gazetteer*, Feb. 5, 1785; "An Elector," ibid.; "Assembly of Pennsylvania," *Pennsylvania Evening Herald*, Jan. 4, 1786.

31. "The PETITION of the Committee of Public Creditors of the City and Liberties of Philadelphia," *Pennsylvania Mercury*, Dec. 14, 1784; "A Message from the General Assembly of the Commonwealth of Pennsylvania," Dec. 24, 1784, *Minutes of the First [–Third] Session of the Ninth General Assembly*; "A proposed ADDRESS from Representatives of the Freemen of the commonwealth of Pennsylvania," *Pennsylvania Mercury*, Jan. 7, 1785; Charles Pettit to Nathanael Greene, Mar. 23, 1785, and "A Mechanic," *Independent Gazetteer*, Jan. 8, 1785, both quoted in Brunhouse, *Counter-Revolution*, 170–171.

32. "A Letter from a respectable farmer in York County," *Pennsylvania Evening Herald*, Mar. 5, 1785.

33. Ibid.

34. For voter turnout data, see Brunhouse, *Counter-Revolution*, 328–342; Robert J. Dinkin, *Voting in Revolutionary America: A Study of Elections in the Original Thirteen States, 1776–1789* (Westport, CT, 1982), 115; Owen S. Ireland, *Religion, Ethnicity, and Politics: Ratifying the Constitution in Pennsylvania* (University Park, PA, 1995), 240; and Ireland, "The Ratification of the Federal Constitution in Pennsylvania" (Ph.D. diss., University of Pittsburgh, 1966), 280. For the taxable population, see "List of Taxables," *Pennsylvania Evening Herald*, Sept. 27, 1786. I adjusted Ireland's voter turnout estimate (37.5 percent of taxables) to reflect the official listing of 4,273 taxables recorded by the state government. Counties elected several representatives to the assembly, and voters were allowed to cast a ballot for each assembly slot. Where winning and losing candidates were listed, I determined turnout by adding the total votes and dividing by the number of offices for which people were allowed to vote. For counties that only listed the tallies for the candidates who won the election, only a rough turnout estimate is possible. To estimate voter turnout here, I added the tallies for the top vote-getter and for the last of the winning candidates and then subtracted one, thus assuming that all the losing candidates received one fewer vote than the lowest winner and that there were an equal number of winning and losing candidates. Since few elections were decided by one vote and most elections had more winners than losers (i.e., five candidates running for three slots), this figure undoubtedly overestimates the actual voter turnout by a considerable margin. Using this

method, Northampton totaled 1,092 votes for a population of 3,967 taxpayers, Dauphin 709 voters in a county of 2,881 taxables, and York had 1,527 ballots cast out of an electorate of 6,254.

35. "Meeting of the Patriotic Convention," *Pittsburgh Gazette*, Feb. 17, 1787.

36. For quotes, see "Petition from York County," 1787, folder 14, box 4, GC, RCG. Also see "Petition from Cumberland County and Franklin County," Aug. 29, 1786, "Petition from Carlisle in Cumberland County," Sept. 12, 1786, both in *Minutes of the First [–Third] Session of the Tenth General Assembly* (Philadelphia, 1785–1786); "Petition from Lancaster, Cumberland, and Franklin Counties," Nov. 9, 1786, *Minutes of the First Session of the Eleventh General Assembly* (Philadelphia, 1786); "Petition from Chester, Lancaster Counties," Mar. 19, 1787, *Minutes of the Second Session of the Eleventh General Assembly* (Philadelphia, 1787); "Petition from Chester County," Nov. 24, 1787, *Proceedings and Debates of the General Assembly . . . Volume the Second* (Philadelphia, 1787).

Chapter 7

1. Pennsylvania Constitution (1776).

2. Of course, the actual process of defending communities usually did not follow such a strict chronology. In most places, all of these protective efforts happened at approximately the same time, and, as might be expected given the circumstances, some people proceeded immediately to violent resistance.

3. The plaintiff listings in county execution dockets and papers read as a roster of the prominent people in each county. These lists also reveal patterns of indebtedness that crossed county lines. For example, execution docket books for Westmoreland and Washington counties disclose that many of the same merchants, lawyers, and county officers regularly sued people in both jurisdictions.

4. Works examining the tax resistance in Pennsylvania include Robert L. Brunhouse, *The Counter-Revolution in Pennsylvania, 1776–1790* (New York, 1971); Lemuel Molovinsky, "Tax Collection Problems in Revolutionary Pennsylvania," *Pennsylvania History* 47, no. 3 (July 1980): 253–259; Dorothy Elaine Fennell, "From Rebelliousness to Insurrection: A Social History of the Whiskey Rebellion, 1765–1802" (Ph.D. diss., University of Pittsburgh, 1981); Thomas P. Slaughter, *The Whiskey Rebellion: Frontier Epilogue to the American Revolution* (New York, 1986); Roger H. Brown, *Redeeming the Republic: Federalists, Taxation, and the Origins of the Constitution* (Baltimore, MD, 1993), 53–68.

5. Commissioners of Bucks County to John Dickinson, July 31, 1783, *Pennsylvania Archives*, ser. 1, vol. 10, 75; William Henderson, John Craig, and Michael Graham, Chester County, to His Excellency and the Supreme Executive Council of the State of Pennsylvania, Dec. 18, 1786, frame 340, reel 22, RPRG; Commissioners of Taxes Northampton County to President

Mifflin, Aug. 19, 1789, *Pennsylvania Archives*, ser. 1, vol. 11, 603; Jacob Rosencrantz, Northampton County, to John Nicholson, Sept. 1, 1786, file 1, box 4, GC, RCG; Jacob Smyser, York County, to Dickinson, Aug. 5, 1783, quoted in Brown, *Redeeming the Republic*, 61; John Thome, Dauphin County, to Nicholson, Sept. 22, 1786, frame 324, reel 19, GC, Sequestered John Nicholson Papers [hereafter Nicholson Papers], PHMCM.

6. John Jordan and Ephraim Steel, Cumberland County, to Nicholson, Sept. 30, 1786, folder 4, box 4, GC, RCG; William Moore, James Lawson, and William Jack, Westmoreland County, to Nicholson, Dec. 1786, file 13, ibid.; Andrew Swearingen, Washington County, to Nicholson, Feb. 4, 1787, file 12, ibid.

7. For examples of reluctant county officers putting the law into force, see Terry Bouton, "A Road Closed: Rural Insurgency in Post-Independence Pennsylvania," *Journal of American History* 87, no. 3 (Dec. 2000): 870.

8. Robert Levers to Nicholson, Jan. 25, June 11, 1783; Feb. 15, Oct. 13, 1786; June 14, 1787, boxes 1, 3, 4, 5, GC, RCG. For the assault, see Dec. session 1785, Northampton County QS Papers, Northampton County Court Annex, Easton, PA.

9. Levers to Nicholson, June 11, 1783; Feb. 16, Aug. 25, Oct. 13, 1786, boxes 1, 3, 4, GC, RCG.

10. Levers to John Nicholson, Oct. 13, 1786, file 6, box 4, GC, RCG.

11. Thomas Crossan and David Stewart, Bedford County, Jan. 16, 1787, file 9, box 4, GC, RCG; Commissioners of Bucks County to Dickinson, July 31, 1783, *Pennsylvania Archives*, ser. 1, vol. 10, 76.

12. James McLene, Canecochique, to George Bryan, Feb. 10, 1784, file 12, box 1, George Bryan Papers, HSP. For most of the postwar period, county judges found themselves removed from the process of tax collection. The tax law of 1782 had placed full control over prosecution in the hands of county tax commissioners. The procedures changed as part of the compromise that produced the 1785 war debt funding act. Rural advocates managed to add a stipulation that before property could be auctioned for nonpayment of taxes, delinquent collectors and taxpayers could have their cases heard before county justices. Brown, *Redeeming the Republic*, 64–65.

13. "Agreeable to the request of the Honorable the Committee on Ways and Means," Dec. 1786, file 8, box 4, GC, RCG.

14. Thomas Crossan to Nicholson, Aug. 22, 1787, file 6, box 5; and Sept. 15, 1787, file 10, box 5, GC, RCG.

15. Ibid.

16. Crossan and Stewart to Nicholson, Apr. 24, 1787, folder 17, box 4, GC, RCG; Crossan to Nicholson, July 27, 1787, folder 5, box 5, ibid.

17. George Clingler, Franklin County, to Nicholson, Oct. 2, 1786, file 7, box 4, GC, RCG; Levers, Northampton County, to Nicholson, June 14, 1787, box 2, file 5, ibid.; Jacob Arndt, Jr., Northampton County, to Nicholson, Apr. 21, 1787, file 17, box 4, ibid.; Richard Parker, Cumberland County, to Nicholson, Sept. 19, 1787, file

7, box 5, ibid.; Christopher Dering, Northumberland County, to Nicholson, Nov. 26, 1787, file 11, ibid.; David Stewart and John Dean, Huntingdon County, to Nicholson, July 5, 1788, file 5, box 6, ibid.; John Thome, Dauphin County, to Nicholson, Dec. 27, 1786, frame 326, reel 19, GC, Nicholson Papers.

18. G. S. Rowe and Jack D. Marietta, *Troubled Experiment: Crime and Justice in Pennsylvania, 1682–1800* (Philadelphia, 2006), ch. 8. These cases generally excluded charges against tax collectors.

19. Richard McAlister to Nicholson, July 31, 1787, file 8, box 5, GC, RCG.

20. Ibid.

21. Levers, Northampton County, to Nicholson, Oct. 13, 1786, file 6, box 4, GC, RCG; William Hamilton, Bush Hill, to Jasper Yeates, Lancaster, Apr. 14, 1787, Yeates Families Papers, HSP.

22. Crossan and Stewart, Bedford County, to Nicholson, Apr. 24, 1787, file 17, box 4, GC, RCG. For the relative wealth of county sheriffs and the poverty of constables, see Harper, *Transformation of Western Pennsylvania*, 168.

23. Jacob Arndt, Jr., Northampton County, to Nicholson, Aug. 25, 1786; Apr. 21, 1787, file 16, box 3, and file 17, box 4, GC, RCG; Jan. 1786, Washington County QS Docket, Washington County Courthouse, Washington, PA.

24. Alexander McKeehen and George Logue, Cumberland County, to Nicholson, Mar. 21, 1789, file 13, box 6, GC, RCG; Commissioners of Bucks County to Dickinson, July 31, 1783, *Pennsylvania Archives*, ser. 1, vol. 10, 75; William Nelson, Lancaster County, to Stephen Collins, Jan. 10, 1789, Correspondence, Collins Papers.

25. Commissioners of Taxes Northampton County, Aug. 25, 1783, *Pennsylvania Archives*, ser. 1, vol. 10, 92; Jacob Rosencrantz, Northampton County, to Nicholson, Sept. 1, 1786, file 1, box 4, GC, RCG; Ephraim Douglass, Fayette County, to Dickinson, July 11, 1784, *Pennsylvania Archives*, ser. 1, vol. 10, 588; John Thome, Dauphin County, to Nicholson, Dec. 27, 1786, frame 326, reel 19, GC, Nicholson Papers. See also Commissioners of Cumberland County to Dickinson, Aug. 14, 1783, *Pennsylvania Archives*, ser. 1, vol. 10, 79–80; Michael Hahn, York County, to Nicholson, Dec. 15, 1786, ibid., vol. 11, 97; William Perry, Westmoreland County, to Nicholson, Sept. 21, 1786, file 3, box 4, GC, RCG; Alexander Boyd, Fayette County, to Nicholson, Feb. 9, 1786, file 6, box 3, ibid.; Mathias Slough, Lancaster County, to Jasper Yeates, Lancaster, Oct. 15, 1785, Yeates Family Papers, HSP.

26. 1783–1786, Westmoreland County Execution Dockets.

27. Petition, Sept. 18, 1780, box 1, Berks 1780, Court Papers, Eastern District, Records of the Supreme Court, PHMC. One of the signers of this covenant was Joseph Hiester, who was later elected to the general assembly from Berks County and who in 1787 voted against ratification of the federal Constitution.

28. Douglass to Nicholson, Jan. 29, 1789, file 11, box 8, GC, RCG.

29. Douglass to Dickinson, July 11, 1784, *Pennsylvania Archives*, ser. 1, vol. 10, 588.

30. For examples, see Bouton, "Road Closed," 874.

31. Apr. 1788, Bedford County QS Dockets and Papers; "Deposition of James Wilson, Apr. 22, 1784," July 1784, Cumberland County QS Papers, Cumberland County Historical Society, Carlisle, PA.

32. For rough music, see E. P. Thompson, "Patrician Society, Plebian Culture," *Journal of Social History* 7 (Summer 1974): 382–405; Thompson, "Rough Music Reconsidered," *Folklore* 103, no. 1 (Apr. 1992): 3–26; Alfred F. Young, "English Plebian Culture and Eighteenth-Century Radicalism," in *The Origins of Anglo-American Radicalism*, ed. Margaret Jacob and James Jacob (London, 1984), 185–212; Fennell, "From Rebelliousness to Insurrection," 4–43, 98–122; and William Pencak, Matthew Dennis, and Simon P. Newman, eds., *Riot and Revelry in Early America* (University Park, PA, 2002).

33. Alexander McClean to President Moore, June 27, 1782, *Pennsylvania Archives*, ser. 1, vol. 9, 565; Douglass to Dickinson, Feb. 2, July 11, 1784, ibid., vol. 10, 553, 588; Douglass to John Armstrong, May 29, 1784, ibid., 582; Armstrong to Michael Huffnagle, Nov. 15, 1783, ibid., 147; "Deposition of James Bell" and "Deposition of Philip Jenkins," 1784, ibid., 594–595.

34. Dorsey Penticost to Council, Apr. 16, 1786, *Pennsylvania Archives*, ser. 1, vol. 10, 757.

35. Ibid.

36. Michael Hahn, York County, to Nicholson, Dec. 15, 1786, *Pennsylvania Archives*, ser. 1, vol. 11, 97–98.

37. *Carlisle Gazette*, May 30, 1787; Hahn to Nicholson, Dec. 15, 1786, *Pennsylvania Archives*, ser. 1, vol. 11, 97–98; Alexander Russell to Nicholson, Dec. 13, 1786, folder 8, box 4, GC, RCG.

38. *Pennsylvania Mercury*, June 8, 1787; Hahn to Nicholson, Dec. 15, 1786, *Pennsylvania Archives*, ser. 1, vol. 11, 97–98.

39. Ibid.

40. Andrew Swearingen, Washington County, to Nicholson, Oct. 13, 1787, file 9, box 5, GC, RCG; Thomas Scott, Washington County, to Nicholson, Feb. 27, 1787, file 17, box 4, ibid.; Jacob Arndt, Berks County, to Nicholson, Apr. 21, 1787, ibid.; John Thome, Dauphin County, to Nicholson, Dec. 27, 1786; Mar. 24, Oct. 20, 1787, frames 326, 328, 332, reel 19, Nicholson Papers.

41. Norman B. Wilkinson, "The `Philadelphia Fever' in Northern Pennsylvania," *Pennsylvania History* 20, no. 1 (Jan. 1953): 42; Peter C. Mancall, *Valley of Opportunity: Economic Culture along the Upper Susquehanna, 1700–1800* (Ithaca, NY, 1991), 166–170; Barbara Ann Chernow, *Robert Morris, Land Speculator, 1790–1801* (New York, 1978), 96–97; for the Pennamite War, see Paul Benjamin Moyer, "Wild Yankees: Settlement, Conflict, and Localism along Pennsylvania's Northeast Frontier, 1760–1820" (Ph.D. diss., College of William and Mary, 1999).

42. Honorable John Boyd and Lieutenant Colonel John Armstrong to President Dickinson, Aug. 7, 1784, frame 409, reel 21, RPRG.

43. "To the Honourable the Worshipful Counsel for the State of Pennsylvania," Dec. 21, 1785, frame 673, reel 22, RPRG; Valentine Eckert to Pres. Franklin, Nov. 9, 1787, *Pennsylvania Archives*, ser. 1, vol. 11.

44. "Petition of Sundry Inhabitants of the Township of Lower Milford in the County of Bucks to President of the Supreme Executive Council," Apr. 15, 1785, frame 39, reel 22, RPRG; Richmond Township, Bucks County, 1785, frame 496, ibid.

45. Ibid.

46. David Rittenhouse to Dickinson, Apr. 27, 1784, quoted in Brown, *Redeeming the Republic*, 63; "State of the Accounts of the Treasury . . . from 1782 . . . to 1785," *Pennsylvania Archives*, ser. 3, vol. 5, 368–373; "Account of Taxes Paid by the Several Counties, from Jan. 1, 1787 to Sept. 6, inclusive," Sept. 20, 1787, in *Proceedings and Debates of the General Assembly . . . Volume the First* (Philadelphia, 1787); "County Tax Accounts, Balances, Effective Supplies Taxes, 1785–1789," RCG. The 1787 deficits ran statewide, ranging from 72 percent of taxes unpaid in Chester and Northampton to 90 percent unpaid in Cumberland and York.

47. For resistance elsewhere, see Louis Maganzin, "Economic Depression in Maryland and Virginia, 1783–1787" (Ph.D. diss., Georgetown University, 1967), 177–202, 265–268; John H. Flannagan, Jr., "Trying Times: Economic Depression in New Hampshire, 1781–1789" (Ph.D. diss., Georgetown University, 1972), 76–132; David P. Szatmary, *Shays' Rebellion: The Making of an Agrarian Insurrection* (Amherst, MA, 1980), 27–31; Jerome J. Nadelhaft, *The Disorders of War: The Revolution in South Carolina* (Orono, ME, 1981), 155–172; Michael Bellesiles, *Revolutionary Outlaws: Ethan Allen and the Struggle for Independence on the Early American Frontier* (Charlottesville, VA, 1993), 246–248, 278; Jean B. Lee, *The Price of Nationhood: The American Revolution in Charles County* (New York, 1994), 228–258; Leonard L. Richards, *Shays's Rebellion: The American Revolution's Final Battle* (Philadelphia, 2002).

Chapter 8

1. Stephen Collins to Colborn Barrell, Aug. 11, Sept. 1, 1786, Letter Books, Collins Papers; Collins to Harrison & Ansley, Feb. 19, 1787, ibid.; Collins to James Swan, Sept. 26, 1786, ibid.; Collins to Pearsall & Glover, Dec. 28, 1786, ibid.

2. James Wilson, *On the Improvement and Settlement of Lands in the United States* (n.d.; reprint, Philadelphia, 1946), 19 (emphasis in original).

3. Etienne Claviére to Jacques Pierre Brissot de Warville, May 18 and undated, 1788, quoted in J. P. Brissot de Warville, *New Travels in the United States of America, 1788*, ed. Durand Echeverria (Cambridge, MA, 1964), 31, 49–50.

4. "Plan of Investigation to be Followed During My Travels in America," quoted in de Warville, *New Travels*, 54; "Extract of a letter from an American Gentleman, now at the Hague," *Pennsylvania Gazette*, Dec. 21, 1785, quoted in Janet Wilson, "The Bank of North America and Pennsylvania Politics: 1781–1787," *Pennsylvania Magazine of History and Biography* 66, no. 1 (Jan. 1942): 14.

5. James Wilson to William Bingham, May 15, 1784, quoted in Robert C. Alberts, *The Golden Voyage: The Life and Times of William Bingham, 1752–1804* (Boston, 1969), 122; Benjamin Rush to Timothy Pickering, Jan. 29, 1788, in Charles W. Upham, *The Life of Timothy Pickering*, 2 vols. (Boston, 1873), vol. 2, 374. For Hollingsworth, see Thomas M. Doerflinger, *A Vigorous Spirit of Enterprise: Merchants and Economic Development in Revolutionary Philadelphia* (Chapel Hill, NC, 1986), 319; Hollingsworth to Enoch Story, Oct. 20, 1787, document 147, DHRCM; Hollingsworth to Doresy Pentacost, May 2, 1789, document 318, DHRCM; Levi Hollingsworth Land Book 1778–1788, Paschall and Hollingsworth Papers, HSP; Collins to Smithson and Greaves, Apr. 30, 1790, Stephen Collins Letterbook, 1782–1793, Daniel Parker Collection, HSP.

6. John Vaughan to Morris, June 2, 1783, *Morris Papers*, vol. 8, 146. Vaughan observed that this assessment applied to all of the colonies and former colonies in the Americas.

7. Collins to Pearsall and Glover, Dec. 28, 1786, Letter Books, Collins Papers; Collins to Colborn Barrell, Sept. 1, 1786, ibid.; Josiah and Samuel Coates, Philadelphia, to Thomas Butler, June 4, 1785, Josiah and Samuel Coates Letter Book, 1784–1790, Coates & Reynell Papers.

8. Bankruptcy File, 1785–1790, reel 34, RPRG.

9. John Montgomery, Philadelphia, to Robert Macgaw, Feb. 11, 1783, James Findley Lamberton Papers, HSP; Charles Coleman Sellers, *Dickinson College: A History* (Middletown, CT, 1973), ch. 4. I converted the figures from pounds to dollars: £257/15/0 was reported in cash, £1,382/17/6 in certificates, and land was valued at £1,200.

10. Marquis de Chastellux to Gouverneur Morris, Dec. 8, 1784, *Morris Papers*, vol. 9, 611–612; Samuel Vaughan to Richard Price, Jan. 4, 1785, reel 108, ser. 9, Peter Force Collection; Wilhem and Jan Willink to Robert Morris, Mar. 26, 1784, *Morris Papers*, vol. 9, 212; James Milligan to David Howell, Dec. 18, 1784, ibid., 319; Etienne Claviére to Jacques Pierre Brissot, May 1788, quoted in de Warville, *New Travels*, 46.

11. Alexander Hamilton, June 18, 1787, in *The Records of the Federal Convention of 1787*, ed. Max Farrand, 3 vols. (New Haven, CT, 1911), vol. 1, 203.

12. U.S. Constitution.

13. U.S. Constitution, Article I, sec. 10.

14. Gouverneur Morris, July 21, 1787, in *Records of the Federal Convention*, vol. 2, 76.

15. Randolph, May 31, 1787, in *Records of the Federal Convention*, vol. 1, 51; Hamilton, June 18, 1787, ibid., 288–289, 299.

16. James Wilson, June 6 and 7, 1787, in *Records of the Federal Convention*, vol. 1, 132–133, 154; James Madison, June 6, 1787, ibid., 134–136.

17. Convention Debates, Nov. 30, Dec. 3, 4, 7, 12, 1787, DHRC, 436, 457, 500, 520, 596. Benjamin Rush used nearly the same language as Wilson, saying that if the Constitution "held forth no other Advantages than a future exemption from paper money & tender laws, it would be eno' to recommend it to

honest men." Benjamin Rush to Jeremy Belknap, Feb. 28, 1788, document 461, frame 1847, DHRCM.

18. Levi Hollingsworth to Enoch Story, Oct. 20, 1787, document 147, frame 789, DHRCM; Miers Fisher to Robert Barclay, Oct. 20, 1787, document 146, frames 778–788, DHRCM.

19. Thomas Forrest to Joseph Ward, Oct. 29, 1787, document 169, frame 896, DHRCM; George Turner to Winthrop Sargent, Nov. 6, 1787, DHRC, 209; Richard Butler to William Irvine, Oct. 11–12, 1787, DHRC, 177 (emphasis in original).

20. Samuel Hodgdon to Timothy Pickering, Sept. 29, 1787, DHRC, 123; "James M'Calmont's Appeal to the Supreme Executive Council," DHRC, 111; Smith, *James Wilson*, 150.

21. Samuel Bryan to Aedanus Burke, Dec. 5, 1789, document 700D, frame 2681, DHRCM.

22. Ibid., frame 2682; William Petrikin to John Nicholson, Mar. 23, 1789, DHFFE, 406; Feb. 24, 1788, DHRC, 695.

23. David Redick to William Irvine, Sept. 24, 1787, DHRC, 135. For a systematic analysis of newspaper coverage before, during, and after the Constitutional Convention, see John K. Alexander, *The Selling of the Constitutional Convention: A History of News Coverage* (Madison, WI, 1990).

24. Convention Debates, Dec. 12, 1787, DHRC, 579, 594.

25. Convention Debates, Dec. 11 and Nov. 28, 1787, DHRC, 558, 388, 387.

26. Samuel Bryan to Aedanus Burke, Dec. 5, 1789, document 700D, frames 2677–2684, DHRCM. For general discussions of the breakdown in voting over the Constitution, see Robert L. Brunhouse, *The Counter-Revolution in Pennsylvania, 1776–1790* (New York, 1971), 191–211; Owen S. Ireland, *Religion, Ethnicity, and Politics: Ratifying the Constitution in Pennsylvania* (University Park, PA, 1995), 147–253; Jackson Turner Main, *The Antifederalists: Critics of the Constitution, 1781–1788* (Chapel Hill, NC, 1961).

27. John Simpson, Northumberland County, to John Nicholson, July 5, 1788, reel 17, Nicholson Papers; Richard Bard to Nicholson, Feb. 1, 1788, DHRC, 712; Charles Nisbet to Alexander Addison, Dec. 7, 1787, document 259, frame 1174, DHRCM; Alexander Fowler, Pittsburgh, to Nicholson, Feb. 9, 1788, document 414, frame 1690, DHRCM. John Bull of Northumberland County declared: "I have the satisfaction to acquaint you that the Majority of the People in this county are much averse to the adoption of the New System of Government without amendments." Dec. 10, 1787, document 260, frame 1177, DHRCM.

28. Convention Debates, Dec. 12, 1787, DHRC, 587–588; "Address and Reasons of Dissent of the Minority," DHRC, 622. For returns, see Convention Election, Nov. 6 and 7, 1787, DHRC, 234–236, 264–265; "List of Taxables," *Pennsylvania Evening Herald*, Sept. 27, 1786.

29. Bard to Nicholson, Feb. 1, 1788, DHRC, 712; Thomas Rodney Journal, May 10, 1788, document 676, frame 2589, DHRCM. Rodney reported the conversation of a Federalist traveler who had stayed at Rodney's home.

30. Rebecca Pickering to Timothy Pickering, Oct. 22 and Nov. 8, 1787, in *Life of Timothy Pickering*, vol. 2, 313, 342. Local Federalists also noted that the inhabitants of Luzerne were "prone to opposition" to the Constitution. One man told Pickering that he had "carefully avoided letting them [the inhabitants] know that any objections were made to the Constitution." Ebenezer Bauman to Timothy Pickering, Nov. 12, 1787, quoted in Main, *Antifederalists*, 188.

31. For a general discussion of the events in Carlisle and accompanying documents, see "The Carlisle Riot and Its Aftermath, Dec. 26, 1787–Mar. 20, 1788," DHRC, 670–708. For an interpretation of the Carlisle uprising and its place in Antifederalism, see Saul Cornell, "Aristocracy Assailed: The Ideology of Backcountry Anti-Federalism," *Journal of American History* 76, no. 4 (Mar. 1990): 1148–1172.

32. John Jordan to John Nicholson, Jan. 26, 1788, DHRC, 693; Receipt, Nov. 5, 1770, folder 9, box 2, Robert Whitehill Papers, Cumberland County Historical Society; "The Scourge" [William Petrikin], *Carlisle Gazette*, Jan. 23, 1788, DHRC, 688–689. For tax assessments of Cumberland protesters and petitioners, see Cornell, "Aristocracy Assailed," 1156.

33. Petrikin to Nicholson, Feb. 24, 1788, DHRC, 694–696; Montgomery to James Wilson, Mar. 2, 1788, DHRC, 701–705.

34. Petrikin to Nicholson, Feb. 24, 1788, DHRC, 694–696.

35. Montgomery to Wilson, Mar. 2, 1788, DHRC, 701–705.

36. Ibid.; *Carlisle Gazette*, Mar. 5, 1788, DHRC, 700; John Shippen to Joseph Shippen, Mar. 3, 1788, DHRC, 706–707.

37. Shippen to Shippen, Mar. 3, 1788; *Carlisle Gazette*, Mar. 5, 1788, DHRC, 699–701.

38. Montgomery to Wilson, Mar. 2, 1788, DHRC, 701–705.

39. "The Federal Joy," *Carlisle Gazette*, Jan. 23, 1788, DHRC, 691–692. For more on the class dimensions of the rhetoric and rituals of the Carlisle protests, see Cornell, "Aristocracy Assailed."

40. *Freeman's Journal*, Mar. 19, 1788, DHRC, 718; 1788, Huntingdon County QS Dockets and Papers; Milton Scott Lytle, *History of Huntingdon County, in the State of Pennsylvania* (Lancaster, PA, 1876), 101–109; Benjamin Elliot to Pres. Mifflin, Feb. 1790, *Pennsylvania Archives*, ser. 1, vol. 11, 665–666.

41. Petrikin to Nicholson, Feb. 24, 1788, DHRC, 696; and Mar. 23, 1789, DHFFE, 1, 406. For an alternative interpretation of the Harrisburg convention, see Paul Leicester Ford, *The Origins, Purpose, and Result of the Harrisburg Convention of 1788: A Study in Popular Government* (Brooklyn, NY, 1890), 15–19.

42. To Francis Hopkinson, Aug. 17, 1788, DHFFE, 252.

43. Petrikin to Nicholson, Feb. 24, 1788, DHRC, 694; and May 8, 1788, document 675, frames 2584–2588, DHRCM. For similar concerns of isolation from Washington County Antifederalists, see Alexander Wright to Nicholson, Sept. 29, 1788, frame 198, reel 20, Nicholson Papers.

44. For Federalist calls to cut out elite Antifederalists, see "A Citizen of Philadelphia," *Pennsylvania Gazette*, Jan. 23, 1788, DHRC, 660. For a strongly worded example, see Peletiah Webster, *Pennsylvania Gazette*, Apr. 18, 1787.

45. "The Petition Campaign for Legislative Rejection or Ratification," DHRC, 709.

46. James Marshel to Nicholson, Feb. 2, 1788, DHRC, 713; John Clark to Nicholson, Mar. 11, 1788, document 506, frame 1997, DHRCM; Petrikin to Nicholson, Feb. 24, 1788, DHRC, 695.

47. "Assembly Proceedings on the Petitions Against the Adoption of the New Constitution, 17–29 Mar.," DHRC, 719–721; "List of Taxables," *Pennsylvania Evening Herald*, Sept. 27, 1786. The taxable figure of 3,939 from Cumberland County is for the year 1786. Using a mean of the 1786 and 1790 figures would be misleading since at the time of the 1790 census, Cumberland had lost territory with the creation of Mifflin County. The 1790 census records a voting-age population of 3,014. Bureau of the Census, *Heads of Families at the First Census of the United States Taken in the Year 1790: Pennsylvania* (Washington, DC, 1908). The taxable population of Franklin County in 1786 was 2,237.

48. William Gray to Tench Coxe, Sunbury, Apr. 26, 1788, document 660, frame 2509, DHRCM; *Freeman's Journal*, Mar. 19, 1788, DHRC, 718; "Assembly Proceedings on the Petitions Against the Adoption of the New Constitution, 17–29 Mar.," DHRC, 719–721.

49. Organizers took their cue from the "dissent of the minority" delegates at the ratification convention, which was a compromise between elite Antifederalists and their rural counterparts: "The Dissent of the Minority of the Convention," DHRC, 617–640. Ordinary Antifederalists continued to talk about paper money, revaluing the war debt, and limiting speculation: "An American Citizen," *Pennsylvania Herald and York General Advertiser*, Jan. 1, 1789; Charles Swift to Robert E. Griffiths, Oct. 18, 1787, DHRC, 198–199; *Pennsylvania Chronicle*, July 16, 1788, DHFFE, 243; Thomas FitzSimons to Samuel Meredith, Philadelphia, Aug. 20, 1788, DHFFE, 253; "A Federal Centinel," *Pennsylvania Gazette*, Sept. 10, 1788, DHFFE, 269; and Tench Coxe to Robert Smith, Philadelphia, Aug. 5, 1788, DHFFE, 248.

50. *Pennsylvania Mercury*, Sept. 13, 1788, DHFFE, 273.

51. Charles Pettit to George Washington, Mar. 19, 1791, document 706, frame 2707, DHRCM.

52. James Hanna to John Vandegrift, Nathan Vansant, and Jacob Vandegrift, Aug. 15, 1788, DHFFE, 1, 250; *Pennsylvania Gazette*, Sept. 3, 1788, DHFFE, 265.

53. Petrikin to Nicholson, Mar. 23, 1789, DHFFE, 406; Proceedings of the Harrisburg Convention, ibid., 258–264.

54. "Civis," *Pennsylvania Packet*, Sept. 19, 1788, DHFFE, 276; Richard Peters to George Washington, Sept. 17, 1788, ibid., 275.

55. Alexander Graydon to Lambert Cadwalader, Sept. 7, 1788, ibid., 265.

56. Pettit to Washington, Mar. 19, 1791, document 706, frames 2707, 2704, DHRCM.

57. On Nicholson's politics after the passage of the federal Constitution, see Robert D. Arbuckle, *Pennsylvania Speculator and Patriot: The Entrepreneurial John Nicholson, 1757–1800* (University Park, PA, 1975), 46–74. On Nicholson's and Morris's land speculations, see ibid., 75–113, 165–208; Chernow, *Robert Morris*; Norman B. Wilkinson, *Land Policy and Speculation in Pennsylvania, 1779–1800: A Test of the New Democracy* (New York, 1979).

58. Petrikin to Nicholson, Mar. 23, 1789, DHFFE, 406.

59. Petrikin to Nicholson, Apr. 14 and May 19, 1789, frames 761–762, reel 14, Nicholson Papers.

60. Tench Coxe to James Madison, Sept. 29, 1787, DHRC, 122.

61. For the entire state, of approximately 70,000 voters, only 14,617 people cast ballots in the election. For election and population data, see "Election Returns for Representatives," DHFFE, 378; "List of Taxables," *Pennsylvania Evening Herald*, Sept. 27, 1786; *First Census: Pennsylvania*.

62. Findley to George Bryan, Aug. 3, 1789, folder 13, box 3, George Bryan Papers, HSP; "Cato," *Pennsylvania Herald and York General Advertiser*, Mar. 27, 1789.

63. Brunhouse, *Counter-Revolution*, 221–227.

64. Pennsylvania Constitution (1790).

Chapter 9

1. Terry Bouton, "A Road Closed: Rural Insurgency in Post-Independence Pennsylvania," *Journal of American History* 87, no. 3 (Dec. 2000): 855–857.

2. Ibid.

3. Ibid., 879–880.

4. Robert Blaine to James Hamilton, n.d., folder 1, box 33, James Hamilton Papers; Aug. and Nov. 1788, Dauphin County QS Papers, Court Papers, PHMCM; Feb. session 1789, Chester County QS Papers, Government Services Building, West Chester, PA. In 1791 in Washington County, two road supervisors were arrested for cutting down timber and building fences across a road. Another supervisor was arrested in June 1791 for "cutting into" the road. Mar. and June 1791, Washington County QS Papers, Washington County Courthouse, Washington, PA.

5. Nov. 1793, Huntingdon County QS Docket, Huntingdon County Courthouse, Huntingdon, PA.

6. "A Supplement to the Act Entitled 'An Act to Enforce the Due Collection and Payment of Taxes Within this Commonwealth,'" Oct. 4, 1788, SALP, vol. 13, 145–149; Sept. 19, 1788, in *Debates of the General Assembly . . . Volume the Fourth* (Philadelphia, 1788).

7. John Nicholson, Mar. 28, 1788, folder 18, box 5, GC, RCG.

8. Findlaw McCowan, Cumberland County, to Nicholson, 1788, folder 7, box 6, GC, RCG; John Thome, Dauphin County, to Nicholson, Apr. 28, 1788, folder 3, box 6, GC, RCG; Andrew Swearingen, Washington County, to Nicholson, Oct. 13, 1787, folder 9, box 5, GC, RCG; Treasurer of Washington County to

Nicholson, Feb. 3, 1788, folder 17, box 5, GC, RCG; Andrew Swearingen, Washington County, to Ferbiger, Aug. 13, 1790, folder 3, box 1, Records of the Treasury Department [hereafter RTD], PHMC; John Cadwallader, Huntingdon County, to Nicholson, May 22, 1788, folder 13, box 9, RCG. For the county balances of unpaid taxes, see "Account of Taxes Paid by the Several Counties, from January 1, 1787 to September 6, inclusive," Sept. 20, 1787, in *Proceedings and Debates of the General Assembly . . . Volume the First* (Philadelphia, 1787).

9. "An Act to Provide a More Effectual Method of Settling the Public Accounts of the Commissioners and Treasurers of the Respective Counties," Mar. 30, 1791, SALP, vol. 14, 41–46.

10. Alexander M'Keehen, Esqr., Treasurer, "List of Deliquent [*sic*] Collectors," Mar. 18, 1791, Carlisle, PA, *Early American Imprints*, ser. 1, Evans number 46255.

11. Andrew Swearingen, Washington County, to Nicholson, Jan. 13, 1790, folder 8, box 7, GC; Swearingen to Christian Ferbiger, Apr. 20, 1791, folder 5, box 1, GC, RTD; William Purdy, Mifflin County, to Ferbiger, Jan. 8, 1791, folder 5, box 1, GC, RTD; William Scott, York County, to John Nicholson, Apr. 30, 1789, folder 16, box 6, GC, RCG. For additional examples of the continued difficulties of county tax officials in collecting back taxes, see R. Terry Bouton, "Tying Up the Revolution: Money, Power, and the Regulation in Pennsylvania, 1765–1800" (Ph.D. diss., Duke University, 1996), 387.

12. Philip Jenkins, Westmoreland County, to Nicholson, 1787, file 12, box 5, GC, RCG; George McCorkhill, Chester County, to Nicholson, Dec. 2, 1788, file 10, box 6, ibid.; Joseph Torrence to Nicholson, Feb. 5, 1790, file 8, box 7, ibid.

13. Report of the Treasurer, Nov. 22, 1790, *Pennsylvania Archives*, ser. 1, vol. 11, 758–761.

14. William Perry, Westmoreland County, to Nicholson, Sept. 21, 1786, file 3, box 4, GC, RCG; Caleb James and Caleb North, Chester County, to Nicholson, Oct. 14, 1787, file 9, box 5, ibid.

15. "A Message from the President and the Supreme Executive Council to the General Assembly," Nov. 8, 1787, in *Colonial Records of Pennsylvania*, 15 vols. (Harrisburg, PA, 1851–1853), vol. 15, 315.

16. "A Supplement to the Act Entitled 'An Act to Enforce the Due Collection and Payment of Taxes Within this Commonwealth,'" Oct. 4, 1788, SALP, vol. 13, 145–149.

17. Sept. 19, 1788, *Debates of the General Assembly . . . Volume the Fourth* (Philadelphia, 1788).

18. Ibid.

19. For quotes, see James Finley to Pres. Franklin, 1788, Minutes of the Supreme Executive Council, *Pennsylvania Archives*, Colonial Series,, vol. 11, 298; Joseph Kerr to Thomas Mifflin, Feb. 26, 1793, folder 6, box 10, GC, RCG. For these and other examples of judicial resistance, see Bouton, "Road Closed," 878.

20. Pennsylvania Constitution (1776, 1790).

21. *Pennsylvania Herald and York General Advertiser*, Nov. 2, 1791.

22. Deposition of William Faulkner, Allegheny County, Sept. 28, 1792, Pennsylvania Whiskey Rebellion Collection, vol. 1, Library of Congress; Deposition of Daniel DePew, Nov. 19, 1794, "Insurrection in Western Pennsylvania," Rawle Family Papers, HSP; Constitution of the Society of United Freemen, Rawle Papers; William Findley, *A History of the Insurrection in the Four Western Counties of Pennsylvania* (Philadelphia, 1796), 56; Hugh Henry Brackenridge, *Incidents of the Insurrection in the Western Parts of Pennsylvania in the Year 1794* (Philadelphia, 1795), vol. 3, 25. The date of the society's creation is unclear. Findley and Brackenridge say that the society formed in early 1794. Court depositions, however, reveal the society to have been active in 1792 and 1793. The dropping of lawsuits suggests that the date probably coincided with the change in the court system.

23. 1791–1794, Washington County Execution Dockets; 1791, Westmoreland County Execution Dockets.

24. For Mifflin County protests, see *Carlisle Gazette*, Sept. 21, 28, Oct. 12, Nov. 10, 1791; and *Pennsylvania Herald and York General Advertiser*, Sept. 21, 1791.

25. Kenneth W. Keller, *Rural Politics and the Collapse of Pennsylvania Federalism* (Philadelphia, 1982), 5.

26. Ephraim Douglass to Nicholson, Jan. 29, 1789, file 11, box 8, GC, RCG.

27. For quotes, see David Stewart and John Dean, Huntingdon County, to Nicholson, July 5, 1788, file 5, box 6, ibid. For other examples of resistance by constables, see Bouton, "Tying Up the Revolution," 390–391.

28. Report of the Treasurer, Nov. 22, 1790, *Pennsylvania Archives*, ser. 1, vol. 11, 758–761; Ann Henry, Lancaster County, to Ferbiger, May 8, 1790, folder 4, box 1, GC, RTD.

29. Richard Parker to Nicholson, May 13, 1788, folder 16, box 6, GC, RCG; Nicholson to Commissioners of Lancaster County, June 27, 1788, Letter Book, RCG. For additional examples of no-bid pacts, see Bouton, "Tying Up the Revolution," 391.

30. In county quarter session dockets, many jail keepers were fined for the crime of "escape." For examples, see Mar. 1790, Mar. 1793, June 1795, Washington County QS Papers; May 1788, Berks County QS Dockets, PHMCM; Apr. 1782, York County QS Dockets, PHMCM.

31. "A Supplement to the Act Entitled 'A Supplement to the Act Entitled 'An Act to Enforce the Due Collection and Payment of Taxes Within this Commonwealth,''" Mar. 28, 1789, SALP, vol. 13, 292–294; "An Act Relating to the Securities to be Given by Sheriffs and Coroners," Mar. 5, 1790, SALP, vol. 13, 455–457.

32. Pennsylvania Constitution (1776, 1790).

33. Nicholson to the Commissioners of Cumberland County, Mar. 31, 1789, Letter Books, RCG.

34. Nicholson to Richard Parker, Cumberland County, June 19, 1788, Letter Books, RCG; Nicholson to the Commissioners of Cumberland County, Mar. 31, 1789, ibid.; Nicholson to Christopher Devring, Northumberland County,

May 16, 1789, ibid.; Samuel Turbett to John Nicholson, Jan. 24, Mar. 14, June 3, 1786; Oct. 1, 4, 1787, frames 881–898, reel 19, Nicholson Papers.

35. Apr. 1788, Lancaster County QS Papers, Historical Society of Lancaster County, Lancaster, PA.

36. G. S. Rowe and Jack D. Marietta, *Troubled Experiment: Crime and Justice in Pennsylvania, 1682–1800* (Philadelphia, 2006), ch. 8.

37. For arson, see *Pennsylvania Herald and York General Advertiser*, Apr. 8, 1789; for forcible entry and rescue, see Rowe and Marietta, *Troubled Experiment*, ch. 8.

38. Bouton, "Road Closed," 881. My crime statistics often differ from those of Rowe and Marietta because I counted every case recorded in the docket books regardless of outcome while they often excluded cases where defendants were acquitted or the charges were thrown out.

39. Douglass, Fayette County, to Nicholson, Jan. 29, 1789, folder 11, box 8, GC, RCG; Robert Galbraith et al. to President Benjamin Franklin, Aug. 23, 1788, DHFFE, vol. 1, 254–255.

40. William Petrikin to Nicholson, May 8, 1788, frame 756, reel 14, Nicholson Papers.

41. Petrikin to Nicholson, Mar. 23, 1789, DHFFE, 406; and May 19, 1789, reel 14, frame 762, Nicholson Papers. On the other companies, see John Jordan to Nicholson, May 19, 1789, frame 13, reel 11, ibid.

42. Jordan to Nicholson, May 19, 1789, frame 13, reel 11, Nicholson Papers. Jordan saw this move as a precursor to the Federalists setting up a peacetime standing army, noting that "a Standing army now would suit their purpose."

43. Benjamin Elliot to Pres. Mifflin, Feb. 1790, *Pennsylvania Archives*, ser. 1, vol. 11, 665–666.

44. "An Act for the Regulation of the Militia of the Commonwealth of Pennsylvania," Apr. 11, 1793, SALP, vol. 14, 454–481.

45. "An Act to Provide for the Settlement of Public Accounts and for Other Purposes Therein Mentioned," Apr. 4, 1792, SALP, vol. 14, 243–249.

46. Apr. and Aug. 1792, Northumberland County QS Papers, Northumberland County Courthouse, Sunbury, PA.

Chapter 10

1. John Wilkins, Pittsburgh, to William Irvine, Aug. 19, 1794, Irvine Family Papers.

2. Ibid.; *Pittsburgh Gazette*, Aug. 2, 1794.

3. Wilkins to Clement Biddle, Aug. 1, 1794, *Pennsylvania Archives*, ser. 2, vol. 4, 69.

4. Thomas P. Slaughter, *The Whiskey Rebellion: Frontier Epilogue to the American Revolution* (New York, 1986); Stanley Elkins and Eric McKitrick, *The Age of Federalism: The Early American Republic, 1788–1800* (New York, 1993), 482, 485; Saul Cornell, *The Other Founders: Anti-Federalism and the Dissenting Tradition in America, 1788–1828* (Chapel Hill, NC, 1999), 200–218; Paul

Douglas Newman, *Fries Rebellion: The Enduring Struggle for the American Revolution* (Philadelphia, 2004). For an exception, see Dorothy Elaine Fennell, "From Rebelliousness to Insurrection: A Social History of the Whiskey Rebellion, 1765–1802" (Ph.D. diss., University of Pittsburgh, 1981).

5. William Findley, *A Review of the Revenue System Adopted by the First Congress under the Federal Constitution: wherein the Principles and Tendency of the Funding System and the Second Congress Are Examined. In Thirteen Letters to a Friend. By a Citizen* (Philadelphia, 1794), 126, 128.

6. Marjoleine Kars, *Breaking Loose Together: The Regulator Rebellion in Pre-Revolutionary North Carolina* (Chapel Hill, NC, 2002).

7. David P. Szatmary, *Shays' Rebellion: The Making of an Agrarian Insurrection* (Amherst, MA, 1980); Leonard L. Richards, *Shays's Rebellion: The American Revolution's Final Battle* (Philadelphia, 2002).

8. Herman Husband, *XIV Sermons on the Characters of Jacob's Fourteen Sons* (Philadelphia, 1789), quoted in Fennell, "From Rebelliousness to Insurrection," 198–199, 215. For Husband's role in the 1794 uprising, see Mark Haddon Jones, "Herman Husband: Millenarian, Carolina Regulator, and Whiskey Rebel" (Ph.D. diss., Northern Illinois University, 1983).

9. Minutes of the Meeting at Pittsburgh, Sept. 7, 1791, *Pennsylvania Archives*, ser. 2, vol. 4, 20–22 (there are two different versions of this volume with slightly different page numbers).

10. E. James Ferguson, *Power of the Purse: A History of American Public Finance, 1776–1790* (Chapel Hill, NC, 1961), 329–330.

11. *Carlisle Gazette*, Jan. 9, 1793; Ferguson, *Power of the Purse*, 329–333.

12. Minutes of the Meeting at Pittsburgh, Sept. 7, 1791, *Pennsylvania Archives*, ser. 2, vol. 4, 20–22.

13. Ibid.

14. Ibid.; Minutes of the Meeting at Pittsburgh, 1792, *Pennsylvania Archives*, ser. 2, vol. 4, 30–31. For an insightful analysis of the economics of the excise tax, see Fennell, "From Rebelliousness to Insurrection," 227–258.

15. Minutes of the Meeting at Pittsburgh, 1791, *Pennsylvania Archives*, ser. 2, vol. 4, 20–22.

16. Robert D. Arbuckle, *Pennsylvania Speculator and Patriot: The Entrepreneurial John Nicholson, 1757–1800* (University Park, PA, 1975), 76–79.

17. Norman B. Wilkinson, *Land Policy and Speculation in Pennsylvania, 1779–1800: A Test of the New Democracy* (New York, 1979), 122, 131.

18. R. Terry Bouton, "Tying Up the Revolution: Money, Power, and the Regulation in Pennsylvania, 1765–1800" (Ph.D. diss., Duke University, 1996), 381–382.

19. James F. Dinsmore, "Courts and Western Pennsylvania Lands: The Origins of the Attack on Pennsylvania's Courts, 1790–1810" (Ph.D. diss., Temple University, 1990), 17–25.

20. *Oracle of Dauphin and Harrisburgh Advertiser*, Jan. 14 and 28, 1793; Hugh Henry Brackenridge, *Incidents of the Insurrection in the Western Parts of Pennsylvania in the Year 1794* (Philadelphia, 1795), vol. 3, 14.

21. The most concise summary of the physical abuse directed against excise tax collectors is the editorial note by John B. Linn, *Pennsylvania Archives*, ser. 2, vol. 4, 1–10. See also Slaughter, *Whiskey Rebellion*, 109–115; and Fennell, "From Rebelliousness to Insurrection," 4–43, 98–122.

22. Aug. 1792, Chester County QS Papers; Tench Coxe to Alexander Hamilton, Oct. 19, 1792, AHP, vol. 12, 594–596; "Circular to the Clerks of the Courts," Nov. 2, 1792, *Pennsylvania Archives*, ser. 2, vol. 4, 35; Lawrence Erb, Northampton Co., to William Powell, Sept. 15, 1792; "Insurrection in Western Pennsylvania," Rawle Family Papers [hereafter Rawle Papers], HSP (the "Insurrection in Western Pennsylvania" section also includes evidence and depositions collected during the investigation of the 1799 uprising); John Herling, East Pennsboro, Cumberland County, to General Edward Hand, Feb. 25, 1793, Rawle Papers; Samuel Hodgdon to Hamilton, May 9, 1794, AHP, vol. 16, 397–399.

23. Deposition of William Faulkner, Allegheny County, Sept. 28, 1792, vol. 1, Pennsylvania Whiskey Rebellion Collection [hereafter WRLC], Library of Congress, Washington, DC; Judge Alexander Addison to Governor Thomas Mifflin, Nov. 4, 1792, *Pennsylvania Archives*, ser. 2, vol. 4, 30–33; George Clymer to Attorney General of the United States, Oct. 4, 1792, WRLC; James Brison to Governor Thomas Mifflin, Nov. 9, 1792, *Pennsylvania Archives*, ser. 2, vol. 4, 44–45; David Redick to Alexander Dallas, Nov. 14, 1792, ibid., 46–47; Judge Thomas Smith to Mifflin, Dec. 10, 1792, ibid., 54–57.

24. Mar. and June 1791; Sept. and Nov. 1792, Washington County QS Papers. Among the other men were Neal Gillespie, a fellow delegate to the Pittsburgh meeting of 1792; William Hays, a delegate to the Parkinson's Ferry meeting in Aug. 1794; and James Miller, who had participated in the militia assembly on Braddock's Field in Aug. 1794.

25. Hamilton to Washington, Sept. 9, 1792, AHP, vol. 12, 344–347.

26. Ibid.; Tench Coxe to Hamilton, Oct. 19, 1792, AHP, vol. 12, 592–601; Slaughter, *Whiskey Rebellion*, 117–119; Mary K. Bonsteel Tachau, "The Federal Courts in Kentucky, 1789–1816" (Ph.D. diss., University of Kentucky, 1972), 66–67; Tachau, "The Whiskey Rebellion in Kentucky: A Forgotten Episode of Civil Disobedience," *Journal of the Early Republic* 2 (Fall 1982): 239–259; and Jeffrey J. Crow, "The Whiskey Rebellion in North Carolina," *North Carolina Historical Review* 66, no. 1 (Jan. 1989): 1–28.

27. Hamilton to Washington, Sept. 9, 1792, AHP, vol. 12, 344–347.

28. Minutes of the Meeting at Pittsburgh, 1792, *Pennsylvania Archives*, ser. 2, vol. 4, 30–31. For the leadership of the western protests, see Fennell, "From Rebelliousness to Insurrection," 44–75, 141–177.

29. Constitution of the Society of United Freemen, Rawle Papers; Brackenridge, *Incidents of the Insurrection*, vol. 1, 86; Deposition of William Faulkner, Allegheny County, Sept. 28, 1792, WRLC; Deposition of Daniel DePew, Nov. 19, 1794, Rawle Papers; *Pittsburgh Gazette*, Feb. 17, 1787; Oct. 10, 1793.

30. Constitution of the Society of United Freemen, Rawle Papers; Minutes of the Meeting at Pittsburgh, 1792, *Pennsylvania Archives*, ser. 2, vol. 4, 30–31.

31. Hamilton to George Washington, Sept. 1 and 9, 1792, AHP, vol. 12, 311–312, 347–365; Hamilton to John Jay, Sept. 3, 1792, AHP, vol. 12, 316–317; Minutes of the Meeting at Pittsburgh, 1792, *Pennsylvania Archives*, ser. 2, vol. 4, 30–31.

32. Edmund Randolph to Alexander Hamilton, Sept. 8, 1792, AHP, vol. 12, 336–340; Jay to Hamilton, Sept. 8, 1792, AHP, vol. 12, 334–335; Washington to Hamilton, Sept. 17, 1792, AHP, vol. 12, 390–391; George Washington, Proclamation, Sept. 15, 1792, *Pennsylvania Archives*, ser. 2, vol. 4, 32–33. See also Richard H. Kohn, "The Washington Administration's Decision to Crush the Whiskey Rebellion," *Journal of American History* 59, no. 3 (Dec. 1972): 567–584.

33. For Clymer's certificate holdings, see Certificate Exchange Proposals, 1789–1793; Hamilton to Coxe, Sept. 1, 1792, AHP, vol. 12, 305–310; Hamilton to Washington, Sept. 1, 1792, AHP, vol. 12, 311–312. For Clymer's subsequent reports to Hamilton, see Clymer to Hamilton, Sept. 18, Oct. 4, 10, 1792, AHP, vol. 12, 495–497, 517–522, 540–542; Clymer to Attorney General of the United States, Oct. 4, 1792, WRLC. For reinforcements of the message to Clymer, see Tench Coxe, Commissioner of Revenue, to George Clymer, Supervisor of Pennsylvania, Sept. 28, 1792, vol. 1: May 11, 1792–Dec. 19, 1795, Letters Sent by the Commissioner of the Revenue and the Revenue Office, 1792–1807, Record Group 58, Records of the Internal Revenue Service, National Archives, College Park, MD.

34. Findley to Thomas Hamilton, Nov. 28, 1792, Thomas Hamilton Papers, Westmoreland County Historical Society, Greensburg, PA; Findley to Alexander Addison, Nov. 30, 1792, Alexander Addison Papers, Darlington Library, University of Pittsburgh, Pittsburgh, PA.

35. William Findley, *A History of the Insurrection in the Four Western Counties of Pennsylvania* (Philadelphia, 1796), 70. For Clymer's accounts, see *Pittsburgh Gazette*, Mar. 2, 16, 30, 1793.

36. See the exchanges between Jeremiah Olney and Hamilton, Mar. 18, Apr. 2, 22, Aug. 19, 1793, AHP, vol. 14, 214–218, 276–277, 333–334.

37. For Miller quotes, see Brackenridge, *Incidents of the Insurrection*, vol. 1, 122. For Neville's participation in popular politics, see *Pittsburgh Gazette*, Feb. 17, 1787; Findley, *History of the Insurrection*, 79.

38. For Neville quotes, see Findley, *History of the Insurrection*, 79–80. For Neville calling the public "rabble," see Neville to Clymer, Sept. 8 and Dec. 12, 1791, quoted in Slaughter, *Whiskey Rebellion*, 114. For Fort Pitt and the excise tax concentrating on the whiskey trade, see Fennell, "From Rebelliousness to Insurrection," 227–258.

39. Findley, *History of the Insurrection*, 77–78; Brackenridge, *Incidents of the Insurrection*, vol. 1, 122.

40. Brackenridge, *Incidents of the Insurrection*, vol. 1, 122; Slaughter, *Whiskey Rebellion*, 176–179.

41. Alexander Fulton to George Washington, 1794, WRLC.

42. For the pledge, see Testimony of John Baldwin, in Robert Porter Trial Transcript, May 18, 1795, Senator John Heinz Pittsburgh Regional History Center, Pittsburgh, PA.

43. Findley, *History of the Insurrection*, 86–90; Slaughter, *Whiskey Rebellion*, 179. For certificates, see *Pittsburgh Gazette*, July 26, 1794.

44. Slaughter, *Whiskey Rebellion*, 188; Robert Porter Trial Transcript. For later appearances of the flag, see Albert Gallatin Testimony, in Brackenridge, *Incidents of the Insurrection*, vol. 3, appendix, 137.

45. David Bradford to David Williamson, July 30, 1794, Jasper Yeates Papers, HSP.

46. Slaughter, *Whiskey Rebellion*, 183–189. For the participation of the Ohio delegations, see William Sutherland, "West of the Ohio River," Oct. 30, 1794, Rawle Papers.

47. Kohn, "The Washington Administration's Decision."

48. *Pittsburgh Gazette*, Sept. 24, 1794; Brackenridge, *Incidents of the Insurrection*, vol. 1, 99, vol. 3, 26; Fennell, "From Rebelliousness to Insurrection," 183–186.

49. William Bradford to the President of the United States, Aug. 17, 1794, WRLC; Bradford to Secretary of State, Sept. 5, 1794, ibid. Two months later, 125 people were brought up on riot charges for this pole raising. See Nov. 1794, Bedford County QS Docket. For the pole's slogan, see Brackenridge, *Incidents of the Insurrection*, vol. 1, 99; *Carlisle Gazette*, Dec. 17, 1794.

50. For evidence of liberty pole raisings, see Slaughter, *Whiskey Rebellion*, 206–209; Fennell, "From Rebelliousness to Insurrection," 260–266; Deposition of Jacob Geiger, June session 1795, Dauphin County QS Papers; "An ODE addressed to his Royal Highness the Liberty Pole of Lewistown," *Carlisle Gazette*, Dec. 17, 1794.

51. "At a Meeting of a number of the inhabitants of the townships of Westpennsbro' & Newton in the county of Cumberland held in the town of Newville," *Carlisle Gazette*, Aug. 20, 1794. For a similar petition, see "Cumberland County Petition," Rawle Papers. People in the neighboring counties of Mifflin and Dauphin held meetings to draw up petitions along these precise lines; see *Oracle of Dauphin and Harrisburgh Advertiser*, Sept. 1, 1794.

52. Deposition of Peter Faulkner, Northumberland Co., Dec. 10, 1794, Rawle Papers; Deposition of Daniel Reese, Northumberland Co., 1794, ibid.; Deposition of Thomas Ashton, Franklin Co., Jan. 31, 1795, ibid.; *Carlisle Gazette*, Aug. 20, 1794.

53. Deposition of Owen Ashton, Franklin Co., Mar. 30, 1795, Rawle Papers.

54. Deposition of Christian Yentzen, Northumberland County, Dec. 27, 1794, Rawle Papers; Deposition of Peter Faulkner, Northumberland Co., Dec. 10, 1794, ibid.; Deposition of John McGrath, Northumberland Co., Dec. 22, 1794, ibid.; Deposition of Flavel Roan, Northumberland Co., Jan. 4, 1795, ibid.; Deposition of Benjamin Young, Northumberland Co., Oct. 16, 1794, ibid.

55. Deposition of John McKibbon, Franklin Co., Feb. 17, 1795, ibid.; Deposition of Robert Scott, Franklin Co., Feb. 2, 1795, ibid.

56. Testimony of Robert Patterson, Cumberland Co., ibid.; Testimony of William Pollock, Cumberland Co., ibid.; Notes on Cumberland County Testimony, Robert Whitehill, ibid.; William Bradford to the President of the United States, Aug. 17, 1794, WRLC.

57. Hugh Henry Brackenridge to Tench Coxe, Aug. 8, 1794, quoted in Brackenridge, *Incidents of the Insurrection*, vol. 3, 130.

58. Deposition of Daniel Reese, Northumberland Co., Oct. 17, 1794, Rawle Papers; Deposition of Thomas Ashton, Franklin Co., Jan. 31, 1795, ibid.; Deposition of James Jenkins, Northumberland County, Nov. 12, 1794, ibid.; Deposition of William Wilson, Northumberland County, Nov. 29, 1794, ibid.; Testimony of William Pollock, Cumberland County, ibid.

59. Fennell, "From Rebelliousness to Insurrection," 264; Sept. 1794, Lancaster County QS Papers; Nov. 1794, Northampton County Criminal Papers; Jacob Rush, Northampton Co., Oct. 2, 1794, Rawle Papers.

60. Thomas Lee to Hamilton, Sept. 12 and 13, 1794, quoted in Fennell, "From Rebelliousness to Insurrection," 262; Tench Coxe to Arthur Lee, Sept. 17, 1794, quoted in Slaughter, *Whiskey Rebellion*, 212; Randolph quoted in John Marshall, *The Life of George Washington*, 5 vols. (Philadelphia, 1807), vol. 5, 581. On the opposition in other states, see Slaughter, *Whiskey Rebellion*, 209–214.

61. William Bradford to the President of the United States, Aug. 17, 1794, WRLC; Bradford to Secretary of State, Sept. 5, 1794, ibid.; Robert Philson to Anthony Emerey, Sept. 6, 1794, in *United States vs. Robert Philson*, 1795, reel 1, Case Files, Records for the United States District Court for the Eastern District, National Archives, College Park, MD; Robert Lusk to William Moorehead, Aug. 26, 1794, *United States vs. Robert Lusk*, ibid.

62. Ross, Yeates, and Bradford, Pittsburgh, to the Secretary of State, Aug. 30, 1794, WRLC.

63. Slaughter, *Whiskey Rebellion*, 214–215.

64. Slaughter, *Whiskey Rebellion*, 200–203, 214–218. For examples of altered submission forms, see WRLC.

65. Capt. David Ford, *Journal of an Expedition Made in the Autumn of 1794* (Newark, NJ, 1856), 5–8.

66. William Irvine, Stoney Creek, to Capt. Webster, Nov. 26, 1794, Irvine Family Papers.

67. Husband quoted in Fennell, "From Rebelliousness to Insurrection," 192, 218–219, 208.

Chapter 11

1. Parts of this chapter appeared in Terry Bouton, "'No wonder the times were troublesome': The Origin of Fries Rebellion, 1783–1799," *Pennsylvania History* 60 (Winter 2000): 21–42.

2. Lee Soltow, *Distribution of Wealth and Income in the United States in 1798* (Pittsburgh, PA, 1989).

3. *Public Statutes at Large of USA* (Boston, 1845), vol. 1, 596–597.

4. Deposition of Michael Bopst, Apr. 10, 1799, Rawle Papers, HSP; Deposition of Daniel Reich, Northampton Co., Jan. 29, 1799, ibid.; Deposition of George Ringer, Northampton Co., Jan. 28, 1799, ibid.; Deposition of Philip Arndt, Sept. 17, 1798, ibid.; Testimony of Colonel William Nichols, in *The Two Trials of John Fries on an Indictment for Treason*, ed. Thomas Carpenter (Philadelphia, 1800), 38; Testimony of James Chapman, ibid., 68; Testimony of Cephas Child, ibid., 76.

5. "Petition of the Subscribers [and] Inhabitants of the County of York in the State of Pennsylvania," *Aurora*, Jan. 22, 1799; Deposition of Henry Ohl, Apr. 27, 1799, Rawle Papers.

6. For estimates of land holding in southeastern Pennsylvania, see Jack D. Marietta, "The Distribution of Wealth in Eighteenth-Century America: Nine Chester County Tax Lists, 1693–1799," *Pennsylvania History* 62 (Oct. 1995): 537–538; James S. Lemon, *The Best Poor Man's Country: A Geographical Study of Early Southeastern Pennsylvania* (Baltimore, MD, 1972), 10–13, 92–96; Lucy Simler, "The Landless Worker: An Index of Economic and Social Change in Chester County, Pennsylvania, 1750–1820," *Pennsylvania Magazine of History and Biography* 114 (Apr. 1990): 163–199; Rodger C. Henderson, *Community Development and the Revolutionary Transition in Eighteenth-Century Lancaster County, Pennsylvania* (New York, 1989), 204. For estimates of land holding among participants in the so-called Fries's Rebellion, see Paul Douglas Newman, *Fries Rebellion: The Enduring Struggle for the American Revolution* (Philadelphia, 2004), 31–35.

7. Testimony of Jacob Eyerly, in *Two Trials of John Fries*, 222; Deposition of Jacob Snyder, Northampton Co., Oct. 7, 1799, Rawle Papers; Deposition of John Butz, Northampton Co., Jan. 29, 1799, ibid.

8. "Millions for Defense, but Not a Cent for Tribute!" *Aurora*, Feb. 21, 1799; "A Citizen of Montgomery County," *Aurora*, Feb. 4, 1799 (emphases in original); *Aurora*, Feb. 25, 1799.

9. Deposition of James Williamson, Northampton County, Apr. 15, 1799, Rawle Papers; Petition, *Aurora*, Jan. 22, 1799; Testimony of Cephas Child, Bucks County, in *Two Trials of John Fries*, 76–77.

10. "JOE BUNKER," *Aurora*, Jan. 12, 1799.

11. Deposition of Frederick Seiberling, Northampton County, Jan. 28, 1799, Rawle Papers; Deposition of Philip Kremer, Berks County, Feb. 13, 1799, ibid.

12. "POLITICAL ARITHMETIC," *Aurora*, Feb. 27, 1799 (emphases in original).

13. For an excellent summary of the protests, see Newman, *Fries Rebellion*, 1, 89–123.

14. Ibid., 48–70.

15. Ibid., 123–137. For connections to the French Revolution, see Simon Newman, "The World Turned Upside Down: Revolutionary Politics, Fries'

and Gabriel's Rebellions, and the Fears of the Federalists," *Pennsylvania History* 67 (Winter 2000): 5–20.

16. Deposition of Michael Bopst, Apr. 10, 1799, Rawle Papers; Deposition of John Lersass, Feb. 1, 1799, ibid.

17. Newman, *Fries Rebellion*, 133–134, 137–138.

18. For quotes, see Testimony of Colonel William Nichols, in *Two Trials of John Fries*, 38. For Fries, see Newman, *Fries Rebellion*, 112–119.

19. Testimony of Colonel William Nichols, in *Two Trials of John Fries*, 38; Deposition of Israel Robert, n.d., Rawle Papers. Due to blurred print in the original document, it was unclear whether the word in the last quote was "snakes" or "shakers."

20. For Fries quote, see Newman, *Fries Rebellion*, 138.

21. For events and the Fries quote, see Newman, *Fries Rebellion*, 138–140.

22. Testimony of George Mitchel, in *Two Trials of John Fries*, 66; Newman, *Fries Rebellion*, 143.

23. Deposition of John Santee, Northampton County, Apr. 26, 1799, Rawle Papers; Deposition of John Butz, Northampton County, Jan. 29, 1799, ibid.; Testimony of James Williamson, Northampton County, in *Two Trials of John Fries*, 187; Testimony of Cephas Child, ibid., 74; Deposition of Sebastian Faust, Berks County, Apr. 18, 1799, Rawle Papers.

24. Deposition of John Romich, Northampton Co., Jan. 29, 1799, Rawle Papers; Testimony of Cephas Child, in *Two Trials of John Fries*, 74; Deposition of Andrew Schlinhter, Berks Co., Apr. 6, 1799, Rawle Papers; Deposition of Michael Bopst, Apr. 10, 1799, Rawle Papers.

25. Testimony of Jacob Eyerly and John Sneider, in *Two Trials of John Fries*, 222–223; Deposition of Jacob Snyder, Northampton County, Oct. 7, 1799, Rawle Papers.

26. Deposition of Adam Wetzel, Apr. 11, 1799, Rawle Papers; Deposition of Michael Bopst, Apr. 10, 1799, ibid.; Testimony of Cephas Child, in *Two Trials of John Fries*, 77.

27. General William MacPherson to Alexander Hamilton, Mar. 22 and 25, 1799, AHP, vol. 22, 579, 584–585; MacPherson to James McHenry, Apr. 8, 1799, quoted in Newman, *Fries Rebellion*, 149, 158.

28. Hugh Henry Brackenridge, *Incidents of the Insurrection in the Western Parts of Pennsylvania in the Year 1794* (Philadelphia, 1795), vol. 3, appendix, 153.

29. *Carlisle Gazette*, Jan. 23, 1799.

30. The drama is ably captured in Newman, *Fries Rebellion*, 165–188.

Conclusion

1. For voting patterns and the rise of the Democratic-Republicans in Pennsylvania, see Kenneth W. Keller, *Rural Politics and the Collapse of Pennsylvania Federalism* (Philadelphia, 1982). For the growing gap between equality and democracy among Jeffersonians in Pennsylvania, see Andrew

Shankman, *Crucible of American Democracy: The Struggle to Fuse Egalitarianism and Capitalism in Jeffersonian Pennsylvania* (Lawrence, KS, 2004).

2. In arguing for the Revolution as a popular victory, many historians have equated democracy with laissez-faire capitalism and suggested that both concepts, as they emerged in the nineteenth century, were in many ways the creation of ordinary folk and that, paradoxically, the popular commitment to unrestrained materialism created a wider wealth gap. For links between democracy and liberalism, see Gordon Wood, *The Radicalism of the American Revolution* (New York, 1991), 245–270, 325–369; Joyce Appleby, *Inheriting the Revolution: The First Generation of Americans* (Cambridge, MA, 2000); Winifred Barr Rothenberg, *From Market Places to a Market Economy* (Chicago, 1992).

3. For a thoughtful examination of long-term wealth inequality and trends in the scholarship on wealth distribution, see Carole Shammas, "A New Look at Long-Term Trends in Wealth Inequality in the United States," *American Historical Review* 98, no. 2 (Apr. 1993): 412–431. For wealth equality as political rhetoric in support of laissez-faire policies, see James L. Huston, *Securing the Fruits of Labor: The American Concept of Wealth Distribution, 1765–1900* (Baton Rouge, LA, 1998). For good examples of co-opted rhetoric and diluted reforms, see Lawrence Goodwyn, *Democratic Promise: The Populist Moment in America* (New York, 1976); Reeve Huston, *Land and Freedom: Rural Society, Popular Protest, and Party Politics in Antebellum New York* (New York, 2000); Charles C. Bolton, *Poor Whites of the Antebellum South: Tenants and Laborers in Central North Carolina and Northeast Mississippi* (Durham, NC, 1994), 139–180.

4. Sam Bass Warner, Jr., *The Private City: Philadelphia in Three Periods of Its Growth* (Philadelphia, 1968), 132–136; Pennsylvania Constitution (1838).

Index